SOURCES FOR *OF THE PEOPLE*

A HISTORY OF THE UNITED STATES
VOLUME II SINCE 1865

EDITED BY

Maxwell Johnson

NEW YORK   OXFORD
OXFORD UNIVERSITY PRESS

Oxford University Press is a department of the University of Oxford.
It furthers the University's objective of excellence in research, scholarship,
and education by publishing worldwide. Oxford is a registered trade mark of
Oxford University Press in the UK and certain other countries.

Published in the United States of America by Oxford University Press
198 Madison Avenue, New York, NY 10016, United States of America.

© 2020 by Oxford University Press

Library of Congress Cataloging-in-Publication Data

Names: Johnson, Maxwell E., 1952- editor.
Title: Sources for Of the people : a history of the United States / edited by
    Maxwell Johnson.
Description: [Fourth edition] | New York, NY : Oxford University Press, 2019. |
    "Sources for Of the People: A History of the United States, Fourth Edition,
    is a two-volume primary source collection, expertly edited by
    Maxwell Johnson, and specifically designed to accompany
    Of the People."—Publisher. | Includes bibliographical references.
Identifiers: LCCN 2018033866| ISBN 9780190910143 (volume 1 : pbk.) |
    ISBN 9780190910150 (volume 2 : pbk.)
Subjects: LCSH: United States—History—Sources.
Classification: LCC E178 .O25 2019 Suppl. | DDC 973—dc23 LC record
    available at https://lccn.loc.gov/2018033866

9 8 7 6 5 4 3 2 1

Printed by LSC Communications, Inc., United States of America

CONTENTS

HOW TO READ A PRIMARY SOURCE

This sourcebook is composed of eighty-five primary sources. A primary source is any text, image, or other information that gives us a first-hand account of the past by someone who witnessed or participated in the historical events in question. While such sources can provide significant and fascinating insight into the past, they must also be read carefully to limit modern assumptions about historical modes of thought. Here are a few elements to keep in mind when approaching a primary source.

AUTHORSHIP

Who produced this source of information? A male or a female? A member of the elite or of the lower class? An outsider looking in at an event or an insider looking out? What profession or lifestyle does the author pursue that might influence how he or she is recording his information?

GENRE

What type of source are you examining? Different genres—categories of material—have different goals and stylistic elements. For example, a personal letter meant exclusively for the eyes of a distant cousin might include unveiled opinions and relatively trivial pieces of information, like the writer's vacation plans. On the other hand, a political speech intended to convince a nation of a leader's point of view might subdue personal opinions beneath artful rhetoric and focus on large issues like national welfare or war. Identifying genre can be useful for deducing how the source may have been received by an audience.

AUDIENCE

Who is reading, listening to, or observing the source? Is it a public or a private audience? National or international? Religious or non-religious? The source may be geared toward the expectations of a particular group; it may be recorded in a language that is specific to a particular group. Identifying audience can help us understand why the author chose a certain tone or included certain types of information.

HISTORICAL CONTEXT

When and why was this source produced? On what date? For what purposes? What historical moment does the source address? It is paramount that we approach primary sources in context to avoid anachronism (attributing an idea or a habit to a past era where it does not belong) and faulty judgment. For example, when considering a medieval history, we must account for the fact that in the Middle Ages, the widespread understanding was that God created the world and could still interfere in the activity of mankind—such as sending a terrible storm when a community had sinned. Knowing the context (Christian, medieval, views of the world) helps us to avoid importing modern assumptions—like the fact that storms are caused by atmospheric pressure—into historical texts. In this way we can read the source more faithfully, carefully, and generously.

BIAS AND FRAMING

Is there an overt argument being made by the source? Did the author have a particular agenda? Did any political or social motives underlie the reasons for writing the document? Does the document exhibit any qualities that offer clues about the author's intentions?

STYLISTIC ELEMENTS

Stylistic features such as tone, vocabulary, word choice, and the manner in which the material is organized and presented should also be considered when examining a source. They can provide insight into the writer's perspective and offer additional context for considering a source in its entirety.

CHAPTER 15

RECONSTRUCTING A NATION, 1865–1877

15.1 JOURDON ANDERSON, LETTER TO HIS FORMER SLAVEOWNER (1864)

Jourdon Anderson (1825–1907) was born in Tennessee, where he was enslaved on various plantations until 1864, when Union soldiers freed him. Subsequently, Anderson moved to Dayton, Ohio, where he worked in various positions and eventually settled as a church maintenance man in 1894. In July 1865, Anderson's former owner, P. H. Anderson, wrote Jourdon to ask him to return to Tennessee and work on the plantation. Jourdon's response became immediately celebrated for Jourdon's careful demands and sarcastic tone. P. H. Anderson later sold his plantation at a major loss in order to escape debt, and he died at age 44 just two years later.

To *my old Master*, COLONEL P. H. ANDERSON, *Big Spring, Tennessee.*

SIR: I got your letter, and was glad to find that you had not forgotten Jourdon, and that you wanted me to come back and live with you again, promising to do better for me than anybody else can. I have often felt uneasy about you. I thought the Yankees would have hung you long before this, for harboring Rebs they found at your house. I suppose they never heard about your going to Colonel Martin's to kill the Union soldier that was left by his company in their stable. Although you shot at me twice before I left you, I did not want to hear of your being hurt, and am glad you are still living. It would do me good to go back to the dear old home again, and see Miss Mary and Miss Martha and Allen, Esther, Green, and Lee. Give my love to them all, and tell them I hope we will meet in the better world, if not in this. I would have gone back to see you all when I was working in the Nashville Hospital, but one of the neighbors told me that Henry intended to shoot me if he ever got a chance.

I want to know particularly what the good chance is you propose to give me. I am doing tolerably well here. I get twenty-five dollars a month, with

Source: L. Maria Child, ed., *The Freedmen's Book* (Boston: Ticknor and Fields, 1865), 265–267. Retrieved from the Internet Archive website, https://babel.hathitrust.org/cgi/pt?id=hvd.32044013553797;view=1up;seq=7 (Accessed June 6, 20188).

victuals and clothing; have a comfortable home for Mandy,—the folks call her Mrs. Anderson,—and the children—Milly, Jane, and Grundy—go to school and are learning well. The teacher says Grundy has a head for a preacher. They go to Sunday School, and Mandy and me attend church regularly. We are kindly treated. Sometimes we overhear others saying, "Them colored people were slaves" down in Tennessee. The children feel hurt when they hear such remarks; but I tell them it was no disgrace in Tennessee to belong to Colonel Anderson. Many darkeys would have been proud, as I used to be, to call you master. Now if you will write and say what wages you will give me, I will be better able to decide whether it would be to my advantage to move back again.

As to my freedom, which you say I can have, there is nothing to be gained on that score, as I got my free papers in 1864 from the Provost-Marshal-General of the Department of Nashville. Mandy says she would be afraid to go back without some proof that you were disposed to treat us justly and kindly; and we have concluded to test your sincerity by asking you to send us our wages for the time we served you. This will make us forget and forgive old scores, and rely on your justice and friendship in the future. I served you faithfully for thirty-two years, and Mandy twenty years. At twenty-five dollars a month for me, and two dollars a week for Mandy, our earnings would amount to eleven thousand six hundred and eighty dollars. Add to this the interest for the time our wages have been kept back, and deduct what you paid for our clothing, and three doctor's visits to me, and pulling a tooth for Mandy, and the balance will show what we are in justice entitled to. Please send the money by Adams's Express, in care of V. Winters, Esq., Dayton, Ohio. If you fail to pay us for faithful labors in the past, we can have little faith in your promises in the future. We trust the good Maker has opened your eyes to the wrongs which you and your fathers have done to me and my fathers, in making us toil for you for generations without recompense. Here I draw my wages every Saturday night; but in Tennessee there was never any pay-day for the negroes any more than for the horses and cows. Surely there will be a day of reckoning for those who defraud the laborer of his hire.

In answering this letter, please state if there would be any safety for my Milly and Jane, who are now grown up, and both good-looking girls. You know how it was with poor Matilda and Catherine. I would rather stay here and starve—and die, if it come to that—than have my girls brought to shame by the violence and wickedness of their young masters. You will also please state if there has been any schools opened for the colored children in your neighborhood. The great desire of my life now is to give my children an education, and have them form virtuous habits.

Say howdy to George Carter, and thank him for taking the pistol from you when you were shooting at me.

From your old servant,
JOURDON ANDERSON.

QUESTIONS TO CONSIDER

1. Are Anderson's demands serious?
2. Why do you think Anderson's letter became so celebrated?

15.2 ABRAHAM LINCOLN'S LAST PUBLIC ADDRESS (1865)

On April 11, 1865, two days after Robert E. Lee surrendered, President Abraham Lincoln spoke from a White House balcony to a crowd of hundreds who had assembled on the lawn below. Far from delivering the joyful speech those in the crowd had expected, Lincoln chose a somber tone in his prepared remarks, and he discussed his strategy toward reincorporating southern states into the Union. Just three days later, John Wilkes Booth shot Lincoln in the back of the head as the President was watching the play "My American Cousin" at Ford's theatre. Lincoln succumbed to his wounds the following morning. This speech, then, provides the clearest hints of Lincoln's potential Reconstruction strategy, one likely more moderate than Radical Republicans would have preferred it to be.

We meet this evening, not in sorrow, but in gladness of heart. The evacuation of Petersburg and Richmond, and the surrender of the principal insurgent army, give hope of a righteous and speedy peace whose joyous expression can not be restrained. In the midst of this, however, He, from Whom all blessings flow, must not be forgotten. A call for a national thanksgiving is being prepared, and will be duly promulgated. Nor must those whose harder part gives us the cause of rejoicing, be overlooked. Their honors must not be parcelled out with others. I myself, was near the front, and had the high pleasure of transmitting much of the good news to you; but no part of the honor, for plan or execution, is mine. To Gen. Grant, his skilful officers, and brave men, all belongs. The gallant Navy stood ready, but was not in reach to take active part.

By these recent successes the re-inauguration of the national authority—reconstruction—which has had a large share of thought from the first, is pressed much more closely upon our attention. It is fraught with great difficulty. Unlike the case of a war between independent nations, there is no authorized organ for us to treat with. No one man has authority to give up the rebellion for any other man. We simply must begin with, and mould from, disorganized and discordant elements. Nor is it a small additional embarrassment that we, the loyal people, differ among ourselves as to the mode, manner, and means of reconstruction.

As a general rule, I abstain from reading the reports of attacks upon myself, wishing not to be provoked by that to which I can not properly offer an answer. In spite of this precaution, however, it comes to my knowledge that I am much censured for some supposed agency in setting up, and seeking to sustain, the new State Government of Louisiana. In this I have done just so much as, and no more than, the public knows. In the Annual Message of Dec. 1863 and accompanying Proclamation, I presented *a* plan of re-construction (as the phrase goes) which, I promised, if adopted by any State, should be acceptable to, and sustained by, the Executive government of the nation. I distinctly stated that this was not the only plan which might possibly be acceptable; and I also distinctly protested that the Executive claimed no right to say when, or whether members should be admitted to seats in Congress from such States. This plan was, in advance, submitted to the then Cabinet, and distinctly approved by every member of it. One of them

Source: Collected Works of Abraham Lincoln, Volume VIII (Ann Arbor: University of Michigan Digital Library Production Services, 2001), **https://quod.lib.umich.edu/l/lincoln/lincoln8/1:850?rgn=div1;singlegenre=All;sort=occur;subview=detail;type=simple;view=fulltext;q1=April+11%2C+1865** (Accessed June 6, 2018).

suggested that I should then, and in that connection, apply the Emancipation Proclamation to the theretofore excepted parts of Virginia and Louisiana; that I should drop the suggestion about apprenticeship for freed-people, and that I should omit the protest against my own power, in regard to the admission of members to Congress; but even he approved every part and parcel of the plan which has since been employed or touched by the action of Louisiana. The new constitution of Louisiana, declaring emancipation for the whole State, practically applies the Proclamation to the part previously excepted. It does not adopt apprenticeship for freed-people; and it is silent, as it could not well be otherwise, about the admission of members to Congress. So that, as it applies to Louisiana, every member of the Cabinet fully approved the plan. The Message went to Congress, and I received many commendations of the plan, written and verbal; and not a single objection to it, from any professed emancipationist, came to my knowledge, until after the news reached Washington that the people of Louisiana had begun to move in accordance with it. From about July 1862, I had corresponded with different persons, supposed to be interested, seeking a reconstruction of a State government for Louisiana. When the Message of 1863, with the plan before mentioned, reached New-Orleans, Gen. Banks wrote me that he was confident the people, with his military co-operation, would reconstruct, substantially on that plan. I wrote him, and some of them to try it; they tried it, and the result is known. Such only has been my agency in getting up the Louisiana government. As to sustaining it, my promise is out, as before stated. But, as bad promises are better broken than kept, I shall treat this as a bad promise, and break it, whenever I shall be convinced that keeping it is adverse to the public interest. But I have not yet been so convinced.

I have been shown a letter on this subject, supposed to be an able one, in which the writer expresses regret that my mind has not seemed to be definitely fixed on the question whether the seceded States, so called, are in the Union or out of it. It would perhaps, add astonishment to his regret, were he to learn that since I have found professed Union men endeavoring to make that question, I have *purposely* forborne any public expression upon it. As appears to me that question has not been, nor yet is, a practically material one, and that any discussion of it, while it thus remains practically immaterial, could have no effect other than the mischievous one of dividing our friends. As yet, whatever it may hereafter become, that question is bad, as the basis of a controversy, and good for nothing at all—a merely pernicious abstraction.

We all agree that the seceded States, so called, are out of their proper practical relation with the Union; and that the sole object of the government, civil and military, in regard to those States is to again get them into that proper practical relation. I believe it is not only possible, but in fact, easier, to do this, without deciding, or even considering, whether these states have even been out of the Union, than with it. Finding themselves safely at home, it would be utterly immaterial whether they had ever been abroad. Let us all join in doing the acts necessary to restoring the proper practical relations between these states and the Union; and each forever after, innocently indulge his own opinion whether, in doing the acts, he brought the States from without, into the Union, or only gave them proper assistance, they never having been out of it.

The amount of constituency, so to to [*sic*] speak, on which the new Louisiana government rests, would be more satisfactory to all, if it contained fifty, thirty, or even twenty thousand, instead of only about twelve thousand, as it does. It is also unsatisfactory to some that the elective franchise is not given to the colored man. I would myself prefer that it were now conferred on the very intelligent, and on those who serve our cause as soldiers. Still the question is not whether the Louisiana government, as it stands, is quite all that is desirable. The question is "Will it be wiser to take it as it is, and help to improve it; or to reject, and disperse it?" "Can Louisiana be brought into proper practical relation with the Union *sooner* by *sustaining*, or by *discarding* her new State Government?"

Some twelve thousand voters in the heretofore slave-state of Louisiana have sworn allegiance to the Union, assumed to be the rightful political power of the State, held elections, organized a State government, adopted a free-state constitution, giving the benefit of public schools equally to black and white, and empowering the Legislature to confer the elective franchise upon the colored man. Their Legislature has already voted to ratify the constitutional amendment recently passed by Congress, abolishing slavery throughout the nation. These twelve thousand persons are thus fully committed to the Union, and to perpetual freedom in the state—committed to the very things, and nearly all the things the nation wants—and they ask the nations recognition, and it's assistance to make good their committal. Now, if we reject, and spurn them, we do our utmost to disorganize and disperse them. We in effect say to the white men "You are worthless, or worse—we will neither help you, nor be helped by you." To the blacks we say "This cup of liberty which these, your old masters, hold to your lips, we will dash from you, and leave you to the chances of gathering the spilled and scattered contents in some vague and undefined when, where, and how." If this course, discouraging and paralyzing both white and black, has any tendency to bring Louisiana into proper practical relations with the Union, I have, so far, been unable to perceive it. If, on the contrary, we recognize, and sustain the new government of Louisiana the converse of all this is made true. We encourage the hearts, and nerve the arms of the twelve thousand to adhere to their work, and argue for it, and proselyte for it, and fight for it, and feed it, and grow it, and ripen it to a complete success. The colored man too, in seeing all united for him, is inspired with vigilance, and energy, and daring, to the same end. Grant that he desires the elective franchise, will he not attain it sooner by saving the already advanced steps toward it, than by running backward over them? Concede that the new government of Louisiana is only to what it should be as the egg is to the fowl, we shall sooner have the fowl by hatching the egg than by smashing it? Again, if we reject Louisiana, we also reject one vote in favor of the proposed amendment to the national constitution. To meet this proposition, it has been argued that no more than three fourths of those States which have not attempted secession are necessary to validly ratify the amendment. I do not commit myself against this, further than to say that such a ratification would be questionable, and sure to be persistently questioned; while a ratification by three fourths of all the States would be unquestioned and unquestionable.

I repeat the question. "Can Louisiana be brought into proper practical relation with the Union *sooner* by *sustaining* or by *discarding* her new State Government?

What has been said of Louisiana will apply generally to other States. And yet so great peculiarities pertain to each state; and such important and sudden changes occur in the same state; and, withal, so new and unprecedented is the whole case, that no exclusive, and inflexible plan can safely be prescribed as to details and colatterals. Such exclusive, and inflexible plan, would surely become a new entanglement. Important principles may, and must, be inflexible.

In the present *"situation"* as the phrase goes, it may be my duty to make some new announcement to the people of the South. I am considering, and shall not fail to act, when satisfied that action will be proper.

QUESTIONS TO CONSIDER

1. What was Lincoln's view of African American rights in the years to come?
2. Which strategy do you think Lincoln would have taken toward Reconstruction? What do you think of this strategy?

15.3 FREEDMEN'S BUREAU BILL TEXT (1865)

In 1865, Congress established the Freedmen's Bureau, formally titled the Bureau of Refugees, Freedmen, and Abandoned Lands. As you will read, the bill aimed to reunite African American families displaced by the war, provide humanitarian aid to African Americans, educate former slaves, assure fair labor conditions for those who returned to work for wages on plantations, and encourage positive relations between former slaves and whites. For the next seven years, the Bureau became an important, controversial part of Reconstruction. Former Confederate states fought the Bureau by issuing Black Codes, which aimed to keep African Americans in semi-bondage. The Ku Klux Klan terrorized Bureau supporters and employees alike. In 1872, Congress did not renew the program, but it remained an important symbol of attempted Federal Reconstruction action.

CHAP. XC.—AN ACT TO ESTABLISH A BUREAU FOR THE RELIEF OF FREEDMEN AND REFUGEES.

Be it enacted by the Senate and House of Representatives of the United States of America in Congress assembled, That there is hereby established in the War Department, to continue during the present war of rebellion, and for one year thereafter, a bureau of refugees, freedmen, and abandoned lands, to which shall be committed, as hereinafter provided, the supervision and management of all abandoned lands, and the control of all subjects relating to refugees and freedmen from rebel states, or from any district of country within the territory embraced in the operations of the army, under such rules and regulations as may be prescribed by the head of the bureau and approved by the President. The Said bureau shall be under the management and control of a commissioner to be appointed by the President, by and with the advice and consent of the Senate, whose compensation shall be three thousand dollars per annum, and such number of clerks as may be assigned to him by the Secretary of War, not exceeding one chief clerk, two of the fourth class, two of the third class, and five of the first class. And the commissioner and all persons appointed under this act, shall, before entering upon their duties, take the oath of office prescribed in an act entitled "An act to prescribe an oath of office, and for other purposes," approved July second, eighteen hundred and sixty-two, and the commissioner and the chief clerk shall, before entering upon their duties, give bonds to the treasurer of the United States, the former in the sum of fifty thousand dollars, and the latter in the sum of ten thousand dollars, conditioned for the faithful discharge of their duties respectively, with securities to be approved as sufficient by the Attorney-General, which bonds shall be filed in the office of the first comptroller of the treasury, to be by him put in suit for the benefit of any injured party upon any breach of the conditions thereof.

SEC. 2. *And be it further enacted,* That the Secretary of War may direct such issues of provisions, clothing, and fuel, as he may deem needful for the immediate and temporary shelter and supply of destitute and suffering refugees and freedmen and their wives and children, under such rules and regulations as he may direct.

Source: An Act to Establish a Bureau for the Relief of Freedmen and Refugees, 38th Congress, Session II, *Congressional Globe* (March 3, 1865), 507–509.

SEC. 3. *And be it further enacted*, That the President may, by and with the advice and consent of the Senate, appoint an assistant commissioner for each of the states declared to be in insurrection, not exceeding ten in number, who shall, under the direction of the commissioner, aid in the execution of the provisions of this act; and he shall give a bond to the Treasurer of the United States, in the sum of twenty thousand dollars, in the form and manner prescribed in the first section of this act. And any military officer may be detailed and assigned to duty under this act without increase of pay or allowances. The commissioner shall, before the commencement of each regular session of congress, make full report of his proceedings with exhibits of the state of his accounts to the President, who shall communicate the same to congress, and shall also make special reports whenever required to do so by the President or either house of congress; and the assistant commissioners shall make quarterly reports of their proceedings to the commissioner, and also such other special reports as from time to time may be required.

SEC. 4. *And be it further enacted*, That the commissioner, under the direction of the President, shall have authority to set apart, for the use of loyal refugees and freedmen, such tracts of land. Within the insurrectionary states as shall have been abandoned, or to which the United States shall have acquired title by confiscation or sale, or otherwise, and to every male citizen, whether refugee or freedman, as aforesaid, there shall be assigned not more than forty acres of such land, and the person to whom it was so assigned shall be protected in the use and enjoyment of the land for the term of three years at an annual rent not exceeding six per centum upon the value of such land, as it was appraised by the state authorities in the year eighteen hundred and sixty, for the purpose of taxation, and in case no such appraisal can be found, then the rental shall be based upon the estimated value of the land in said year, to be ascertained in such manner as the commissioner may by regulation prescribe. At the end of said term, or at any time during said term, the occupants of any parcels so assigned may purchase the land and receive such title thereto as the United States can convey, upon paying therefore the value of the land, as ascertained and fixed for the purpose of determining the annual rent aforesaid.

SEC. 5. *And be it further enacted*, That all acts and parts of acts Repealing inconsistent with the provisions of this act, are hereby repealed.

APPROVED, March 3, 1865.

QUESTIONS TO CONSIDER

1. What did the Bill do?
2. Do you think the Bill was an overreach of Federal power?

15.4 ANDREW JOHNSON DEFENDS PASSIVE RECONSTRUCTION POLICIES (1866)

Andrew Johnson (1808–875) became President after Lincoln's 1865 assassination. Lincoln had added the Democratic Johnson, a U.S. Senator from Tennessee, to his National Union Party ticket to propagate a bipartisan message during the 1864 election. Upon assuming the Presidency, Johnson quickly tried to reincorporate former Confederate states into the Union. He clashed with Radical Republicans, such as Thaddeus Stevens (see Reading 15.5), who desired a slower reincorporation policy that was more punitive toward previous Confederate politicians and ensured greater African American rights. In 1867, Johnson vetoed the First Reconstruction Act, which placed the Confederacy under martial law and required former Confederate states to ratify the Fourteenth Amendment in order to rejoin the Union. Congress then overrode his veto, and the House of Representatives impeached Johnson, though the Senate later acquitted him. Johnson delivered the following speech during an ill-fated speaking tour he completed in 1866 to try to rouse support for his non-punitive Reconstruction plans. Johnson later failed in his bid to receive the 1868 Democratic nomination for President, but he pardoned all major Confederate officials before leaving office.

Fellow Citizens of Cleveland:—It is not for the purpose of making a speech I came here to-night. I am aware of the great curiosity that exists on the part of strangers in reference to seeing individuals who are here amongst us. [Louder.] You must remember there are a good many people here to-night, and it requires a great voice to reach the utmost verge of this vast audience. I have used my voice so constantly for some days past that I do know as I shall be able to make you all hear, but I will do my best to make myself heard.

What I am going to say is: There is a large number here who would like to see General Grant, and hear him speak, and hear what he would have to say; but the fact is General Grant is not here. He is extremely ill. His health will not permit of his appearing before this audience to-night. It would be a greater pleasure to me to see him here and have him speak than to make a speech of my own. So then it will not be expected that he will be here to-night, & you cannot see him on account of his extreme indisposition.

Fellow Citizens: In being before you to-night it is not for the purpose of making a speech, but simply to make your acquaintance, and while I am telling you how to do, and at the same time tell you goodbye. We are here to-night on our tour towards a sister State for the purpose of participating in and witnessing the laying of the chief corner stone over a monument to one of our fellow citizens who is no more. It is not necessary for me to mention the name of Stephen A. Douglas to the citizens of Ohio. It is a name familiar to you all, and being on a tour to participate in the ceremonies, and passing through your State and section of country and witnessing the demonstration and manifestation of regard & respect which has been paid to me, I am free to say to you that so far as I am concerned, and I think I am speaking for all the company, when I say we feel extremely gratified and flattered at the demonstration made by the country through which we have passed, and in being flattered, I want to state at the same time that I don't consider that

Source: Andrew Johnson speech included in 40th Congress, 2d Session, *Supplement to the Congressional Globe* (April 3, 1868), 109–110.

entirely personal, but as evidence of what is pervading the public mind, that there is a great issue before the country, and that this demonstration of feeling, is more than anything else, an indication of a deep interest among the great mass of the people in regard to all these great questions that agitate the public mind. In coming before you to-night, I come before you as an American citizen, and not simply as your Chief Magistrate. I claim to be a citizen of the Southern States, and an inhabitant of one of the States of the Union. I know that it has been said, and contended for on the part of some, that I was an alien, for I did not reside in any one of the States of the Union, and therefore I could not be Chief Magistrate, though the States declared I was.

But all that was necessary was simply to introduce a resolution declaring the office vacant or depose the occupant, or under some pretext to prefer articles of impeachment, & the individual who occupies the Chief Magistracy would be deposed and deprived of power.

But, fellow-citizens, a short time since you had a ticket before you for the Presidency and Vice Presidency; I was placed upon that ticket, in conjunction with a distinguished fellow citizen who is now no more. (Voice, "a great misfortune too"). I know there are some who will exclaim, "unfortunate." I admit the ways of Providence are mysterious and unfortunate but uncontrolable by those who would exclaim unfortunate. I was going to say my countrymen, but a short time since, I was selected and placed upon a ticket. There was a platform prepared and adopted by those who placed me upon it, and now, notwithstanding all kinds of misrepresentation: notwithstanding since after the sluice of misrepresentation has been poured out, notwithstanding a subsidized gang of hirelings have traduced me and maligned me ever since I have entered upon the discharge of my official duties, yet I will say had my predecessor have lived, the vials of wrath would have been poured out on him (cries of never, never, never.) I come here to-night in passing along, and being called upon, for the purpose of exchanging opinions and views as time would permit, and to ascertain if we could who was in the wrong.

I appear before you to-night and I want to say this: that I have lived and been among all American people, and have represented them in some capacity for the last twenty-five years. And where is the man living, or the woman in the community, that I have wronged, or where is the person that can place their finger upon one single hair breadth of deviation from one single pledge I have made, or one single violation of the Constitution of the country. What tongue does he speak? What religion does he profess? Let him come forward and place his finger upon one pledge I have violated. (A voice, "Hang Jeff Davis"): (Mr. President resumes.) Hang Jeff Davis? Hang Jeff Davis? Why don't you? (Applause.) Why don't you? (Applause.) Have you not got the Court? Have you not got the Court? Have not you got the Attorney General? Who is your Chief Justice— and that refused to sit upon the trial? (Applause.) I am not the Prosecuting Attorney. I am not the jury. But I will tell you what I did do: I called upon your Congress, that is trying to break up the Government, (immense applause.) Yes, did your Congress order hanging Jeff Davis? (Prolonged applause, mingled with hisses.)

But, fellow citizens, we had as well let feelings and prejudices pass; let passion subside; let reason resume her empire. In presenting myself to you in the few remarks I intended to make, my intention was to address myself to your judgment and to your good sense, and not to your anger or the malignity of your hearts. This was my object in presenting myself on this occasion, and at the same time to tell you good-bye. I have heard the remark made in this crowd to-night. "Traitor, traitor!" (Prolonged confusion.) My countrymen, will you hear me for my cause? For the Constitution of my country? I want to know when, where and under what circumstances Andrew Johnson, either as Chief Executive, or in any other capacity over violated the Constitution of his country. Let me ask this large and intelligent audience here to-night, if your Secretary of State, who served four years under Mr. Lincoln, who was placed under the butcher's blow and exposed to the assassin's knife, when he turned traitor. If I were disposed to play orator, and deal in declamation, here to-night. I would imitate one of the ancient tragedies we have such account of—I would take William HSeward and open to you the scars he has received. I would exhibit his bloody garment and show the rent caused by the assassin's knife. [Three cheers for Seward.] Yes, I would unfold his bloody garments here to-night and ask who had committed treason. I would ask why Jeff Davis was not hung? Why don't you hang Thad Stevens and Wendell Phillips? I can tell you, my countrymen I have been fighting traitors in the South, [prolonged applause,] and they have been whipped, and say they were wrong, acknowledge their error and accept the terms of the Constitution.

And now as I pass around the circle, having fought traitors at the South, I am prepared to fight traitors at the North. God being willing with your help ["You can't have it." and prolonged confusion,] they would be crushed worse than the traitors of the South, and this glorious Union of ours will be preserved. In coming here to-night, it was not coming as Chief Magistrate of twenty-five States, but I come here as the Chief Magistrate of thirty-six States. I came here to-night with the flag of my country in my hand, with a constellation of thirty-six and not twenty-five stars. I came here to-night with the Constitution of my country intact, determined to defend the Constitution, let the consequences be what they may. I came here to-night for the Union: the entire circle of these States. [A Voice, "How many States made you President?"] How many States made me President? Was you against secession? Do you want to dissolve the Union? [A voice, No.] Then I am President of the whole United States, and I will tell you one thing. I understand the discordant notes in this audience here to-night. And I will tell you furthermore, that he that is opposed to the restoration of the Government and the union of the States, is as great a traitor as Jeff Davis, and I am against both of them. I fought traitors at the South, now I fight them at the North. (Immense applause.)

QUESTIONS TO CONSIDER

1. How did Johnson defend himself?
2. Do you find the speech to be persuasive?

15.5 THADDEUS STEVENS' SPEECH ON RECONSTRUCTION (1867)

Thaddeus Stevens (1792–1868) held very different views than Johnson (see Reading 15.4). A member of the U.S. House of Representatives from Pennsylvania, Stevens was a "Radical Republican" who demanded a stronger version of Federal Reconstruction in order to punish prominent Confederates and secure African American rights after the war. Stevens, who found Lincoln's delayed acceptance of complete abolitionism to be appalling, especially clashed with President Andrew Johnson, who advocated friendly policies toward the former Confederacy. In January 1867, Stevens delivered the following speech. In it, he demanded greater Federal action to quell southern dissent and violence toward Freedmen. Two months later, Stevens led the effort in the House of Representatives to remove Johnson from office via impeachment. Stevens passed away in 1868, shortly after the Senate acquitted Johnson in its impeachment trial.

Mr. Speaker, I am very anxious that this bill should be proceeded with until finally acted upon. I desire that as early as possible, without curtailing debate, this House shall come to some conclusion as to what shall be done with the rebel States. This becomes more and more necessary every day; and the late decision of the Supreme Court of the United States has rendered immediate action by Congress upon the question of the establishment of governments in the rebel States absolutely indispensable.

That decision, although in terms perhaps not as infamous as the Dred Scott decision, is yet far more dangerous in its operation upon the lives and liberties of the loyal men of this country. That decision has taken away every protection in every one of these rebel States from every loyal man, black or white, who resides there. That decision has unsheathed the dagger of the assassin, and places the knife of the rebel at the throat of every man who dares proclaim himself to be now, or to have been heretofore, a loyal Union man. If the doctrine enunciated in that decision be true, never were the people of any country anywhere, or at any time, in such terrible peril as are our loyal brethren at the South, whether they be black or white, whether they go there from the North or are natives of the rebel States.

Now, Mr. Speaker, unless Congress proceeds at once to do something to protect these people from the barbarians who are now daily murdering them; who are murdering the loyal whites daily and daily putting into secret graves not only hundreds but thousands of the colored people of that country; unless Congress proceeds at once to adopt some means for their protection, I ask you and every man who loves liberty whether we will not be liable to the just censure of the world for our negligence or our cowardice or our want of ability to do so?

Now, sir, it is for these reasons that I insist on the passage of some such measure as this. This is a bill designed to enable loyal men, so far as I could discriminate them in these States, to form governments which shall be in loyal hands, that they may protect themselves from such outrages as I have mentioned. . . .

. . . May I ask, without offense, will Congress have the courage to do its duty? Or will it be deterred by the clamor of ignorance, bigotry, and despotism from perfecting a revolution begun without their consent, but which ought not to be ended without their full

Source: Beverly Wilson Palmer, ed., *The Selected Papers of Thaddeus Stevens, Volume II* (Pittsburgh: University of Pittsburgh Press, 1998), 211–221.

participation and concurrence? Possibly the people would not have inaugurated this revolution to correct the palpable incongruities and despotic provisions of the Constitution; but having it forced upon them, will they be so unwise as to suffer it to subside without erecting this nation into a perfect Republic?

Since the surrender of the armies of the confederate States of America a little has been done toward establishing this Government upon the true principles of liberty and justice; and but a little if we stop here. We have broken the material shackles of four million slaves. We have unchained them from the stake so as to allow them locomotion, provided they do not walk in paths which are trod by white men. We have allowed them the unwonted privilege of attending church, if they can do so without offending the sight of their former masters. We have even given them that highest and most agreeable evidence of liberty as defined by the "great plebeian," the "right to work." But in what have we enlarged their liberty of thought? In what have we taught them the science and granted them the privilege of self-government? We have imposed upon them the privilege of fighting our battles, of dying in defense of freedom, and of bearing their equal portion of taxes; but where have we given them the privilege of ever participating in the formation of the laws for the government of their native land? By what civil weapon have we enabled them to defend themselves against oppression and injustice? Call you this liberty? Call you this a free Republic where four millions are subjects but not citizens? Then Persia, with her kings and satraps, was free; then Turkey is free! Their subjects had liberty of motion and of labor, but the laws were made without and against their will; but I must declare that, in my judgment, they were as really free governments as ours is to-day. I know they had fewer rulers and more subjects, but those rulers were no more despotic that ours, and their subjects had just as large privileges in governing the country as ours have. Think not I would slander my native land; I would reform it. Twenty years ago I denounced it as a despotism. Then, twenty million white men enchained four million black men. I pronounce it no nearer to a true Republic now when twenty-five million of a privileged class exclude five million from all participation in the rights of government.

The freedom of a Government does not depend upon the quality of its laws, but upon the power that has the right to enact them. During the dictatorship of Pericles his laws were just, but Greece was not free. During the last century Russia has been blessed with most remarkable emperors, who have generally decreed wise and just laws, but Russia is not free.

No Government can be free that does not allow all its citizens to participate in the formation and execution of her laws. There are degrees of tyranny. But every other government is despotism. It has always been observed that the larger the number of the rulers the more cruel the treatment of the subject races. It were better for the black man if he were governed by one king than by twenty million. . . .

But it will be said, as it has been said, "This is negro equality!" What is negro equality, about which so much is said by knaves, and some of which is believed by men who are not fools? It means, as understood by honest Republicans, just this much, and no more: every man, no matter what his race or color; every earthly being who has an immortal soul, has an equal right to justice, honesty, and fair play with every other man; and the law should secure him these rights. The same law which condemns or acquits an African should condemn or acquit a white man. The same law which gives a verdict in a white man's favor should give a verdict in a black man's favor on the same state of facts. Such is the law of God and such ought to be the law of man. The doctrine does not mean that a negro shall sit on the same seat or eat at the same table with a white man. That is a matter of taste which every man must decide for himself. The law has nothing to do with it. If there be any who are afraid of the rivalry of the black man in office or in business, I have only to advise them to try and beat their competitor in knowledge and business capacity, and there is no danger that his white neighbors will prefer his African rival to himself. I know there is between those who are influenced by this cry of "negro equality" and the opinion that there is still danger that the negro will be the smartest, for I never saw even a contraband slave that had not more sense than such men.

There are those who admit the justice and ultimate utility of granting impartial suffrage to all men, but they think it is impolitic. An ancient philosopher, whose antagonist admitted that what he required was just but deemed it impolitic, asked him: "Do you believe in Hades?" I would say to those above referred to, who admit the justice of human equality before the law but doubt its policy: "Do you believe in hell?"

How do you answer the principle inscribed in our political scripture, "That to secure these rights governments are instituted among men, deriving their just powers from the consent of the governed?" Without such consent government is a tyranny, and you exercising it are tyrants. Of course, this does not admit malefactors to power, or there would soon be no penal laws and society would become an anarchy. But this step forward is an assault upon ignorance and prejudice, and timid men shrink from it. Are such men fit to sit in the places of statesmen?

There are periods in the history of nations when statesmen can make themselves names for posterity; but such occasions are never improved by cowards. In the acquisition of true fame courage is just as necessary in the civilian as in the military hero. In the Reformation there were men engaged as able and perhaps more learned than Martin Luther. Melancthon and others were ripe scholars and sincere reformers, but none of them had his courage. He alone was willing to go where duty called though "devils were as thick as the tiles on the houses." And Luther is the great luminary of the Reformation, around whom the others revolve as satellites and shine by his light. We may not aspire to fame. But great events fix the eye of history on small objects and magnify their meanness. Let us at least escape that condition.

QUESTIONS TO CONSIDER

1. How did Stevens make his case for greater Federal action?
2. Do you find the speech to be persuasive?

15.6 ULYSSES S. GRANT, "USE OF THE ARMY IN CERTAIN OF THE SOUTHERN STATES" (1876)

Ulysses S. Grant (1822–1885) was the Commanding General of the Union Army at the end of the Civil War and the eighteenth President of the United States. In the 1868 election, Grant defeated Democrat Horatio Seymour by a wide margin and, once in office, worked with his fellow Republicans to secure the rights gained by Union victory in the Civil War. In 1970, he campaigned for the ratification of the Fifteenth Amendment, which prohibited denying suffrage based on "race, color, or previous condition of servitude." Grant continued to struggle, however, with southern violence toward both freed slaves and the state Republican governments that protected them. In 1876, Grant delivered the following speech. In it, he defended sending the military into Virginia, South Carolina, Louisiana, and Florida to protect African American voting right, quell violence, and protect Republican governments in those states. Grant's presidency was undone by a series of corruption strategies that involved senior officials in his administration. His successor, Rutherford B. Hayes, ended the Federal military occupation of the South.

To the House of Representatives :

On the 9th day of December, 1876, the following resolution of the House of Representatives was received, viz :

Resolved, That the President be requested, if not incompatible with the public interest, to transmit to this House copies of any and all orders or directions emanating from him or from either of the Executive Departments of the Government to any military commander or civil officer, with reference to the service of the Army, or any portion thereof, in the States of Virginia, South Carolina, Louisiana, and Florida, since the 1st of August last, together with reports, by telegraph or otherwise, from either or any of said military commanders or civil officers.

It was immediately, or soon thereafter, referred to the Secretary of War and the Attorney-General, the custodians of all retained copies of "orders or directions" given by the executive department of the Government covered by the above inquiry, together with all information upon which such "orders or directions" were given.

The information, it will be observed, is voluminous, and, with the limited clerical force in the Department of Justice, has consumed the time up to the present. Many of the communications accompanying this have been already made public in connection with messages heretofore sent to Congress. This class of information includes the important documents received from the governor of South Carolina, and sent to Congress with my message on the subject of the Hamburgh massacre ; also the documents accompanying my response to the resolution of the House of Representatives in regard to the soldiers stationed at Petersburgh.

There have also come to me and to the Department of Justice, from time to time, other earnest written communications from persons holding public trusts and from others residing in the South, some of which I append hereto as bearing upon the precarious condition of the public peace in those States. These communications I have reason to regard as made by

Source: Ulysses S. Grant, "Use of the Army in Certain of the Southern States," 44th Congress, 2d Session, *Congressional Globe* (January 24, 1877), 1–4.

respectable and responsible men. Many of them deprecate the publication of their names as involving danger to them personally,

The reports heretofore made by committees of Congress of the results of their inquiries in Mississippi and in Louisiana, and the newspapers of several States recommending "the Mississippi plan," have also furnished important data for estimating the danger to the public peace and order in those States.

It is enough to say that these different kinds and sources of evidence have left no doubt whatever in my mind that intimidation has been used, and actual violence, to an extent requiring the aid of the United States Government, where it was practicable to furnish such aid, in South Carolina, in Florida, and in Louisiana, as well as in Mississippi, in Alabama, and in Georgia.

The troops of the United States have been but sparingly used, and in no case so as to interfere with the free exercise of the right of suffrage. Very few troops were available for the purpose of preventing or suppressing the violence and intimidation existing in the States above named. In no case except that of South Carolina was the number of soldiers in any State increased in anticipation of the election, saving that twenty-four men and an officer were sent from Fort Foote to Petersburgh, Va., where disturbances were threatened prior to the election.

No troops were stationed at the voting-places. In Florida and in Louisiana, respectively, the small number of soldiers already in the said States were stationed at such points in each State as were most threatened with violence, where they might be available as a *posse* for the officer whose duty it was to preserve the peace and prevent intimidation of voters, Such a disposition of the troops seemed to me reasonable, and justified by law and precedent, while its omission would have been inconsistent with the constitutional duty of the President of the United States "to take care that the laws be faithfully executed." The statute expressly forbids the bringing of troops to the polls, "except where it is necessary to keep the peace," implying that to keep the peace it may be done. But this even, so far as I am advised, has not in any case been done. The Stationing of a company or part of a company in the vicinity, where they would be available to prevent riot, has been

the only use made of troops prior to and at the time of the elections. Where so stationed, they could be called, in an emergency requiring it, by a marshal or deputy marshal as a *posse* to aid in suppressing unlawful violence. The evidence which has come to me has left me no ground to doubt that if there had been more military force available, it would have been my duty to have disposed of it in several States with a view to the prevention of the violence and intimidation which have undoubtedly contributed to the defeat of the election-law in Mississippi, Alabama, and Georgia, as well as in South Carolina, Louisiana, and Florida.

By article 4, section 4, of the Constitution, "The United States shall guarantee to every State in this Union a republican form of government, and on application of the legislature, or of the executive, (when the legislature cannot be convened,) shall protect each of them against domestic violence."

By act of Congress (R. S. U. S., sec, 1034,1035) the President, in case of "insurrection in any State," or of "unlawful obstruction to the enforcement of the laws of the United States by the ordinary course of judicial proceedings," or whenever "domestic violence in any State so obstructs the execution of the laws thereof, and of the United States, as to deprive any portion of the people of such State" of their civil or political rights, is authorized to employ such parts of the land and naval forces as he may deem necessary to enforce the execution of the laws and preserve the peace, and sustain the authority of the State and of the United States. Acting under this title (69) of the Revised Statutes, United States, I accompanied the sending of troops to South Carolina with a proclamation such as is therein prescribed.

The President is also authorized by act of Congress "to employ such part of the land or naval forces of the United States" ✳ ✳ "as shall be necessary to prevent the violation and to enforce the due execution of the provisions" of Title 24 of the Revised Statutes of the United States for the protection of the civil rights of citizens, among which is the provision against conspiracies "to prevent by force, intimidation, or threat, any citizen who is lawfully entitled to vote, from giving his support or advocacy in a legal manner toward or in favor of the election of any lawfully qualified person as an elector for President or Vice President, or as a member of Congress of the United States." (U. S. Rev. Stat., 1989.)

In cases falling under this title I have not considered it necessary to issue a proclamation to precede or accompany the employment of such part of the Army as seemed to be necessary.

In case of insurrection against a State government, or against the Government of the United States, a proclamation is appropriate ; but in keeping the peace of the United States at an election at which members of Congress are elected, no such call from the State or proclamation by the President is prescribed by statute or required by precedent.

In the case of South Carolina, insurrection and domestic violence against the State government were clearly shown, and the application of the governor founded thereon was duly presented, and I could not deny his constitutional request without abandoning my duty as the Executive of the National Government.

The companies stationed in the other States have been employed to secure the better execution of the laws of the United States and to preserve the peace of the United States.

After the election had been had, and where violence was apprehended by which the returns from the counties and precincts might be destroyed, troops were ordered to the State of Florida, and those already in Louisiana were ordered to the points in greatest danger of violence.

I have not employed troops on slight occasions, nor in any case where it has not been necessary to the enforcement of the laws of the United States. In this I have been guided by the Constitution and the laws which have been enacted and the precedents which have been formed under it.

It has been necessary to employ troops occasionally to overcome resistance to the internal-revenue laws, from the time of the resistance to the collection of the whisky-tax in Pennsylvania, under Washington, to the present time.

In 1854, when it was apprehended that resistance would be made in Boston to the seizure and return to his master of a fugitive slave, the troops there stationed were employed to enforce the master's right under the Constitution, and troops stationed at New York were ordered to be in readiness to go to Boston if it should prove to be necessary.

In 1859, when John Brown with a small number of men made his attack upon Harper's Ferry, the President ordered United States troops to assist in the apprehension and suppression of him and his party, without a formal call of the legislature or governor of Virginia, and without proclamation of the President.

Without citing further instances, in which the Executive has exercised his power as commander of the Army and Navy to prevent or suppress resistance to the laws of the United States, or where he has exercised like authority in obedience to a call from a State to suppress insurrection, I desire to assure both Congress and the country that it has been my purpose to administer the executive powers of the Government fairly, and in no instance to disregard or transcend the limits of the Constitution.

QUESTIONS TO CONSIDER

1. How did Grant make the case for Federal military involvement in the South?
2. Do you find the speech to be persuasive?

CHAPTER 16

THE TRIUMPH OF INDUSTRIAL CAPITALISM, 1850–1890

16.1 JOHN GAST, *AMERICAN PROGRESS* (1872)

Artist John Gast's 1872 painting, "American Progress," is a prime example of nascent American Western art and of contemporary views relating to Manifest Destiny. Gast, who lived in Brooklyn, was not particularly well-known except for this painting. In 1872, a publisher of American Western travel guides commissioned the work from Gast, and "American Progress" has since been widely displayed and studied. The woman in the foreground, "Progress," leads the way to the West, and settlers follow in her wake.

Source: John Gast, "American Progress," http://www.loc.gov/pictures/item/97507547/ (Accessed June 11, 2018).

1. What details do you notice in the painting, and what do you make of them?

2. How did Gast use different colors to make an argument in the painting?

16.2 ANDREW CARNEGIE, "WEALTH" (1899)

The life of Andrew Carnegie (1835–1919) illustrates well the rise of industrial capitalism in America during the mid to late nineteenth century. Carnegie, who was born in Scotland, emigrated to the United States in 1848. During the 1860s, Carnegie purchased investments in railroads and oil. In the 1880s, Carnegie formed a major steel company in the Pittsburgh area and then set about trying to vertically integrate the company by purchasing its supply chains. Carnegie Steel became one of the largest steel companies in the world, and Carnegie one of the world's richest men. In 1901, Carnegie sold Carnegie Steel to banker J. P. Morgan for $480 million. As he accumulated wealth, Carnegie began to evangelize about the need for the rich to give back to society through philanthropy. His 1899 essay, "Wealth," codified these ideals. In the essay, Carnegie espoused a specific viewpoint about the role of the rich in a healthy society. Indeed, in the early twentieth century, Carnegie donated some $350 million to charity—around ninety percent of his fortune. Among other ventures, he supported thousands of free libraries, founded the Carnegie Institute of Technology (now Carnegie Mellon University), and created a charitable trust for Scottish universities.

The problem of our age is the proper administration of wealth, so that the ties of brotherhood may still bind together the rich and poor in harmonious relationship. The conditions of human life have not only been changed, but revolutionized, within the past few hundred years. In former days there was little difference between the dwelling, dress, food, and environment of the chief and those of his retainers. The Indians are to-day where civilized man then was. When visiting the Sioux, I was led to the wigwam of the chief. It was just like the others in external appearance, and even within the difference was trifling between it and those of the poorest of his braves. The contrast between the palace of the millionaire and the cottage of the laborer with us today measures the change which has come with civilization.

This change, however, is not to be deplored, but welcomed as highly beneficial. It is well, nay, essential for the progress of the race, that the houses of some should be homes for all that is highest and best in literature and the arts, and for all the refinements of civilization, rather than that none should be so. Much better this great irregularity than universal squalor. Without wealth there can be no Maecenas. The "good old times" were not good old times.

Neither master nor servant was well situated then as to-day. A relapse to old conditions would be disastrous to both—not the least so to him who serves and

Source: Andrew Carnegie, "Wealth," *The North American Review* 266 no. 3 (September, 1981), 60–64.

would sweep away civilization with it. But whether the change be for good or ill, it is upon us, beyond our power to alter, and therefore to be accepted and made the best of. It is a waste of time to criticize the inevitable.

It is easy to see how the change has come. One illustration will serve for almost every phase of the cause. In the manufacture of products we have the whole story. It applies to all combinations of human industry, as stimulated and enlarged by the inventions of this scientific age. Formerly articles were manufactured at the domestic hearth or in small shops which formed part of the household. The master and his apprentices worked side by side, the latter living with the master, and therefore subject to the same conditions. When these apprentices rose to be masters, there was little or no change in their mode of life, and they, in turn, educated in the same routine succeeding apprentices. There was, substantially, social equality, and even political equality, for those engaged in industrial pursuits had then little or no political voice in the State.

But the inevitable result of such a mode of manufacture was crude articles at high prices. To-day the world obtains commodities of excellent quality at prices which even the generation preceding this would have deemed incredible. In the commercial world similar causes have produced similar results, and the race is benefited thereby. The poor enjoy what the rich could not before afford. What were the luxuries have become the necessaries of life. The laborer has now more comforts than the farmer had a few generations ago. The farmer has more luxuries than the landlord had, and is more richly clad and better housed. The landlord has books and pictures rarer, and appointments more artistic, than the King could then obtain.

The price we pay for this salutary change is, no doubt, great. We assemble thousands of operatives in the factory, in the mine, and in the counting-house, of whom the employer can know little or nothing, and to whom the employer is little better than a myth. All intercourse between them is at an end. Rigid Castes are formed, and, as usual, mutual ignorance breeds mutual distrust. Each Caste is without sympathy for the other, and ready to credit anything disparaging in regard to it. Under the law of competition, the employer of thousands is forced into the strictest economies, among

which the rates paid to labor figure prominently, and often there is friction between the employer and the employed, between capital and labor, between rich and poor. Human society loses homogeneity.

The price which society pays for the law of competition, like the price it pays for cheap comforts and luxuries, is also great; but the advantages of this law are also greater still, for it is to this law that we owe our wonderful material development, which brings improved conditions in its train. But, whether the law be benign or not, we must say of it, as we say of the change in the conditions of men to which we have referred: It is here; we cannot evade it; no substitutes for it have been found; and while the law may be sometimes hard for the individual, it is best for the race, because it insures the survival of the fittest in every department. We accept and welcome, therefore, as conditions to which we must accommodate ourselves, great inequality of environment, the concentration of business, industrial and commercial, in the hands of a few, and the law of competition between these, as being not only beneficial, but essential for the future progress of the race. Having accepted these, it follows that there must be great scope for the exercise of special ability in the merchant and in the manufacturer who has to conduct affairs upon a great scale. That this talent for organization and management is rare among men is proved by the fact that it invariably secures for its possessor enormous rewards, no matter where or under what laws or conditions. The experienced in affairs always rate the *man* whose services can be obtained as a partner as not only the first consideration, but such as to render the question of his capital scarcely worth considering, for such men soon create capital; while, without the special talent required, capital soon takes wings. Such men become interested in firms or corporations using millions; and estimating only simple interest to be made upon the capital invested, it is inevitable that their income must exceed their expenditures, and that they must accumulate wealth. Nor is there any middle ground which such men can occupy, because the great manufacturing or commercial concern which does not earn at least interest upon its capital soon becomes bankrupt. It must either go forward or fall behind; to stand still is impossible. It is a condition essential for its successful operation that it should be thus far profitable, and even that, in addition to interest on capital, it should make profit. It is a law, as certain as any of the others named, that men possessed of this peculiar talent for affairs, under the free play of economic forces, must, of necessity, soon be in receipt of more revenue than can be judiciously expended upon themselves; and this law is as beneficial for the race as the others.

Objections to the foundations upon which society is based are not in order, because the condition of the race is better with these than it has been with any others which have been tried. Of the effect of any new substitutes proposed we cannot be sure. The Socialist or Anarchist who seeks to overturn present conditions is to be regarded as attacking the foundation upon which civilization itself rests, for civilization took its start from the day that the capable, industrious workman said to his incompetent and lazy fellow, "If thou dost not sow, thou shalt not reap," and thus ended primitive Communism by separating the drones from the bees. One who studies this subject will soon be brought face to face with the conclusion that upon the sacredness of property civilization itself depends—the right of the laborer to his hundred dollars in the savings bank, and equally the legal right of the millionaire to his millions. To those who propose to substitute Communism for this intense Individualism the answer, therefore, is: The race has tried that. All progress from that barbarous day to the present time has resulted from its displacement. Not evil, but good, has come to the race from the accumulation of wealth by those who have the ability and energy that produce it. But even if we admit for a moment that it might be better for the race to discard its present foundation, Individualism,—that it is a nobler ideal that man should labor, not for himself alone, but in and for a brotherhood of his fellows, and share with them all in common, realizing Swedenborg's idea of Heaven, where, as he says, the angels derive their happiness, not from laboring for self, but for each other,—even admit all this, and a sufficient answer is, This is not evolution, but revolution. It necessitates the changing of human nature itself—a work of aeons, even if it were good to change it, which we cannot know. It is not practicable in our day or in our age. Even if desirable theoretically, it belongs to another and long-succeeding sociological

stratum. Our duty is with what practicable now; with the next step possible in our day and generation. It is criminal to waste our energies in endeavoring to uproot, when all we can profitably or possibly accomplish is to bend the universal tree of humanity a little in the direction most favorable to the production of good fruit under existing circumstances. We might as well urge the destruction of the highest existing type of man because he failed to reach our ideal as to favor the destruction of Individualism, Private Property, the Law of Accumulation of Wealth, and the Law of Competition; for these are the highest results of human experience, the soil in which society so far has produced the best fruit. Unequally or unjustly, perhaps, as these laws sometimes operate, and imperfect as they appear to the Idealist, they are nevertheless, like the highest type of man, the best and most valuable of all that humanity has yet accomplished.

* * *

We start, then, with a condition of affairs under which the best interests of the race are promoted, but which inevitably gives wealth to the few. Thus far, accepting conditions as they exist, the situation can be surveyed and pronounced good. The question then arises,—and, if the foregoing be correct, it is the only question with which we have to deal,—What is the proper mode of administering wealth after the laws upon which civilization is founded have thrown it into the hands of the few? And it is of this great question that I believe I offer the true solution. It will be understood that *fortunes* are here spoken of, not moderate sums saved by many years of effort, the returns from which are required for the comfortable maintenance and education of families. This is not *wealth*, but only *competence*, which it should be the aim of all to acquire.

There are but three modes in which surplus wealth can be disposed of. It can be left to the families of the decedents; or it can be bequeathed for public purposes; or, finally, it can be administered during their lives by its possessors. Under the first and second modes most of the wealth of the world that has reached the few has hitherto been applied. Let us in turn consider each of these modes. The first is the most injudicious. In monarchical countries, the estates and the greatest portion of the wealth are left to the first son, that the vanity of the parent may be gratified by the thought that his name and title are to descend to succeeding generations unimpaired. The condition of this class in Europe today teaches the futility of such hopes or ambitions. The successors have become impoverished through their follies or from the fall in the value of land. Even in Great Britain the strict law of entail has been found inadequate to maintain the status of an hereditary class. Its soil is rapidly passing into the hands of the stranger. Under republican institutions the division of property among the children is much fairer, but the question which forces itself upon thoughtful men in all lands is: Why should men leave great fortunes to their children? If this is done from affection, is it not misguided affection? Observation teaches that, generally speaking, it is not well for the children that they should be so burdened. Neither is it well for the state. Beyond providing for the wife and daughters moderate sources of income, and very moderate allowances indeed, if any, for the sons, men may well hesitate, for it is no longer questionable that great sums bequeathed oftener work more for the injury than for the good of the recipients. Wise men will soon conclude that, for the best interests of the members of their families and of the state, such bequests are an improper use of their means.

It is not suggested that men who have failed to educate their sons to earn a livelihood shall cast them adrift in poverty. If any man has seen fit to rear his sons with a view to their living idle lives, or, what is highly commendable, has instilled in them the sentiment that they are in a position to labor for public ends without reference to pecuniary considerations, then, of course, the duty of the parent is to see that such are provided for *in moderation*. There are instances of millionaires' sons unspoiled by wealth, who, being rich, still perform great services in the community. Such are the very salt of the earth, as valuable as, unfortunately, they are rare; still it is not the exception, but the rule, that men must regard, and, looking at the usual result of enormous sums conferred upon legatees, the thoughtful man must shortly say, "I would as soon leave to my son a curse as the almighty dollar," and admit to himself that it is not the welfare of the children, but family pride, which inspires these enormous legacies.

As to the second mode, that of leaving wealth at death for public uses, it may be said that this is only a means for the disposal of wealth, provided a man is content to wait until he is dead before it becomes of much good in the world. Knowledge of the results of legacies bequeathed is not calculated to inspire the brightest hopes of much posthumous good being accomplished. The cases are not few in which the real object sought by the testator is not attained, nor are they few in which his real wishes are thwarted. In many cases the bequests are so used as to become only monuments of his folly. It is well to remember that it requires the exercise of not less ability than that which acquired the wealth to use it so as to be really beneficial to the community. Besides this, it may fairly be said that no man is to be extolled for doing what he cannot help doing, nor is he to be thanked by the community to which he only leaves wealth at death. Men who leave vast sums in this way may fairly be thought men who would not have left it at all, had they been able to take it with them. The memories of such cannot be held in grateful remembrance, for there is no grace in their gifts. It is not to be wondered at that such bequests seem so generally to lack the blessing.

The growing disposition to tax more and more heavily large estates left at death is a cheering indication of the growth of a salutary change in public opinion. The State of Pennsylvania now takes—subject to some exceptions—one-tenth of the property left by its citizens. The budget presented in the British Parliament the other day proposes to increase the death-duties; and, most significant of all, the new tax is to be a graduated one. Of all forms of taxation, this seems the wisest. Men who continue hoarding great sums all their lives, the proper use of which for public ends would work good to the community, should be made to feel that the community, in the form of the state, cannot thus be deprived of its proper share. By taxing estates heavily at death the state marks its condemnation of the selfish millionaire's unworthy life.

It is desirable that nations should go much further in this direction. Indeed, it is difficult to set bounds to the share of a rich man's estate which should go at his death to the public through the agency of the state, and by all means such taxes should be graduated, beginning at nothing upon moderate sums to dependents, and increasing rapidly as the amounts swell, until of the millionaire's hoard, as of Shylock's at least

"____The other half Comes to the privy coffer of the state."

This policy would work powerfully to induce the rich man to attend to the administration of wealth during his life, which is the end that society should always have in view, as being that by far most fruitful for the people. Nor need it be feared that this policy would sap the root of enterprise and render men less anxious to accumulate, for to the class whose ambition it is to leave great fortunes and be talked about after their death, it will attract even more attention, and indeed, be a somewhat nobler ambition to have enormous sums paid over to the state from their fortunes.

* * *

There remains, then, only one mode of using great fortunes; but in this we have the true antidote for the temporary unequal distribution of wealth, the reconciliation of the rich and the poor—a reign of harmony—another ideal, differing, indeed, from that of the Communist in requiring only the further evolution of existing conditions. It is founded upon the present most intense individualism, and the race is prepared to put it in practice by degrees whenever it pleases. Under its sway we shall have an ideal state, in which the surplus wealth of the few will become, in the best sense, the property of the many, because administered for the common good, and this wealth, passing through the hands of the few, can be made a much more potent force for the elevation of our race than if it had been distributed in small sums to the people themselves. Even the poorest can be made to see this, and to agree that great sums gathered by some of their fellow-citizens and spent for public purposes, from which the masses reap the principal benefit, are more valuable to them than if scattered among them through the course of many years in trifling amounts.

If we consider what results flow from the Cooper Institute, for instance, to the best portion of the race in New York not possessed of means, and compare these with those which would have arisen for the good of the masses from an equal sum distributed by Mr. Cooper in his lifetime in the form of wages, which is the highest form of distribution, being for work done

and not for charity, we can form some estimate of the possibilities for the improvement of the race which lie embedded in the present law of the accumulation of wealth. Much of this sum, if distributed in small quantities among the people, would have been wasted in the indulgence of appetite, some of it in excess, and it may be doubted whether even the part put to the best use, that of adding to the comforts of the home, would have yielded results for the race, as a race, at all comparable to those which are flowing and are to flow from the Cooper Institute from generation to generation. Let the advocate of violent or radical change ponder well this thought.

We might even go so far as to take another instance, that of Mr. Tilden's bequest of five millions of dollars for a free library in the city of New York, but in referring to this one cannot help saying involuntarily, How much better if Mr. Tilden had devoted the last years of his own life to the proper administration of this immense sum; in which case neither legal contest nor any other cause of delay could have interfered with his aims. But let us assume that Mr. Tilden's millions finally become the means of giving to this city a noble public library, where the treasures of the world contained in books will be open to all forever, without money and without price. Considering the good of that part of the race which congregates in and around Manhattan Island, would its permanent benefit have been better promoted had these millions been allowed to circulate in small sums through the hands of the masses? Even the most strenuous advocate of Communism must entertain a doubt upon this subject. Most of those who think will probably entertain no doubt whatever.

Poor and restricted are our opportunities in this life; narrow our horizon; our best work most imperfect; but rich men should be thankful for one inestimable boon. They have it in their power during their lives to busy themselves in organizing benefactions from which the masses of their fellows will derive lasting advantage, and thus dignify their own lives. The highest life is probably to be reached, not by such imitation of the life of Christ as Count Tolstoi gives us, but, while animated by Christ's spirit, by recognizing the changed conditions of this age, and adopting modes of expressing this spirit suitable to the changed conditions under which we live; still laboring for the good of our fellows, which was the essence of His life and teaching, but laboring in a different manner.

This, then, is held to be the duty of the man of Wealth: First, to set an example of modest, unostentatious living, shunning display or extravagance; to provide moderately for the legitimate wants of those dependent upon him; and after doing so to consider all surplus revenues which come to him simply as trust funds, which he is called upon to administer, and strictly bound as a matter of duty to administer in the manner which, in his judgment, is best calculated to produce the most beneficial result for the community—the man of wealth thus becoming the mere agent and trustee for his poorer brethren, bringing to their service his superior wisdom, experience, and ability to administer, doing for them better than they would or could do for themselves.

We are met here with the difficulty of determining what are moderate sums to leave to members of the family; what is modest, unostentatious living; what is the test of extravagance. There must be different standards for different conditions. The answer is that it is as impossible to name exact amounts or actions as it is to define good manners, good taste, or the rules of propriety; but, nevertheless, these are verities, well known although undefinable. Public sentiment is quick to know and to feel what offends these. So in the case of wealth. The rule in regard to good taste in the dress of men or women applies here. Whatever makes one conspicuous offends the canon. If any family be chiefly known for display, for extravagance in home, table, equipage, for enormous sums ostentatiously spent in any form upon itself,—if these be its chief distinctions, we have no difficulty in estimating its nature or culture. So likewise in regard to the use or abuse of its surplus wealth, or to generous, free-handed coöperation in good public uses, or to unabated efforts to accumulate and hoard to the last, whether they administer or bequeath. The verdict rests with the best and most enlightened public sentiment. The community will surely judge, and its judgments will not often be wrong. . . .

Thus is the problem of Rich and Poor to be solved. The laws of accumulation will be left free; the laws of distribution free. Individualism will continue, but the millionaire will be but a trustee for the poor; intrusted for a season with a great part of the increased wealth of the community far better than it could or would have done for itself. The best minds will thus have reached a stage in the development of the race in which it is clearly seen that there is no mode of disposing of surplus wealth creditable to thoughtful and earnest men into whose hands it flows save by using it year by year for the general good. This day already dawns. But a little while, and although, without incurring the pity of their fellows, men may die sharers in great business enterprises from which their capital cannot be or has not been withdrawn, and is left chiefly at death for public uses, yet the man who dies leaving behind him millions of available wealth, which was his to administer during life, will pass away "unwept, unhonored, and unsung," no matter to what uses he leaves the dross which he cannot take with him. Of such as these the public verdict will then be: "The man who dies thus rich dies disgraced."

Such, in my opinion, is the true Gospel concerning Wealth, obedience to which is destined some day to solve the problem of the Rich and the Poor, and to bring "Peace on earth, among men Good-Will."

QUESTIONS TO CONSIDER

1. What did Carnegie see as the role of the rich in society?
2. Do you find his argument convincing?

16.3 IDA TARBELL, EXCERPT FROM *THE HISTORY OF THE STANDARD OIL COMPANY* (1904)

In the late nineteenth and early twentieth centuries, the Standard Oil Company dominated the American oil market. John D. Rockefeller, the company's founder, ensured both vertical integration (Standard Oil controlled its supply chains) and horizontal integration (Standard Oil negotiated for cheaper railroad rates to transport the oil, which kept the company's prices low and eliminated competitors, allowing Rockefeller to monopolize the oil refining business). In 1900, the muckraking journalist Ida Tarbell decided to take on the Standard Oil behemoth. Tarbell, whose father had worked for Standard Oil, started researching Rockefeller and uncovering evidence about the ways in which Standard Oil had rigged railroad rates to its advantage. In 1902, Tarbell began publishing the nineteen articles that would become *The History of the Standard Oil Company* in *McClure's Magazine*. The essays were later collected in one volume. In part because of Tarbell's work, in 1911 the U.S. Supreme Court found that Standard Oil had violated the 1890 Sherman Antitrust Act, which forbid companies from forming monopolies "in restraint of trade or commerce." The Court's decision forced Standard Oil to break into 34 smaller companies.

Among the many young men of Cleveland who, from the start, had an eye on the oil-refining business and had begun to take an active part in its development as soon as it was demonstrated that there was a reasonable hope of its being permanent, was a young firm of produce commission merchants. Both members of this firm were keen business men, and one of them had remarkable commercial vision—a genius for seeing the possibilities in material things. This man's name was Rockefeller—John D. Rockefeller. He was but twenty-three years old when he first went into the oil business, but he had already got his feet firmly on the business ladder, and had got them there by his own efforts. The habit of driving good bargains and of saving money had started him. He himself once told how he learned these lessons so useful in money-making, in one of his frequent Sunday-school talks to young men on success in business. The value of a good bargain he learned in buying cord-wood for his father: "I knew what a cord of good solid beech and maple wood was. My father told me to select only the solid wood and the straight wood and not to put any limbs in it or any punky wood. That was a good training for me. I did not need any father to tell me or anybody else how many feet it took to make a cord of wood."

And here is how he learned the value of investing money:

"Among the early experiences that were helpful to me that I recollect with pleasure was one in working a few days for a neighbor in digging potatoes—a very enterprising, thrifty farmer, who could dig a great many potatoes. I was a boy of perhaps thirteen or fourteen years of age, and it kept me very busy from morning until night. It was a ten-hour day. And as I was saving these little sums I soon learned that I could get as much interest for fifty dollars loaned at seven per cent.—the legal rate in the state of New York at that time for a year—as I could earn by digging potatoes for 100 days. The impression was gaining ground with me that it was a good thing to let the money be my slave

Source: Ida Tarbell, *The History of the Standard Oil Company* (New York: McClure, Phillips & Co., 1904), 39–43, 148–157. Retrieved from the Internet Archive website, https://archive.org/details/historyofstandar00tarbuoft (Accessed June 11, 2018).

and not make myself a slave to money." Here we have the foundation principles of a great financial career.

When young Rockefeller was thirteen years old, his father moved from the farm in Central New York, where the boy had been born (July 8, 1839), to a farm near Cleveland, Ohio. He went to school in Cleveland for three years. In 1855 it became necessary for him to earn his own living. It was a hard year in the West and the boy walked the streets for days looking for work. He was about to give it up and go to the country when, to quote the story as Mr. Rockefeller once told it to his Cleveland Sunday-school, "As good fortune would have it I went down to the dock and made one more application, and I was told that if I would come in after dinner—our noon-day meal was dinner in those days—they would see if I could come to work for them. I went down after dinner and I got the position, and I was permitted to remain in the city." The position, that of a clerk and bookkeeper, was not lucrative. According to a small ledger which has figured frequently in Mr. Rockefeller's religious instructions, he earned from September 26, 1855, to January, 1856, fifty dollars. "Out of that," Mr. Rockefeller told the young men of his Sunday-school class, "I paid my washerwoman and the lady I boarded with, and I saved a little money to put away."

He proved an admirable accountant—one of the early-and-late sort, who saw everything, forgot nothing and never talked. In 1856 his salary was raised to twenty-five dollars a month, and he went on always "saving a little money to put away." In 1858 came a chance to invest his savings. Among his acquaintances was a young Englishman, M. B. Clark. Older by twelve years than Rockefeller he had left a hard life in England when he was twenty to seek fortune in America. He had landed in Boston in 1847, without a penny or a friend, and it had taken three months for him to earn money to get to Ohio. Here he had taken the first job at hand, as man-of-all-work, wood-chopper, teamster. He had found his way to Cleveland, had become a valuable man in the houses where he was employed, had gone to school at nights, had saved money. They were two of a kind, Clark and Rockefeller, and in 1858 they pooled their earnings and started a produce commission business on the Cleveland docks. The venture succeeded. Local historians credit Clark and

Rockefeller with doing a business of $450,000 the first year. The war came on, and as neither partner went to the front, they had full chance to take advantage of the opportunity for produce business a great army gives. A greater chance than furnishing army supplies, lucrative as most people found that, was in the oil business (so Clark and Rockefeller began to think), and in 1862, when an Englishman of ability and energy, one Samuel Andrews, asked them to back him in starting a refinery, they put in $4,000 and promised to give more if necessary. Now Andrews was a mechanical genius. He devised new processes, made a better and better quality of oil, got larger and larger percentages of refined from his crude. The little refinery grew big, and Clark and Rockefeller soon had $100,000 or more in it. In the meantime Cleveland was growing as a refining centre. The business which in 1860 had been a gamble was by 1865 one of the most promising industries of the town. It was but the beginning—so Mr. Rockefeller thought—and in that year he sold out his share of the commission business and put his money into the oil firm of Rockefeller and Andrews. . . .

The first intimation that the Oil Region had that Mr. Rockefeller was pushing another combination was in March of 1875, when it was announced that an organization of refiners, called the Central Association, of which he was president, had been formed. Its main points were that if a refiner would lease to the association his plant for a term of months he would be allowed to subscribe for stock of the new company. The lease allowed the owner manufacturing, but gave Mr. Rockefeller's company "irrevocable authority" to make all purchases of crude oil and sales of refined, to decide how much each refinery should manufacture, and *to negotiate for all freight and pipe-line expenses.* The Central Association was a most clever device. It furnished the secret partners of Mr. Rockefeller a plausible proposition with which to approach the firms of which they wished to obtain control.

Little as the Oil Regions knew of the real meaning of the Central Association, the news of its organisation raised a cry of monopoly, and the advocates of the new scheme felt called upon to defend it. The defense took the line that the conditions of the trade made such a combination of refineries necessary. Altogether the ablest explanation was that of H. H. Rogers, of Charles

Pratt and Company, to a reporter of the New York Tribune:

"There are five refining points in the country," said Mr. Rogers, "Pittsburg, Philadelphia, Cleveland, the Oil Regions and New York city. Each of these has certain local advantages which may be briefly stated as follows: Pittsburg, cheap oil; Philadelphia, the seaboard; Cleveland, cheap barrels, and canal as well as railroad transportation; the Oil Regions, crude oil at the lowest figure; and all the products of petroleum have the best market in New York city. The supply of oil is three or four times greater than the demand. If the oil refineries were run to their full capacity, the market would be overstocked. The business is not regular, but spasmodic. When the market is brisk and oil is in demand, all the oil interests are busy and enjoy a fair share of prosperity. At other times, the whole trade is affected by the dullness. It has been estimated that not less than twenty millions of dollars are invested in the oil business. It is therefore to the interest of every man who has put a dollar in it to have the trade protected and established on a permanent footing. Speculators have ruined the market. The brokers heretofore have been speculating upon the market with disastrous effects upon the trade, and this new order of things will force them to pursue their legitimate calling, and realise their profits from their industry and perseverance. Two years ago an attempt was made to organise an oil refiners' association, but it was subsequently abandoned. There was no cohesion of interests, and agreements were not kept. The movement at the present time is a revival of the former idea, and, it is believed, has already secured fully nine-tenths of the oil refiners in the country in its favour. I do not believe there is any intention among the oil men to 'bull' the market. The endeavour is to equalize all around and protect the capital invested. If by common consent, in good faith, the refiners agree to reduce the quantities to an allotment for each, made in view of the supply and demand, and the capacity for production, the market can be regulated with a reasonable profit for all. The price of oil to-day is fifteen cents per gallon. The proposed allotment of business would probably advanced price to twenty cents. To make an artificial increase, with immense profits, would be recognized as speculative instead of legitimate, and the oil interests would suffer accordingly. Temporary capital would compete with permanent investment and ruin everything. The oil producers to-day are bankrupt. There have been more failures during the last five months than in five years previously. An organisation to protect the oil capital is imperatively needed. Oil to yield a fair profit should be sold for twenty-five cents per gallon. That price would protect every interest and cover every outlay for getting out the crude petroleum, transporting by railroad, refining and the incidental charges of handling, etc. The foreign markets will regulate the price to a great extent, because they are the greatest consumers. The people of China, Germany, and other foreign countries cannot afford to pay high prices. Kerosene oil is luxury to them, and they do not receive sufficient compensation for their labour to enable them to use this oil at an extravagant price. The price, therefore, must be kept within reasonable limits."

The Oil Regions refused flatly to accept this view of the situation. The world would not buy refined at twenty-five cents, they argued. "Your injured the foreign market in 1872 by putting up the price. Our only hope is in increasing consumption. The world is buying more oil to-day than ever before, because it is cheap. We must learn to accept small profits, as other industries do." "The formation of the Refiners' Association has thrust upon the trade an element of uncertainty that has unsettled all sound views as to the general outlook," said the Derrick. "The scope of the Association," wrote a Pittsburg critic, "is an attempt to control the refining of oil, with the ultimate purpose of advancing its price and reaping a rich harvest in profits. This can only be done by reducing the production of refined oil, and this will in turn act on crude oil, making the stock so far in excess of the demand as to send it down to a lower figure than it has yet touched."

"The most important feature of this contract," said a "veteran refiner," "is perhaps that part which provides that the Executive Committee of the Central Association are to have the exclusive power to arrange with the railroads for the carrying of the crude and refined oil. It is intended by this provision to enable the Executive Committee to speak for the whole trade in securing special rates of freight, whereby independent shippers of crude oil, and such refiners as refuse to join the combination, and any new refining interest that may be started, may be driven out of the trade. The whole general purpose of the combination is to reap a large margin by depressing crude and raising the price of refined oil, and the chief means employed is the system of discrimination in railroad freights to the seaboard."

"The veteran refiner" was right in his supposition that Mr. Rockefeller intended to use the enormous power his combination gave him to get a special rate. . . .

Mr. Rockefeller was certainly now in an excellent condition to work out his plan of bringing under his own control all the refineries of the country. The Standard Oil Company owned in each of the great refining centres, New York, Pittsburg and Philadelphia, a large and aggressive plant run by the men who had built it up. These works were, so far as the public knew, still independent and their only relation that of the "Central Association." As a matter of fact they were the "Central Association." Not only had Mr. Rockefeller brought these powerful interests into his concern; he had secured for them a rebate of ten per cent. On a rate which should always be as low as any one of the roads gave any of his competitors. He had done away with middlemen, that is, he was" paying nobody profit." He had undeniably a force wonderfully constructed for what he wanted to do and one made practically impregnable as things were in the oil business then, by virtue of its special transportation rate.

As soon as his new line was complete the work of acquiring all outside refineries began at each of the oil centres. Unquestionably the acquisitions were made through persuasion when this was possible. If the party approached refused to lease or sell, he was told firmly what Mr. Rockefeller had told the Cleveland refiners when he went to them in 1872 with the South Improvement contracts, that there was no hope for him; that a combination was in progress which was bound to work; and that those who stayed out would inevitably go to the wall. Naturally the first fruits to fall into the hands of the new alliance were those refineries which were embarrassed or discouraged by the conditions which Mr. Rogers explains above. Take as an example the case of the Citizens' Oil Refining Company of Pittsburg, as it was explained in 1888 to the House

Committee on Manufactures in its trust investigation. A. H. Track, a partner in the company, told the story:

"We began in 1869 with a capacity of 1,000 barrels a day. At the start everything was *couleur de rose*, so much so that we put our works in splendid shape. We manufactured all the products. We even got it down to making wax, and using the very last residuum in the boilers. We got the works in magnificent order and used up everything. We began to feel the squeeze in 1872. We did not know what was the matter. Of course we were all affected the same way in Pennsylvania, and of course we commenced shifting about, and meeting together, and forming delegations, and going down to Philadelphia to see the Pennsylvania Railroad, meeting after meeting and delegation after delegation. We suspected there was something wrong, and told those men there was something wrong somewhere; that we felt, so far as position was concerned, we had the cheapest barrels, the cheapest labour, and the cheapest coal, and the route from the crude district was altogether in our favour. We had a railroad and a river to bring us our raw material. We had made our investment based on the seaboard routes, and we wanted the Pennsylvania Railroad to protect us. But none of our meetings or delegations ever amounted to anything. They were always repulsed in some way, put off, and we never got any satisfaction. The consequence was that in two or three years there was no margin or profit. In order to overcome that we commenced speculating, in the hope that there would be a change some time or other for the better. We did not like the idea of giving up the ship. Now, during these times the Standard Oil Company increased so perceptibly and so strong that we at once recognized it as the element. Instead of looking to the railroad I always looked to the Standard Oil Company. In 1874 I went to see Rockefeller to find if we could make arrangements with him by which we could run a portion of our works. It was a very brief interview. He said there was no hope for us at all. He remarked this—I cannot give the exact quotation—'There is no hope for us,' and probably he said, 'There is no hope for any of us'; but he says, 'The weakest must go first.' And we went."

All over the country the refineries in the same condition as Mr. Track's firm sold or leased. Those who felt the hard times and had any hope of weathering them resisted at first. With many of them the resistance was due simply to their love for their business and their unwillingness to share its control with outsiders. The thing which a man has begun, cared for, led to a healthy life, from which he has begun to gather fruit, which he knows he can make greater and richer, he loves as he does his life. It is one of the fruits of his life. He is jealous of it—wishes the honour of it, will not divide it with another. He can suffer heavily his own mistakes, learn from them, correct them. He can fight opposition, bear all—so long as the work is his. There were refiners in 1875 who loved their business in this way. Why one should love an oil refinery the outsider may not see; but to the man who had begun with one still and had seen it grow by his own energy and intelligence to ten, who now sold 500 barrels a day where he once sold five, the refinery was the dearest spot on earth save his home. He walked with pride among its evil-smelling places, watched the processes with eagerness, experimented with joy and recounted triumphantly every improvement. To ask such a man to give up his refinery was to ask him to give up the thing which, after his family, meant most in life to him.

To Mr. Rockefeller this feeling was a weak sentiment. To place love of independent work above love of profits was as incomprehensible to him as a refusal to accept a rebate because it was *wrong!* Where persuasion

failed then, it was necessary, in his judgment, that pressure be applied—simply a pressure sufficient to demonstrate to these blind or recalcitrant individuals the impossibility of their long being able to do business independently. It was a pressure varied according to locality. Usually it took the form of cutting their market. The system of "predatory competition" was no invention of the Standard Oil Company. It has prevailed in the oil business from the start. Indeed, it was one of the evils Mr. Rockefeller claimed his combination would cure, but until now it had been used spasmodically. Mr. Rockefeller never did anything spasmodically. He applied underselling for destroying his rivals' market with the same deliberation and persistency that characterized all his efforts, and in the long run he always won. There were other forms of pressure. Sometimes the independents found it impossible to get oil; again, they were obliged to wait days for cars to ship in; there seemed to be no end to the ways of making it hard for men to do business, of discouraging them until they would sell or lease, and always at the psychological moment a purchaser was at their side. . . .

QUESTIONS TO CONSIDER

1. How did Tarbell portray Rockefeller?
2. Do you think the Standard Oil Company should have been broken up?

16.4 SUPREME COURT, MAJORITY OPINION IN *LOCHNER V. NEW YORK* (1905)

Though the U.S. Supreme Court did vote to break up the Standard Oil Company in 1911 (see Reading 16.3), the Court more often deferred to business interests during the early twentieth century. Much of the ideology behind the Court's deference appeared in the 1905 case *Lochner v. New York.* Joseph Lochner owned a small bakery in Utica, New York. Regulators fined Lochner multiple times for violating New York's Bakeshop Act of 1865, which barred employees from working in bakeries for more than 10 hours per day or 60 hours per week. In 1901, after the second fine, Lochner appealed the decision all the way up to the Supreme Court, where he finally received a favorable judgement. Associate Justice Rufus W. Peckham's controversial majority opinion in Lochner's favor, from which the following document is excerpted, ushered in the "Lochner Era" of Supreme Court decisions for the next four decades, during which the Court struck down multiple state and federal laws intended to regulate working conditions.

MR. JUSTICE PECKHAM, after making the foregoing statement of the facts, delivered the opinion of the court.

The indictment, it will be seen, charges that the plaintiff in error violated the one hundred and tenth section of article 8, chapter 415, of the Laws of 1897, known as the labor law of the State of New York, in that he wrongfully and unlawfully required and permitted an employé working for him to work more than sixty hours in one week. There is nothing in any of the opinions delivered in this case, either in the Supreme Court or the Court of Appeals of the State, which construes the section, in using the word "required," as referring to any physical force being used to obtain the labor of an employé. It is assumed that the word means nothing more than the requirement arising from voluntary contract for such labor in excess of the number of hours specified in the statute. There is no pretense in any of the opinions that the statute was intended to meet a case of involuntary labor in any form. All the opinions assume that there is no real distinction, so far as this question is concerned, between the words "required" and "permitted." The mandate of the statute that "no employé shall be required or permitted to work," is the substantial equivalent of an enactment that "no employé shall contract or agree to work," more than ten hours per day, and as there is no provision for special emergencies the statute is mandatory in all cases. It is not an act merely fixing the number of hours which shall constitute a legal day's work, but an absolute prohibition upon the employer, permitting, under any circumstances, more than ten hours work to be done in his establishment. The employé may desire to earn the extra money, which would arise from his working more than the prescribed time, but this statute forbids the employer from permitting the employé to earn it.

The statute necessarily interferes with the right of contract between the employer and employés, concerning the number of hours in which the latter may labor in the bakery of the employer. The general right to make a contract in relation to his business is part of the liberty of the individual protected by the Fourteenth Amendment of the Federal Constitution.

Source: "Lochner v. New York," https://cdn.loc.gov/service/ll/usrep/usrep198/usrep198045/usrep198045.pdf (Accessed June 11, 2018)

Allgeyer v *Louisiana*, 165 U. S. 578. Under that provision no State can deprive any person of life, liberty or property without due process of law[.] The right to purchase or to sell labor is part of the liberty protected by this amendment, unless there are circumstances which exclude the right. There are, however, certain powers, existing in the sovereignty of each State in the Union, somewhat vaguely termed police powers, the exact description and limitation of which have not been attempted by the courts. Those powers, broadly stated and without, at present, any attempt at a more specific limitation, relate to the safety, health, morals and general welfare of the public. Both property and liberty are held on such reasonable conditions as may be imposed by the governing power of the State in the exercise of those powers, and with such conditions the Fourteenth Amendment was not designed to interfere. *Mugler* v *Kansas*, 123 U. S. 623, *In re Kemmler*, 136 U. S. 436, *Crowley* v. *Christensen*, 137 U S. 86, *In re Converse*, 137 U. S. 624.

The State, therefore, has power to prevent the individual from making certain kinds of contracts, and in regard to them the Federal Constitution offers no protection. If the contract be one which the State, in the legitimate exercise of its police power, has the right to prohibit, it is not prevented from prohibiting it by the Fourteenth Amendment. Contracts in violation of a statute, either of the Federal or state government, or a contract to let one's property for immoral purposes, or to do any other unlawful act, could obtain no protection from the Federal Constitution, as coming under the liberty of person or of free contract. Therefore, when the State, by its legislature, in the assumed exercise of its police powers, has passed an act which seriously limits the right to labor or the right of contract in regard to their means of livelihood between persons who are *sui juris* (both employer and employé), it becomes of great importance to determine which shall prevail—the right of the individual to labor for such time as he may choose, or the right of the State to prevent the individual from laboring or from entering into any contract to labor, beyond a certain time prescribed by the State. . . .

It must, of course, be conceded that there is a limit to the valid exercise of the police power by the State. There is no dispute concerning this general proposition. Otherwise the Fourteenth Amendment would have no efficacy and the legislatures of the States would have unbounded power, and it would be enough to say that any piece of legislation was enacted to conserve the morals, the health or the safety of the people; such legislation would be valid, no matter how absolutely without foundation the claim might be. The claim of the police power would be a mere pretext—become another and delusive name for the supreme sovereignty of the State to be exercised free from constitutional restraint. This is not contended for. In every case that comes before this court, therefore, where legislation of this character is concerned and where the protection of the Federal Constitution is sought, the question necessarily arises: Is this a fair, reasonable and appropriate exercise of the police power of the State, or is it an unreasonable, unnecessary and arbitrary interference with the right of the individual to his personal liberty or to enter into those contracts in relation to labor which may seem to him appropriate or necessary for the support of himself and his family? Of course the liberty of contract relating to labor includes both parties to it. The one has as much right to purchase as the other to sell labor.

This is not a question of substituting the judgment of the court for that of the legislature. If the act be within the power of the State it is valid, although the judgment of the court might be totally opposed to the enactment of such a law[.] But the question would still remain. Is it within the police power of the State? and that question must be answered by the court.

The question whether this act is valid as a labor law, pure and simple, may be dismissed in a few words. There is no reasonable ground for interfering with the liberty of person or the right of free contract, by determining the hours of labor, in the occupation of a baker. There is no contention that bakers as a class are not equal in intelligence and capacity to men in other trades or manual occupations, or that they are not able to assert their rights and care for themselves without the protecting arm of the State, interfering with their independence of judgment and of action. They are in no sense wards of the State. Viewed in the light of a purely labor law, with no reference whatever, to the question of health, we think that a law like the one before us involves neither the safety, the morals nor the welfare of the public, and that the interest of the public is not in the slightest degree affected by such an act. The law must be upheld, if at all, as a law pertaining to the health of the individual engaged in the occupation of a baker. It does not affect any other portion of the public than those who are engaged in that occupation. Clean and wholesome bread does not depend upon whether the baker works but ten hours per day or only sixty hours a week. The limitation of the hours of labor does not come within the police power on that ground.

It is a question of which of two powers or rights shall prevail—the power of the State to legislate or the right of the individual to liberty of person and freedom of contract. The mere assertion that the subject relates though but in a remote degree to the public health does not necessarily render the enactment valid. The act must have a direct relation, as a means to an end, and the end itself must be appropriate and legitimate, before an act can be held to be valid which interferes with the general right of an individual to be free in his person and in his power to contract in relation to his own labor.

This case has caused much diversity of opinion in the state courts. In the Supreme Court two of the five judges composing the Appellate Division dissented from the judgment affirming the validity of the act. In the Court of Appeals three of the seven judges also dissented from the judgment upholding the statute. Although found in what is called a labor law of the State, the Court of Appeals has upheld the act as one relating to the public health—in other words, as a health law[.] One of the judges of the Court of Appeals, in upholding the law, stated that, in his opinion, the regulation in question could not be sustained unless they were able to say, from common knowledge, that working in a bakery and candy factory was an unhealthy employment. The judge held that, while the evidence was not uniform, it still led him to the conclusion that the occupation of a baker or confectioner was unhealthy and tended to result in diseases of the respiratory organs. Three of the judges dissented from that view, and they thought the occupation of a baker was not to such an extent unhealthy

as to warrant the interference of the legislature with the liberty of the individual.

We think the limit of the police power has been reached and passed in this case. There is, in our judgment, no reasonable foundation for holding this to be necessary or appropriate as a health law to safeguard the public health or the health of the individuals who are following the trade of a baker. If this statute be valid, and if, therefore, a proper case is made out in which to deny the right of an individual, *sui juris*, as employer or employé, to make contracts for the labor of the latter under the protection of the provisions of the Federal Constitution, there would seem to be no length to which legislation of this nature might not go. The case differs widely, as we have already stated, from the expressions of this court in regard to laws of this nature, as stated in *Holden* v *Hardy* and *Jacobson* v *Massachusetts, supra....*

It is impossible for us to shut our eyes to the fact that many of the laws of this character, while passed under what is claimed to be the police power for the purpose of protecting the public health or welfare, are, in reality, passed from other motives. We are justified in saying so when, from the character of the law and the subject upon which it legislates, it is apparent that the public health or welfare bears but the most remote relation to the law[.] The purpose of a statute must be determined from the natural and legal effect of the language employed; and whether it is or is not repugnant to the Constitution of the United States must be determined from the natural effect of statutes when put into operation, and not from their proclaimed purpose. *Minnesota* v *Barber*, 136 U S. 313, *Brimmer* v *Rebman*, 138 U. S. 78. The court looks beyond the mere letter of the law in such cases. *Yick Wo* v *Hopkins*, 118 U. S. 356.

It is manifest to us that the limitation of the hours of labor as provided for in this section of the statute under which the indictment was found, and the plaintiff in error convicted, has no such direct relation to and no such substantial effect upon the health of the employé, as to justify us in regarding the section as really a health law It seems to us that the real object and purpose were simply to regulate the hours of labor between the master and his employés (all being men, *sui juris*), in a private business, not dangerous in any degree to morals or in any real and substantial degree, to the health of the employés. Under such circumstances the freedom of master and employé to contract with each other in relation to their employment, and in defining the same, cannot be prohibited or interfered with, without violating the Federal Constitution.

The judgment of the Court of Appeals of New York as well as that of the Supreme Court and of the County Court of Oneida County must be reversed and the case remanded to the County Court for further proceedings not inconsistent with this opinion.

Reversed.

QUESTIONS TO CONSIDER

1. How did the Court defend its decision?
2. Do you find the opinion convincing? Should states be able to regulate working conditions?

16.5 ROSE COHEN, EXCERPT FROM
OUT OF THE SHADOW (1918)

Rose Cohen's *Out of the Shadow* gives a detailed look at the life of an ordinary person who experienced the effects of rising immigration and industrial capitalism around the turn of the twentieth century. Cohen (1880–1925) was born in Belarus and immigrated to the United States in 1892 with her aunt, Masha. Rose and Masha joined Rose's father, who had previously settled in the Lower East Side of New York City. In New York, Cohen worked in a sweatshop of the clothing industry and later helped to teach courses at the Manhattan Trade School for Girls. Cohen's 1918 autobiography *Out of the Shadow*, from which the following document is excerpted, depicts her early life and her time in New York City. In the excerpt, Cohen describes the experience of waiting for a boat from Hamburg, Germany, to the United States, along with her travails on the transatlantic journey and her first impressions of America.

ONE day, I don't remember how soon after we crossed the border, we arrived in Hamburg. We stopped in a large, red building run in connection with the steamship company. We were all shown (really driven) into a large room where many dirty, narrow cots stood along the walls. Aunt Masha shivered as she looked at the one in which we two were to sleep.

"The less we stay in these beds the better," she said. So, although we were dead tired we went to bed quite late. But before we were on our cot very long we saw that sleep was out of the question.

The air in the room was so foul and thick that it felt as if it could be touched. From every corner came sounds of groaning ad snoring. But worst of all were the insects in the cot. After battling with these for some time Aunt Masha sat up.

"I feel I'll go mad," she gasped, clutching her hair. After sitting up a while she remembered seeing a wagon with some hay in it under the shed in the yard, and we decided to go there. We took our shoes in our hands and slipped out noiselessly.

It was a dark night and Aunt Masha was almost as much afraid in the dark as I was. With one arm clasped about each other's waists we groped about an endless time, until we crossed the yard and found the wagon. Fortunately, no one had thought of sleeping in it. Aunt Masha gave a sigh of relief and satisfaction as she nestled comfortably into the hay. Soon she was asleep.

To me sleep did not come so readily. My mind always seemed more active when I lay down at night than at any other time. And since we had been on the journey I could not sleep because of the new and strange things about me.

As I lay thinking, listening, I suddenly caught a whiff of cigarette smoke. I sat up quickly and peered into the darkness. In the direction where I knew the door was I saw a tiny light. My first thought was to wake Aunt Masha. Then it occurred to me that it must be some one like ourselves who could not sleep and so came to stay outside. But as I sat watching the light I saw that it was coming toward the shed, though very slowly.

Nearer and nearer it came and soon I discerned a tall, dark form coming along stealthily. I recognized the slow cat-like tread. It was he with the red eyes and grinning mouth.

Source: Rose Cohen, *Out of the Shadow* (New York: George H. Doran Company, 1918), 57–74. Retrieved from the Internet Archive website, https://archive.org/details/outofshadow00cohe (Accessed June 11, 2018).

I was almost beside myself with fear now that I knew who it was and I pressed closer to Aunt Masha. As he stopped a short distance from the shed and stood listening, I coughed to let him know that some one was in the wagon.

Then only, it seemed as if he realized that the light from his cigarette could be seen and he put his hand behind him. For a minute or so he stood still, listening. Then he went away as stealthily as he came and I saw him crouch down in a corner of the yard.

I sat wondering whether he knew that it was Aunt Masha and I that were in the wagon, and whether he would come again. He did, after a good while passed. Again I coughed to warn him. But this time he came right into the shed and craning his neck he tried to see.

"Why don't you lie down and go to sleep," he whispered feigning friendly concern. Now I saw that he knew us.

"I am not sleepy," I said, loudly.

"But you will fall asleep if you lie down," he insisted.

I noticed that he looked around as if he were uneasy when I spoke loud. So I answered still louder:

"I am not going to lie down. I am going to sit up all night, and if you don't go away at once I'll shout and wake the whole house." Then he turned quickly and tiptoed away, cursing under his breath.

At first I thought I would let Aunt Masha sleep a while and then wake her. But when some time passed it occurred to me that if I could stay up all night without waking Aunt Masha, no one could ever again call me that hated name, "'Fraid-cat." So I clasped my hands tightly in my lap and sat watching, listening. At the least sound in the yard I felt my hair rise on my head. Several times Aunt Masha moved restlessly in her sleep. Then I too, moved, half hoping that she would hear me and wake up. But she slept on. At one time it grew so dark and so cold that I could not keep my teeth still and it seemed as if the night would never end.

"Oh, now I must wake her." But at the very thought of it I seemed to hear, "Ah, you are a 'Fraid-cat after all." And so I pressed my hand over my mouth and waited.

At last a faint grey light came creeping slowly into the yard. With unspeakable joy I watched the house loom out of the darkness, but it was only when the smaller objects in the yard took on their natural forms, and people began to come and go, that I lay down.

My head scarcely seemed to have touched the hay when I heard Aunt Masha say, teasingly, "Oh, you sleepy head, the night is never long enough for you. Why, your eyes are actually swollen from too much sleep. Get up."

I sat up, not knowing at first where I was or what had happened. Then recollecting my experience of the night I wondered whether I should tell Aunt Masha or not. She had never invited any confidence from me. And this particularly seemed hard to tell. As I sat, hesitating, I half saw, half felt the red eyes glaring at me from the doorway. And so I jumped out of the wagon and ran to get washed.

Our breakfast, which was boiled potatoes and slices of white bread, was served on long bare tables in a room like the sleeping room. No sooner was the food put on the tables than it was gone, and some of us were left with empty plates. Aunt Masha and I looked at each other and burst out laughing. To see the bread grabbed up and the fingers scorched on the boiled potatoes was ugly and pathetic but also funny.

"To-morrow," Aunt Masha said, "we too shall have to grab. For the money sewed in your waist won't last if we have to buy more than one meal a day for a week." But the next day it was almost the same thing. Going hungry seemed easy in comparison with the shame we felt to put out our hands for the bread while there was such a struggle.

Aunt Masha managed to get one slice which she held out to me. "Here, eat it." When I refused she gave me a look that was as bad as a blow. "Take it at once," she said angrily. I took it. I found it hard to swallow the bread, knowing that she was hungry.

We stayed in Hamburg a week. Every day from ten in the morning until four in the afternoon we stayed in a large, bare hall waiting for our names to be called. On the left side of the hall there was a heavy door leading into the office, where the emigrants were called in one by one.

I used to sit down on the floor opposite the door and watch the people's faces as they came and went into the office. Some looked excited and worried when they came out, and others looked relieved.

When our names were called I rose quickly and followed Aunt Masha. The clerk who always came to the door, which the opened only a little, looked at us and asked our names. Then he let Aunt Masha go in and pushing me away roughly without a word he shut the heavy door in my face.

I stood nearby waiting, until my feet ached. When Aunt Masha came out at last her face was flushed and there were tears in her eyes. Immediately she went over to her friends (she had many friends by that time) and began to talk to them excitedly. I followed her but she stopped talking when she saw me. I understood that I was not to listen. And so I went away.

This went on for almost a week. Each day her face looked more worried and perplexed.

One afternoon the door of the office opened wider than usual and a different clerk came out holding a paper in his hand. He told us that the English steamer for which we had been waiting was in. And then he read the names of those who were to go on it.

I'll never forget Aunt Masha's joy when she heard that we were to sail the next day. She ran from one to the other of her friends, crying and laughing at once.

QUESTIONS TO CONSIDER

1. What surprised you about Cohen's remembrance?
2. Does it change how you think about late nineteenth-century immigration?

CHAPTER 17

THE CULTURE AND POLITICS OF INDUSTRIAL AMERICA, 1870–1892

17.1 KNOW-NOTHING PARTY PLATFORM (1857)

In the mid-1850s, the American Party, often termed the "Know-Nothing Party," formed to combat purported issues relating to growing immigration rates. The Know Nothings were extremely xenophobic and very anti-Catholic—they sought to oppose the perceived political power of the Catholic Church in America, which, the Party feared, would only grow as more Catholics immigrated to America. Though the Party faded into obscurity in just a few years, its 1857 Party Platform (the "American Platform of Principles") illustrates the rising debate in America about immigration and ethnicity.

1. An humble acknowledgement to the Supreme Being, for his protecting care vouchsafed to our fathers in their successful Revolutionary struggle, and hitherto manifested to us, their descendants, in the preservation of the liberties, the independence and the union of these States.

2. The perpetuation of the Federal Union and Constitution, as the palladium of our civil and religious liberties, and the only sure bulwarks of American Independence.

3. Americans must rule America, and to this end native-born citizens should be selected for all State, Federal, and municipal offices of government employment, in preference to all others. Nevertheless,

4. Persons born of American parents residing temporarily abroad, should be entitled to all the rights of native-born citizens.

5. No person should be selected for political station (whether of native or foreign birth), who recognizes any allegiance or obligation of any description to any foreign prince, potentate or power, or who refuses to recognize the Federal and State Constitution (each within its sphere) as paramount to all other laws, as rules of political action.

6. The unequalled recognition and maintenance of the reserved rights of the several States, and the cultivation of harmony and fraternal good will between the citizens of the several States, and to this end, non-interference by Congress with questions

Source: "American Platform of Principles," https://glc.yale.edu/american-platform-principles (Accessed May 20, 2018).

appertaining solely to the individual States, and non-intervention by each State with the affairs of any other State.

7. The recognition of the right of native-born and naturalized citizens of the United States, permanently residing in any Territory thereof, to frame their constitution and laws, and to regulate their domestic and social affairs in their own mode, subject only to the provisions of the Federal Constitution, with the privilege of admission into the Union whenever they have the requisite population for one Representative in Congress: Provided, always, that none but those who are citizens of the United States, under the Constitution and laws thereof, and who have a fixed residence in any such territory, ought to participate in the formation of the Constitution, or in the enactment of laws for said Territory or State.

8. An enforcement of the principles that no State or Territory ought to admit others than citizens to the right of suffrage, or of holding political offices of the United States.

9. A change in the laws of naturalization, making a continued residence of twenty-one years, of all not heretofore provided for, an indispensable requisite for citizenship hereafter, and excluding all paupers, and persons convicted of crime, from landing upon our shores; but no interference with the vested rights of foreigners.

10. Opposition to any union between Church and State; no interference with religious faith or worship, and no test oaths for office.

11. Free and thorough investigation into any and all alleged abuses of public functionaries, and a strict economy in public expenditures.

12. The maintenance and enforcement of all laws constitutionally enacted until said laws shall be repealed, or shall be declared null and void by competent judicial authority.

13. Opposition to the reckless and unwise policy of the present Administration in the general management of our national affairs, and more especially as shown in removing "Americans" (by designation) and Conservatives in principle, from office, and placing foreigners and Ultraists [extremists] in their places; as shown in a truckling subserviency to the stronger, and an insolent and cowardly bravado towards the weaker powers; as shown in re-opening sectional agitation; by the repeal of the Missouri Compromise; as shown in granting to unnaturalized foreigners the right of suffrage in [the] Kansas and Nebraska question; as shown in the corruptions which pervade some of the Departments of the Government; as shown in disgracing meritorious naval officers through prejudice or caprice; and as shown in the blundering mismanagement of our foreign relations.

14. Therefore, to remedy existing evils, and prevent the disastrous consequences otherwise resulting therefrom, we would build up the "American Party" upon the principles hereinbefore stated.

15. That each State Council shall have authority to amend their several Constitutions, so as to abolish the several degrees and substitute a pledge of honor, instead of other obligations, for fellowship and admission into the party.

16. A free and open discussion of all political principles embraced in our platform.

QUESTIONS TO CONSIDER

1. On what did the platform especially focus?
2. Who, in the American Party's mind, counted as an American during this time?

17.2 TEXT OF THE CHINESE EXCLUSION ACT (1882)

Beginning in the mid-nineteenth century, Chinese laborers increasingly flocked to the American west coast. First lured by the 1848 California Gold Rush, Chinese labor, under harsh conditions, was crucial to completion of the First Transcontinental Railroad. Afterward, many Chinese eventually formed Chinatowns in Los Angeles and San Francisco. After the Civil War, white Californians began to blame Chinese laborers for low wage levels. In Los Angeles on October 24, 1871, for instance, a mob of 500 Anglos stormed into Chinatown and murdered around twenty Chinese immigrants after a white police officer was killed during an altercation in the neighborhood. Rising western animus towards Chinese immigration led the Federal government to pass the Chinese Exclusion Act in 1882. The government did not repeal the act until 1943.

An Act to execute certain treaty stipulations relating to Chinese.

Whereas in the opinion of the Government of the United States the coming of Chinese laborers to this country endangers the good order of certain localities within the territory thereof: Therefore,

Be it enacted by the Senate and House of Representatives of the United States of America in Congress assembled, That from and after the expiration of ninety days next after the passage of this act, and until the expiration of ten years next after the passage of this act, the coming of Chinese laborers to the United States be, and the same is hereby, suspended; and during such suspension it shall not be lawful for any Chinese laborer to come, or having so come after the expiration of said ninety days to remain within the United States.

SEC. 2. That the master of any vessel who shall knowingly bring within the United States on such vessel, and land or permit to be landed, any Chinese laborer, from any foreign port or place, shall be deemed guilty of a misdemeanor, and on conviction thereof shall be punished by a fine of not more than five hundred dollars for each and every such Chinese laborer so brought, and maybe also imprisoned for a term not exceeding one year.

SEC. 3. That the two foregoing sections shall not apply to Chinese laborers who were in the United States on the seventeenth day of November, eighteen hundred and eighty, or who shall have come into the same before the expiration of ninety days next after the passage of this act, and who shall produce to such master before going on board such vessel, and shall produce to the collector of the port in the United States at which such vessel shall arrive, the evidence hereinafter in this act required of his being one of the laborers in this section mentioned; nor shall the two foregoing sections apply to the case of any master whose vessel, being bound to a port not within the United States, shall come within the jurisdiction of the United States by reason of being in distress or in stress of weather, or touching at any port of the United States on its voyage to any foreign port or place: Provided, That all Chinese laborers brought on such vessel shall depart with the vessel on leaving port.

SEC. 4. That for the purpose of properly identifying Chinese laborers who were in the United States on the seventeenth day of November eighteen hundred and eighty, or who shall have come into the same before the expiration of ninety days next after the passage of this act, and in order to furnish them with the

Source: "Transcript of Chinese Exclusion Act (1882)," https://www.ourdocuments.gov/doc.php?flash=false&doc=47&page=transcript (Accessed May 20, 2018).

proper evidence of their right to go from and come to the United States of their free will and accord, as provided by the treaty between the United States and China dated November seventeenth, eighteen hundred and eighty, the collector of customs of the district from which any such Chinese laborer shall depart from the United States shall, in person or by deputy, go on board each vessel having on board any such Chinese laborers and cleared or about to sail from his district for a foreign port, and on such vessel make a list of all such Chinese laborers, which shall be entered in registry-books to be kept for that purpose, in which shall be stated the name, age, occupation, last place of residence, physical marks of peculiarities, and all facts necessary for the identification of each of such Chinese laborers, which books shall be safely kept in the custom-house; and every such Chinese laborer so departing from the United States shall be entitled to, and shall receive, free of any charge or cost upon application therefor, from the collector or his deputy, at the time such list is taken, a certificate, signed by the collector or his deputy and attested by his seal of office, in such form as the Secretary of the Treasury shall prescribe, which certificate shall contain a statement of the name, age, occupation, last place of residence, personal description, and facts of identification of the Chinese laborer to whom the certificate is issued, corresponding with the said list and registry in all particulars. In case any Chinese laborer after having received such certificate shall leave such vessel before her departure he shall deliver his certificate to the master of the vessel, and if such Chinese laborer shall fail to return to such vessel before her departure from port the certificate shall be delivered by the master to the collector of customs for cancellation. The certificate herein provided for shall entitle the Chinese laborer to whom the same is issued to return to and re-enter the United States upon producing and delivering the same to the collector of customs of the district at which such Chinese laborer shall seek to re-enter; and upon delivery of such certificate by such Chinese laborer to the collector of customs at the time of re-entry in the United States said collector shall cause the same to be filed in the custom-house . . .

. . . SEC. 5. That any Chinese laborer mentioned in section four of this act being in the United States, and desiring to depart from the United States by land, shall have the right to demand and receive, free of charge or cost, a certificate of identification similar to that provided for in section four of this act to be issued to such Chinese laborers as may desire to leave the United States by water; and it is hereby made the duty of the collector of customs of the district next adjoining the foreign country to which said Chinese laborer desires to go to issue such certificate, free of charge or cost, upon application by such Chinese laborer, and to enter the same upon registry-books to be kept by him for the purpose, as provided for in section four of this act.

SEC. 6. That in order to the faithful execution of articles one and two of the treaty in this act before mentioned, every Chinese person other than a laborer who may be entitled by said treaty and this act to come within the United States, and who shall be about to come to the United States, shall be identified as so entitled by the Chinese Government in each case, such identity to be evidenced by a certificate issued under the authority of said government, which certificate shall be in the English language or (if not in the English language) accompanied by a translation into English, stating such right to come, and which certificate shall state the name, title or official rank, if any, the age, height, and all physical peculiarities, former and present occupation or profession, and place of residence in China of the person to whom the certificate is issued and that such person is entitled, conformably to the treaty in this act mentioned to come within the United States. Such certificate shall be prima-facie evidence of the fact set forth therein, and shall be produced to the collector of customs, or his deputy, of the port in the district in the United States at which the person named therein shall arrive.

SEC. 7. That any person who shall knowingly and falsely alter or substitute any name for the name written in such certificate or forge any such certificate, or knowingly utter any forged or fraudulent certificate, or falsely personate any person named in any such certificate, shall be deemed guilty of a misdemeanor; and upon conviction thereof shall be fined in a sum not exceeding one thousand dollars, and imprisoned in a penitentiary for a term of not more than five years.

SEC. 8. That the master of any vessel arriving in the United States from any foreign port or place shall, at the same time he delivers a manifest of the cargo, and if there be no cargo, then at the time of making a report of the entry of the vessel pursuant to law, in addition to the other matter required to be reported, and before landing, or permitting to land, any Chinese passengers, deliver and report to the collector of customs of the district in which such vessels shall have arrived a separate list of all Chinese passengers taken on board his vessel at any foreign port or place, and all such passengers on board the vessel at that time. Such list shall show the names of such passengers (and if accredited officers of the Chinese Government traveling on the business of that government, or their servants, with a note of such facts), and the names and other particulars, as shown by their respective certificates; and such list shall be sworn to by the master in the manner required by law in relation to the manifest of the cargo. Any willful refusal or neglect of any such master to comply with the provisions of this section shall incur the same penalties and forfeiture as are provided for a refusal or neglect to report and deliver a manifest of the cargo.

SEC. 9. That before any Chinese passengers are landed from any such line vessel, the collector, or his deputy, shall proceed to examine such passenger, comparing the certificate with the list and with the passengers; and no passenger shall be allowed to land in the United States from such vessel in violation of law.

SEC. 10. That every vessel whose master shall knowingly violate any of the provisions of this act shall be deemed forfeited to the United States, and shall be liable to seizure and condemnation in any district of the United States into which such vessel may enter or in which she may be found.

SEC. 11. That any person who shall knowingly bring into or cause to be brought into the United States by land, or who shall knowingly aid or abet the same, or aid or abet the landing in the United States from any vessel of any Chinese person not lawfully entitled to enter the United States, shall be deemed guilty of a misdemeanor, and shall, on conviction thereof, be fined in a sum not exceeding one thousand dollars, and imprisoned for a term not exceeding one year.

SEC. 12. That no Chinese person shall be permitted to enter the United States by land without producing to the proper officer of customs the certificate in this act required of Chinese persons seeking to land from a vessel. And any Chinese person found unlawfully within the United States shall be caused to be removed therefrom to the country from whence he came, by direction of the President of the United States, and at the cost of the United States, after being brought before some justice, judge, or commissioner of a court of the United States and found to be one not lawfully entitled to be or remain in the United States.

SEC. 13. That this act shall not apply to diplomatic and other officers of the Chinese Government traveling upon the business of that government, whose credentials shall be taken as equivalent to the certificate in this act mentioned, and shall exempt them and their body and household servants from the provisions of this act as to other Chinese persons.

SEC. 14. That hereafter no State court or court of the United States shall admit Chinese to citizenship; and all laws in conflict with this act are hereby repealed.

SEC. 15. That the words "Chinese laborers", wherever used in this act shall be construed to mean both skilled and unskilled laborers and Chinese employed in mining.

Approved, May 6, 1882.

QUESTIONS TO CONSIDER

1. What did the Chinese Exclusion Act do, and how did the government seek to enforce it?
2. How does the Chinese Exclusion Act reflect contemporary tensions about immigration and ethnicity?

17.3 FRANCES WILLARD, EXCERPT FROM *WOMAN AND TEMPERANCE* (1883)

In the early nineteenth century, the temperance movement came about in conjunction with other movements for moral reform, especially the Second Great Awakening. By the 1870s, however, temperance advocates wanted to create a more powerful, centralized organization to direct their activism. Their efforts culminated in the creation of the Women's Christian Temperance Organization (WCTU) in 1874, which tried to eliminate alcohol from American society as a means to solve larger social problems, such as domestic violence and poverty. Frances Willard (1839–1898) worked for the WCTU and became its president in 1879, a position she would hold until her death. Under Willard's leadership, the WCTU grew from about 22,000 members in 1881 to 138,000 members a decade later. In 1883, Willard published *Women and Temperance,* from which the following excerpt is taken. *Women and Temperance* summarized the work of the WCTU and portrayed the work of specific women involved in the organization on a grassroots level. In the excerpt, Willard discusses one of the early movements that led to the founding of the WCTU.

THE date is memorable. Some day its anniversaries will be ranked among our national festivals. . . . But the first eddy of that Whirlwind of the Lord, which in a few weeks had swept over the great State of Ohio, and grown to the huge proportions of the Woman's Temperance Crusade, began in Hillsboro', Ohio, December 23, 1873. By common consent of her sisters in the united churches of the village where almost her whole life had been spent, Mrs. Eliza J. Thompson was chosen to lead the first band on its first visit to a saloon. Never did character and circumstance conspire to form a central figure better suited to the significant occasion. "The first Crusader," a gentle-mannered lady of sixty years, had been from her early days a member of Christ's church and always prominent in charitable work, thus endearing herself to the class whose antagonism her new departure would naturally arouse. She is a wife, mother, and grandmother, loving and beloved ; with marks upon her face of the grief which renders sacred, which disarms criticism, and in this instance, has a significance too deep for tears. She is the only daughter of Governor Trimble, than whom Ohio never had a chief magistrate more true.

Nearly forty years before, she had accompanied that noble father when he went as a delegate to the earliest national temperance convention, which was so small that its opening meeting was held in the dining-room of a Saratoga hotel of that period. Going with him to the door of this dignified assembly, where the white cravats of the clergy were a feature of prominence, the timid Ohio girl whispered, "O, papa, I'm afraid to enter, those gentlemen may think it an intrusion. I should be the only lady, don't you see?" Upon this the Governor replied, "My daughter should never be afraid, even if she is alone in a good cause," and taking her by the arm, he drew her into the convention. What a prophecy was the first entrance of a woman—and *this* woman—upon a temperance convention made up

Source: Frances Willard, *Women and Temperance: On the Work and Workers of The Woman's Christian Temperance Union* (Hartford, CT: Park Publishing Co., 1883), 52–57. Retrieved from the Internet Archive website, https://archive.org/details/womantemperance00willa (Accessed June 11, 2018).

of men! Read its fulfillment in her now happy home, her lawyer husband's leadership of the home protection movement in Ohio, and in the procession of white-ribbon workers that belts the world to-day.

Kneeling hand in hand with this dear friend and leader, in the room where first the "Crusade Psalm" was read and prayer of consecration offered, my heart was newly laid upon the altar of our blessed cause. Upon the thousands of faithful temperance women all over the land, let me lovingly urge some special annual commemoration of the twenty-third of December, as a day in which all our hearts shall be warmed with new love, stirred to fresh zeal, and lifted into clearer faith.

It is worth while to preserve in her own language the account of that strange "call" which came to Mrs. Thompson in 1873. She wrote it out for a near friend in the following words :

"On the evening of Dec. 22, 1873, Dio Lewis, a Boston physician and lyceum lecturer, delivered in Music Hall, Hillsboro, Ohio, a lecture on 'Our Girls.'

"He had been engaged by the Lecture Association some months before to fill one place in the winter course of lectures 'merely for the entertainment of the people.' But finding that he could remain another evening and still reach his next appointment (Washington C. H.), he consented to give another lecture on the evening of the 23d. At the suggestion of Judge Albert Matthews, an old-line temperance man and Democrat, a free lecture on Temperance became the order of the evening.

"I did not hear Dio Lewis lecture (although he was our guest), because of home cares that required my presence, but my son, a youth of sixteen, was there, and he came to me upon his return home and in a most excited manner related the thrilling incidents of the evening— how Dr. Lewis told of his own mother and several of her good Christian friends uniting in prayer with and for the liquor sellers of his native town until they gave up their soul-destroying business, and then said,—'Ladies, you might do the same thing in Hillsboro if you had the same faith,'—and, turning to the ministers and temperance men who were upon the platform, added, 'Suppose I ask the ladies of this audience to signify their opinions upon the subject?' They all bowed their consent, and fifty or more women stood up in token of approval. He then asked the gentlemen how many of them would

stand as 'backers,' should the ladies undertake the work, and sixty or seventy arose. 'And now, mother,' said my boy, 'they have got you into business, for you are on a committee to do some work at the Presbyterian Church in the morning at nine o'clock, and then the ladies want you to go out with them to the saloons.'

"My husband, who had returned from Adams County court that evening and was feeling very tired, seemed asleep as he rested upon the couch, while my son in an undertone had given me all the above facts ; but as the last sentence was uttered, he raised himself up upon his elbow and said, 'What tom-foolery is all that?' My son slipped out of the room quietly, and I betook myself to the task of consoling my husband with the promise that I should not be led into any foolish act by Dio Lewis or any association of human beings. But after he had relaxed into a milder mood, continuing to call the whole plan, as he understood it, 'tom-foolery,' I ventured to remind him that the men had been in the 'tom-foolery' business a long time, and suggested that it might be 'God's will' that the women should now take their part. (After this he fell asleep quietly, and I resumed my Bible reading.) Nothing further was said upon the subject that had created such interest the night before until after breakfast, when we gathered in the 'family room.' First, my son approached me and gently placing his hand upon my shoulder, in a very subdued tone said, 'Mother, are you not going over to the church, this morning?' As I hesitated, and doubtless showed in my countenance the burden upon my spirit, he emphatically said, 'But, my dear mother, you know you have to go.' Then my daughter, who was sitting on a stool by my side, leaning over in a most tender manner, and looking up in my face, said, 'Don't you think you will go?' All this time my husband had been walking the floor, uttering not a word. He stopped, and placing his hand upon the family Bible that lay upon my work-table, he said emphatically, 'Children, you know where your mother goes to settle all vexed questions. Let us leave her alone,' withdrawing as he spoke, and the dear children following him. I turned the key, and was in the act of kneeling before God and his 'holy word' to see what would be sent me, when I heard a gentle tap at my door. Upon opening it, I saw my dear daughter, with her little Bible open, and the tears coursing down her young cheeks, as she said, "I opened to this, mother. It must be for you.' She immediately left the room, and I sat down to read the wonderful message of the great 'I Am' contained in the 146th Psalm.

"No longer doubting, I at once repaired to the Presbyterian church, where quite a large assembly of earnest people had gathered.

"I was at once unanimously chosen as the President (or leader) ; Mrs. Gen. McDowell, Vice-President ; and Mrs. D. K. Finner, Secretary of the strange work that was to follow.

"Appeals were drawn up to druggists, saloon-keepers, and hotel proprietors. Then the Presbyterian minister (Dr. McSurely), who had up to this time occupied the chair, called upon the chairman-elect to come forward to the 'post of honor,' but your humble servant could not ; her limbs refused to bear her. So Dr. McSurely remarked, as he looked around upon the gentlemen : 'Brethren, I see that the ladies will do nothing while we remain ; let us adjourn, leaving this new work with God and the women.'

"As the last man closed the door after him, strength before unknown came to me, and without any hesitation or consultation I walked forward to the minister's table, took the large Bible, and, opening it, explained the incidents of the morning ; then read and briefly (as my tears would allow) commented upon its new meaning to me. I then called upon Mrs. McDowell to lead in prayer, and such a prayer! It seemed as though the angel had brought down 'live coals' from off the altar and touched her lips—she who had never before heard her own voice in prayer!

"As we rose from our knees (for there were none sitting on that morning). I asked Mrs. Cowden (our M. E. minister's wife) to start the good old hymn 'Give to the winds thy fears' to a familiar tune, and turning to the dear women, I said : 'As we all join in singing this hymn, let us form in line, two and two, the small women in front, leaving the tall ones to bring up the rear, and let us at once proceed to our sacred mission, trusting alone in the God of Jacob.' It was all done in less time than it takes to write it ; every heart was throbbing, and every woman's countenance betrayed her solemn realization of the fact that she was "going about her Father's business."

As this band of "mysterious beings" first encountered the outside gaze, and as they passed from the door of the old church and reached the street beyond the large churchyard, they were singing these prophetic words :

"Far, far above thy thought,
His counsel shall appear,
"When fully He the work hath wrought
That caused thy needless fear."

On they marched in solemn silence up Main street, first to Dr. Wm. Smith's drug store. After calling at all the drug stores, four in number, their pledge being signed by all save one, they encountered saloons and hotels with varied success, until by continuous, daily visitations, with persuasion, prayer, song, and Scripture readings, the drinking places of the town were reduced from thirteen to one drug store, one hotel, and two saloons, and they sold 'very cautiously.'

QUESTIONS TO CONSIDER

1. How did Mrs. Thompson get involved in the movement?
2. What can you glean about the temperance movement and contemporary America through Mrs. Thompson's story?

17.4 HELEN HUNT JACKSON, EXCERPT FROM *RAMONA* (1884)

In 1881, American writer Helen Hunt Jackson (1830–1885) gained acclaim for her controversial *A Century of Dishonor,* an expose about the Federal government's mistreatment of Native Americans. Just three years later, she delved into popular fiction with her novel *Ramona,* from which the following excerpt is taken. Jackson set *Ramona* in Southern California, just after the Mexican-American War. Ramona, an orphan girl, is raised by Señora Gonzaga Moreno, a formerly powerful figure in the area who has lost much of that power due to the outcome of the war. In the novel, Ramona falls in love with a Native American sheep shearer, Alessandro, and marries him. The couple elopes and finds only hardship in the changing American landscape. Alessandro eventually dies tragically, and Ramona returns to the Moreno estate, where she remarries and lives out her life. *Ramona* was a huge commercial success for Jackson and heavily contributed to a sentimentalized vision of Southern California based in Mexican heritage but removed from the violence of Americanization. This excerpt is from the beginning of the novel, where Jackson recounts Moreno's past.

THE Senora Moreno's house was one of the best specimens to be found in California of the representative house of the half barbaric, half elegant, wholly generous and free-handed life led there by Mexican men and women of degree in the early part of this century, under the rule of the Spanish and Mexican viceroys, when the laws of the Indies were still the law of the land, and its old name, "New Spain," was an ever-present link and stimulus to the warmest memories and deepest patriotisms of its people.

It was a picturesque life, with more of sentiment and gayety in it, more also that was truly dramatic, more romance, than will ever be seen again on those sunny shores. The aroma of it all lingers there still; industries and inventions have not yet slain it; it will last out its century,—in fact, it can never be quite lost, so long as there is left standing one such house as the Senora Moreno's.

When the house was built, General Moreno owned all the land within a radius of forty miles,—forty miles westward, down the valley to the sea; forty miles eastward, into the San Fernando Mountains; and a good forty miles more or less along the coast. The boundaries were not very strictly defined; there was no occasion, in those happy days, to reckon land by inches. It might be asked, perhaps, just how General Moreno owned all this land, and the question might not be easy to answer. It was not and could not be answered to the satisfaction of the United States Land Commission, which, after the surrender of California, undertook to sift and adjust Mexican land titles; and that was the way it had come about that the Senora Moreno now called herself a poor woman. Tract after tract, her lands had been taken away from her; it looked for a time as if nothing would be left. Every one of the claims based on deeds of gift from Governor Pio Fico, her husband's most intimate friend, was disallowed. They all went by the board in one batch, and took away from the Senora in a day the greater part of her best pasture-lands. They were lands which had belonged to the Bonaventura Mission, and lay along

Source: Helen Hunt Jackson, *Ramona* (Champaign-Urbana, IL: Project Gutenberg, 2008) https://www.gutenberg.org/files/2802/2802-h/2802-h.htm (Accessed May 20, 2018)

the coast at the mouth of the valley down which the little stream which ran past her house went to the sea; and it had been a great pride and delight to the Senora, when she was young, to ride that forty miles by her husband's side, all the way on their own lands, straight from their house to their own strip of shore. No wonder she believed the Americans thieves, and spoke of them always as hounds. The people of the United States have never in the least realized that the taking possession of California was not only a conquering of Mexico, but a conquering of California as well; that the real bitterness of the surrender was not so much to the empire which gave up the country, as to the country itself which was given up. Provinces passed back and forth in that way, helpless in the hands of great powers, have all the ignominy and humiliation of defeat, with none of the dignities or compensations of the transaction.

Mexico saved much by her treaty, spite of having to acknowledge herself beaten; but California lost all. Words cannot tell the sting of such a transfer. It is a marvel that a Mexican remained in the country; probably none did, except those who were absolutely forced to it.

Luckily for the Senora Moreno, her title to the lands midway in the valley was better than to those lying to the east and the west, which had once belonged to the missions of San Fernando and Bonaventura; and after all the claims, counter-claims, petitions, appeals, and adjudications were ended, she still was left in undisputed possession of what would have been thought by any new-comer into the country to be a handsome estate, but which seemed to the despoiled and indignant Senora a pitiful fragment of one. Moreover, she declared that she should never feel secure of a foot of even this. Any day, she said, the United States Government might send out a new Land Commission to examine the decrees of the first, and revoke such as they saw fit. Once a thief, always a thief. Nobody need feel himself safe under American rule. There was no knowing what might happen any day; and year by year the lines of sadness, resentment, anxiety, and antagonism deepened on the Senora's fast aging face.

It gave her unspeakable satisfaction, when the Commissioners, laying out a road down the valley, ran it at the back of her house instead of past the front. "It is well," she said. "Let their travel be where it belongs, behind our kitchens; and no one have sight of the front doors of our houses, except friends who have come to visit us." Her enjoyment of this never flagged. Whenever she saw, passing the place, wagons or carriages belonging to the hated Americans, it gave her a distinct thrill of pleasure to think that the house turned its back on them. She would like always to be able to do the same herself; but whatever she, by policy or in business, might be forced to do, the old house, at any rate, would always keep the attitude of contempt,—its face turned away.

One other pleasure she provided herself with, soon after this road was opened,—a pleasure in which religious devotion and race antagonism were so closely blended that it would have puzzled the subtlest of priests to decide whether her act were a sin or a virtue. She caused to be set up, upon every one of the soft rounded hills which made the beautiful rolling sides of that part of the valley, a large wooden cross; not a hill in sight of her house left without the sacred emblem of her faith. "That the heretics may know, when they go by, that they are on the estate of a good Catholic," she said, "and that the faithful may be reminded to pray. There have been miracles of conversion wrought on the most hardened by a sudden sight of the Blessed Cross."

There they stood, summer and winter, rain and shine, the silent, solemn, outstretched arms, and became landmarks to many a guideless traveller who had been told that his way would be by the first turn to the left or the right, after passing the last one of the Senora Moreno's crosses, which he couldn't miss seeing. And who shall say that it did not often happen that the crosses bore a sudden message to some idle heart journeying by, and thus justified the pious half of the Senora's impulse? Certain it is, that many a good Catholic halted and crossed himself when he first beheld them, in the lonely places, standing out in sudden relief against the blue sky; and if he said a swift short prayer at the sight, was he not so much the better?

The house was of adobe, low, with a wide veranda on the three sides of the inner court, and a still broader one across the entire front, which looked to the south. These verandas, especially those on the inner court, were supplementary rooms to the house. The greater part of the family life went on in them. Nobody stayed inside the walls, except when it was necessary. All the kitchen work, except the actual cooking, was done here, in front of the kitchen doors and windows. Babies slept, were washed, sat in the dirt, and played, on the veranda. The women said their prayers, took their naps, and wove their lace there. Old Juanita shelled her beans there, and threw the pods down on the tile floor, till towards night they were sometimes piled up high around her, like corn-husks at a husking. The herdsmen and shepherds smoked there, lounged there, trained their dogs there; there the young made love, and the old dozed; the benches, which ran the entire length of the walls, were worn into hollows, and shone like satin; the tiled floors also were broken and sunk in places, making little wells, which filled up in times of hard rains, and were then an invaluable addition to the children's resources for amusement, and also to the comfort of the dogs, cats, and fowls, who picked about among them, taking sips from each.

The arched veranda along the front was a delight-some place. It must have been eighty feet long, at least, for the doors of five large rooms opened on it. The two westernmost rooms had been added on, and made four steps higher than the others; which gave to that end of the veranda the look of a balcony, or loggia. Here the Senora kept her flowers; great red water-jars, hand-made by the Indians of San Luis Obispo Mission, stood in close rows against the walls, and in them were always growing fine geraniums, carnations, and yellow-flowered musk. The Senora's passion for musk she had inherited from her mother. It was so strong that she sometimes wondered at it; and one day, as she sat with Father Salvierderra in the veranda, she picked a handful of the blossoms, and giving them to him, said, "I do not know why it is, but it seems to me if I were dead I could be brought to life by the smell of musk."

"It is in your blood, Senora," the old monk replied. "When I was last in your father's house in Seville, your mother sent for me to her room, and under her window was a stone balcony full of growing musk, which so filled the room with its odor that I was like to faint. But she said it cured her of diseases, and without it she fell ill. You were a baby then."

"Yes," cried the Senora, "but I recollect that balcony. I recollect being lifted up to a window, and looking down into a bed of blooming yellow flowers; but I did not know what they were. How strange!"

"No. Not strange, daughter," replied Father Salvierderra. "It would have been stranger if you had not acquired the taste, thus drawing it in with the mother's milk. It would behoove mothers to remember this far more than they do."

Besides the geraniums and carnations and musk in the red jars, there were many sorts of climbing vines,—some coming from the ground, and twining around the pillars of the veranda; some growing in great bowls, swung by cords from the roof of the veranda, or set on shelves against the walls. These bowls were of gray stone, hollowed and polished, shining smooth inside and out. They also had been made by the Indians, nobody knew how many ages ago, scooped and polished by the patient creatures, with only stones for tools.

Among these vines, singing from morning till night, hung the Senora's canaries and finches, half a dozen of each, all of different generations, raised by the Senora. She was never without a young bird-family on hand; and all the way from Bonaventura to Monterey, it was thought a piece of good luck to come into possession of a canary or finch of Senora Moreno's 'raising.

Between the veranda and the river meadows, out on which it looked, all was garden, orange grove, and almond orchard; the orange grove always green, never without snowy bloom or golden fruit; the garden never without flowers, summer or winter; and the almond orchard, in early spring, a fluttering canopy of pink and white petals, which, seen from the hills on the opposite side of the river, looked as if rosy sunrise clouds had fallen, and become tangled in the tree-tops. On either hand stretched away other orchards,—peach, apricot, pear, apple, pomegranate; and beyond these, vineyards. Nothing was to be seen but verdure or bloom or fruit, at whatever time of year you sat on the Senora's south veranda.

A wide straight walk shaded by a trellis so knotted and twisted with grapevines that little was to be seen of the trellis wood-work, led straight down from the veranda steps, through the middle of the garden, to a little brook at the foot of it. Across this brook, in the shade of a dozen gnarled old willow-trees, were set the broad flat stone washboards on which was done all the family washing. No long dawdling, and no running away from work on the part of the maids, thus close to the eye of the Senora at the upper end of the garden; and if they had known how picturesque they looked there, kneeling on the grass, lifting the dripping linen out of the water, rubbing it back and forth on the stones, sousing it, wringing it, splashing the clear water in each other's faces, they would have been content to stay at the washing day in and day out, for there was always somebody to look on from above. Hardly a day passed that the Senora had not visitors. She was still a person of note; her house the natural resting-place for all who journeyed through the valley; and whoever came, spent all of his time, when not eating, sleeping, or walking over the place, sitting with the Senora on the sunny veranda. Few days in winter were cold enough, and in summer the day must be hot indeed to drive the Senora and her friends indoors. There stood on the veranda three carved oaken chairs, and a carved bench, also of oak, which had been brought to the Senora for safe keeping by the faithful old sacristan of San Luis Rey, at the time of the occupation of that Mission by the United States troops, soon after the conquest of California. Aghast at the sacrilegious acts of the soldiers, who were quartered in the very church itself, and amused themselves by making targets of the eyes and noses of the saints' statues, the sacristan, stealthily, day by day and night after night, bore out of the church all that he dared to remove, burying some articles in cottonwood copses, hiding others in his own poor little hovel, until he had wagon-loads of sacred treasures. Then, still more stealthily, he carried them, a few at a time, concealed in the bottom of a cart, under a load of hay or of brush, to the house of the Senora, who felt herself deeply honored by his confidence, and received everything as a sacred trust, to be given back into the hands of the Church again, whenever the Missions should be restored, of which at that time all Catholics had good hope. And so it had come about that no bedroom in the Senora's house was without a picture or a statue of a saint or of the Madonna; and some had two; and in the little chapel in the garden the altar was surrounded by a really imposing row of holy and apostolic figures, which had looked down on the splendid ceremonies of the San Luis Rey Mission, in Father Peyri's time, no more

benignly than they now did on the humbler worship of the Senora's family in its diminished estate. That one had lost an eye, another an arm, that the once brilliant colors of the drapery were now faded and shabby, only enhanced the tender reverence with which the Senora knelt before them, her eyes filling with indignant tears at thought of the heretic hands which had wrought such defilement. Even the crumbling wreaths which had been placed on some of the statues' heads at the time of the last ceremonial at which they had figured in the Mission, had been brought away with them by the devout sacristan, and the Senora had replaced each one, holding it only a degree less sacred than the statue itself. . . .

Any race under the sun would have been to the Senora less hateful than the American. She had scorned them in her girlhood, when they came trading to post after post. She scorned them still. The idea of being forced to wage a war with pedlers was to her too monstrous to be believed. In the outset she had no doubt that the Mexicans would win in the contest.

"What!" she cried, "shall we who won independence from Spain, be beaten by these traders? It is impossible!"

When her husband was brought home to her dead, killed in the last fight the Mexican forces made, she said icily, "He would have chosen to die rather than to have been forced to see his country in the hands of the enemy." And she was almost frightened at herself to see how this thought, as it dwelt in her mind, slew the grief in her heart. She had believed she could not live if her husband were to be taken away from her; but she found herself often glad that he was dead,— glad that he was spared the sight and the knowledge of the things which happened; and even the yearning tenderness with which her imagination pictured him among the saints, was often turned into a fierce wondering whether indignation did not fill his soul, even in heaven, at the way things were going in the land for whose sake he had died.

QUESTIONS TO CONSIDER

1. How does Jackson seek to gain sympathy for Moreno?
2. Why do you think the novel was so successful?

17.5 WILLIAM A. PEFFER, EXCERPT FROM *THE FARMER'S SIDE: HIS TROUBLES AND THEIR REMEDY* (1891)

William A. Peffer (1831–1912) was an American politician who in 1891 became the first Populist Party member to be elected to the U.S. Senate. The Populist Party received much of its support from small farmers and poor urban dwellers during the late nineteenth century. As a whole, the party pledged to make society more economically fair by, among other things, reforming banking, instituting a graduated income tax and an eight-hour workday, nationalizing the railroads, and abolishing the gold standard. In *The Farmer's Side,* Peffer outlined the various problems facing farmers and advocated for the rise of a new political party. In the following excerpt, Peffer introduced his main argument.

I.—STUDY BY COMPARISON—THE FARMER.

We learn much, and as to a great many things we learn best, by comparison. Contrast impresses the memory and sinks into the heart. If there were nothing white nobody would know that there is anything red or green. If the sky were never blue we would not know that it is ever black or gray. Without pain we would have no conception of pleasure. The sweetness of hope is intensified by the gloom of despair. Looking upon an object without knowledge of other objects with which to compare it, we have no satisfactory method or test of measurement. And this is true of properties and qualities as well as of form, dimension, and color. While any particular thing may be of a certain shape, size, and hue, without reference to the observer's capacity for discernment, yet, as to the observer himself, he will measure all these properties by his knowledge of things with which he may properly compare them. A farmer's estimate of the quality and value of his products is based upon what he knows of the quality and value of other similar articles with which he

compares them. He recognizes the greater worth of improved methods in agriculture in their superiority over other methods with which he was once familiar. He measures the value of pure-bred Durhams, Devons, Herefords, Galloways, and Jerseys, by the merits of "scrubs" which he handled in his younger days. The merits of the steel plow impress his mind more forcibly when he notes the contrast between that and the sheet-iron mold-board of a century ago. The value of a self-binder is best measured in comparison with the sickle and the cradle which our fathers used to cut their grain with. The man of toil whose wasting energy follows him through the cheerless years, who shivers in the storm while hunger is gnawing at his vitals, knows he is poor because he feels all these cruel pangs. But how shall he measure the extent of his poverty? By what means shall he learn how poor he is? Let him watch currents flowing in the highway where all sorts and conditions of men are passing to and fro through the hours of the busy day. There he sees what accompanies ease and affluence, what follows wealth and fame. And as he looks upon the sparkling eyes and ruddy cheeks of playful children, and as he listens to

Source: W. A. Peffer, *The Farmer's Side: His Troubles and Their Remedy* (New York: D. Appleton and Company, 1891), 1–9. Retrieved from the Internet Archive website, https://archive.org/details/cu31924031175460 (Accessed June 11, 2018).

the joyous laughter of merry-making sons and daughters of the well-to-do and rich, he turns toward the pale face, the sunken eye of the thinly clad child of his own home; how he sickens at the contrast, how his heart bleeds, how his soul weeps, how the poor man groans in agony when he beholds the depth of his poverty! He sees it in comparison.

Is the farmer in trouble? To what extent? Is he really poor? How shall we know? Is he worse off than men engaged in other lines of work? By what rule shall we measure the rate of his progress? Let him but look at the world about him and note the contrasts. Let him hold up a mirror, if you please—a mirror which reflects what has passed, what is passing, and foreshadows what is yet to come. Look and think. Behold, compare, and learn. Follow the guide.

Two hundred and seventy years have we been at work in this country. We conquered the wilderness, we peopled the solitudes, we civilized the continent. We cleared away forests, opened highways, established commerce, and built a nation that leads all the rest in agriculture and manufactures, having half the railroad mileage of the world, with an internal trade which, measured either in dollars or in tons, exceeds the foreign commerce of any half-dozen other countries. Yet, with all that we have done, we find our necessities are multiplying while our profits are dividing. Society makes more demands upon us than our incomes will satisfy. Our ancient prerogatives have been wrested from us, our statesmen have been led away from the people, and money presides over the destinies of the republic.

One hundred years ago, when Benjamin Franklin was at the head of our postal system, there were only seventy-five post-offices in the country, and the aggregate length of all the mail routes was 1,875 miles. The entire cost of the service for the year 1790 was a little over $22,000, while the receipts for the year were nearly $28,000. The mail was carried mostly on horses. The trip from New York to Boston required five days, and from New York to Philadelphia the time was three days. At the beginning of the present century it required thirty-two days to carry a letter from Philadelphia to Lexington, Ky., and to reach Nashville on the same trip the time was extended to forty-four days. Now fifty-six railway mail trains, each with a post-office aboard, go into Chicago every day, and an equal number go out. The mail from Philadelphia to New York runs thirteen times daily, and from New York to Philadelphia ten times daily; the time is about two hours, with an aggregate weight of forty tons of mail. On the 30th day of June, 1890, the number of post-offices in the country was 62,401. The number of mail routes was over 26,000, and their aggregate length is 428,000 miles. The total length of all the trips made on all the routes both ways daily is equal to a line that would encircle the earth at the equator forty-one times. Packages sent through the mails during the year, all told, amounted to 4,500,408,206—over four thousand million—more than half of which were letters. The total expense of the system last year was $66,645,083, and the total revenue amounted to $60,858,783. The estimated cost of carrying mails on railroads alone for the year 1891 is $22,610,128.

The first passenger locomotive was put on the track sixty years ago. On the 30th day of June, 1889, the aggregate length of our railroads was 157,758 miles, and the entire railroad system of the country was capitalized at $9,015,175,374. (Total mileage January 1, 1891, was 160,554 miles.) In 1834, upon completing connection between Philadelphia and Pittsburg, it cost $1.12½ to carry a barrel of flour eastward over the route; now a bushel of wheat is carried from Kansas City to New York for 25 cents.

One hundred years ago there was not a cotton or a woolen factory in the United States outside of the dwellings of the people, and as late as fifty years ago cards and spinning wheels and weaving looms were in use on more than half the farms. Now we have about 260,000 manufacturing establishments. In 1880, the number was 253,840, with a capital of $2,790,223,506, using raw material valued at $3,394,340,029, turning out a finished product valued at $5,369,667,706. It required 2,738,930 persons to perform the work, and they received $947,919,674 wages during the year.

A hundred years ago 90 per cent of our population lived on farms, and transportation was so expensive that surplus wheat and corn had no market value fifty miles away from a market town. Now great cities have grown up, the market has been distributed all over the country, and distance is practically annihilated. From a small area along the Atlantic coast, we have spread across the continent, and we travel in palace cars from Boston to San Francisco in less than six working days. We have about 5,000,000 farms, though less than half of our people live on them. They are valued at something over eleven thousand million dollars. Ten years ago the value of farm machinery was $406,520,055, and our farm live stock on hand was worth $1,500,464,609. Our average annual production of wheat the last ten years has been about 500,000,000 bushels, and of corn we raised nearly four times that much. Learning, enterprise, and invention have added 75 per cent to the productive power of the people in the last fifty years. The opening of the Suez Canal shortened the distance between Bombay and Liverpool 10,000 miles and cheapened transportation 50 per cent. Wheat grown in India can be landed in Britain for 50 cents a bushel total cost. Many men now living remember when wheat, one hundred miles west, of our large cities on the seaboard, was valueless except for home use, its carriage that distance being worth its full value in the market. One man and three horses plow as much ground with one plow as two men and four horses did with two plows formerly; one man with a seed drill will sow seed on twice as much ground as he could if sowing broadcast by hand; one man with a self-binder will put in sheaf as much wheat as twelve persons did before the reaper was invented. On the whole, one man does as much work on the farm now as two men did under the old *régime*, and more in some lines of work. The farmer produces as much grain to the acre, raises as many cattle, hogs, sheep, and horses, works as hard and steadily as he did then—but is he gaining? Has he saved anything? On the contrary, is he not in debt and falling behind? Is he not losing rather than gaining ground compared with his fellow-men? His crops have not fallen off, but their value in the market is less by 30 to 50 per cent than they were a dozen years ago, and before that time. He is paying all the way from 8 to 40 per cent for the use of money—money which goes up in value while his products go down. His taxes have not diminished a penny, while his crops are cut short one-half in paying power. The census reports have shown well for the farmer. In number and value farms have increased, farm implements have been multiplied many times, and live stock increases yearly. But the average farmer is not growing richer. In the last thirty-eight years railroad interests in

the United States have developed 1,580 per cent, banking 918 per cent, manufactures 408 per cent, while agriculture has not gone beyond 200 per cent. He plows and sows and reaps with machines. A machine cuts his wheat and puts it in sheaf, and steam drives his thrashers. He may read the morning paper while he plows, and sit under an awning while he reaps. Surely, considering all these things, and in view of them, the farmer ought to be in his best estate, but he is not. He ought to be the richest, the most happy, the most ·influential and powerful citizen in the republic. Who is bold enough to assert that he is?

II.—THE WAGE WORKER.

AND what shall we say of the wage worker, the artisan, the mechanic, the farm-hand, the common day laborer? Machinery has invaded his kingdom also. It does 75 per cent of his work; but how much better off is he than his father was fifty years ago? Who gets the benefit of invention—the hired man or his employer? One person now accomplishes as much work in a given time as four persons did before muscles were made of iron and nerves of steel. And what has become of the displaced hands, and what better off are the workers to-day in view of the altered conditions of living? The farm tenant, with his garden and potato patch, his cow pasture and fire-wood, his pigs, and his home-spun clothes, is not common now. A man's work is worth more than it was when everything was done by hand, because he can do more in a given time, and he receives more in wages; but things over which he has no control have so changed that his expenses are now necessarily greater than they were then, so that, while it need not, yet in fact it does cost him more to live than it did in the days of the flail and the hand loom. It is true that the farm laborer of to-day, whatever be his wages, is no better off—does not save any more money—than his predecessor of half a century ago. And how is it with the wage worker in other lines—mechanics, builders, and skilled workers? They, too, are apparently better off than they were in the days when blacksmiths and wagon-makers and shoe-makers were in every neighborhood, and carders and spinsters and weavers in every home. For these the figures show well on paper. Manufactures have developed enormously. One person in many instances can now do as much work in a factory as a dozen did in the same line when hand work was common. An engineer and his fireman will haul as much wheat or corn at one load over a railroad as would have required 100 wagons, 600 horses, and 100 men on the Philadelphia and Pittsburg turnpike only fifty years ago. Speaking generally, one person now does as much work in manufactures and commerce as four persons did when everybody was his own master[.] But, though the productive power of individual workers has increased 300 per cent in forty years, their wages have not gone beyond 50 per cent on the average—taking the census figures of 1850 and 1880 as authority. Cost of manufactured products has been reduced 25 per cent, and of transportation 75 per cent on the general average, and to that extent the people have reaped substantial benefits from the use of machinery. But what has taken the place of the little shop at the cross roads, and what became of the worker there? Our wage workers earn more and receive more than they did formerly. But do they receive enough? Do they receive as large a share of the profit on their labor as their fathers did when they worked in their own little shops by the wayside, half a century ago? What profit is there for the workman on a 33-cent pair of shoes, or on a 3-cent yard of cloth? The shoe factories and the cloth factories are owned by rich men. Do they receive more than their proper share of the profit, what little there is, on the men's work? And the women—ah, yes, the women! Three cents for making a shirt, 13 cents for a pair of trousers, 50 cents for a coat—there is no need of asking what share of the profit they get. Work and starvation the daily round all through the weary years. We have steam engines and electric motors. We have sewing machines, perfecting printing presses, and telephones. We have pneumatic tubes to carry our mail. We talk over a wire to a friend a hundred miles distant. We preserve speech on a cylinder, and have music repeated to us by a machine. We travel at the rate of a mile a minute and dine as we go. The lightning carries messages for us, and we float ships on the air. But what good has all this wrought for the man of toil? Is he any the richer, happier, or more content than his ancestor was when the old-fashioned wagon shop stood by the highway, and the carpenter made his own sashes and doors, and the neighborhood mechanic owned the house he lived in?

Briefly, while the world has been moving ahead with long and rapid strides, while invention has multiplied machinery a thousand fold, giving every worker ten hands and increasing wealth at marvelous rate; while the country has advanced without parallel in the history of nations; while statisticians flood reports with bewildering figures; while politicians grow big with patriotic conceptions and eloquent with fervid speech, the men and women who do the manual work are growing relatively poorer, and the few who live off of the profits of other men's labor, or off of the interest on money, or rent on buildings and land, and they who gamble in labor's products and play with the fortunes of men as if they were foot-balls or dice, and to whom the toil and sweat of the poor have no more value than the drip of the roof, are growing richer. Advances in wages, real though they are, have not kept pace with the growing necessities of the working people. Is not the workman worthy of his hire? Ought not the producer to be first paid? Who may rightfully despoil him?

QUESTIONS TO CONSIDER

1. How did Peffer set up his argument?
2. Do you find the argument convincing?

CHAPTER 18

INDUSTRY AND EMPIRE, 1890–1900

18.1 ALFRED THAYER MAHAN, EXCERPT FROM *THE INFLUENCE OF SEA POWER UPON HISTORY* (1890)

In 1890, Alfred Thayer Mahan (1840–1914) asked the world to think more seriously about naval power. Mahan, a former U.S. Naval Officer, was by the mid-1880s a lecturer at the Naval War College. In his lectures, he synthesized the history of naval power into a broader argument about the contemporary applicability of naval technology and fleet strength. As a result of Mahan's forceful argument, French, British, German, and Japanese officials took up his ideas and began urging their respective nations to building stronger and more advanced fleets. In the excerpt you will read, Mahan discussed the elements he believed aided in achieving naval power.

The first and most obvious light in which the sea presents itself from the political and social point of view is that of a great highway; or better, perhaps, of a wide common, over which men may pass in all directions, but on which some well-worn paths show that controlling reasons have led them to choose certain lines of travel rather than others. These lines of travel are called trade routes; and the reasons which have determined them are to be sought in the history of the world. . . .

Under modern conditions . . . home trade is but a part of the business of a country bordering on the sea. Foreign necessaries or luxuries must be brought to its ports, either in its own or in foreign ships, which will return, bearing in exchange the products of the country, whether they be the fruits of the earth or the works of men's hands; and it is the wish of every nation that this shipping business should be done by its own vessels. The ships that thus sail to and fro must have secure ports to which to return, and must, as far as possible, be followed by the protection of their country throughout the voyage.

This protection in time of war must be extended by armed shipping. The necessity of a navy, in the restricted

Source: Alfred Thayer Mahan, *The Influence of Sea Power upon History, 1660–1783* (Boston: Little Brown and Company, 1890). Retrieved from the Project Gutenberg website, http://www.gutenberg.org/files/13529/13529-h/13529-h.htm (Accessed June 11, 2018).

sense of the word, springs, therefore, from the existence of a peaceful shipping, and disappears with it, except in the case of a nation which has aggressive tendencies, and keeps up a navy merely as a branch of the military establishment. As the United States has at present no aggressive purposes, and as its merchant service has disappeared, the dwindling of the armed fleet and general lack of interest in it are strictly logical consequences. When for any reason sea trade is again found to pay, a large enough shipping interest will reappear to compel the revival of the war fleet. It is possible that when a canal route through the Central-American Isthmus is seen to be a near certainty, the aggressive impulse may be strong enough to lead to the same result. This is doubtful, however, because a peaceful, gain-loving nation is not far-sighted, and far-sightedness is needed for adequate military preparation, especially in these days. . . .

The principal conditions affecting the sea power of nations may be enumerated as follows: I. Geographical Position. II. Physical Conformation, including, as connected therewith, natural productions and climate. III. Extent of Territory. IV. Number of Population. V. Character of the People. VI. Character of the Government, including therein the national institutions.

I. GEOGRAPHICAL POSITION.

It may be pointed out, in the first place, that if a nation be so situated that it is neither forced to defend itself by land nor induced to seek extension of its territory by way of the land, it has, by the very unity of its aim directed upon the sea, an advantage as compared with a people one of whose boundaries is continental. This has been a great advantage to England over both France and Holland as a sea power. The strength of the latter was early exhausted by the necessity of keeping up a large army and carrying on expensive wars to preserve her independence; while the policy of France was constantly diverted, sometimes wisely and sometimes most foolishly, from the sea to projects of continental extension. These military efforts expended wealth; whereas a wiser and consistent use of her geographical position would have added to it.

The geographical position may be such as of itself to promote a concentration, or to necessitate a dispersion, of the naval forces. Here again the British Islands have an advantage over France. The position of the latter,

touching the Mediterranean as well as the ocean, while it has its advantages, is on the whole a source of military weakness at sea. The eastern and western French fleets have only been able to unite after passing through the Straits of Gibraltar, in attempting which they have often risked and sometimes suffered loss. The position of the United States upon the two oceans would be either a source of great weakness or a cause of enormous expense, had it a large sea commerce on both coasts. . . .

II. PHYSICAL CONFORMATION.

The peculiar features of the Gulf coast, just alluded to, come properly under the head of Physical Conformation of a country, which is placed second for discussion among the conditions which affect the development of sea power.

The seaboard of a country is one of its frontiers; and the easier the access offered by the frontier to the region beyond, in this case the sea, the greater will be the tendency of a people toward intercourse with the rest of the world by it. If a country be imagined having a long seaboard, but entirely without a harbor, such a country can have no sea trade of its own, no shipping, no navy. This was practically the case with Belgium when it was a Spanish and an Austrian province. The Dutch, in 1648, as a condition of peace after a successful war, exacted that the Scheldt should be closed to sea commerce. This closed the harbor of Antwerp and transferred the sea trade of Belgium to Holland. The Spanish Netherlands ceased to be a sea power.

Numerous and deep harbors are a source of strength and wealth, and doubly so if they are the outlets of navigable streams, which facilitate the concentration in them of a country's internal trade; but by their very accessibility they become a source of weakness in war, if not properly defended. . . .

III. EXTENT OF TERRITORY.

The last of the conditions affecting the development of a nation as a sea power, and touching the country itself as distinguished from the people who dwell there, is Extent of Territory. This may be dismissed with comparatively few words.

As regards the development of sea power, it is not the total number of square miles which a country contains, but the length of its coast-line and the character of its harbors that are to be considered. As to these it is to be said that, the geographical and physical conditions being the same, extent of sea-coast is a source of strength or weakness according as the population is large or small. A country is in this like a fortress; the garrison must be proportioned to the *enceinte*. A recent familiar instance is found in the American War of Secession. Had the South had a people as numerous as it was warlike, and a navy commensurate to its other resources as a sea power, the great extent of its sea-coast and its numerous inlets would have been elements of great strength. The people of the United States and the Government of that day justly prided themselves on the effectiveness of the blockade of the whole Southern coast. It was a great feat, a very great feat; but it would have been an impossible feat had the Southerners been more numerous, and a nation of seamen. What was there shown was not, as has been said, how such a blockade can be maintained, but that such a blockade is possible in the face of a population not only unused to the sea, but also scanty in numbers. Those who recall how the blockade was maintained, and the class of ships that blockaded during a great part of the war, know that the plan, correct under the circumstances, could not have been carried out in the face of a real navy. Scattered unsupported along the coast, the United States ships kept their places, singly or in small detachments, in face of an extensive network of inland water communications which favored secret concentration of the enemy. Behind the first line of water communications were long estuaries, and here and there strong fortresses, upon either of which the enemy's ships could always fall back to elude pursuit or to receive protection. Had there been a Southern navy to profit by such advantages, or by the scattered condition of the United States ships, the latter could not have been distributed as they were; and being forced to concentrate for mutual support, many small but useful approaches would have been left open to commerce. . . .

IV. NUMBER OF POPULATION.

After the consideration of the natural conditions of a country should follow an examination of the characteristics of its population as affecting the development of sea power; and first among these will be taken, because of its relations to the extent of the territory, which has just been discussed, the number of the people who live in it. It has been said that in respect of dimensions it is not merely the number of square miles, but the extent and character of the sea-coast that is to be considered with reference to sea power; and so, in point of population, it is not only the grand total, but the number following the sea, or at least readily available for employment on ship-board and for the creation of naval material, that must be counted. . . .

If time be, as is everywhere admitted, a supreme factor in war, it behooves countries whose genius is essentially not military, whose people, like all free people, object to pay for large military establishments, to see to it that they are at least strong enough to gain the time necessary to turn the spirit and capacity of their subjects into the new activities which war calls for. If the existing force by land or sea is strong enough so to hold out, even though at a disadvantage, the country may rely upon its natural resources and strength coming into play for whatever they are worth,—its numbers, its wealth, its capacities of every kind. If, on the other hand, what force it has can be overthrown and crushed quickly, the most magnificent possibilities of natural power will not save it from humiliating conditions, nor, if its foe be wise, from guarantees which will postpone revenge to a distant future. The story is constantly repeated on the smaller fields of war: "If so-and-so can hold out a little longer, this can be saved or that can be done;" as in sickness it is often said: "If the patient can only hold out so long, the strength of his constitution may pull him through." . . .

V. NATIONAL CHARACTER.

The effect of national character and aptitudes upon the development of sea power will next be considered.

If sea power be really based upon a peaceful and extensive commerce, aptitude for commercial pursuits must be a distinguishing feature of the nations that have at one time or another been great upon the sea. History almost without exception affirms that this is true. Save the Romans, there is no marked instance to the contrary.

All men seek gain and, more or less, love money; but the way in which gain is sought will have a marked effect upon the commercial fortunes and the history of the people inhabiting a country. . . .

. . . Of colonization, as of all other growths, it is true that it is most healthy when it is most natural. Therefore colonies that spring from the felt wants and natural impulses of a whole people will have the most solid foundations; and their subsequent growth will be surest when they are least trammelled from home, if the people have the genius for independent action. . . .

This truth stands out the clearer because the general attitude of all the home governments toward their colonies was entirely selfish. However founded, as soon as it was recognized to be of consequence, the colony became to the home country a cow to be milked; to be cared for, of course, but chiefly as a piece of property valued for the returns it gave. Legislation was directed toward a monopoly of its external trade; the places in its government afforded posts of value for occupants from the mother-country; and the colony was looked upon, as the sea still so often is, as a fit place for those who were ungovernable or useless at home. The military administration, however, so long as it remains a colony, is the proper and necessary attribute of the home government. . . .

It seems scarcely necessary, however, to do more than appeal to a not very distant past to prove that, if legislative hindrances be removed, and more remunerative fields of enterprise filled up, the sea power will not long delay its appearance. The instinct for commerce, bold enterprise in the pursuit of gain, and a keen scent for the trails that lead to it, all exist; and if there be in the future any fields calling for colonization, it cannot be doubted that Americans will carry to them all their inherited aptitude for self-government and independent growth.

VI. CHARACTER OF THE GOVERNMENT.

In discussing the effects upon the development of a nation's sea power exerted by its government and institutions, it will be necessary to avoid a tendency to over-philosophizing, to confine attention to obvious and immediate causes and their plain results, without prying too far beneath the surface for remote and ultimate influences.

Nevertheless, it must be noted that particular forms of government with their accompanying institutions, and the character of rulers at one time or another, have exercised a very marked influence upon the development of sea power. The various traits of a country and its people which have so far been considered constitute the natural characteristics with which a nation, like a man, begins its career; the conduct of the government in turn corresponds to the exercise of the intelligent will-power, which, according as it is wise, energetic and persevering, or the reverse, causes success or failure in a man's life or a nation's history.

It would seem probable that a government in full accord with the natural bias of its people would most successfully advance its growth in every respect; and, in the matter of sea power, the most brilliant successes have followed where there has been intelligent direction by a government fully imbued with the spirit of the people and conscious of its true general bent. Such a government is most certainly secured when the will of the people, or of their best natural exponents, has some large share in making it; but such free governments have sometimes fallen short, while on the other hand despotic power, wielded with judgment and consistency, has created at times a great sea commerce and a brilliant navy with greater directness than can be reached by the slower processes of a free people. The difficulty in the latter case is to insure perseverance after the death of a particular despot. . . .

. . . [I]t is seen that that influence can work in two distinct but closely related ways.

First, in peace: The government by its policy can favor the natural growth of a people's industries and its tendencies to seek adventure and gain by way of the sea; or it can try to develop such industries and such sea-going bent, when they do not naturally exist; or, on the other hand, the government may by mistaken action check and fetter the progress which the people left to themselves would make. In any one of these ways the influence of the government will be felt, making or marring the sea power of the country in the matter of peaceful commerce; upon which alone, it cannot be too often insisted, a thoroughly strong navy can be based.

Secondly, for war: The influence of the government will be felt in its most legitimate manner in maintaining an armed navy, of a size commensurate with the growth of its shipping and the importance of the interests connected with it. More important even than the size of the navy is the question of its institutions, favoring a healthful spirit and activity, and providing for rapid development in time of war by an adequate reserve of men and of ships and by measures for drawing out that general reserve power which has before been pointed to, when considering the character and pursuits of the people. Undoubtedly under this second head of warlike preparation must come the maintenance of suitable naval stations, in those distant parts of the world to which the armed shipping must follow the peaceful vessels of commerce. . . .

It may be urged that, with the extensive sea-coast of the United States, a blockade of the whole line cannot be effectively kept up. No one will more readily concede this than officers who remember how the blockade of the Southern coast alone was maintained. But in the present condition of the navy, and, it may be added, with any additions not exceeding those so far proposed by the government, the attempt to blockade Boston, New York, the Delaware, the Chesapeake, and the Mississippi, in other words, the great centres of export and import, would not entail upon one of the large maritime nations efforts greater than have been made before. England has at the same time blockaded Brest, the Biscay coast, Toulon, and Cadiz, when there were powerful squadrons lying within the harbors. It is true that commerce in neutral ships can then enter other ports of the United States than those named; but what a dislocation of the carrying traffic of the country, what failure of supplies at times, what inadequate means of transport by rail or water, of dockage, of lighterage, of warehousing, will be involved in such an enforced change of the ports of entry! Will there be no money loss, no suffering, consequent upon this? And when with much pain and expense these evils have been partially remedied, the enemy may be led to stop the new inlets as he did the old. The people of the United States will certainly not starve, but they may suffer grievously. As for supplies which are contraband of war, is there not reason to fear that the United States is not now able to go alone if an emergency should arise?

QUESTIONS TO CONSIDER

1. What factors did Mahan argue were important in achieving "sea power"?
2. How convincing do you find his argument?

18.2 FREDERICK JACKSON TURNER, EXCERPT FROM "THE SIGNIFICANCE OF THE FRONTIER IN AMERICAN HISTORY" (1893)

Frederick Jackson Turner's "Frontier Thesis" has come to be a foundational piece in studying America at the turn-of-the-twentieth century. Turner was a historian who taught at the University of Wisconsin from 1890 to 1910 and then Harvard University from 1910 to 1922. At the Chicago World's Columbian Exposition in 1893, Jackson gave a version of his now-famous paper "The Significance of the Frontier in American History," from which the following document is excerpted. Turner began with a recent development: the 1890 census indicated that the American frontier had ceased to exist. He laid out a specific argument about the importance of the frontier to democracy. While historians have challenged many of Turner's points, his arguments provide pivotal insights into contemporary debates about American expansion. Through Turner, we can get a sense of a changing America.

In a recent bulletin of the Superintendent of the Census for 1890 appear these significant words: "Up to and including 1880 the country had a frontier of settlement, but at present the unsettled area has been so broken into by isolated bodies of settlement that there can hardly be said to be a frontier line. In the discussion of its extent, its westward movement, etc., it can not, therefore, any longer have a place in the census reports." This brief official statement marks the closing of a great historic movement. Up to our own day American history has been in a large degree the history of the colonization of the Great West. The existence of an area of free land, its continuous recession, and the advance of American settlement westward, explain American development.

Behind institutions, behind constitutional forms and modifications, lie the vital forces that call these organs into life and shape them to meet changing conditions. The peculiarity of American institutions is, the fact that they have been compelled to adapt themselves to the changes of an expanding people—to the changes involved in crossing a continent, in winning a wilderness, and in developing at each area of this progress out of the primitive economic and political conditions of the frontier into the complexity of city life. Said Calhoun in 1817, "We are great, and rapidly— I was about to say fearfully—growing!" So saying, he touched the distinguishing feature of American life. All peoples show development; the germ theory of politics has been sufficiently emphasized. In the case of most nations, however, the development has occurred in a limited area; and if the nation has expanded, it has met other growing peoples whom it has conquered. But in the case of the United States we have a different phenomenon. Limiting our attention to the Atlantic coast, we have the familiar phenomenon of the evolution of institutions in a limited area, such as the rise of representative government; the differentiation of simple colonial governments into complex organs; the progress from primitive industrial society, without division of labor, up to manufacturing civilization. But we have in addition to this a recurrence of the process of evolution in each western area reached in the process of expansion. Thus American development has exhibited not merely advance along a single line, but a return to primitive conditions on a continually advancing frontier line, and a new development for that area. American

Source: Frederick Jackson Turner, *The Frontier in American History* (New York: Henry Holt and Company, 1931). Retrieved from the Project Gutenberg website, http://www.gutenberg.org/files/22994/22994-h/22994-h.htm (Accessed June 11, 2018).

social development has been continually beginning over again on the frontier. This perennial rebirth, this fluidity of American life, this expansion westward with its new opportunities, its continuous touch with the simplicity of primitive society, furnish the forces dominating American character. The true point of view in the history of this nation is not the Atlantic coast, it is the Great West. Even the slavery struggle, which is made so exclusive an object of attention by writers like Professor von Holst, occupies its important place in American history because of its relation to westward expansion.

In this advance, the frontier is the outer edge of the wave—the meeting point between savagery and civilization. Much has been written about the frontier from the point of view of border warfare and the chase, but as a field for the serious study of the economist and the historian it has been neglected.

The American frontier is sharply distinguished from the European frontier—a fortified boundary line running through dense populations. The most significant thing about the American frontier is, that it lies at the hither edge of free land. In the census reports it is treated as the margin of that settlement which has a density of two or more to the square mile. The term is an elastic one, and for our purposes does not need sharp definition. We shall consider the whole frontier belt, including the Indian country and the outer margin of the "settled area" of the census reports. This paper will make no attempt to treat the subject exhaustively; its aim is simply to call attention to the frontier as a fertile field for investigation, and to suggest some of the problems which arise in connection with it.

In the settlement of America we have to observe how European life entered the continent, and how America modified and developed that life and reacted on Europe. Our early history is the study of European germs developing in an American environment. Too exclusive attention has been paid by institutional students to the Germanic origins, too little to the American factors. The frontier is the line of most rapid and effective Americanization. The wilderness masters the colonist. It finds him a European in dress, industries, tools, modes of travel, and thought. It takes him from the railroad car and puts him in the birch canoe. It strips off the garments of civilization and arrays him in the hunting shirt and the moccasin. It puts him in the

log cabin of the Cherokee and Iroquois and runs an Indian palisade around him. Before long he has gone to planting Indian corn and plowing with a sharp stick; he shouts the war cry and takes the scalp in orthodox Indian fashion. In short, at the frontier the environment is at first too strong for the man. He must accept the conditions which it furnishes, or perish, and so he fits himself into the Indian clearings and follows the Indian trails. Little by little he transforms the wilderness, but the outcome is not the old Europe, not simply the development of Germanic germs, any more than the first phenomenon was a case of reversion to the Germanic mark. The fact is, that here is a new product that is American. At first, the frontier was the Atlantic coast. It was the frontier of Europe in a very real sense. Moving westward, the frontier became more and more American. As successive terminal moraines result from successive glaciations, so each frontier leaves its traces behind it, and when it becomes a settled area the region still partakes of the frontier characteristics. Thus the advance of the frontier has meant a steady movement away from the influence of Europe, a steady growth of independence on American lines. And to study this advance, the men who grew up under these conditions, and the political, economic, and social results of it, is to study the really American part of our history. . . .

Having now roughly outlined the various kinds of frontiers, and their modes of advance, chiefly from the point of view of the frontier itself, we may next inquire what were the influences on the East and on the Old World. A rapid enumeration of some of the more noteworthy effects is all that I have time for.

First, we note that the frontier promoted the formation of a composite nationality for the American people. . . .

It was this nationalizing tendency of the West that transformed the democracy of Jefferson into the national republicanism of Monroe and the democracy of Andrew Jackson. The West of the War of 1812, the West of Clay, and Benton and Harrison, and Andrew Jackson, shut off by the Middle States and the mountains from the coast sections, had a solidarity of its own with national tendencies. On the tide of the Father of Waters, North and South met and mingled into a nation. Interstate migration went steadily on—a process of cross-fertilization of ideas and institutions. The fierce struggle of the sections over slavery on the western frontier does not diminish the truth of this statement; it proves the truth of it. Slavery was a sectional trait that would not down, but in the West it could not remain sectional. It was the greatest of frontiersmen who declared: "I believe this Government can not endure permanently half slave and half free. It will become all of one thing or all of the other." Nothing works for nationalism like intercourse within the nation. Mobility of population is death to localism, and the western frontier worked irresistibly in unsettling population. The effect reached back from the frontier and affected profoundly the Atlantic coast and even the Old World.

But the most important effect of the frontier has been in the promotion of democracy here and in Europe. As has been indicated, the frontier is productive of individualism. Complex society is precipitated by the wilderness into a kind of primitive organization based on the family. The tendency is anti-social. It produces antipathy to control, and particularly to any direct control. The tax-gatherer is viewed as a representative of oppression. Prof. Osgood, in an able article, has pointed out that the frontier conditions prevalent in the colonies are important factors in the explanation of the American Revolution, where individual liberty was sometimes confused with absence of all effective government. The same conditions aid in explaining the difficulty of instituting a strong government in the period of the confederacy. The frontier individualism has from the beginning promoted democracy.

The frontier States that came into the Union in the first quarter of a century of its existence came in with democratic suffrage provisions, and had reactive effects of the highest importance upon the older States whose peoples were being attracted there. An extension of the franchise became essential. It was *western* New York that forced an extension of suffrage in the constitutional convention of that State in 1821; and it was *western* Virginia that compelled the tide-water region to put a more liberal suffrage provision in the constitution framed in 1830, and to give to the frontier region a more nearly proportionate representation with the tide-water aristocracy. The rise of democracy as an effective force in the nation came in with western

preponderance under Jackson and William Henry Harrison, and it meant the triumph of the frontier—with all of its good and with all of its evil elements. An interesting illustration of the tone of frontier democracy in 1830 comes from the same debates in the Virginia convention already referred to. A representative from western Virginia declared:

But, sir, it is not the increase of population in the West which this gentleman ought to fear. It is the energy which the mountain breeze and western habits impart to those emigrants. They are regenerated, politically I mean, sir. They soon become *working politicians*; and the difference, sir, between a *talking* and a *working* politician is immense. The Old Dominion has long been celebrated for producing great orators; the ablest metaphysicians in policy; men that can split hairs in all abstruse questions of political economy. But at home, or when they return from Congress, they have negroes to fan them asleep. But a Pennsylvania, a New York, an Ohio, or a western Virginia statesman, though far inferior in logic, metaphysics, and rhetoric to an old Virginia statesman, has this advantage, that when he returns home he takes off his coat and takes hold of the plow. This gives him bone and muscle, sir, and preserves his republican principles pure and uncontaminated.

So long as free land exists, the opportunity for a competency exists, and economic power secures political power. But the democracy born of free land, strong in selfishness and individualism, intolerant of administrative experience and education, and pressing individual liberty beyond its proper bounds, has its dangers as well as its benefits. Individualism in America has allowed a laxity in regard to governmental affairs which has rendered possible the spoils system and all the manifest evils that follow from the lack of a highly developed civic spirit. In this connection may be noted also the influence of frontier conditions in permitting lax business honor, inflated paper currency and wild-cat banking. The colonial and revolutionary frontier was the region whence emanated many of the worst forms of an evil currency. The West in the War of 1812 repeated the phenomenon on the frontier of that day, while the speculation and wild-cat banking of the period of the crisis of 1837 occurred on the new frontier belt of the next tier of States. Thus each one of the periods of lax financial integrity coincides with periods when a new set of frontier communities had arisen, and coincides in area with these successive frontiers, for the most part. The recent Populist agitation is a case in point. Many a State that now declines any connection with the tenets of the Populists, itself adhered to such ideas in an earlier stage of the development of the State. A primitive society can hardly be expected to show the intelligent appreciation of the complexity of business interests in a developed society. The continual recurrence of these areas of paper-money agitation is another evidence that the frontier can be isolated and studied as a factor in American history of the highest importance. . . .

From the conditions of frontier life came intellectual traits of profound importance. The works of travelers along each frontier from colonial days onward describe certain common traits, and these traits have, while softening down, still persisted as survivals in the place of their origin, even when a higher social organization succeeded. The result is that to the frontier the American intellect owes its striking characteristics. That coarseness and strength combined with acuteness and inquisitiveness; that practical, inventive turn of mind, quick to find expedients; that masterful grasp of material things, lacking in the artistic but powerful to effect great ends; that restless, nervous energy; that dominant individualism, working for good and for evil, and withal that buoyancy and exuberance which comes with freedom—these are traits of the frontier, or traits called out elsewhere because of the existence of the frontier. Since the days when the fleet of Columbus sailed into the waters of the New World, America has been another name for opportunity, and the people of the United States have taken their tone from the incessant expansion which

has not only been open but has even been forced upon them. He would be a rash prophet who should assert that the expansive character of American life has now entirely ceased. Movement has been its dominant fact, and, unless this training has no effect upon a people, the American energy will continually demand a wider field for its exercise. But never again will such gifts of free land offer themselves. For a moment, at the frontier, the bonds of custom are broken and unrestraint is triumphant. There is not *tabula rasa*. The stubborn American environment is there with its imperious summons to accept its conditions; the inherited ways of doing things are also there; and yet, in spite of environment, and in spite of custom, each frontier did indeed furnish a new field of opportunity, a gate of escape from the bondage of the past; and freshness, and confidence, and scorn of older society, impatience of its restraints and its ideas, and indifference to its lessons, have accompanied the frontier. What the Mediterranean Sea was to the Greeks, breaking the bond of custom, offering new experiences, calling out new institutions and activities, that, and more, the ever retreating frontier has been to the United States directly, and to the nations of Europe more remotely. And now, four centuries from the discovery of America, at the end of a hundred years of life under the Constitution, the frontier has gone, and with its going has closed the first period of American history.

QUESTIONS TO CONSIDER

1. What was, to Turner, "The Significance of the Frontier"?
2. Do you find his argument persuasive? How might you challenge it?

18.3 WILLIAM JENNINGS BRYAN, "THE CROSS OF GOLD" (1896)

Like William Peffer (see Reading 17.5), William Jennings Bryan (1860–1925) gained support from—and catered to—the Populist movement. Bryan moved from his native Illinois to Nebraska in the 1880s and there began his political career. He first gained election to Congress in 1890 as a member of the Democratic Party and served in that role until 1895. In 1896, Bryan ran for the Democratic nomination for President. As one of the finest orators of his time, Bryan found great success in traveling through the United States and campaigning on a platform of removing America from the gold standard in favor of bimetallism, the "Free Silver" movement. At the 1896 Democratic National Convention in Chicago, Bryan took his movement to a broader audience. In his "Cross of Gold" speech, from which the following document is excerpted, Bryan captivated his audience. Often cited as one of the greatest speeches in American political history, "The Cross of Gold" catapulted Bryan into the Democratic nomination and cemented the Democratic Party as one temporarily controlled by its agrarian base. Bryan went on to lose the election to William McKinley. Bryan again won the Democratic nomination in 1900 and 1908, but he lost both of these elections as well. Regardless, "The Cross of Gold" revealed a deep cultural split in America over the nation's future economic policy.

Mr. Chairman and Gentlemen of the Convention: I would be presumptuous, indeed, to present myself against the distinguished gentlemen to whom you have listened if this were but a measuring of ability; but this is not a contest among persons. The humblest citizen in all the land, when clad in armor of a righteous cause, is stronger than all the whole hosts of error that they can bring. I come to speak to you in defense of a cause as holy as the cause of liberty—the cause of humanity. When this debate is concluded a motion will be made to lay upon the table the resolution offered in commendation of the administration and also the resolution in condemnation of the Administration. I shall object to bringing this question down to a level of person. The individual is but an atom; he is born, he acts, he dies but principles are eternal; and this has been a contest of principle.

Never before in the history of this country has there been witnessed such a contest as that through which we have passed. Never before in the history of American politics has a great issue been fought out, as this issue has been, by the voters themselves.

On the 4th of March, 1895, a few Democrats, most of them members of Congress, issued an address to the Democrats of the nation asserting that the money question was the paramount issue of the hour; asserting also the right of a majority of the Democratic party to control the position of the party on this paramount issue; concluding with the request that all believers in free coinage of silver in the Democratic party should

Source: *Official Proceedings of the Democratic National Conventions Held in Chicago, ILL., July 7th, 8th, 9th, 10th and 11th, 1896* (Logansport, IN: Wilson, Humphreys and Co.: 1896), 226–235. Retrieved from the Internet Archive website, https://archive.org/stream/officialproceedi1896demo/officialproceedi1896demo_djvu.txt (Accessed June 11, 2018).

organize and take charge of and control the policy of the Democratic party. Three months later, at Memphis, and organization was perfected, and the silver Democrats went forth openly and boldly and courageously proclaiming their belief and declaring that if successful they would crystallize in a platform the declaration what they had made; and then began the conflict with a zeal approaching the zeal which inspired the crusaders who followed PETER the Hermit. Our silver Democrats went forth from victory unto victory until they are assembled now, not to discuss, not to debate, but to enter up the judgment rendered by the plain people of this country.

But in this contest, brother has been arrayed against brother, and father against son. The warmest ties of love and acquaintance and association have been disregarded. Old leaders have been cast aside when they refused to give expression to the sentiments of those whom they would lead, and new leaders have sprung up to give direction to this cause of freedom. Thus has the contest been waged, and we have assembled here under as binding and solemn instructions as were ever fastened upon the representatives of a people. . . .

Now, my friends, let me come to the great paramount issue. If they ask us here why it is we say more on the money question than we say upon the tariff question, I reply that if protection has slain its thousands the gold standard has slain its tens of thousands. If they ask us why we did not embody all these things in our platform which we believe, we reply to them that when we have restored the money of the constitution all other necessary reforms will be possible, and that until that is done there is no reform that can be accomplished.

Why is it that within three months such a change has come over the sentiments of the country? Three months ago, when it was confidently asserted that those who believed in the gold standard would frame our platforms and nominate our candidates, even the advocates of the gold standard did not think that we could elect a President; but they had good reasons for the suspicion, because there is scarcely a State here to-day asking for the gold standard that is not within the absolute control of the Republican party. But not the change. Mr. McKINLEY was nominated at St. Louis upon a platform that declared for the maintenance of the gold standard until it should be changed into bimetallism by an international agreement. Mr. McKINLEY was the most popular man among the Republicans and everybody three months ago in the Republican party prophesied his election. How is it to-day? Why, that man who used to boast that he looked like NAPOLEON, that man shudders to-day when he thinks that he was nominated on the anniversary of the battle of Waterloo. Not only that, but as he listens he can hear with ever-increasing distinctness the sound of the waves as they beat upon the lonely shores of St. Helena.

Why this change? Ah, my friends, is not the change evident to anyone who will look at the matter? It is because no private character, however pure, no personal popularity, however great, can protect from the avenging wrath of an indignant people the man who will either declare that he is in favor of fastening the gold standard upon this people, or who is willing to surrender the right of self-government and place legislative control in the hands of foreign potentates and powers.

My friends, the prospect—

(The continued cheering made it impossible for the speaker to proceed. Finally Mr. BRYAN raising his hand, obtained silence, and said: I have only ten minutes left, and I ask you to let me occupy that time.)

We go forth confident that we shall win. Why? Because upon the paramount issue in this campaign there is not a spot of ground upon which the enemy will dare to challenge battle. Why, if they tell us that the gold standard is a good thing, we point to their platform and tell them that their platform pledges the party to get rid of a gold standard, and substitute bimetallism. If the gold standard is a good thing why try to get rid of it? If the gold standard, and I might call your attention to the fact that some of the very people who are in this convention to-day and who tell you that we ought to declare in favor of international bimetallism and thereby declare that the gold standard is wrong, and that the principles of bimetallism are better—these very people four months ago were open and avowed advocates of the gold standard and telling us that we could not legislate two metals together even with all the world.

I want to suggest this truth, that if the gold standard is a good thing we ought to declare in favor of its retention and not in favor of abandoning it; and if the gold standard is a bad thing why should we wait until some other nations are willing to help us to let it go?

Here is the line of battle. We care not upon which issue they force the fight. We are prepared to meet them on either issue or on both. If they tell us that the gold standard is the standard of civilization we reply to them that this, the most enlightened of all nations of the earth, has never declared for a gold standard, and both the parties this year are declaring against it. If the gold standard is the standard of civilization, why, my friends, should we not have it? So if they come to meet us on that we can present the history of our nation. More than that. We can tell them this, that they will search the pages of history in vain to find a single instance in which the common people of any land ever declared themselves in favor of a gold standard. They can find where the holders of fixed investments have.

MR. CARLISLE said in 1878 that this was a struggle between the idle holders of idle capital and the struggling masses who produce the wealth and pay the taxes of the country; and my friends, it is simply a question that we shall decide upon which side shall the Democratic party fight? Upon the side of the idle holders of idle capital, or upon the side of the struggling masses? That is the question that the party must answer first; and then it must be answered by each individual hereafter. The sympathies of the Democratic party, as described by the platform, are on the side of the struggling masses, who have ever been the foundation of the Democratic party.

There are two ideas of government. There are those who believe that if you just legislate to make the well-to-do prosperous that their prosperity will leak through on those below. The Democratic idea has been that if you legislate to make the masses prosperous their prosperity will find its way up and through every class that rests upon it.

You come to us and tell us that the great cities are in favor of the gold standard. I tell you that the great cities rest upon these broad and fertile prairies. Burn down your cities and leave our farms, and your cities will spring up again as if by magic. But destroy our farms and the grass will grow in the streets of every city in this country.

My friends, we shall declare that this nation is able to legislate for its own people on every question, without waiting for the aid or consent of any other nation on earth, and upon that issue we expect to carry every single State in this Union.

I shall not slander the fair State of Massachusetts nor the State of New York by saying that when its citizens are confronted with the proposition, "Is this nation able to attend to its own business?"—I will not slander either one by saying that the people of those States will declare our helpless impotency as a nation to attend to our own business. It is the issue of 1776 over again. Our ancestors, when but 3,000,000, had the courage to declare their political independence of every other nation upon earth. Shall we, their descendants, when we have grown to 70,000,000, declare that we are less independent than our forefathers? No, my friends, it will never be the judgment of this people. Therefore, we care not upon what lines the battle is fought. If they say bimetallism is good, but we cannot have it till some nation helps us, we reply that, instead of having a gold standard because England has, we shall restore bimetallism, and then let England have bimetallism because the United States have.

If they dare to come out and in the open defend the gold standard as a good thing, we shall fight them to the uttermost, having behind us the producing masses of the Nation and the world. Having behind us the commercial interests and the laboring interests and all the toiling masses, we shall answer their demands for a gold standard by saying to them, you shall not press down upon the brow of labor this crown of thorns. You shall not crucify mankind upon a cross of gold.

QUESTIONS TO CONSIDER

1. How did Bryan support his argument? Do you find it effective?
2. Why do you think the speech was and is so highly regarded?

18.4 RUDYARD KIPLING, "THE WHITE MAN'S BURDEN" (1899), AND MARK TWAIN, EXCERPT FROM "THE WAR PRAYER" (1905)

The issue of American imperialism increasingly divided Americans at the turn-of-the-twentieth century. The following two literary pieces show two different sides of the issue. First, Rudyard Kipling's "The White Man's Burden" argues that white civilization had a duty to take over less powerful, non-white countries. Kipling originally wrote the poem for Queen Victoria of England but rewrote it in response to the Philippine-American War, in which American forces fought Filipino independence fighters after the United States took over the islands in the wake of the Spanish-American War. Second, Mark Twain's short story "The War Prayer" disparaged American imperialism. Twain, an active member of the American Anti-Imperialist League, also wrote in response to the Spanish-American and Philippine-American wars. The Philippines would not gain its independence until 1946.

THE WHITE MAN'S BURDEN

TAKE up the White Man's burden—
    Send forth the best ye breed—
Go bind your sons to exile
    To serve your captives' need;
To wait in heavy harness
    On fluttered folk and wild—
Your new-caught, sullen peoples,
    Half devil and half child.

Take up the White Man's burden—
    In patience to abide,
To veil the threat of terror
    And check the show of pride;

By open speech and simple,
    An hundred times made plain.
To seek another's profit,
    And work another's gain.

Take up the White Man's burden—
    The savage wars of peace—
Fill full the mouth of Famine
    And bid the sickness cease;
And when your goal is nearest
    The end for others sought,
Watch Sloth and heathen Folly
    Bring all your hope to nought.

Sources: Rudyard Kipling's Verse: Definitive Edition (London: Hodder and Stoughton, Ltd.: 1940), 321–323. Retrieved from the Internet Archive website, https://archive.org/stream/rudyardkiplingsvkipl/rudyardkiplingsvkipl_djvu.txt (Accessed June 11, 2018); *The Complete Works of Mark Twain: Europe and Elsewhere* (New York: Harper and Brothers, 1923), 394–398. Retrieved from the Internet Archive website, https://archive.org/details/completeworksofm20twai (Accessed June 11, 2018).

Take up the White Man's burden—
　　No tawdry rule of kings,
But toil of serf and sweeper—
　　The tale of common things.
The ports ye shall not enter,
　　The roads ye shall not tread,
Go make them with your living,
　　And mark them with your dead!

Take up the White Man's burden—
　　And reap his old reward:
The blame of those ye better,
　　The hate of those ye guard—
The cry of hosts ye humour
　　(Ah, slowly!) toward the light:—
"Why brought ye us from bondage,
　　Our loved Egyptian night?"

Take up the White Man's burden—
　　Ye dare not stoop to less—
Nor call too loud on Freedom
　　To cloak your weariness;
By all ye cry or whisper,
　　By all ye leave or do,
The silent, sullen peoples
　　Shall weigh your Gods and you.

Take up the White Man's burden—
　　Have done with childish days—
The lightly proffered laurel,
　　The easy, ungrudged praise.
Comes now, to search your manhood
　　Through all the thankless years,
Cold-edged with dear-bought wisdom,
　　The judgment of your peers!

THE WAR PRAYER

It was a time of great and exalting excitement. The country was up in arms, the war was on, in every breast burned the holy fire of patriotism; the drums were beating, the bands playing, the toy pistols popping, the bunched firecrackers hissing and spluttering; on every hand and far down the receding and fading spread of roofs and balconies a fluttering wilderness of flags flashed in the sun; daily the young volunteers marched down the wide avenue gay and fine in their new uniforms, the proud fathers and mothers and sisters and sweethearts cheering them with voices choked with happy emotion as they swung by; nightly the packed mass meetings listened, panting, to patriot oratory which stirred the deepest deeps of their hearts, and which they interrupted at briefest intervals with cyclones of applause, the tears running down their cheeks the while; in the churches the pastors preached devotion to flag and country, and invoked the God of Battles, beseeching His aid in our good cause in outpouring of fervid eloquence which moved every listener. It was indeed a glad and gracious time, and the half dozen rash spirits that ventured to disapprove of the war and cast a doubt upon its righteousness straightway got such a stern and angry warning that for their personal safety's sake they quickly shrank out of sight and offended no more in that way.

Sunday morning came—next day the battalions would leave for the front; the church was filled; the volunteers were there, their young faces alight with martial dreams—visions of the stern advance, the gathering momentum, the rushing charge, the flashing sabers, the flight of the foe, the tumult, the enveloping smoke, the fierce pursuit, the surrender!—them home from the war, bronzed heroes, welcomed, adored, submerged in golden seas of glory! With the volunteers sat their dear ones, proud, happy, and envied by the neighbors and friends who had no sons and brothers to send forth to the field of honor, there to win for the flag, or, failing, die the noblest of noble deaths. The service proceeded; a war chapter from the Old Testament was read; the first prayer was said; it was followed by an organ burst that shook the building, and with one impulse the house rose, with glowing eyes and beating hearts, and poured out that tremendous invocation—

"God the all-terrible! Thou who ordainest,
Thunder thy clarion and lightning thy sword!"

Then came the "long" prayer. None could remember the like of it for passionate pleading and moving and beautiful language. The burden of its supplication was, that an ever-merciful and benignant Father of us all would watch over our noble young soldiers, and aid, comfort, and encourage them in their patriotic work; bless them, shield them in the day of battle and the hour of peril, bear them in His mighty hand, make them strong and confident, invincible in the bloody onset; help them to crush the foe, grant to them and to their flag and country imperishable honor and glory—

An aged stranger entered and moved with slow and noiseless step up the main aisle, his eyes fixed upon the minister, his long body clothed in a robe that reached to his feet, his head bare, his white hair descending in a frothy cataract to his shoulders, his seamy face unnaturally pale, pale even to ghastliness. With all eyes following him and wondering, he made his silent way; without pausing, he ascended to the preacher's side and stood there, waiting. With shut lids the preacher, unconscious of his presence, continued his moving prayer, and at last finished it with the words, uttered in fervent appeal, "Bless our arms, grant us the victory, O Lord our God, Father and Protector of our land and flag!"

The stranger touched his arm, motioned him to step aside—which the startled minister did—and took his place. During some moments he surveyed the spellbound audience with solemn eyes, in which burned an uncanny light; then in a deep voice he said:

"I come from the Throne—bearing a message from Almighty God!" The words smote the house with a shock; if the stranger perceived it he gave no attention. "He has heard the prayer of His servant your shepherd, and will grant it if such shall be your desire after I, His messenger, shall have explained to you its import—that is to say, its full import. For it is like unto many of the prayers of men, in that it asks for more than he who utters it is aware of—except he pause and think.

"God's servant and yours has prayed his prayer. Has he paused and taken thought? Is it one prayer?

No, it is two—one uttered, the other not. Both have reached the ear of Him Who heareth all supplications, the spoken and the unspoken. Ponder this—keep it in mind. If you would beseech a blessing upon yourself, beware! lest without intent you invoke a curse upon a neighbor at the same time. If you pray for the blessing of rain upon your crop which needs it, by that act you are possibly praying for a curse upon some neighbor's crop which may not need rain and can be injured by it.

"You have heard your servant's prayer—the uttered part of it. I am commissioned of God to put into words the other part of it—that part which the pastor—and also you in your hearts—fervently prayed silently. And ignorantly and unthinkingly? God grant that it was so! You heard these words: 'Grant us the victory, O Lord our God!' That is sufficient. The *whole* of the uttered prayer is compact into those pregnant words Elaborations were not necessary. When you have prayed for victory you have prayed for many unmentioned results which follow victory—*must* follow it, cannot help but follow it. Upon the listening spirit of God the Father fell also the unspoken part of the prayer. He commandeth me to put it into words. Listen!

"O Lord our Father, our young patriots, idols of our hearts, go forth to battle—be Thou near them! With them—in spirit—we also go forth from the sweet peace of our beloved firesides to smite the foe. O Lord our God, help us to tear their soldiers to bloody shreds with our shells; help us to cover their smiling fields with the pale forms of their patriot dead; help us to drown the thunder of the guns with the shrieks of their wounded, writhing in pain; help us to lay waste their humble homes with a hurricane of fire; help us to wring the hearts of their unoffending widows with unavailing grief; help us to turn them out roofless with their little children to wander unfriended the wastes of their desolated land in rags and hunger and thirst, sports of the sun flames of summer and the icy winds of winter, broken in spirit, worn with travail, imploring Thee for the refuge of the grave and denied it—for our sakes who adore Thee, Lord, blast their hopes, blight their lives, protract their bitter pilgrimage, make heavy their steps, water their way with their tears, stain the white snow with the blood of their wounded feet! We ask it, in the spirit of love, of Him Who is the Source of Love, and Who is the ever-faithful refuge and friend of all that are sore beset and seek His aid with humble and contrite hearts. Amen."

(*After a pause.*) "Ye have prayed it; if ye still desire it, speak! The messenger of the Most High waits."

It was believed afterward that the man was a lunatic, because there was no sense in what he said.

QUESTIONS TO CONSIDER

1. How did the two authors justify their arguments?
2. Which literary methods did the two authors use to make their points?

CHAPTER 19

A UNITED BODY OF ACTION, 1900–1916

19.1 IDA B. WELLS-BARNETT, EXCERPT FROM *THE RED RECORD* (1895)

Ida Wells (1862–1931) led a remarkable life. Born into slavery in Mississippi, she gained her freedom at the end of the Civil War. Both of her parents died when Wells was just sixteen, and she began working to support her siblings. Eventually, she moved into the newspaper business. During the 1890s, as co-owner of the *Memphis Free Speech and Headlight*, Wells began investigating the extent of lynching in the South after one of her good friends fell victim to a mob. Her initial articles so enraged the white community in Memphis that a mob burned her newspaper offices to the ground. In 1895, Wells published a longer-form version of her lynching investigation, *The Red Record*. The 100-page pamphlet described the history of lynching, accumulated statistics about its prevalence, and delved into specific cases. Afterward, Wells became a prominent African American activist and twice toured Europe to speak about lynching. The excerpt here comes from Wells' exploration of specific lynching cases.

LYNCHED ON ACCOUNT OF RELATIONSHIP

If no other reason appealed to the sober sense of the American people to check the growth of Lynch Law, the absolute unreliability and recklessness of the mob in inflicting punishment for crimes done, should do so. Several instances of this spirit have occurred in the year past. In Louisiana, near New Orleans, in July, 1893, Roselius Julian, a colored man, shot and killed a white judge, named Victor Estopinal. The cause of the shooting has never been definitely ascertained. It is claimed that the Negro resented an insult to his wife, and the killing of the white man was an act of a Negro (who dared) to defend his home. The judge was killed

Source: Ida B. Wells-Barnett, *The Red Record: Tabulated Statistics and Alleged Causes of Lynching in the United States* (Champaign-Urbana, IL: Project Gutenberg, 2005) https://www.gutenberg.org/files/14977/14977-h/14977-h.htm

in the court house, and Julian, heavily armed, made his escape to the swamps near the city. He has never been apprehended, nor has any information ever been gleaned as to his whereabouts. A mob determined to secure the fugitive murderer and burn him alive. The swamps were hunted through and through in vain, when, being unable to wreak their revenge upon the murderer, the mob turned its attention to his unfortunate relatives. Dispatches from New Orleans, dated September 19, 1893, described the affair as follows:

"Posses were immediately organized and the surrounding country was scoured, but the search was fruitless so far as the real criminal was concerned. The mother, three brothers and two sisters of the Negro were arrested yesterday at the Black Ridge in the rear of the city by the police and taken to the little jail on Judge Estopinal's place about Southport, because of the belief that they were succoring the fugitive.

About 11 o'clock twenty-five men, some armed with rifles and shotguns, came up to the jail. They unlocked the door and held a conference among themselves as to what they should do. Some were in favor of hanging the five, while others insisted that only two of the brothers should be strung up. This was finally agreed to, and the two doomed negroes were hurried to a pasture one hundred yards distant, and there asked to take their last chance of saving their lives by making a confession, but the Negroes made no reply. They were then told to kneel down and pray. One did so, the other remained standing, but both prayed fervently. The taller Negro was then hoisted up. The shorter Negro stood gazing at the horrible death of his brother without flinching. Five minutes later he was also hanged. The mob decided to take the remaining brother out to Camp Parapet and hang him there. The other two were to be taken out and flogged, with an order to get out of the parish in less than half an hour. The third brother, Paul, was taken out to the camp, which is about a mile distant in the interior, and there he was hanged to a tree."

Another young man, who was in no way related to Julian, who perhaps did not even know the man and who was entirely innocent of any offense in connection therewith, was murdered by the same mob. The same paper says:

"During the search for Julian on Saturday one branch of the posse visited the house of a Negro family in the neighborhood of Camp Parapet, and failing to find the object of their search, tried to induce John Willis, a young Negro, to disclose the whereabouts of Julian. He refused to do so, or could not do so, and was kicked to death by the gang." . . .

LYNCHED BECAUSE THE JURY ACQUITTED HIM

The entire system of the judiciary of this country is in the hands of white people. To this add the fact of the inherent prejudice against colored people, and it will be clearly seen that a white jury is certain to find a Negro prisoner guilty if there is the least evidence to warrant such a finding.

Meredith Lewis was arrested in Roseland, La., in July of last year. A white jury found him not guilty of the crime of murder wherewith he stood charged. This did not suit the mob. A few nights after the verdict was rendered, and he declared to be innocent, a mob gathered in his vicinity and went to his house. He was called, and suspecting nothing, went outside. He was seized and hurried off to a convenient spot and hanged by the neck until he was dead for the murder of a woman of which the jury had said he was innocent.

LYNCHED AS A SCAPEGOAT

Wednesday, July 5, about 10 o'clock in the morning, a terrible crime was committed within four miles of Wickliffe, Ky. Two girls, Mary and Ruby Ray, were found murdered a short distance from their home. The news of this terrible cowardly murder of two helpless young girls spread like wild fire, and searching parties scoured the territory surrounding Wickliffe and Bardwell. Two of the searching party, the Clark brothers, saw a man enter the Dupoyster cornfield; they got their guns and fired at the fleeing figure, but without effect; he got away, but they said he was a white man or nearly so. The search continued all day without effect, save the arrest of two or three strange Negroes. A bloodhound was brought from the penitentiary and put on the trail which he followed from the scene of the murder to the river and into the boat of a fisherman named Gordon. Gordon stated that he had ferried one man and only one across the river about half past six the evening of July 5; that his passenger sat in front of him, and he was a white man or a very bright mulatto, who could not be told from a white man. The bloodhound was put across the river in the boat, and he struck a trail again at Bird's Point on the Missouri side, ran about three hundred yards to the cottage of a white farmer named Grant and there lay down refusing to go further.

Thursday morning a brakesman on a freight train going out of Sikeston, Mo., discovered a Negro stealing a ride; he ordered him off and had hot words which terminated in a fight. The brakesman had the Negro arrested. When arrested, between 11 and 12 o'clock, he had on a dark woolen shirt, light pants and coat, and no vest. He had twelve dollars in paper, two silver dollars and ninety-five cents in change; he had also four rings in his pockets, a knife and a razor which were rusted and stained. The Sikeston authorities immediately jumped to the conclusion that this man was the murderer for whom the Kentuckians across the river were searching. They telegraphed to Bardwell that their prisoner had on no coat, but wore a blue vest and pants which would perhaps correspond with the coat found at the scene of the murder, and that the names of the murdered girls were in the rings found in his possession.

As soon as this news was received, the sheriffs of Ballard and Carlisle counties and a posse of thirty well-armed and determined Kentuckians, who had pledged their word the prisoner should be taken back to the scene of the supposed crime, to be executed there if proved to be the guilty man, chartered a train and at nine o'clock Thursday night started for Sikeston. Arriving there two hours later, the sheriff at Sikeston, who had no warrant for the prisoner's arrest and detention, delivered him into the hands of the mob without authority for so doing, and accompanied them to Bird's Point. The prisoner gave his name as Miller, his home at Springfield, and said he had never been in Kentucky in his life, but the sheriff turned him over to the mob to be taken to Wickliffe, that Frank Gordon, the fisherman, who had put a man across the river might identify him.

In other words, the protection of the law was withdrawn from C.J. Miller, and he was given to a mob by this sheriff at Sikeston, who knew that the prisoner's life depended on one man's word. After an altercation

with the train men, who wanted another $50 for taking the train back to Bird's Point, the crowd arrived there at three o'clock, Friday morning. Here was anchored *The Three States*, a ferryboat plying between Wickliffe, Ky, Cairo, Ill., and Bird's Point, Mo. This boat left Cairo at twelve o'clock, Thursday, with nearly three hundred of Cairo's best citizens and thirty kegs of beer on board. This was consumed while the crowd and the bloodhound waited for the prisoner.

When the prisoner was on board *The Three States* the dog was turned loose, and after moving aimlessly around, followed the crowd to where Miller sat handcuffed and there stopped. The crowd closed in on the pair and insisted that the brute had identified him because of that action. When the boat reached Wickliffe, Gordon, the fisherman, was called on to say whether the prisoner was the man he ferried over the river the day of the murder.

The sheriff of Ballard County informed him sternly that if the prisoner was not the man, he (the fisherman) would be held responsible as knowing who the guilty man was. Gordon stated before, that the man he ferried across was a white man or a bright colored man; Miller was a dark brown skinned man, with kinky hair, "neither yellow nor black," says the *Cairo Evening Telegram* of Friday, July 7. The fisherman went up to Miller from behind, looked at him without speaking for fully five minutes, then slowly said, "Yes, that's the man I crossed over." This was about six o'clock, Friday morning, and the crowd wished to hang Miller then and there. But Mr. Ray, the father of the girls, insisted that he be taken to Bardwell, the county seat of Ballard, and twelve miles inland. He said he thought a white man committed the crime, and that he was not satisfied that was the man. They took him to Bardwell and at ten o'clock, this same excited, unauthorized mob undertook to determine Miller's guilt. One of the Clark brothers who shot at a fleeing man in the Dupoyster cornfield, said the prisoner was the same man; the other said he was not, but the testimony of the first was accepted. A colored woman who had said she gave breakfast to a colored man clad in a blue flannel suit the morning of the murder, said positively that she had never seen Miller before. The gold rings found in his possession had no names in them, as had been asserted, and Mr. Ray said they did not belong to his daughters. Meantime a funeral pyre for the purpose of burning Miller to death had been erected in the center of the village. While the crowd swayed by passion was clamoring that he be burnt, Miller stepped forward and made the following statement: "My name is C.J. Miller. I am from Springfield, Ill.; my wife lives at 716 N. 2d Street. I am here among you today, looked upon as one of the most brutal men before the people. I stand here surrounded by men who are excited, men who are not willing to let the law take its course, and as far as the crime is concerned, I have committed no crime, and certainly no crime gross enough to deprive me of my life and liberty to walk upon the green earth."

A telegram was sent to the chief of the police at Springfield, Ill., asking if one C.J. Miller lived there. An answer in the negative was returned. A few hours after, it was ascertained that a man named Miller, and his wife, did live at the number the prisoner gave in his speech, but the information came to Bardwell too late to do the prisoner any good. Miller was taken to jail, every stitch of clothing literally torn from his body and examined again. On the lower left side of the bosom of his shirt was found a dark reddish spot about the size of a dime. Miller said it was paint which he had gotten on him at Jefferson Barracks. This spot was only on the right side, and could not be seen from the under side at all, thus showing it had not gone through the cloth as blood or any liquid substance would do.

Chief-of-Police Mahaney, of Cairo, Ill., was with the prisoner, and he took his knife and scraped at the spot, particles of which came off in his hand. Miller told them to take his clothes to any expert, and if the spot was shown to be blood, they might do anything they wished with him. They took his clothes away and were gone some time. After a while they were brought back and thrown into the cell without a word. It is needless to say that if the spot had been found to be blood, that fact would have been announced, and the shirt retained as evidence. Meanwhile numbers of rough, drunken men crowded into the cell and tried to force a confession of the deed from the prisoner's lips. He refused to talk save to reiterate his innocence. To Mr. Mahaney, who talked seriously and kindly to him, telling him the mob meant to burn and torture him at three o'clock, Miller said: "Burning and torture here lasts but a little while, but if I die with a lie on my soul, I shall be tortured forever. I am innocent." For more than three hours, all sorts of pressure in the way of threats, abuse and urging, was brought to bear to force him to confess to the murder and thus justify the mob in its deed of murder. Miller remained firm; but as the hour drew near, and the crowd became more impatient, he asked for a priest. As none could be procured, he then asked for a Methodist minister, who came, prayed with the doomed man, baptized him and exhorted Miller to confess. To keep up the flagging spirits of the dense crowd around the jail, the rumor went out more than once, that Miller had confessed. But the solemn assurance of the minister, chief-of-police, and leading editor—who were with Miller all along—is that this rumor is absolutely false.

At three o'clock the mob rushed to the jail to secure the prisoner. Mr. Ray had changed his mind about the promised burning; he was still in doubt as to the prisoner's guilt. He again addressed the crowd to that effect, urging them not to burn Miller, and the mob heeded him so far, that they compromised on hanging instead of burning, which was agreed to by Mr. Ray. There was a loud yell, and a rush was made for the prisoner. He was stripped naked, his clothing literally torn from his body, and his shirt was tied around his loins. Some one declared the rope was a "white man's death," and a log-chain, nearly a hundred feet in length, weighing over one hundred pounds, was placed round Miller's neck and body, and he was led and dragged through the streets of the village in that condition followed by thousands of people. He fainted from exhaustion several times, but was supported to the platform where they first intended burning him.

The chain was hooked around his neck, a man climbed the telegraph pole and the other end of the chain was passed up to him and made fast to the crossarm. Others brought a long forked stick which Miller was made to straddle. By this means he was raised several feet from the ground and then let fall. The first fall broke his neck, but he was raised in this way and let fall a second time. Numberless shots were fired into the dangling body, for most of that crowd were heavily armed, and had been drinking all day.

Miller's body hung thus exposed from three to five o'clock, during which time, several photographs of him as he hung dangling at the end of the chain were taken, and his toes and fingers were cut off. His body was taken down, placed on the platform, the torch applied, and in a few moments there was nothing left of C.J. Miller save a few bones and ashes. Thus perished another of the many victims of Lynch Law, but it is the honest and sober belief of many who witnessed the scene that an innocent man has been barbarously and shockingly put to death in the glare of the nineteenth-century civilization, by those who profess to believe in Christianity, law and order.

QUESTIONS TO CONSIDER

1. What is the overall theme that ties the cases together?
2. How did Wells use language to reach her readers?

19.2 W. E. B. DUBOIS, "OF MR. BOOKER T. WASHINGTON AND OTHERS" (1903)

W. E. B. DuBois (1868–1963) was one of the most important intellectuals of his time. Born in Great Barrington, Massachusetts, he first encountered southern Jim Crow tactics during his time at Fisk University, a historically black college in Nashville, Tennessee. In 1895, DuBois was the first African American to receive a Ph.D. from Harvard University, and he then took a job as professor at Atlanta University. In that role, he published widely on issues relating to race. He especially began to oppose the activism of Booker T. Washington, probably the most prominent African American spokesperson of the time, because DuBois felt that Washington was too accommodating with Southerners who wished to keep African Americans subjugated. "Of Mr. Booker T. Washington and Others" appeared in DuBois' seminal *The Souls of Black Folk,* a collection of his essays on African American history, literature, and sociology. In the essay, he attacked Washington for his stances. In 1910, DuBois helped to found the National Associations for the Advancement of Colored Persons (NAACP), which would grow into the foremost African American activist organization in the country. Over the next five decades, DuBois continued to publish widely and fight for African American rights. Just a year after his death, Congress passed the Civil Rights Act of 1964.

Easily the most striking thing in the history of the American Negro since 1876 is the ascendancy of Mr. Booker T. Washington. It began at the time when war memories and ideals were rapidly passing; a day of astonishing commercial development was dawning; a sense of doubt and hesitation overtook the freedmen's sons,—then it was that his leading began. Mr. Washington came, with a simple definite programme, at the psychological moment when the nation was a little ashamed of having bestowed so much sentiment on Negroes, and was concentrating its energies on Dollars. His programme of industrial education, conciliation of the South, and submission and silence as to civil and political rights, was not wholly original; the Free Negroes from 1830 up to war-time had striven to build industrial schools, and

Source: W. E. B. DuBois, *The Souls of Black Folk* (Champaign-Urbana, IL: Project Gutenberg, 2008) http://www.gutenberg.org/files/408/408-h/408-h.htm

the American Missionary Association had from the first taught various trades; and Price and others had sought a way of honorable alliance with the best of the Southerners. But Mr. Washington first indissolubly linked these things; he put enthusiasm, unlimited energy, and perfect faith into his programme, and changed it from a by-path into a veritable Way of Life. And the tale of the methods by which he did this is a fascinating study of human life.

It startled the nation to hear a Negro advocating such a programme after many decades of bitter complaint; it startled and won the applause of the South, it interested and won the admiration of the North; and after a confused murmur of protest, it silenced if it did not convert the Negroes themselves.

To gain the sympathy and cooperation of the various elements comprising the white South was Mr. Washington's first task; and this, at the time Tuskegee was founded, seemed, for a black man, well-nigh impossible. And yet ten years later it was done in the word spoken at Atlanta: "In all things purely social we can be as separate as the five fingers, and yet one as the hand in all things essential to mutual progress." This "Atlanta Compromise" is by all odds the most notable thing in Mr. Washington's career. The South interpreted it in different ways: the radicals received it as a complete surrender of the demand for civil and political equality; the conservatives, as a generously conceived working basis for mutual understanding. So both approved it, and to-day its author is certainly the most distinguished Southerner since Jefferson Davis, and the one with the largest personal following. . . .

Mr. Washington's cult has gained unquestioning followers, his work has wonderfully prospered, his friends are legion, and his enemies are confounded. To-day he stands as the one recognized spokesman of his ten million fellows, and one of the most notable figures in a nation of seventy millions. One hesitates, therefore, to criticise a life which, beginning with so little, has done so much. And yet the time is come when one may speak in all sincerity and utter courtesy of the mistakes and shortcomings of Mr. Washington's career, as well as of his triumphs, without being thought captious or envious, and without forgetting that it is easier to do ill than well in the world.

The criticism that has hitherto met Mr. Washington has not always been of this broad character. In the South especially has he had to walk warily to avoid the harshest judgments,—and naturally so, for he is dealing with the one subject of deepest sensitiveness to that section. Twice—once when at the Chicago celebration of the Spanish-American War he alluded to the color-prejudice that is "eating away the vitals of the South," and once when he dined with President Roosevelt—has the resulting Southern criticism been violent enough to threaten seriously his popularity. In the North the feeling has several times forced itself into words, that Mr. Washington's counsels of submission overlooked certain elements of true manhood, and that his educational programme was unnecessarily narrow. Usually, however, such criticism has not found open expression, although, too, the spiritual sons of the Abolitionists have not been prepared to acknowledge that the schools founded before Tuskegee, by men of broad ideals and self-sacrificing spirit, were wholly failures or worthy of ridicule. While, then, criticism has not failed to follow Mr. Washington, yet the prevailing public opinion of the land has been but too willing to deliver the solution of a wearisome problem into his hands, and say, "If that is all you and your race ask, take it."

Among his own people, however, Mr. Washington has encountered the strongest and most lasting opposition, amounting at times to bitterness, and even today continuing strong and insistent even though largely silenced in outward expression by the public opinion of the nation. Some of this opposition is, of course, mere envy; the disappointment of displaced demagogues and the spite of narrow minds. But aside from this, there is among educated and thoughtful colored men in all parts of the land a feeling of deep regret, sorrow, and apprehension at the wide currency and ascendancy which some of Mr. Washington's theories have gained. These same men admire his sincerity of purpose, and are willing to forgive much to honest endeavor which is doing something worth the doing. They cooperate with Mr. Washington as far as they conscientiously can; and, indeed, it is no ordinary tribute to this man's tact and power that, steering as he must between so many diverse interests and opinions, he so largely retains the respect of all.

But the hushing of the criticism of honest opponents is a dangerous thing. It leads some of the best of the critics to unfortunate silence and paralysis of effort, and others to burst into speech so passionately and intemperately as to lose listeners. Honest and earnest criticism from those whose interests are most nearly touched,—criticism of writers by readers,—this is the soul of democracy and the safeguard of modern society. . . .

Mr. Washington represents in Negro thought the old attitude of adjustment and submission; but adjustment at such a peculiar time as to make his programme unique. This is an age of unusual economic development, and Mr. Washington's programme naturally takes an economic cast, becoming a gospel of Work and Money to such an extent as apparently almost completely to overshadow the higher aims of life. Moreover, this is an age when the more advanced races are coming in closer contact with the less developed races, and the race-feeling is therefore intensified; and Mr. Washington's programme practically accepts the alleged inferiority of the Negro races. Again, in our own land, the reaction from the sentiment of war time has given impetus to race-prejudice against Negroes, and Mr. Washington withdraws many of the high demands of Negroes as men and American citizens. In other periods of intensified prejudice all the Negro's tendency to self-assertion has been called forth; at this period a policy of submission is advocated. In the history of nearly all other races and peoples the doctrine preached at such crises has been that manly self-respect is worth more than lands and houses, and that a people who voluntarily surrender such respect, or cease striving for it, are not worth civilizing.

In answer to this, it has been claimed that the Negro can survive only through submission. Mr. Washington distinctly asks that black people give up, at least for the present, three things,—

First, political power,

Second, insistence on civil rights,

Third, higher education of Negro youth,—and concentrate all their energies on industrial education, and accumulation of wealth, and the conciliation of the South. This policy has been courageously and insistently advocated for over fifteen years, and has been triumphant for perhaps ten years. As a result of this

tender of the palm-branch, what has been the return? In these years there have occurred:

1. The disfranchisement of the Negro.
2. The legal creation of a distinct status of civil inferiority for the Negro.
3. The steady withdrawal of aid from institutions for the higher training of the Negro.

These movements are not, to be sure, direct results of Mr. Washington's teachings; but his propaganda has, without a shadow of doubt, helped their speedier accomplishment. The question then comes: Is it possible, and probable, that nine millions of men can make effective progress in economic lines if they are deprived of political rights, made a servile caste, and allowed only the most meagre chance for developing their exceptional men? If history and reason give any distinct answer to these questions, it is an emphatic NO. And Mr. Washington thus faces the triple paradox of his career:

1. He is striving nobly to make Negro artisans business men and property-owners; but it is utterly impossible, under modern competitive methods, for workingmen and property-owners to defend their rights and exist without the right of suffrage.
2. He insists on thrift and self-respect, but at the same time counsels a silent submission to civic inferiority such as is bound to sap the manhood of any race in the long run.
3. He advocates common-school and industrial training, and depreciates institutions of higher learning; but neither the Negro common-schools, nor Tuskegee itself, could remain open a day were it not for teachers trained in Negro colleges, or trained by their graduates.

This triple paradox in Mr. Washington's position is the object of criticism by two classes of colored Americans. One class is spiritually descended from Toussaint the Savior, through Gabriel, Vesey, and Turner, and they represent the attitude of revolt and revenge; they hate the white South blindly and distrust the white race generally, and so far as they agree on definite action, think that the Negro's only hope lies in emigration beyond the borders of the United States. And yet, by the irony of fate, nothing has more effectually made this programme seem hopeless than the recent course of the United States toward weaker and darker peoples in the West Indies, Hawaii, and the Philippines,—for where in the world may we go and be safe from lying and brute force?

The other class of Negroes who cannot agree with Mr. Washington has hitherto said little aloud. They deprecate the sight of scattered counsels, of internal disagreement; and especially they dislike making their just criticism of a useful and earnest man an excuse for a general discharge of venom from small-minded opponents. Nevertheless, the questions involved are so fundamental and serious that it is difficult to see how men like the Grimkes, Kelly Miller, J. W. E. Bowen, and other representatives of this group, can much longer be silent. Such men feel in conscience bound to ask of this nation three things:

1. The right to vote.
2. Civic equality.
3. The education of youth according to ability.

They acknowledge Mr. Washington's invaluable service in counselling patience and courtesy in such demands; they do not ask that ignorant black men vote when ignorant whites are debarred, or that any reasonable restrictions in the suffrage should not be applied; they know that the low social level of the mass of the race is responsible for much discrimination against it, but they also know, and the nation knows, that relentless color-prejudice is more often a cause than a result of the Negro's degradation; they seek the abatement of this relic of barbarism, and not its systematic encouragement and pampering by all agencies of social power from the Associated Press to the Church of Christ. They advocate, with Mr. Washington, a broad system of Negro common schools supplemented by thorough industrial training; but they are surprised that a man of Mr. Washington's insight cannot see that no such educational system ever has rested or can rest on any other basis than that of the well-equipped college and university, and they insist that there is a demand for a few such institutions throughout the South to train the best of the Negro youth as teachers, professional men, and leaders.

This group of men honor Mr. Washington for his attitude of conciliation toward the white South; they accept the "Atlanta Compromise" in its broadest interpretation; they recognize, with him, many signs of promise, many men of high purpose and fair judgment, in this section; they know that no easy task has been laid upon a region already tottering under heavy burdens. But, nevertheless, they insist that the way to truth and right lies in straightforward honesty, not in indiscriminate flattery; in praising those of the South who do well and criticising uncompromisingly those who do ill; in taking advantage of the opportunities at hand and urging their fellows to do the same, but at the same time in remembering that only a firm adherence to their higher ideals and aspirations will ever keep those ideals within the realm of possibility. They do not expect that the free right to vote, to enjoy civic rights, and to be educated, will come in a moment; they do not expect to see the bias and prejudices of years disappear at the blast of a trumpet; but they are absolutely certain that the way for a people to gain their reasonable rights is not by voluntarily throwing them away and insisting that they do not want them; that the way for a people to gain respect is not by continually belittling and ridiculing themselves; that, on the contrary, Negroes must insist continually, in season and out of season, that voting is necessary to modern manhood, that color discrimination is barbarism, and that black boys need education as well as white boys.

In failing thus to state plainly and unequivocally the legitimate demands of their people, even at the cost of opposing an honored leader, the thinking classes of American Negroes would shirk a heavy responsibility,—a responsibility to themselves, a responsibility to the struggling masses, a responsibility to the darker races of men whose future depends so largely on this American experiment, but especially a responsibility to this nation,—this common Fatherland. It is wrong to encourage a man or a people in evil-doing; it is wrong to aid and abet a national crime simply because it is unpopular not to do so. The growing spirit of kindliness and reconciliation between the North and South after the frightful difference of a generation ago ought to be a source of deep congratulation to all, and especially to those whose mistreatment caused the war; but if that reconciliation is to be marked by the industrial slavery and civic death of those same black men, with permanent legislation into a position of inferiority, then those black men, if they are really men, are called upon by every consideration of patriotism and loyalty to oppose such a course by all civilized methods, even though such opposition involves disagreement with Mr. Booker T. Washington. We have no right to sit silently by while the inevitable seeds are sown for a harvest of disaster to our children, black and white.

First, it is the duty of black men to judge the South discriminatingly. The present generation of Southerners are not responsible for the past, and they should not be blindly hated or blamed for it. Furthermore, to no class is the indiscriminate endorsement of the recent course of the South toward Negroes more nauseating than to the best thought of the South. The South is not "solid"; it is a land in the ferment of social change, wherein forces of all kinds are fighting for supremacy; and to praise the ill the South is today perpetrating is just as wrong as to condemn the good. Discriminating and broad-minded criticism is what the South needs,—needs it for the sake of her own white sons and daughters, and for the insurance of robust, healthy mental and moral development. . . .

The South ought to be led, by candid and honest criticism, to assert her better self and do her full duty to the race she has cruelly wronged and is still wronging. The North—her co-partner in guilt—cannot salve her conscience by plastering it with gold. We cannot settle this problem by diplomacy and suaveness, by

"policy" alone. If worse come to worst, can the moral fibre of this country survive the slow throttling and murder of nine millions of men?

The black men of America have a duty to perform, a duty stern and delicate,—a forward movement to oppose a part of the work of their greatest leader. So far as Mr. Washington preaches Thrift, Patience, and Industrial Training for the masses, we must hold up his hands and strive with him, rejoicing in his honors and glorying in the strength of this Joshua called of God and of man to lead the headless host. But so far as Mr. Washington apologizes for injustice, North or South, does not rightly value the privilege and duty of voting, belittles the emasculating effects of caste distinctions, and opposes the higher training and ambition of our brighter minds,—so far as he, the South, or the Nation, does this,—we must unceasingly and firmly oppose them. By every civilized and peaceful method we must strive for the rights which the world accords to men, clinging unwaveringly to those great words which the sons of the Fathers would fain forget: "We hold these truths to be self-evident: That all men are created equal; that they are endowed by their Creator with certain unalienable rights; that among these are life, liberty, and the pursuit of happiness."

QUESTIONS TO CONSIDER

1. How did DuBois portray Washington?
2. Do you find DuBois' argument persuasive? Why or why not?

19.3 GIFFORD PINCHOT, "THE A B C OF CONSERVATION" (1909)

Gifford Pinchot (1865–1946) had a foundational impact on American conservation. From 1898 to 1910, he held major roles in the Federal government related to the management of the nation's forest—first as the Chief of the Division of Forestry and then as the Chief of the U.S. Forest Service. Pinchot was a Progressive and believed that the Federal government should play a major role in the scientific management of forests, but he also pushed back against what he viewed as overly restrictive ideologies espoused by conservationists such as John Muir. Pinchot published the following piece in the *Outlook* magazine in 1909. In it, he set down his views on conservation in a brief, accessible manner. After leaving the Federal government in 1910, Pinchot remained active in the Progressive Party and twice served as governor of Pennsylvania. In that role, he encouraged the state to develop a power plan, co-operated with the Federal government during the Great Depression, and discouraged the sale of alcohol in Pennsylvania.

THE questions contained in your letter of November 18 are well worth answering, and I am glad to reply :

1. What does Conservation stand for ?

The central thing for which Conservation stands is to make this country the best possible place to live in, both for us and for our descendants. It stands against the waste of the natural resources which cannot be renewed, such as coal and iron ; it stands for the perpetuation of the resources which can be renewed, like the food-producing soils and the forests ; and, most of all, it stands for an equal opportunity for every American citizen to get his fair share of benefit from these resources, both now and hereafter.

Conservation stands for the same kind of practical common-sense management of this country by the people that every business man stands for in the handling of his own business. It believes in prudence and foresight instead of reckless blindness ; it holds that resources now public property should not become the basis for oppressive private monopoly ; and it demands the complete and orderly development of all our resources for the benefit of all the people, instead of the partial exploitation of them for the benefit of a few. It recognizes fully the right of the present generation to use what it needs and all it needs of the natural resources now available, but it recognizes equally our obligation so to use what we need that our descendants shall not be deprived of what they need.

2. What has Conservation to do with the welfare of the average man to-day ?

Conservation has much to do with the welfare of the average man to-day. It proposes to secure a continuous and abundant supply of the necessaries of life, which means a reasonable cost of living and business stability. It advocates fairness in the distribution of the benefits which flow from the natural resources. It will matter very little to the average citizen when scarcity comes and prices rise, whether he cannot get what he needs because there is none left or because he cannot afford to pay for it. In both cases the essential fact is that he cannot get what he needs. Conservation holds that it is about as important to

Source: =Gifford Pinchot, "The A B C of Conservation," *Outlook*, December 4, 1909, 770.

see that the people in general get the benefit of our natural resources as to see that there shall be natural resources left.

Conservation is the most democratic movement this country has known for a generation. It holds that the people have not only the right but the duty to control the use of the natural resources, which are the great sources of prosperity. And it regards the absorption of these resources by the special interests, unless their operations are under effective public control, as a moral wrong. Conservation is the application of common sense to the common problems for the common good, and I believe it stands nearer to the desires, aspirations, and purposes of the average man than any other policy now before the American people.

3. What is the danger to the Conservation policies in the coming session of Congress ?

The danger to the Conservation policies in the coming session of Congress is that the privileges of the few may continue to obstruct the rights of the many, especially in the matter of water power and coal. Congress must decide at this session whether the great coal-fields still in public ownership shall remain so, in order that their use may be controlled with due regard to the interest of the consumer, or whether they shall pass into private ownership and be controlled in the monopolistic interest of a few.

Congress must decide also whether immensely valuable rights to the use of water power shall be given away to special interests in perpetuity and without compensation, instead of being held and controlled by the public. In most cases, actual development of water power can best be done by private interests acting under public control, but it is neither good sense nor good morals to let these valuable privileges pass from the public ownership for nothing and forever. Other Conservation matters will doubtless require action ; but these two, the Conservation of water power and of coal, the chief sources of power of the present and the future, are clearly the most pressing.

4. Why is it important to protect the water powers ?

It is of the first importance to prevent our water powers from passing into private ownership as they have been doing, because the greatest source of power we know is falling water. Furthermore, it is the only great unfailing source of power. Our coal, the experts

say, is likely to be exhausted during the next century, our natural gas and oil in this. Our rivers, if the forests on the watersheds are property handled, will never cease to deliver power. Under our form of civilization, if a few men ever succeed in controlling the sources of power, they will eventually control all industry as well. If they succeed in controlling all industry, they will necessarily control the country. This country has achieved political freedom ; what our people are fighting for now is industrial freedom. And unless we win our industrial liberty we cannot keep our political liberty. I see no reason why we should deliberately keep on helping to fasten the handcuffs of corporate control upon ourselves for all time merely because the few men who would profit by it most have heretofore had the power to compel it.

5. How must it be done ?

The essential things that must be done to protect the water powers for the people are few and simple. First, the granting of water powers forever, either on non-navigable or navigable streams, must absolutely stop. It is perfectly clear that one hundred, fifty, or even twenty-five years ago our present industrial conditions and industrial needs were completely beyond the imagination of the wisest of our predecessors. It is just as true that we cannot imagine or foresee the industrial conditions and needs of the future. But we do know that our descendants should be left free to meet their own necessities as they arise. It cannot be right, therefore, for us to grant perpetual rights to the one great permanent source of power. It is just as wrong as it is foolish, and just as needless as it is wrong, to mortgage the welfare of our children in such a way as this. Water powers must and should be developed mainly by private capital, and they must be developed under conditions which make investment in them profitable and safe. But neither profit nor safety requires perpetual rights, as many of the best water power men now freely acknowledge.

Second, the men to whom the people grant the right to use water power should pay for what they get. The water power sites now in the public hands are enormously valuable. There is no reason whatever why special interests should be allowed to use them for profit without making some direct payment to the people for the valuable rights derived from the people.

This is important not only for the revenue the Nation will get. It is at least equally important as a recognition that the public control their own property and have a right to share in the benefits arising from its development.

There are other ways in which public control of water power must be exercised, but these two are the most important.

6. Does the same principle apply to navigable streams as to non-navigable ?

Water power on non-navigable streams usually results from dropping a little water a long way. In the mountains water is dropped many hundreds of feet upon the turbines which move the dynamos that produce the electric current. Water power on navigable streams is usually produced by dropping immense volumes of water a short distance, as twenty feet, fifteen feet, or even less. Every stream is a unit from its source to its mouth, and the people have the same stake in the control of water power in one part of it as in another. Under the Constitution the United States exercises direct control over navigable streams. It exercises control over non-navigable and source streams only through its ownership of the lands through which they pass, as in the public domain and National forests. It is just as essential for the public welfare that the people should retain and exercise control of water power monopoly on navigable as on non-navigable streams. If the difficulties are greater, then the danger that the water powers may pass out of the people's hands on the lower navigable parts of the streams is greater than on

the upper non-navigable parts, and it may be harder, but in no way less necessary, to prevent it.

These answers to your questions will, I hope, give you the information for which you wrote. It must be clear to any man who has followed the development of the Conservation idea that no other policy now before the American people is so thoroughly democratic in its essence and in its tendencies as the Conservation policy. It asserts that the people have the right and the duty, and that it is their duty no less than their right, to protect themselves against the uncontrolled monopoly of the natural resources which yield the necessaries of life. We are beginning to realize that the Conservation question is a question of right and wrong, as any question must be which may involve the difference between prosperity and poverty, health and sickness, ignorance and education, well-being and misery, to hundreds of thousands of families. Seen from the point of view of human welfare and human progress, questions which begin as purely economic often end as moral issues; Conservation is a moral issue because it involves the rights and the duties of our people— their rights to prosperity and happiness, and their duties to themselves, to their descendants, and to the whole future progress and welfare of this Nation.

QUESTIONS TO CONSIDER

1. How did Pinchot define conservation?
2. Does his view of conservation match your own? Why or why not?

19.4 WILLIAM "BIG BILL" HAYWOOD, EXCERPT FROM *THE GENERAL STRIKE* (1911)

In the early twentieth century, William "Big Bill" Haywood (1869–1928) helped to found the Industrial Workers of the World (IWW), one of the most important radical labor organizations of its time. The IWW believed in fighting for the rights of all laborers in all professions—much different from other labor unions, which confined themselves to specific professions or job types. On a large scale, the IWW aimed for nothing less than a working-class takeover of the means of production. Haywood gained national fame during a 1907 murder trial, when a jury acquitted him of conspiracy to murder an Idaho politician who had clashed with mineworkers. During the trial, prominent lawyer Clarence Darrow defended Haywood and revealed how mine owners had tried to frame Haywood for conspiracy. In 1912, Haywood helped to run a textile strike in Lawrence, Massachusetts, which raised textile wages by up to 20 percent. Haywood's *The General Strike* set out the ideals of the IWW. Later, the Federal government arrested Haywood and other IWW leaders for anti-war activism as a part of a crackdown on the organization during World War I. Released on bail, Haywood fled to Soviet Russia, where he lived for the rest of his life.

Thousands of thoughtful and class-conscious workers in years past have looked to the General Strike for deliverance from wage slavery. Today their hopes are stronger than ever. Their number has been increased with additional thousands who are confident that the General Strike, and the General Strike alone, can save Humanity from the torture and degradation of the continuation of capitalism and the misery and privation of its recurrent wars and depressions.

The General Strike is the child of the Labor Movement. It is Labor's natural reaction to a system of society based upon the private ownership of the machinery of production. It is Labor's ultimate attitude in the class struggle. It is Labor's answer to the problem of economic disorganization.

Logically enough the General Strike has become the rallying-cry of millions of persons the world over who favor it simply because they do not wish to see the highly industrialized modern world sink into chaos, and human society sink to the level of savage survival.

The idea of the General Strike is here to stay. It came into being with the perfection of the machine process and the centralization of control which made it possible. And it will remain as a constant challenge to capitalism as long as the machinery of production is operated for profit instead of for use. . . .

CRAFT UNIONS AND THE GENERAL STRIKE

The purpose of industrial unionism is to give the working class the greatest possible organized power in industry. Unquestionably the General Strike, either on or off the job, is the most perfect manifestation of this power. If the craft unions of today are examined in regard to their adaptability to this end it will

Source: William Dudley Haywood, *The General Strike* (Chicago: Published by the Industrial Workers of the World, 1946), 3–4, 25–26, 42–48. Retrieved from the Internet Archive website, https://archive.org/details/HaywoodTheGeneralStrike (Accessed June 12, 2018).

put the revolutionary industrial union movement in an entirely new light. Also it will reveal clearly the shortcomings of conventional unionism in general and the craft union movement in particular. After all, the full measure of power is the acid test of any labor organization.

A cursory glance at the craft union movement will reveal the fact that it is constructed in such way as to divide rather than to unify the forces of labor. The craft union is not designed to enable labor to use its full power. This type of union came into existence during the period of industrial evolution known as small production when the tools of the craft and the skill of the craftsman were important things. In those days the organized power of the tradesman consisted in his having monopoly of the skill necessary to make the tools of his trade industrially productive. The withdrawal of this skill during periods of strikes was all that was necessary to force the old-time employer of labor to terms. Thus it happened that the craft union was organized around the, then important, tools of the tradesmen.

TOOLS AND SKILL OBSOLETE

But all this has been changed. The onward march of the machine process has to a large extent made both tools and skill unnecessary. This great advance in technical development has made the old fashioned trades union unable to cope with modern conditions. Craft unions still carry on as a matter of habit, it is true, but they are anachronisms in this modern world. Some of them merely serve as pie-cards for the tired business men who are their officials and all such unions serve more or less as props of the existing order. But they are not unions in the modern sense at all. They are merely the shells of once useful unions operating to secure advantages for a few favored groups of workers without regard to the interests of the working class as a whole. They are organized within the capitalist system which they have been taught to take for granted, and they have no thought or program of anything beyond this system.

In relation to the manifest weakness of the trade union structure and concept the I. W. W. Preamble points out with telling emphasis: "We find that the centering of the management of industries into fewer and fewer hands makes the trades unions unable to cope with the ever growing power of the employing class. The trade unions foster a state of affairs which allows one set of workers to be pitted against another set of workers in the same industry, thereby helping to defeat one another in wage wars. Moreover the trade unions aid the employing class to mislead the workers into the belief that the workers have interests in common with their employers." . . .

MASS OPPOSITION TO EXPLOITATION

The General Strike is conditioned upon the WILL of the workers to make it effective and their stubborn determination to put an end to exploitation by producing goods for USE instead of PROFIT. Unlike the small strike the General Strike does not necessarily depend upon the complete withdrawal of productive effort from machinery, but rather upon their ability to withdraw or withhold only such effort as will put a complete stop to the profits of the parasitic 'owners.'

The ultimate aim of the General Strike as regards wages is to give to each producer the full product of his labor. The demand for better wages becomes revolutionary only when it is coupled with the demand that the exploitation of labor must cease. Labor is exploited at the point of production, and it is at the point of production alone that Labor can stop the idle, absentee drones from receiving any more than they produce. Only the complete disallowal of any share whatever to nonproducers will guarantee economic justice to the working class. Working conditions under capitalism have occasioned many bitter controversies but even the most necessary demands for their betterment could hardly be called revolutionary. Even under Industrial Democracy such things will be matters of expediency and consistently sustained improvement, in keeping with recognized needs.

SHORT HOURS, THE REVOLUTIONARY DEMAND

The demand for shorter hours however is decidedly a revolutionary demand. On the basis of an eight hour day less than three hours are all that is necessary for the worker to earn his wage; the rest of the day he is employed in producing surplus value for the boss. Each hour of the shortened workday means for the employer one hour's less profits from every man employed—one hour less opportunity to exploit. This accounts for the fact that the worker's demands for shorter hours have always been contested more vigorously than demands for better conditions or even increased wages.

The reason is obvious: The difference between the six hour day and the eight hour day is the difference between three hours and five hours given to the employer in which to sweat profits from the hides of his help, each hour of reduction being made at the expense of the exploiter. The difference between the six hour day and, say, the three hour day is the difference between three hours of profit-sweating and none at all. Therefore, if the employer wishes to continue to live off the labor of his wage slaves he must (and does) guard jealously the length of the toiler's work day. Upon it depends not only the amount of his unearned income but also the continuation of his privilege to live without producing.

The chief demand of the General Strike would therefore logically be a demand for an average workday of not longer than three hours or whatever length of time is technologically necessary to carry on production on a non-profit basis. This is the most revolutionary of all demands because it dries up the possibility of class exploitation at its source. Under a planned industrial system and with the perfected machinery of modern production placed at the disposal of the human race even with the present staff of competent directors there is no reason at all (apart from the profit system) why any one should be forced to work longer than two and a half or three hours per day. Any workday longer than that required to do the actual necessary work of the world simply serves to fatten the already hog-fat parasites of industry. The General Strike for the three hour day would not only put the millions of unemployed back to work, but it would also put the Thieves of Big Business to work alongside of them. In this regard it is well to remember that I. W. W. loggers in the northwest won the eight hour day by the simple expedient of blowing the whistle at the end of eight hours and then walking off the job en-masse. . . .

LET COME WHAT MAY . . .

Already the world is a tumult of disorder and rebellion due to starvation and misrule. No individual or organization can predict with blue-print precision what course events may take in each of the civilized countries, during the last days of the expiring social order. All that we are able to see in the light of social science is that the industries must be taken over by the ones who use them and need them and be operated for use instead of profit. The socialization of the means of production, transportation and exchange is now necessary for the survival of the human race. Only the workers are in a position to do this and it is their duty AT ALL COSTS to see that it is done. Properly organized and disciplined no power on earth can stop the aroused working class from coming into its own.

The scientifically sound and thoroughly constructive character of the I. W. W. program has never been stressed more forcibly than in the concluding paragraphs of its Preamble: "It is the historic mission of the working class to do away with capitalism. The army of production must be organized not only for the everyday struggle with capitalists, but also to carry on production when capitalism shall have been overthrown. By organizing industrially we are forming the structure of the new society within the shell of the old."

"LABOR SHALL BE ALL"

"Seize the industries," is at present a discredited slogan, for, by inference, we are led to understand that this means to seize the industries from the outside. But, frankly, is it necessary for workers to "seize" something they already have?

Every day, on the job, workers are in possession of the industries. The problem is not how to "seize" them, but how to keep from giving them up. The scientific modern General Strike would have a much simpler slogan and a much more sensible program: For the employed: "Retain the industries, but refuse to produce for profit." For the unemployed: "Picket the industries and refuse to scab or to let anyone else scab."

It is vitally necessary for the present "owners" that machinery and resources be manned by labor. It is equally necessary, during the revolutionary transition, that labor refuse to relinquish its hold on machinery either to the "owners" or to their scabs or mercenaries.

That labor will defend its own interests goes without saying. The I. W. W. has taught and is teaching workers to fight, not to beg—to demand, not to plead for what they want. And in this final struggle to free the world from social parasitism, courage, clear-thinking and fearless fighting spirit are needed as never before.

Realizing that the control of industry can only come into the hands of the producing class when the producers have sufficient power to keep and to hold this control, the I. W. W. advocates the General Strike on the job reinforced by formidable, determined revolutionary picket-lines of unemployed. The change from private to social ownership being inevitable, only thus can the danger of serious destruction and bloodshed be minimized.

The working class should bend every effort to this end. The full current of the revolutionary movement should be directed from the streets to the industries. The revolutionary struggle should be thought out and fought out in terms of industrial action—control, defense, operation. The class struggle, in the last analysis, must be a struggle to control the means of production, transportation and exchange. It will probably be a bitter fight, but on that can have but one ending—complete victory for the workers in the world's industries.

Let come what may, no worker should count the cost. Even at the worst a General Strike could scarcely entail more privation and suffering than one of capitalism's many and all too frequent depressions. The General Strike is saner than insurrection and surer than political action. And beyond it—after the storm—is a scientifically planned and ordered world based on peace, plenty and security for martyrized humanity. What other thing is more worth striving for by courageous men and women than the ideal of this classless Industrial Democracy for which the I. W. W. has battled so valorously and for so many years?

QUESTIONS TO CONSIDER

1. How did Haywood portray the IWW's work?
2. Why do you think the organization gained in popularity during the early twentieth century?

19.5 PROGRESSIVE PARTY PLATFORM (1912)

The Progressive movement was characterized by activism toward making government more account-able, business more fair, and people more moral. In 1912, former President Theodore Roosevelt took up the mantle of the Progressives when he put together a third-party bid for the Presidency. Roosevelt, who was president from 1901 to 1909, had lost the 1912 Republican Party nomination for President to William Howard Taft, and his Progressive Party—also nicknamed the Bull Moose Party—fought for a "Square Deal" set of programs to reform business and politics. Though he did not have the support of all Progressives, he took on many of their ideals. In the general election, Roosevelt outperformed Taft 27.4 percent to 23.2 percent, but both men lost to Woodrow Wilson's 41.8 percent. Four years later, Roosevelt declined the Progressive Party nomination, and the Party mostly collapsed. Roosevelt's 1912 bid, however, received the highest percentage of the vote of any third-party campaign in American history.

The conscience of the people, in a time of grave national problems, has called into being a new party, born of the nation's sense of justice. We of the Progressive party here dedicate ourselves to the fulfillment of the duty laid upon us by our fathers to maintain the government of the people, by the people and for the people whose foundations they laid.

We hold with Thomas Jefferson and Abraham Lincoln that the people are the masters of their Constitution, to fulfill its purposes and to safeguard it from those who, by perversion of its intent, would convert it into an instrument of injustice. In accordance with the needs of each generation the people must use their sovereign powers to establish and maintain equal opportunity and industrial justice, to secure [that] which this Government was founded and without which no republic can endure.

This country belongs to the people who inhabit it. Its resources, its business, its institutions and its laws should be utilized, maintained or altered in whatever manner will best promote the general interest.

It is time to set the public welfare in the first place.

THE OLD PARTIES

Political parties exist to secure responsible government and to execute the will of the people.

From these great tasks both of the old parties have turned aside. Instead of instruments to promote the general welfare, they have become the tools of corrupt interests which use them impartially to serve their selfish purposes. Behind the ostensible government sits enthroned an invisible government owing no allegiance and acknowledging no responsibility to the people.

To destroy this invisible government, to dissolve the unholy alliance between corrupt business and corrupt politics is the first task of the statesmanship of the day.

The deliberate betrayal of its trust by the Republican party, the fatal incapacity of the Democratic party to deal with the new issues of the new time, have compelled the people to forge a new instrument of government through which to give effect to their will in laws and institutions.

Unhampered by tradition, uncorrupted by power, undismayed by the magnitude of the task, the new party offers itself as the instrument of the people to sweep away old abuses, to build a new and nobler commonwealth.

A COVENANT WITH THE PEOPLE

This declaration is our covenant with the people, and we hereby bind the party and its candidates in State and Nation to the pledges made herein. . . .

Source: "Progressive Party Platform of 1912," http://www.presidency.ucsb.edu/ws/index.php?pid=29617 (Accessed May 20, 2018).

EQUAL SUFFRAGE

The Progressive party, believing that no people can justly claim to be a true democracy which denies political rights on account of sex, pledges itself to the task of securing equal suffrage to men and women alike.

CORRUPT PRACTICES

We pledge our party to legislation that will compel strict limitation of all campaign contributions and expenditures, and detailed publicity of both before as well as after primaries and elections. . . .

SOCIAL AND INDUSTRIAL JUSTICE

The supreme duty of the Nation is the conservation of human resources through an enlightened measure of social and industrial justice. We pledge ourselves to work unceasingly in State and Nation for:

Effective legislation looking to the prevention of industrial accidents, occupational diseases, overwork, involuntary unemployment, and other injurious effects incident to modern industry;

The fixing of minimum safety and health standards for the various occupations, and the exercise of the public authority of State and Nation, including the Federal Control over interstate commerce, and the taxing power, to maintain such standards;

The prohibition of child labor;

Minimum wage standards for working women, to provide a "living wage" in all industrial occupations;

The general prohibition of night work for women and the establishment of an eight hour day for women and young persons;

One day's rest in seven for all wage workers;

The eight hour day in continuous twenty-four hour industries;

The abolition of the convict contract labor system; substituting a system of prison production for governmental consumption only; and the application of prisoners' earnings to the support of their dependent families;

Publicity as to wages, hours and conditions of labor; full reports upon industrial accidents and diseases, and the opening to public inspection of all tallies, weights, measures and check systems on labor products;

Standards of compensation for death by industrial accident and injury and trade disease which will transfer the burden of lost earnings from the families of working people to the industry, and thus to the community;

The protection of home life against the hazards of sickness, irregular employment and old age through the adoption of a system of social insurance adapted to American use;

The development of the creative labor power of America by lifting the last load of illiteracy from American youth and establishing continuation schools for industrial education under public control and encouraging agricultural education and demonstration in rural schools;

The establishment of industrial research laboratories to put the methods and discoveries of science at the service of American producers;

We favor the organization of the workers, men and women, as a means of protecting their interests and of promoting their progress.

DEPARTMENT OF LABOR

We pledge our party to establish a department of labor with a seat in the cabinet, and with wide jurisdiction over matters affecting the conditions of labor and living.

COUNTRY LIFE

The development and prosperity of country life are as important to the people who live in the cities as they are to the farmers. Increase of prosperity on the farm will favorably affect the cost of living, and promote the interests of all who dwell in the country, and all who depend upon its products for clothing, shelter and food.

We pledge our party to foster the development of agricultural credit and co-operation, the teaching of agriculture in schools, agricultural college extension, the use of mechanical power on the farm, and to re-establish the Country Life Commission, thus directly promoting the welfare of the farmers, and bringing the benefits of better farming, better business and better living within their reach.

HIGH COST OF LIVING

The high cost of living is due partly to worldwide and partly to local causes; partly to natural and partly to artificial causes. The measures proposed in this platform on various subjects such as the tariff, the trusts and conservation, will of themselves remove the artificial causes.

There will remain other elements such as the tendency to leave the country for the city, waste, extravagance, bad system of taxation, poor methods of raising crops and bad business methods in marketing crops.

To remedy these conditions requires the fullest information and based on this information, effective government supervision and control to remove all the artificial causes. We pledge ourselves to such full and immediate inquiry and to immediate action to deal with every need such inquiry discloses.

HEALTH

We favor the union of all the existing agencies of the Federal Government dealing with the public health into a single national health service without discrimination against or for any one set of therapeutic methods, school of medicine, or school of healing with such additional powers as may be necessary to enable it to perform efficiently such duties in the protection of the public from preventable diseases as may be properly undertaken by the Federal authorities, including the executing of existing laws regarding pure food, quarantine and cognate subjects, the promotion of vital statistics and the extension of the registration area of such statistics, and co-operation with the health activities of the various States and cities of the Nation.

BUSINESS

We believe that true popular government, justice and prosperity go hand in hand, and, so believing, it is our purpose to secure that large measure of general prosperity which is the fruit of legitimate and honest business, fostered by equal justice and by sound progressive laws.

We demand that the test of true prosperity shall be the benefits conferred thereby on all the citizens, not confined to individuals or classes, and that the test of corporate efficiency shall be the ability better to serve the public; that those who profit by control of business affairs shall justify that profit and that control by sharing with the public the fruits thereof.

We therefore demand a strong National regulation of inter-State corporations. The corporation is

an essential part of modern business. The concentration of modem business, in some degree, is both inevitable and necessary for national and international business efficiency. But the existing concentration of vast wealth under a corporate system, unguarded and uncontrolled by the Nation, has placed in the hands of a few men enormous, secret, irresponsible power over the daily life of the citizen—a power insufferable in a free Government and certain of abuse.

This power has been abused, in monopoly of National resources, in stock watering, in unfair competition and unfair privileges, and finally in sinister influences on the public agencies of State and Nation. We do not fear commercial power, but we insist that it shall be exercised openly, under publicity, supervision and regulation of the most efficient sort, which will preserve its good while eradicating and preventing its ill.

To that end we urge the establishment of a strong Federal administrative commission of high standing, which shall maintain permanent active supervision over industrial corporations engaged in inter-State commerce, or such of them as are of public importance, doing for them what the Government now does for the National banks, and what is now done for the railroads by the Inter-State Commerce Commission.

Such a commission must enforce the complete publicity of those corporation transactions which are of public interest; must attack unfair competition, false capitalization and special privilege, and by continuous trained watchfulness guard and keep open equally all the highways of American commerce.

Thus the business man will have certain knowledge of the law, and will be able to conduct his business easily in conformity therewith; the investor will find security for his capital; dividends will be rendered more certain, and the savings of the people will be drawn naturally and safely into the channels of trade.

Under such a system of constructive regulation, legitimate business, freed from confusion, uncertainty and fruitless litigation, will develop normally in response to the energy and enterprise of the American business man.

We favor strengthening the Sherman Law by prohibiting agreement to divide territory or limit output; refusing to sell to customers who buy from business rivals; to sell below cost in certain areas while maintaining higher prices in other places; using the power of transportation to aid or injure special business concerns; and other unfair trade practices. . . .

CONSERVATION

The natural resources of the Nation must be promptly developed and generously used to supply the people's needs, but we cannot safely allow them to be wasted, exploited, monopolized or controlled against the general good. We heartily favor the policy of conservation, and we pledge our party to protect the National forests without hindering their legitimate use for the benefit of all the people.

Agricultural lands in the National forests are, and should remain, open to the genuine settler. Conservation will not retard legitimate development. The honest settler must receive his patent promptly, without hindrance, rules or delays.

We believe that the remaining forests, coal and oil lands, water powers and other natural resources still in State or National control (except agricultural lands) are more likely to be wisely conserved and utilized for the general welfare if held in the public hands.

In order that consumers and producers, managers and workmen, now and hereafter, need not pay toll to private monopolies of power and raw material, we demand that such resources shall be retained by the State or Nation, and opened to immediate use under laws which will encourage development and make to the people a moderate return for benefits conferred.

In particular we pledge our party to require reasonable compensation to the public for water power rights hereafter granted by the public.

We pledge legislation to lease the public grazing lands under equitable provisions now pending which will increase the production of food for the people and thoroughly safeguard the rights of the actual homemaker. Natural resources, whose conservation is necessary for the National welfare, should be owned or controlled by the Nation. . . .

TARIFF

We believe in a protective tariff which shall equalize conditions of competition between the United States and foreign countries, both for the farmer and the manufacturer, and which shall maintain for labor an adequate standard of living.

Primarily the benefit of any tariff should be disclosed in the pay envelope of the laborer. We declare that no industry deserves protection which is unfair to labor or which is operating in violation of Federal law. We believe that the presumption is always in favor of the consuming public.

We demand tariff revision because the present tariff is unjust to the people of the United States. Fair dealing toward the people requires an immediate downward revision of those schedules wherein duties are shown to be unjust or excessive.

We pledge ourselves to the establishment of a nonpartisan scientific tariff commission, reporting both to the President and to either branch of Congress, which shall report, first, as to the costs of production, efficiency of labor, capitalization, industrial organization and efficiency and the general competitive position in this country and abroad of industries seeking protection from Congress; second, as to the revenue producing power of the tariff and its relation to the resources of Government; and, third, as to the effect of the tariff on prices, operations of middlemen, and on the purchasing power of the consumer.

We believe that this commission should have plenary power to elicit information, and for this purpose to prescribe a uniform system of accounting for the great protected industries. The work of the commission should not prevent the immediate adoption of acts reducing these schedules generally recognized as excessive.

We condemn the Payne-Aldrich bill as unjust to the people. The Republican organization is in the hands of those who have broken, and cannot again be trusted to keep, the promise of necessary downward revision.

The Democratic party is committed to the destruction of the protective system through a tariff for revenue only—a policy which would inevitably produce widespread industrial and commercial disaster.

We demand the immediate repeal of the Canadian Reciprocity Act.

INHERITANCE AND INCOME TAX

We believe in a graduated inheritance tax as a National means of equalizing the obligations of holders of property to Government, and we hereby pledge our party to enact such a Federal law as will tax large inheritances, returning to the States an equitable percentage of all amounts collected.

We favor the ratification of the pending amendment to the Constitution giving the Government power to levy an income tax.

PEACE AND NATIONAL DEFENSE

The Progressive party deplores the survival in our civilization of the barbaric system of warfare among nations with its enormous waste of resources even in time of peace, and the consequent impoverishment of the life of the toiling masses. We pledge the party to use its best endeavors to substitute judicial and other peaceful means of settling international differences.

We favor an international agreement for the limitation of naval forces. Pending such an agreement, and as the best means of preserving peace, we pledge ourselves to maintain for the present the policy of building two battleships a year.

TREATY RIGHTS

We pledge our party to protect the rights of American citizenship at home and abroad. No treaty should receive the sanction of our Government which discriminates between American citizens because of birthplace, race, or religion, or that does not recognize the absolute right of expatriation.

THE IMMIGRANT

Through the establishment of industrial standards we propose to secure to the able-bodied immigrant and to his native fellow workers a larger share of American opportunity.

We denounce the fatal policy of indifference and neglect which has left our enormous immigrant population to become the prey of chance and cupidity.

We favor Governmental action to encourage the distribution of immigrants away from the congested cities, to rigidly supervise all private agencies dealing with them and to promote their assimilation, education and advancement.

PENSIONS

We pledge ourselves to a wise and just policy of pensioning American soldiers and sailors and their widows and children by the Federal Government. And we approve the policy of the southern States in granting pensions to the ex-Confederate soldiers and sailors and their widows and children. . . .

GOVERNMENT SUPERVISION OVER INVESTMENTS

The people of the United States are swindled out of many millions of dollars every year, through worthless investments. The plain people, the wage earner and the men and women with small savings, have no way of knowing the merit of concerns sending out highly colored prospectuses offering stock for sale, prospectuses that make big returns seem certain and fortunes easily within grasp.

We hold it to be the duty of the Government to protect its people from this kind of piracy. We, therefore, demand wise, carefully thought out legislation that will give us such Governmental supervision over this matter as will furnish to the people of the United States this much-needed protection, and we pledge ourselves thereto.

CONCLUSION

On these principles and on the recognized desirability of uniting the Progressive forces of the Nation into an organization which shall unequivocally represent the Progressive spirit and policy we appeal for the support of all American citizens, without regard to previous political affiliations

QUESTIONS TO CONSIDER

1. What were the Party's stated goals? How did they emerge from the time?

2. Why do you think the Progressive Party platform was so popular?

19.6 ROBERT LA FOLLETTE, EXCERPT FROM *LA FOLLETTE'S AUTOBIOGRAPHY* (1913)

Robert La Follette was perhaps the most important public spokesperson for the Progressive movement in America. As a Wisconsin politician in the 1890s, he led a nascent wing of the Republican Party that opposed the power of big business and demanded greater governmental accountability. From 1901 to 1906, La Follette was the Governor of Wisconsin, a role in which he fought for numerous Progressive reforms, including greater oversight of the railroads, a direct primary system, a minimum wage bill, and women's suffrage. The state legislature blocked the vast majority of his agenda. In the following excerpt from his autobiography, La Follette describes how he tried to pass Progressive legislation in Wisconsin. After his governorship, La Follette served as a U.S. Senator from 1905 until his death in 1926. In that role, he continued to champion Progressive ideals, and he gained controversial fame for his lonely fight against U.S. entry into World War I. In the 1924 Presidential election, La Follette gained 17 percent of the national vote while running on the Progressive Party ticket. His platform pledged to nationalize railroads; pass child labor laws, pro-union legislation, and laws to protect civil liberties; and end American imperialism.

REFORMERS often stop fighting before the battle is really won: before the new territory is completely occupied. I felt that the campaign of 1904 was the very crux of our whole movement. We had passed our railroad taxation and direct primary measures in 1903; but the railroad taxation law would be a barren victory until it was supplemented by a commission to control railroad rates; and the direct nomination of candidates would fail unless we carried the election and secured the adoption of the primary bill at the referendum that fall. Without the direct primary law it would be an easy matter for the old machine to regain control of the legislature and not only prevent further progressive legislation, but undo part, if not all, of the work already accomplished. . . .

Now, it is never safe to be satisfied with victory at an election. The real test comes later, when the bills incorporating new principles are written. It is one thing to talk of general propositions on the stump: it is quite another thing to perform the careful, cautious, thoughtful task of reducing those propositions into closely worded legal provisions which will afterward serve the public interest and stand the scrutiny of the courts. The trouble comes when the powerful opposition appears to cease, when the skilful corporation lawyer comes to you and says:

"You shall have no further opposition. All we ask is that the measure be fair and reasonable. We have had large practical experience, and we can make a few suggestions really for the good of the legislation."

He then presents changes which seem very plausible, but in which may lurk the weaknesses and uncertainties that will afterward lead the court to break down the statute by construction. It is then that sincere friends of reform may be misled, because they have not the expert knowledge to meet the situation. . . .

It was a very strong regulatory bill. It provided for a commission with power not only to fix rates but to control service and to make a complete physical valuation of all the railroad property in the state. It was

Source: Robert M. La Follette, *La Follette's Autobiography* (Madison, WI: The Robert M. La Follette Co., 1913), 319–370. Retrieved from the Library of Congress website, https://www.loc.gov/item/13007510/ (Accessed June 12, 2018).

more sweeping than any legislation enacted by any state up to that time; and there is still, I believe, no law which compares with it—and none, certainly, more successfully enforced both to the advantage of the railroads and to that of the people—as I shall show later.

Of course, the railroad representatives opposed the bill at every step. The hearings continued for many weeks, and the strain was at times serious.

While we were in the stress of the fight I was called one evening from the dinner table to answer the telephone. Some one said:

"Hello, Governor! how are you getting on with your legislation?"

I answered instantly, for I recognized his voice: "Colonel Bryan, where are you?"

He told me that he was to speak in Milwaukee that night, and the next day at Oshkosh. I said:

"Colonel, come this way. Some of the best provisions of our railroad bill are in danger. Come this way and help us."

He was in doubt about being able to do so without interfering with his engagement at Oshkosh, but the next morning a telegram from him was delivered to me at the breakfast table. It said, "I am just taking the train for Madison; will arrive at 10.45."

I went down to the capitol early and called into the executive office several leading members of the legislature, both Republicans and Democrats. I informed them Colonel Bryan would be in Madison that day a couple of hours between trains, and suggested that the legislature adopt a resolution inviting him to address them in joint session at about eleven o'clock. This suggestion met with the favor of the men whom I had called in, and they secured the passage of the resolution.

I met Colonel Bryan at the train. He was in fine spirits, keenly alive to the situation and deeply interested in a non-partisan way in our achieving the very best results we could in that important session. The galleries of the assembly chamber were crowded with citizens, and all the members of the legislature were present on the floor. I presented Colonel Bryan, and he made one of the finest speeches I ever listened to. He was witty and eloquent; he appealed to the patriotism of the legislature without regard to party, especially urging the Democratic members to support our measure. He said

he was not afraid of Republicans stealing Democratic thunder; that he would be willing to leave all the good Democratic propositions that had ever been advanced out on the porch over night if only the Republicans would steal them and enact them into law.

I had Bryan's speech taken down by a stenographer and circulated it widely in Democratic districts, thus starting a back fire on the Democratic legislators who were doubtful. The result justified the effort. It aided us materially, and when the bill came up for the final vote it was passed unanimously.

I have always felt grateful to Colonel Bryan for this broadminded and patriotic action. It showed that his interest in principles was truly uppermost. I first met Bryan near the close of the last session of the 49th Congress. I had been defeated and was going out; he had just been elected and was coming in. He was then a tall, slender, handsome fellow who looked like a young divine. Since then I have met him very often, and have come to feel a strong personal attachment for him. He helped us often during our long fight in Wisconsin when the Democratic machine as well as the Republican machine was opposing the things we stood for. He helped us in *The Commoner* with his support of our campaign for direct primaries. I have brought audiences to their feet by quoting Bryan . . .

All through our fight for railroad control the lobbyists and the railroad newspapers made the most mournful prophecies of disaster: they predicted that capital would fly from the state, that new construction would stop, that equipment would deteriorate, and so on and so on. What are the facts?

The object of our legislation was not to "smash" corporations, but to drive them out of politics, and then to treat them exactly the same as other people are treated. Equality under the law was our guiding star. It is the special discriminations and unjust rates that are being corrected; the privileges, unfair advantages, and political corruption that have been abolished. Where these do not exist the object has been to foster and encourage business activity. Consequently, no state in the union to-day offers better security for the savings of its people than Wisconsin. The honest investor, or business man, or farmer, or laborer, who simply wants equal opportunity with others and security for what he honestly earns, is protected and encouraged by the laws. The mere speculator, or monopolist, or promoter, who wants to take advantage of others under protection of law, is held down or driven out. The result is that instead of falling behind, the state has actually gone forward more rapidly than the rest of the country. This may be shown by incontrovertible facts and figures in practically every direction where there has been progressive legislation affecting business.

The Railroad Commission keeps accurate account of all the business of every railroad and public utility in the state. It has jurisdiction over property whose total value amounts to $450,000,000. The books are kept exactly as the commission orders them to be kept. These accounts show that while during the first five years of its existence the commission reduced rates by more than $2,000,000 a year, the *net earnings* of the railroads of Wisconsin increased relatively just a little more than the net earnings for all railways in the United States. The increase in Wisconsin was 18.45 per cent., and in the United States it was 18.41 per cent.

How did this come about? Simply from the fact that the decrease in rates for freight and passengers was followed by an enormous increase in the amount of freight and number of passengers carried. So it happened that, notwithstanding the *reduction in rates*, there was an actual increase of nearly 20 per cent in the revenue, while the increase of revenue of all the railroads in the United States was only 16 per cent.

This remarkable increase took place notwithstanding the fact that, mainly on account of the greatly improved service which the commission required the railroads to perform, the expense of railroad operation in Wisconsin increased 33 per cent[,] more than the average rate of increase in the entire United States.

Much of what the railroads lost in the reduction of open rates that everybody shares they recovered by being compelled to abolish free passes and secret cut rates that went only to insiders and grafters. The special examiners whom I appointed in 1903 uncovered $5,992,731.58 as Wisconsin's share of rebates paid by twelve roads during the six years 1898 to 1903. By stopping rebates alone the railroads have gained at least $1,000,000 a year toward offsetting $2,000,000 they lost by reduction of rates. At the end of another fifteen months, in July, 1911, after such an increase in profits following the reduction in rates, the company accepted without protest another reduction to 12 cents. No additional investigation was necessary, because the books of the company had been kept in the way prescribed by the commission so as to show every item of expense, income, and investment. Supervision by the state commission has thus proven of great benefit to the private corporation itself.

How has it been possible that both the people of Wisconsin and the investors in public utilities have been so greatly benefited by this regulation? *Simply because the regulation is scientific.* The Railroad Commission has found out through its engineers, accountants, and statisticians what it actually costs to build and operate the road and utilities. Watered stock and balloon bonds get no consideration. On the other hand, since the commission knows the costs, it knows exactly the point below which rates cannot be reduced. It even raises rates when they are below the cost, including reasonable profit.

The people are benefited because they are not now paying profits on inflated capital. The investors are benefited because the commission has all the facts needed to prevent a reduction of rates below a fair profit on their true value. So honestly, capably, and scientifically has the work of our commission been done that the railroads and other utility corporations have accepted their reductions without any contest at all. Our law makes it perfectly easy for the railroads to seek redress in the courts if they feel wronged in any way. Yet it is significant that there has never been an appeal taken in any railroad rate case decided by the Railroad Commission. The corporations know that the Railroad Commission has all the data for making rates that they (the railroads) have, and that it can go into court and show that it is making rates not by guess, not by estimate, but by the most careful calculation based upon definite information. Thus while the railroad companies do not enjoy having their rates cut down, they are not over-eager to advertise the Wisconsin system of rate making. When the other states of the country and the federal government make rates as we do in Wisconsin, the shippers of the country will be saved millions of dollars every year in excessive transportation charges.

In Wisconsin we regulate services as well as rates. When the services of a railroad are not satisfactory to the public, complaint can be made to the Railroad Commission. Under our law that complaint does not need to be a formal legal document, but a simple statement of grievance by letter or postal card. In 1906 I rode over the branch of the Chicago, Milwaukee and St. Paul road which runs from Madison to Prairie du Chien. The train was not so very crowded when I got on two or three stations east of Prairie du Chien, but it kept filling up and pretty soon I found myself standing in the aisle. I kept being crowded back and back until when I got to Madison I was sitting on the tail end of the train, and I was thoroughly angry. I had a canvass made of the regular patrons of the train who were aboard, to find out how the service that morning compared with the average service. I found it was the usual thing, and I wrote at once on the back of an envelope which I took from my pocket something like this:

"Mr. Commissioner: I call your attention to the bad service on the Prairie du Chien division of the Chicago, Milwaukee and St. Paul road. It is not adequately equipped either with cars or trains. Passenger train so-and-so crowded to the platforms. I think the matter should be investigated by your commission."

I think inside of ten days there was a new train running on that road. The travelling men called it the "Bob" train in honor of me, but I am sure that no more attention was paid to my complaint than would have been paid to one from any other source.

The complaint is taken up by the commission in an informal way. A representative of the railroad and the party making complaint are then brought together, quite informally. I should say hundreds of cases of that sort are disposed of and adjusted to the satisfaction of both parties to one case requiring a formal presentation and the employment of counsel. This system makes it cheaper for the railroads, cheaper for the people, and it is a speedy way to get justice in a lot of little things. Most people deal with railroads in a large way only a few times in their lives. But they are brought into intimate contact with the railroad on little freight shipments, or with relation to crossings and depots— small annoyances which often cause more bitterness than large matters. As the result of the easy and just settlement of such difficulties I think to-day there is

a better feeling in the state toward the railroads and railroad men than ever before in our history.

In other ways our progressive legislation has materially benefited all the people of the state. For example, beginning in 1903, I secured in every water-power franchise the insertion of a provision that the rates charged should be regulated by arbitration. Since that time the water powers of the state serving as public utilities have been placed under the control of the Railroad Commission, and a great corporation, supervised by the Railroad Commission, with its profits limited to 6 per cent on actual cost, has been created and has improved the headwaters of the Wisconsin River in order to secure a steady flow through the year. Several enormous power dams have been constructed, and through these means the state has gone far toward utilizing its 1,000,000 available horsepower, while protecting the state against water-power monopoly.

Wisconsin began in 1905 to build up a state forest reserve on the headwaters of its principal rivers. It now ranks next to New York and Pennsylvania in its areas of forests belonging to the state, and has adopted a permanent policy of adding annually to the reserve.

Wisconsin has also taken hold of the insurance problem with vigor. The special session of the legislature which I called in 1905 provided for a committee to investigate insurance corporations. This was about the time of the Hughes investigation in New York, and the committee appointed pursuant to that legislation rendered a very signal service to our state. As a member of that committee H. L. Ekern, who was then Speaker of the Assembly—a legislator of real creative power—developed a very remarkable aptitude for the insurance problem. It was most extraordinary. Ekern is a Norwegian, a university graduate, a lawyer. In the legislature of 1907 he appeared before the committee having charge of the insurance legislation, and there demonstrated his ability to more than hold his own against the ablest actuaries and lawyers representing the largest insurance companies in the United States.

In 1910 he was elected Insurance Commissioner of the state and in the legislature of 1911 he brought about a complete recodification of our insurance laws. He has indeed practically laid the basis for a system of state insurance—the first, I think, in the United States.

The public service of the state has been democratized by a civil service law opening it to men and women on an equal footing independent of everything excepting qualification and fitness for office. I think the passing of this law was the only case of the kind where the employees then holding office were not blanketed into the service, but were required to take the regular competitive examinations in order to retain their jobs. The law has worked to the great advantage of the service and to the general improvement of political standards. There is no longer any political pull in Wisconsin. . . .

These are a few of the conclusive proofs that progressive legislation in Wisconsin has not been destructive, as its enemies predicted. Instead of driving capital out of the state it has attracted capital more than other states. It has made investments safe for all, instead of speculative for a few. It has been conservative and constructive as well as progressive. Only one of the progressive laws—a law passed in 1911, declaring flowing water public property—has been overturned by the supreme court of the state, and not one has been carried into the federal courts.

No account of the long and successful struggle in Wisconsin would be fair and complete that did not record the splendid services of the men who led the fight for progressive principles. I regret that I cannot here give to each the individual recognition that is merited. That must wait for a more detailed history of the Wisconsin movement. It was a day-and-night service with them; they left their offices and business interests and devoted years to the great constructive work which

has made Wisconsin the safest guide in dealing with the political, economic and social problems of our time.

This closes the account of my services in Wisconsin—a time full of struggle, and yet a time that I like to look back upon. It has been a fight supremely worth making, and I want it to be judged, as it will be ultimately, by results actually attained. If it can be shown that Wisconsin is a happier and better state to live in, that its institutions are more democratic, that the opportunities of all its people are more equal, that social justice more nearly prevails, that human life is safer and sweeter—then I shall rest content in the feeling that the Progressive movement has been successful. And I believe all these things can really be shown, and that there is no reason now why the movement should not expand until it covers the entire nation. While much has been accomplished, there is still a world of problems yet to be solved; we have just begun; there is hard fighting, and a chance for the highest patriotism, still ahead of us. The fundamental problem as to which shall rule, men or property, is still unsettled; it will require the highest qualities of heroism, the profoundest devotion to duty in this and in the coming generation, to reconstruct our institutions to meet the requirements of a new age. May such brave and true leaders develop that the people will not be led astray.

QUESTIONS TO CONSIDER

1. How did La Follette portray his work in the state?
2. Is his defense of Progressivism convincing to you? Why or why not?

CHAPTER 20

A GLOBAL POWER, 1914–1919

20.1 WOODROW WILSON, "ADDRESS TO A JOINT SESSION OF CONGRESS ON THE TAMPICO INCIDENT" (1914)

Woodrow Wilson (1856–1924) became President at a crucial time in American history. The former President of Princeton University and Governor of New Jersey, Wilson served during a period of increasing turmoil domestically and abroad. At the end of World War I, he led the Paris Peace Conference and fought for the formation of the League of Nations (see Reading 20.4). He also spearheaded numerous reforms, including passing an income tax and creating the Federal Reserve System. His involvement in Mexico, however, is less well known. In 1911, William Howard Taft, Wilson's predecessor, had supported a revolution in Mexico against Porfirio Díaz, a dictator who had rule since 1876. The revolution first brought Francisco Madero to power. Just two years later, Victoriano Huerta, one of Madero's generals, carried out a coup and had Madero assassinated, probably with the support of Taft's ambassador, Henry Lane Wilson. Upon assuming office, Wilson clashed with Huerta, especially after Huerta arrested members of the U.S. Navy in the port of Tampico in 1914. Wilson then gave the following statement to Congress. In it, he outlined the situation and asked Congress to support his policies. The following day, Wilson sent the U.S. Navy to occupy the Mexican port of Veracruz. U.S. forces held the port until late November, but the two nations averted war after a series of diplomatic negotiations.

Gentlemen of the Congress:

It is my duty to call your attention to a situation which has arisen in our dealings with General Victoriano Huerta at Mexico City which calls for action, and to ask your advice and cooperation in acting upon it.

On the 9th of April a paymaster of the U.S.S. *Dolphin* landed at the Iturbide Bridge landing at Tampico with a whaleboat and boat's crew to take off certain supplies needed by his ship, and while engaged in loading the boat was arrested by an officer and squad of men of

Source: Woodrow Wilson, "Address to a Joint Session of Congress on the Tampico Incident," http://www.presidency.ucsb.edu/ws/?pid=65376 (Accessed May 20, 2018).

the army of General Huerta. Neither the paymaster nor anyone of the boat's crew was armed. Two of the men were in the boat when the arrest took place and were obliged to leave it and submit to be taken into custody, notwithstanding the fact that the boat carried, both at her bow and at her stern, the flag of the United States. The officer who made the arrest was proceeding up one of the streets of the town with his prisoners when met by an officer of higher authority, who ordered him to return to the landing and await orders; and within an hour and a half from the time of the arrest orders were received from the commander of the Huertista forces at Tampico for the release of the paymaster and his men. The release was followed by apologies from the commander and later by an expression of regret by General Huerta himself. General Huerta urged that martial law obtained at the time at Tampico; that orders had been issued that no one should be allowed to land at the Iturbide Bridge; and that our sailors had no right to land there. Our naval commanders at the port had not been notified of any such prohibition; and, even if they had been, the only justifiable course open to the local authorities would have been to request the paymaster and his crew to withdraw and to lodge a protest with the commanding officer of the fleet. Admiral Mayo regarded the arrest as so serious an affront that he was not satisfied with the apologies offered, but demanded that the flag of the United States be saluted with special ceremony by the military commander of the port.

The incident cannot be regarded as a trivial one, especially as two of the men arrested were taken from the boat itself—that is to say, from the territory of the United States—but had it stood by itself it might have been attributed to the ignorance or arrogance of a single officer. Unfortunately, it was not an isolated case. A series of incidents have recently occurred which cannot but create the impression that the representatives of General Huerta were willing to go out of their way to show disregard for the dignity and rights of this Government and felt perfectly safe in doing what they pleased, making free to show in many ways their irritation and contempt. A few days after the incident at Tampico an orderly from the U.S.S. *Minnesota* was arrested at Vera Cruz while ashore in uniform to obtain the ship's mail, and was for a time thrown into jail. An official dispatch from this Government to its embassy at Mexico City was withheld by the authorities of the telegraphic service until peremptorily demanded by our chargé d'affaires in person. So far as I can learn, such wrongs and annoyances have been suffered to occur only against representatives of the United States. I have heard of no complaints from other Governments of similar treatment. Subsequent explanations and formal apologies did not and could not alter the popular impression, which it is possible it had been the object of the Huertista authorities to create, that the Government of the United States was being singled out, and might be singled out with impunity, for slights and affronts in retaliation for its refusal to recognize the pretensions of General Huerta to be regarded as the constitutional provisional President of the Republic of Mexico.

The manifest danger of such a situation was that such offenses might grow from bad to worse until something happened of so gross and intolerable a sort as to lead directly and inevitably to armed conflict. It was necessary that the apologies of General Huerta and his representatives should go much further, that they should be such as to attract the attention of the whole population to their significance, and such as to impress upon General Huerta himself the necessity of seeing to it that no further occasion for explanations and professed regrets should arise. I, therefore, felt it my duty to sustain Admiral Mayo in the whole of his demand and to insist that the flag of the United States should be saluted in such a way as to indicate a new spirit and attitude on the part of the Huertistas.

Such a salute General Huerta has refused, and I have come to ask your approval and support in the course I now purpose to pursue.

This Government can, I earnestly hope, in no circumstances be forced into war with the people of Mexico. Mexico is torn by civil strife. If we are to accept the tests of its own constitution, it has no government. General Huerta has set his power up in the City of Mexico, such as it is, without right and by methods for which there can be no justification. Only part of the country is under his control. If armed conflict should unhappily come as a result of his attitude of personal resentment toward this Government, we should be fighting only General Huerta and those who adhere to him and give him their support, and our object would be only to restore to the people of the distracted Republic the opportunity to set up again their own laws and their own government.

But I earnestly hope that war is not now in question. I believe that I speak for the American people when I say that we do not desire to control in any degree the affairs of our sister Republic. Our feeling for the people of Mexico is one of deep and genuine friendship, and everything that we have so far done or refrained from doing has proceeded from our desire to help them, not to hinder or embarrass them. We would not wish even to exercise the good offices of friendship without their welcome and consent. The people of Mexico are entitled to settle their own domestic affairs in their own way, and we sincerely desire to respect their right. The present situation need have none of the grave implications of interference if we deal with it promptly, firmly, and wisely.

No doubt I could do what is necessary in the circumstances to enforce respect for our Government without recourse to the Congress, and yet not exceed my constitutional powers as President; but I do not wish to act in a matter possibly of so grave consequence except in close conference and cooperation with both the Senate and House. I, therefore, come to ask your approval that I should use the armed forces of the United States in such ways and to such an extent as may be necessary to obtain from General Huerta and his adherents the fullest recognition of the rights and dignity of the United States, even amidst the distressing conditions now unhappily obtaining in Mexico.

There can in what we do be no thought of aggression or of selfish aggrandizement. We seek to maintain the dignity and authority of the United States only because we wish always to keep our great influence unimpaired for the uses of liberty, both in the United States and wherever else it may be employed for the benefit of mankind.

QUESTIONS TO CONSIDER

1. How did Wilson portray the situation?
2. Do you agree with Wilson's tactics? Should he have done something else or nothing at all?

20.2 LETTERS FROM BRITISH SOLDIERS IN WORLD WAR I (1915)

In the United States, World War I is sometimes overlooked. America's late entry into the war and relatively limited involvement can sometimes render the war an afterthought to World War II. In Europe, however, World War I remains a major part of the historical narrative. From 1914 to 1918, European nations mobilized some 70 million people to fight. Over nine million soldiers and seven million civilians died during the war, in a ghastly display of the impact of technology on modern warfare. Much of the war was fought in the close confines of trenches, where armies might battle for months over relatively small pieces of land. The following letters are chosen from a series of British World War I soldiers' letters kept by the U.K. National Archives. Both letters discuss life in the trenches and the horrors the two soldiers experienced while fighting.

TRENCHES: "THEY WERE MOSTLY MERE BOYS"

My dear Mother,

Have just come through a particularly nasty period. We went into the trenches on Wednesday night and on Sunday morning at 5am our Artillery commenced bombarding the German trenches and after 20 minutes had elapsed we went over the parapet. My goodness what a reception the Huns had in store for us, they simply swept the ground with machine gun fire and shrapnel. Poor old 'C' coy. caught it hot and Neuve Chapelle seemed to be a fleabite compared with this. It was found impossible to make any advance in our quarter, so I dug myself in and awaited events. It was horrible suspense, as I seemed to be the only man untouched, all around me, and being personally acquainted with each man made matters worse, in fact, it's all wrong to call them men, as they were mostly mere boys.

About early afternoon I was hailed from the trench as to whether it was possible for me to get back. I replied in the affirmative and decided to run the risk of getting potted on the way. So I commenced crawling on my stomach until about a few yards from the parapet, then made a spring and rushed headlong over the top, nearly spoiling the features of a few who happened to be in the trench and were not expecting me. We were relieved that afternoon, but some of the fellows did not get in until nightfall and these experienced another bombardment . . . Billy Hastings is quite fit and the only pal left. We have been resting since and getting information about the [illegible] but by all reports we shall be up again soon. No rest for the wicked it is said, and if true we must surely be a bad lot.

What a terrible thing about the Lusitania, and with so many Americans aboard. Should imagine there will be more trouble. Have received box and letter dated 6th and am most thankful for everything you are all doing for me. (censored.)

As regards the pads [masks of cotton pads which served as gas masks], all we were served out with were made 'on the spot' and consisted of a piece of gauze and tape and were steeped in a solution of bicarbonate of soda, prior to this charge. I lost all my belongings except the Gillette [razor] so should be glad of a few toilet requisites when next you are sending a parcel. Do not trouble about towel and perhaps Frank would get me a shaving brush. Must now close. Much love to all. From your affectionate son,

Dick

Source: "Letters from the First World War, 1915," *The National Archives,* http://www.nationalarchives.gov.uk/education/resources/letters-first-world-war-1915 (Accessed June 12, 2018).

DARDANELLES: "AN EVERLASTING NIGHTMARE"

Dear Arthur,

I expect you are wondering why I have not written, but it is an awful effort to get all correspondence off, and be on active service at the same time. I can't say that I am enjoying myself out here. It's awfully hot, and we are eaten up by millions of flies. Life in the trenches is not a picnic either we have about four or five days out of them and eight or nine in them. When we are out supposed to be resting, we have to go on working parties, digging etc., then wherever we are, we are always under shell fire, so it's not much rest after all. The last shell we had in camp, there was four killed and seventeen wounded.

We have been under fire for three months now, and we should like a rest as the strain is tremendous on one's nerves. I don't think the troops in France get it quite as bad. Then again, the only comforts we have are sent from home, as the country here is quite barren, and we cannot buy anything in shops, I would give a quid for a pint of beer down the club. Our food consists of half a loaf of bread per day, bacon and tea for breakfast, Bully beef and biscuits for dinner and Jam for tea and cheese. Lime juice is served out about four times per week, that is a drop is put into a dixie of water and a cup full served out per man, and rum is served out twice a week (sometimes) that is about four table spoonful each.

We live in a trench and it is a mercy it don't rain otherwise we'd be washed away. The fighting just lately has been terrible. Our shells knock the enemy all ways and the sight in the trenches that we take is awful. We wear our respirators because of the awful smell of the dead. I'll never get the sight out of my eyes, and it will be an everlasting nightmare. If I am spared to come home, I'll be able to tell you all about it, but I cannot possibly write as words fail me. I can't describe things.

Wouldn't it be nice to be at Walmer again and you come down and see me again, I did enjoy that time, and also seeing Billy Dawson and Richardson. There seem to be a lot of French troops out here, but there seems to be no relief for us. Nobody loves us now Churchill has gone, we are nobody's pets. It's the army first here, except when there is work to be done, and then the Naval Division have to do it. You know both my brothers have commissions in the 4th Bedfordshires and are at Dovercourt. My wife tells me she has sent me three boxes of stuff, I received one box, and I fear that one transport has been floundered [sunk] and another has been torpedoed, so I expect that is where my other two boxes are. It's awfully disappointing because I do look forward so to a bit of chocolate and a few biscuits from home. We get cigarettes and baccy served out to us, but it is too hot to smoke much, so that I don't miss that so much. I get a bath in a biscuit tin when I can, but when in the trenches I have to go all the time without a wash, so you can tell I am used to being dirty.

How are they all down the club, and is Emmie still there, and is she better or not? Is Paice going to Looe this year? And where are you spending your holidays? Lord how I'd like a holiday, I am so tired and would give anything to get away from this continual banging.

Please remember me to all fellows who are left in the office. Mr. Miller and Goff & Hills and George Williams, and all the boys generally. I can't write to all separately, also for details of my experiences you must wait until I get back, if ever I do, of which sometimes I despair.

The papers tell you pretty full accounts, although they are rather anticipating events as to our advancing. Now I must close old chap, and thank you very much for all your kindness. Wishing you all the best

Yours very sincerely,
Harold Watts.

QUESTIONS TO CONSIDER

1. What especially stands out to you after reading the letters?
2. Does this change at all how you think about World War I?

20.3 ATLEE POMERENE DENOUNCES ROBERT LA FOLLETTE (1918)

Robert La Follette (see Chapter 19, Reading 19.6) was a U.S. Senator from Wisconsin and a major leader of the Progressive movement. During World War I, La Follette also became one of the few American politicians to vehemently oppose the war. He famously spoke out against American entry in a speech on the Senate floor in April 1917, and he was one of just six senators to vote against the war resolution. Afterward, La Follette continued to denounce the war and the Espionage and Sedition Acts. In response to La Follette's anti-war activism, several members of the Senate, led by Ohio Senator Atlee Pomerene, worked to expel La Follette for an allegedly treasonous speech La Follette had given in St. Paul, Minnesota. After fourteen months of hearings, a Senate investigative committee recommended dismissing all charges against Follette. Pomerene then submitted his own minority report, which defended the investigation and recommended removing La Follette from the Senate and an excerpt from which appears here. In the end, the Senate dismissed all charges, and La Follette served as Senator until his death in 1926.

I regret not being able to concur in the report of the majority of the Committee on Privileges and Elections recommending the dismissal of the proceedings pending against the Senator from Wisconsin. . . .

ESPIONAGE ACT OF JUNE 15, 1917

Now, in light of what I conceive to be the unlimited power of the Senate to determine the rules of its proceedings, to punish its members for disorderly behavior, and with the concurrence of two-thirds, to expel a member, let us examine the situation as it must present itself to the mind while considering the charges which have been filed with the Senate against Senator La Follette.

On April 6, 1917, the Congress of the United States declared a state of war against the German Imperial Government, the greatest military power of modern times.

On May 18, 1917, Congress passed a draft law providing for the creation of an army to carry on the war, and by its terms required all male persons between the ages of 21 and 31, inclusive, to enroll or register for military service, excluding, of course, aliens who had not declared their intention to become citizens, and made them subject to call by the President from time to time into the military and naval forces of the United States; and by the law of the land these men constituted a part of the military and naval forces of the country.

On June 5, 1917, the registration of all men within the military age began throughout the entire country.

On June 15, 1917, the Congress passed the so-called espionage act making it a penal offense, punishable by fine or imprisonment, or both, for anyone when the United States is at war—

First. "To willfully make or convey false reports or false statements with intent to interfere with the operation or success of the military or naval forces of the United States, or to promote the success of its enemies;" or

Second. "To willfully cause or attempt to cause insubordination, disloyalty, mutiny, or refusal of duty in the military or naval forces of the United States;" or

Source: Atlee Pomerene, "Views of a Minority," Report submitted to the 65th Congress, 3rd Session, Calendar No. 560 (December 14, 1918), 3–11.

Third. "To willfully obstruct the recruiting or enlistment service of the United States to the injury of the service of the United States."

MILITARY CONDITIONS IN THE COUNTRY

On September 5, 1917, the first call was issued for 687,000 men, and other calls were made thereafter at short intervals. The young men thus called, and to be called, to the colors, came from all sections of the country. With rare exceptions they responded with alacrity for the defense of their country and for the protection of humanity.

On September 20, 1917, Senator La Follette made the speech which is the subject of controversy, before the Nonpartisan League in St. Paul, Minn.

At this time it was within common knowledge of the people generally that the I. W. W.'s, the extreme Socialists, the well-intentioned but misguided pacifists, and certain German propagandists were sowing the seeds of dissension and insubordination, and spreading their poison throughout the country for the purpose of discrediting the Government in its prosecution of the war. Some of them were taking this course because they were opposed to all war; others because they were opposed to this war; and still others because they were using their utmost endeavors to aid the enemy and to render impotent, so far as they could, our own forces. State and local authorities and the loyal citizens of the land, with the approval of the Government, were organizing associations for the purpose of checking acts of disloyalty and sedition in their respective communities, and among these organizations was the Minnesota Public Safety Commission, which filed the complaint now under consideration.

On May 7, 1915, the *Lusitania* was sunk by a German submarine with a loss of more than 1,100 lives, 114 of whom were American citizens, without warning, and without providing for the safety of the passengers and crew—an act of piracy, so recognized by everyone save Germany and those who sympathized with her.

But this was not all. Before Congress passed the joint resolution declaring a state of war, the German submarines had sunk in the same way and by the same means 20 American vessels with a total loss of human life aggregating nearly 300 American lives. After repeated

negotiations covering almost a year, on the 4th day of May, 1916, the German Imperial Government sent its note to the United States advising this Government that Germany had given instructions to her submarine commanders not to sink vessels without giving warning and without caring for the safety of passengers and crew in conformity with the rules of international law, unless they sought to escape; but intimated that upon certain contingencies this mode of warfare might be resumed. With this announcement the country believed the crisis had passed and all minor controversies could be adjusted, and except for Germany's subsequent aggressions there would have been no war.

But on January 31, 1917, the United States was advised that after February 1, 1917, Germany would resume without restrictions her submarine warfare on belligerent and neutral ships alike that would pass through a war zone estimated to be 1,400 miles long and 400 miles wide, through which nine-tenths of its commerce, aggregating at that time more than $6,000,000,000 annually would have to pass; that only one ship could go each week, on Thursday, into Great Britain from the United States, and one ship return on Sunday, each week, from Great Britain. Only one day's notice was given to us, notwithstanding the fact that the German Imperial Government had determined as early as January 19 to resume this warfare, as is evidenced by the message which was sent to Bernstorff to be transmitted to the German ambassador in Mexico urging him to incite Mexico and Japan to begin war against us.

These were among the causes that led to the war, and these facts must have been known to the Senator from Wisconsin, and yet in his speech at St. Paul he said:

Now fellow citizens, we are in the midst of a war. For my own part I was not in favor of beginning the war. [Cheers and applause.]

I don't mean to say that we hadn't suffered grievances; we had—[A voice: "Yes!"] at the hands of Germany. Serious grievances! [A voice: "You bet!"]

We had cause for complaint. *They had interfered with the right of American citizens to travel upon the high seas—on ships loaded with munitions for Great Britain.* [Laughter, cheers, and applause.]

Let me have the time; I have got to catch a train—unless I am stopped by somebody [laughter], and I have never been stopped yet! [Laughter and applause.]

Cut it out. Let me have the time. I would not be understood as saying that we didn't have grievances. We did. And upon those grievances, which I regarded as insufficient, considering the amount involved and the rights involved, *which was the right to ship munitions to Great Britain with, American passengers on board to secure a safe transit.* [Laughter and applause.]

We had a right, a technical right, to ship the munitions, and the *American citizens* have a *technical right to ride on those vessels.* I was not in favor of the riding on them [laughter], because it seemed to me that the consequences resulting from any destruction of life that might occur, would be so awful—[A voice: "Yellow!"]

What did you say? [A voice: "Yellow!"]

Any man who says that in an audience where he can conceal his identity is yellow himself. [Many cries: "Put him out!" "Put him out!"]

Sit down everybody. I don't want any of that in an audience where I am speaking. [Cries of "Order!" "Order!"]

All I want is order. I will take care of everybody that interrupts if you will just give me the chance. [Cheers and applause.]

I say this, that the comparatively *small privilege of the right of an American citizen to ride on a munition-loaded ship, flying a foreign flag* is too small to involve this Government in the loss of millions and millions of lives! [Cheers and applause.]

Now—[A voice interrupting: "Where is the yellow guy now?"] [Another voice: "Give it to him, La Follette!"] [Order!]

Now, fellow citizens, I didn't believe that we should have gone into this war for that poor privilege. [A voice: "Nobody else!"]

The right of an *American citizen to travel upon a foreign vessel loaded with munitions of war.* Because—[Another interruption.]

Wait just a minute. Let me state my position. Because *a foreign vessel loaded with munitions of war is technically foreign territory*—[cheers and applause]—and an American citizen takes his life in his own hands, just as much as he would if he were on the territory of France and camped in the neighborhood of an arsenal! [Cheers and applause.]

Mr. President, it has sometimes occurred to me that the shippers of munitions of war, who were making enormous profits out of the business, invited and encouraged *American citizens to ride on those ships,* in order to give a sort of semblance of safety to the passage of their profiteering cargo abroad. [Cheers and applause.]

But, Mr. President, we went into the war by the adoption by Congress of a declaration of war in constitutional form. [Applause.] I was not in favor of going into the war illegally.

I resisted the right to arm merchantmen, when I knew that that would result in producing a condition that would bring about war without a declaration by Congress; and the Constitution says that Congress, not the acts of the President, shall bring on a war with a foreign government. [Cheers and applause.]

But war was declared, and lawfully declared,

It was not brought about by an unlawful and piratical arming of merchant ships. I had a little bit to do with stopping that on the 4th of March, and I put it to my everlasting credit that I was able to do it. [Cheers and applause.]

We are in the war, And, at least, we are lawfully in the war.

Now, then, the war entails expenses. [Laughter.]

You can not run a war in these days without paying for it. [Laughter.]

It is a costly enterprise. Everyone of the nations, the belligerent nations of Europe, are reeling under the financial burdens that war, this war of all wars in the history of the world, has laid upon them. Everyone of the foreign nations up to last April, when we entered the war, had passed the line of safety so far as ever being able to redeem their financial obligations were concerned. Everyone except Great Britain. Whenever any government is paying out for Its obligations more than—for its current obligations—more than 25 per cent of its income, that nation has passed the line where it is safe to loan to it. [Applause.]

Every belligerent nation in Europe last April, except Great Britain, had passed that line. Never—this is tritism to say—never before in the history of the human race was a war in progress that so, day by day, hour by hour, moment by moment, sapped the very life blood, the financial life blood, of the existence of the nation as a stable entity.

And, fellow citizens, it behooves a nation to consider well before it enters upon a war of that sort, how much it has got at stake. If all it has got at stake is the loans of the house of Morgan made to foreign governments, and the profits that the munition makers will earn in shipping their products to foreign countries, then I think it ought to be weighed not in a common hay scale but in an apothecary's scale. [Laughter and applause.]

Ah, but somebody will tell you, American rights are involved.

What American rights? *The right of some person to ride upon a munition-laden vessel in violation of an American statute,* that no vessel that carries explosives shall carry passengers. [Cheers and applause.]

Four days before the *Lusitania* sailed President Wilson was warned in person by Secretary of State Bryan, that the *Lusitania* had 6,000,000 rounds of ammunition on board, besides explosives; and that the passengers who proposed to sail on that vessel were sailing in violation of a statute of this country; that no passenger shall sail or travel upon a railroad train or upon a vessel which carries dangerous explosives. [Cheers and applause.]

And Secretary Bryan appealed to President Wilson to stop passengers from sailing on the *Lusitania.*

I am giving you some history that probably has not been given you here before. [Cheers.]

So, I say that the grievances that carried this country into war, into a war the limits of which, as to the loss of life, and the burdens, financial burdens, that shall be laid upon us, can not be calculated by any man—I say that the conditions that carried us into that war needed to be weighed carefully. For I enunciate no new doctrine. I say what Daniel Webster said when the Mexican war was on at full tilt—that it is the right of the people of this country to determine for themselves whether there has been a sufficient grievance for the people to incur all of the burdens and risks that go with the entrance into war.

DISCUSSION OF SPEECH

For the purposes of this report I shall pass over that part of Senator La Follette's address which describes his personal services in the West, or give his views concerning the financing of the war, and deal only with that portion which speaks of the causes leading up to the war and of our motives for entering it.

Seven different times in less than two pages of printed matter, with little variation, he tells his audience in substance either that we went to war to establish the right of an American citizen to travel upon the high seas on a foreign-owned munition-laden ship or that he did not believe that we should have gone into the war for

that "poor privilege." And each time he uses this language the stenographic reports of the speech show that his sentiments were met by the audience with "laughter, cheers, and applause" or "with cheers and applause," clearly indicating the influence of his statements upon his audience. Either they believed his statement that the United States had gone to war for this "poor privilege" and applauded it because they did not think it sufficient cause for war, or they knew it was not true and approved this slander upon the Government. Whatever may have been the reason for these demonstrations, the effect of the speech was wholly vicious.

Again he says:

Mr. President, it has sometimes occurred to me that the shippers of munitions of war, who are making enormous profits out of the business, should not have encouraged American citizens to ride on those ships in order to give a sort of semblance of safety to the passage of their profiteering cargoes abroad.

And again the sentiment is met with "applause." What inference can be drawn except that it was the intention of the speaker to make it appear to his audience that the manufacturers of munitions were in fact encouraging American citizens to ride on those ships in order to give a semblance of safety to their business? What proof can be adduced for such an assertion? Everyone knows that Senator La Follette was opposed to entering the war, but that was no reason why he should misrepresent the attitude of the President or of 82 Senators and of 373 Congressmen who voted in favor of a declaration of a state of war. Why should he seek thus to discredit the cause of America? Is not the Senate interested in finding out? . . .

Presumably he familiar with the causes which led up to the war, and yet with all the prestige of a long service in the Senate, at the capital of the nation, he tells his audience that we went to war "for the poor privilege of establishing the right of an American citizen to travel upon a foreign-owned vessel loaded with munitions of war." He wholly ignores the real causes which led to the war, and which I have in part detailed in the earlier part of this report. He ignores the fact that a compliance with the German Imperial Government's order of January 31, giving notice that after February 1, 1917, all vessels which appeared in the war zone would be sunk, would, if put in effect, deny to 110,000,000 of people a foreign commerce aggregating $6,000,000,000 annually.

What excuse has the Senator from Wisconsin made for these statements? I have heard none. What must have been the effect upon his audience? The transcript of his speech shows that these particular parts of it were punctured with applause. Were those who applauded disloyal at heart, or were they ignorant of the real causes of our having gone to war, and agreed with him that we did not have cause for entering the war?

Presumably there were in this audience men and women of all classes and shades of opinion, men who constituted a part of the military and naval forces of the United States, as well as those who were older or younger—parents, perhaps, of boys who had gone to the front to serve their country. What effect would such language have upon these people gathered together for the purpose of hearing a message from the capital of the Nation?

If it were true that we only went to war for the purpose of establishing the right of an American citizen to sail on a munition-laden, foreign-owned vessel, without warning and without caring for the safety of passengers and crew, it would have been justified, but does anyone feel that the war would have received the same united and enthusiastic support given to it by the American people? If young men of military age were in the audience, who were about to be called to arms, would not their ardor have cooled if they believed his speech? If the fathers and mothers of these young men were present, might they not have been persuaded that they ought not to be asked to make so great a sacrifice as the war would entail for "that poor privilege"? Would not it have helped to arouse their indignation? Would not its natural effect have been to cause "insubordination" or acts of "disloyalty" or "failure of duty" if an attempt were made to compel young men to go into the service for such a cause? Would it not have

tended to obstruct the recruiting or enlistment service of the United States to the injury of that service? Men usually intend what they say. In peace-loving America my belief is that the less the cause for war the less will be the enthusiasm for it.

If these statements had been made by one who was not accustomed to public speaking, or by a private individual who did not appear upon the platform in the habiliments of his office, less serious consequences might be expected to follow. But when one of the Senators of a great Commonwealth, exercising the functions of his office, appears upon the platform to discuss in the presence of his fellow citizens such commanding questions as the cause of the war, while we are in the midst of preparations for it, we must not overestimate or underestimate the weight of his words.

These statements could not have been made by accident or slip of the tongue, because the same thought, if not the very same language, is repeated several times within the space of a few minutes.

Counsel for Senator La Follete in his argument before the committee, had much to say on the subject of freedom of speech. I yield to no one in my desire to preserve this right in its entirety; but he has cited the committee to no authority, and Senators will look in vain for any authority which makes freedom of speech a shield by which the speaker may protect himself from the consequences of misstatement. Freedom of speech can not be pleaded in defense to justify the slander of the chastity of a woman or the honor of a man, or the cause of a country when in the throes of the most terrific war ever waged. . . .

QUESTIONS TO CONSIDER

1. What was Pomerene's argument? How did he defend it?
2. Do you agree more with La Follette or with Pomerene?

20.4 HENRY CABOT LODGE, SENATE SPEECH OPPOSING THE LEAGUE OF NATIONS (1919)

At the Paris Peace Conference in 1919, the Allied Powers agreed on a number of controversial items. They imposed extensive financial reparations on Germany and blamed the war on German aggression, among other parts of the agreement. Perhaps most controversially, however, the assembled nations agreed to form a League of Nations to theoretically prevent future wars on the scale of World War I. American President Woodrow Wilson was one of the leaders of the League of Nations effort, and after the Paris Conference agreed to terms, he sent the treaty for ratification by the U.S. Senate. There, the treaty encountered serious resistance, led by Senator Henry Cabot Lodge of Massachusetts. Lodge especially opposed Article X of the Treaty, which mandated that all member nations join to fight aggression if asked to do so by the League of Nations. He delivered the following speech in the Senate on February 28, 1919. In the end, the Senate never ratified the Treaty, and the much-weakened League of Nations was unable to deal with the events leading to World War II.

Mr. President, all people, men and women alike, who are capable of connected thought abhor war and desire nothing so much as to make secure the future peace of the world. Everybody hates war. Everyone longs to make it impossible. We ought to lay aside once and for all the unfounded and really evil suggestion that because men may differ as to the best method of assuring the world's peace in the future, anyone is against permanent peace, if it can be obtained, among all the nations of mankind. Because one man goes to the Capitol in Washington by one street and another man by a different street it does not follow that they are not both going to the Capitol. We all earnestly desire to advance toward the preservation of the world's peace, and difference in method makes no distinction in purpose. It is almost needless to say that the question now before us is so momentous that it transcends all party lines. Party considerations and party interests disappear in dealing with such a question as this. I will follow any man and vote for any measure which in my honest opinion will make for the maintenance of the world's peace. I will follow no man and vote for no measures which, however well intended, seem in my best judgment to lead to dissensions rather than to harmony among the nations or to injury, peril, or injustice to my country. No question has ever confronted the United States Senate which equals in importance that which is involved in the league of nations intended to secure the future peace of the world. There should be no undue haste in considering it. My one desire is that not only the Senate, which is charged with responsibility, but that the press and the people of the country should investigate every proposal with the utmost thoroughness and weigh them all carefully before they make up their minds. If there is any proposition or any plan which will not bear, which will not court the most thorough and most public discussion, that fact makes it an object of suspicion at the very outset. Beware of it; be on your guard against it. Demand that those who oppose the plan now offered present arguments and reasons, based on facts and history, and that those who favor it meet objections with something more relative than rhetoric, personal denunciation, and shrill shrieks that virtue is

Source: Henry Cabot Lodge, "Constitution of the League of Nations," Robert C. Byrd, ed., *The Senate 1789–1989: Classic Speeches, 1830–1993* (Washington D.C.: Government Printing Office, 1994), https://www.senate.gov/artandhistory/history/resources/pdf/LodgeLeagueofNations.pdf (Accessed June 12, 2018)

to be preferred to vice and that peace is better than war. Glittering and enticing generalities will not serve. We must have facts, details, and sharp, clear-cut definitions. The American people cannot give too much thought to this subject, and that they shall look into it with considerate eyes is all that I desire. . . .

"IF THE UNITED STATES AGREES TO GUARANTIES . . . WE MUST MAINTAIN THEM"

Two other general propositions, and I shall proceed to examine these league articles in detail. In article 10 we, in common, of course, with the other signatories and members of the projected league, guarantee the territorial integrity and the political independence of every member of the league. That means that we ultimately guarantee the independence and the boundaries, as now settled or as they may be settled by the treaty with Germany, of every nation on earth. If the United States agrees to guaranties of that sort we must maintain them.

The word of the United States, her promise to guarantee the independence and the boundaries of any country, whether she does it alone or in company with other nations, whether she guarantees one country or all the countries of the world, is just as sacred as her honor—far more important than the maintenance of every financial pledge, which the people of this country would never consent to break.

I do not now say the time has not come when, in the interest of future peace, the American people may not decide that we ought to guarantee the territorial integrity of the far-flung British Empire, including her self-governing dominions and colonies, of the Balkan States, of China or Japan, or of the French, Italian, and Portuguese colonies in Africa; but I do suggest that it is a very grave, a very perilous promise to make, because there is but one way by which such guaranties, if ever invoked, can be maintained, and that way is the way of force—whether military or economic force, it matters not. If we guarantee any country on the earth, no matter how small or how large, in its independence or its boundaries, that guarantee we must maintain at any cost when our word is once given, and we must be in constant possession of fleets and armies capable of enforcing these guaranties at a moment's notice. There is no need of arguing

whether there is to be compulsive force behind this league. It is there in article 10 absolutely and entirely by the mere fact of these guaranties. The ranks of the armies and the fleets of the navy made necessary by such pledges are to be filled and manned by the sons, husbands, and brothers of the people of America. I wish them carefully to consider, therefore, whether they are willing to have the youth of America ordered to war by other nations without regard to what they or their representatives desire. I would have them determine after much reflection whether they are willing to have the United States forced into war by other nations against her own will. They must bear in mind constantly that we have only one vote in the executive council, only one vote in the body of delegates, and a majority of the votes rules and is decisive.

I am not here to discuss the constitutional question of the sole right of Congress to declare war. That is a detail, as it relates only to Constitution, which we may decide later. In my own opinion, we shall be obliged to modify the Constitution. I do not think, and I never can admit, that we can change or modify the Constitution by a treaty negotiated by the president and ratified by the Senate. I think that must be done, and can only be done, in the way prescribed by the Constitution itself, and to promise to amend our Constitution is a serious task and a doubtful undertaking.

I hope the American people will take time to consider this promise before they make it—because when it is once made it cannot be broken—and ask themselves whether this is the best way of assuring perfect peace throughout the future years, which is what we are aiming at, for we all are aiming at the same object. A world's peace which requires at the outset preparation for war—for war either economic or military—in order to maintain that peace presents questions and awakens thoughts which certainly ought to be soberly and discreetly considered.

"ARE WE PREPARED TO HAVE A LEAGUE OF NATIONS . . . OPEN OUR DOORS?"

The second general proposition to which I would call attention is this: We now in this draft bind ourselves to submit every possible international dispute or difference either to the league court or to the control of the executive council of the league. That includes immigration, a very live question, to take a single example. Are we ready to give to other nations the power to say who shall come into the United States and become citizens of the Republic? If we are ready to do this, we are prepared to part with the most precious of sovereign rights, that which guards our existence and our character as a nation. Are we ready to leave it to other nations to determine whether we shall admit to the United States a flood of Japanese, Chinese, and Hindu labor? If we accept this plan for a league, this is precisely what we promise to do. I know that by following out all the windings of the provision for referring to the council or allowing the council to take charge of what has been called hitherto a nonjusticiable question, we shall probably reach a point where it would not be possible to secure unanimous action by the league upon the question of immigration. But, Mr. President, I start with the proposition that there should be no jurisdiction in the league at all over that question; that it should be separated absolutely and entirely from any jurisdiction of the league. Are we prepared to have a league of nations—in which the United States has only one vote, which she could not cast on a dispute to which she was a party—open our doors, if they see fit, to any and all immigration from all parts of the world?

Mr. Taft[10] has announced, in an article which appeared in the *Nation Geographic* Magazine, that the question of immigration will go before the international tribunal, and he says now that all organized labor is for the league. If American labor favors putting the restriction of immigration in the control of other nations they must have radically changed their minds and abandoned their most cherished policy. Certainly the gravity of such promises as are involved in the points I have suggested is sufficient to forbid haste. If such promises are to be given they must be given in cold blood with a full realization of what they mean and after the American people and those who represent them here have considered all that is involved with a serious care such as we have never been called upon to exercise before. We are asked to abandon the policies which we have adhered to during all our life as a nation. We are asked to guarantee the political independence and the territorial integrity of every nation which chooses to join the league—and that means all nations, as the president stated in his speech at Manchester. We are asked to leave to the decision of other nations, or to the jurisdiction of other nations, the question of what immigrants shall come to the United States. We are asked also to give up in part our sovereignty and our independence and to subject our own will to the will of other nations, if there is a majority against our desires. We are asked, therefore, in a large and important degree to substitute internationalism for nationalism and an international state for pure Americanism. Certainly such things as these deserve reflection, discussion, and earnest thought.

I am not contending now that these things must not be done. I have no intention of opposing a blank negative to propositions which concern the peace of he world, which I am as anxious to see promoted as any living man can be; but I do say, in the strongest terms, that these things I have pointed out are of vast importance not only to us but to the entire world, and a mistake now in making the league of nations might result in more war and trouble than the old system in its worst days. What I ask, and all I ask, is consideration, time, and thought. . . .

That which I desire above everything else, that which is nearest to my heart, is to bring our soldiers home. The making of a league of nations will not do that. We can only bring our soldiers home, entirely and completely, when the peace with Germany is made and proclaimed. Let that peace be made and I can assure the world that when the treaty of peace with Germany comes to this chamber there will be no delay in the Senate of the United States. We must bring our men back from France—the men who fought the war, the men who made the personal sacrifice. Let us get them back at once, and to that end let us have the peace made with Germay, made now, and not delay it until the complicated questions of the league of nations can be settle

10. William Howard Taft (1857–1930), who was president of the United States, 1909–1913, served as joint-chairman of the War Labor Board during World War I, before being appointed chief justice of the United States in 1921.

with the care and consideration which they demand. What is it that delays the peace with Germany? Discussions over the league of nations; nothing else. Let us have peace now, in this year of grace 1919. That is the first step to the future peace of the world. The next step will be to make sure if we can that the world shall have peace in the year 1950 or 2000. Let us have the peace with Germany and bring our boys home.

This is the immediate thing to do toward the establishment of the world's peace, but there is an issue involved in the league constitution presented to us which far overshadows all others. We are asked to depart now for the first time from the foreign policies of Washington. We are invited to move away from George Washington toward the other end of the line at which stands the sinister figure of Trotzky, the champion of internationalism.

We have in this country a government of the people, for the people, and by the people, the freest and best government in the world, and we are the great rampart today against the anarchy and disorder which have taken possession of Russia and are trying to invade every peaceful country in the world. For Lincoln's government of the people, for the people, and by the people we are asked to substitute in the United States on many vital points government of, for, and by other people. Pause and consider well before you take this fateful step. I do not say that agreements may not be made among the nations which stand for ordered freedom and civilization, which will do much to secure and preserve the peace of the world; but no such agreement has yet been presented to us. We must beware of the dangers which beset our path. We must not lose by an improvident attempt to reach eternal peace all that we have won by war and sacrifice. We must build no bridges across the chasm which now separates American freedom and order from Russian anarchy and destruction. We must see to it that the democracy of the United States, which has prospered so mightily in the past, is not drawn by any hasty error or by any glittering delusions, through specious devices of supernational government, within the toils of international socialism and anarchy. I wish nothing but good to all the races of men. I hope and pray that peace, unbroken peace, may reign everywhere on earth. But America and the American people are first in my heart now and always. I can never assent to any scheme no matter how fair its outward seeming which is not for the welfare and for the highest and best interest of my own beloved people of whom I am one—the American people—the people of the United States.

QUESTIONS TO CONSIDER

1. How did Lodge defend his argument?
2. Do you find the argument persuasive?

CHAPTER 21

THE MODERN NATION, 1919–1928

21.1 WILLIAM 'BILLY' SUNDAY: *THE MAN AND HIS MESSAGE* (1914)

William "Billy" Sunday (1862–1935) was perhaps the foremost evangelical minister of his time. Sunday played Major League Baseball for eight years before leaving to become a minister in the 1880s. He made a name for himself with his charisma and fast-paced delivery. In the mid-1890s, Sunday decided to take his message beyond the Chicago church where he had been preaching. For the next forty years, he traveled the nation. Initially, Sunday preached in a tent. Later, he preached to large crowds in wooden structures he asked each city to build for him. Eventually, Sunday grew so popular that he had twenty-six people working for him full time on the revival campaigns. During his career, Sunday likely reached over 100 million people in face-to-face sermons, and he probably converted over one million of them. Especially before World War I, Sunday was a phenomenon. The following excerpt is taken from *Billy Sunday: The Man and His Message*, a 1914 biography of Sunday that incorporated some of his sermons in full. Here, you will read a portion of Sunday's sermon "The Unpardonable Sin."

"THE UNPARDONABLE SIN"

"Wherefore I say unto you, All manner of sin and blasphemy shall be forgiven unto men: but the blasphemy against he Holy Ghost shall not be forgiven unto men.

"And whosoever speaketh a word against the Son of man, it shall be forgiven him: but whosoever speaketh against the Holy Ghost, it shall not be forgiven him, neither in this world, neither in the world to come."

I'd like to know where anybody ever found any authority for a belief in future probation. Jesus Christ was either human or he was divine. And if he was only human then I am not obligated to obey his word any more than I am that of any other philosopher.

The Pharisees charged Jesus with being in league with the devil. They said to him, "You have a devil." They grew bolder in their denunciation and said: "You do

Source: William T. Ellis, *"Billy" Sunday: The Man and His Message: With His Own Words Which Have Won Thousands for Christ* (Philadelphia: L. T. Myers, 1914), 370–382, Retrieved from the Internet Archive website, https://archive.org/details/billysundaythema000428mbp (Accessed June 12, 2018).

what you do through Beelzebub, the prince of devils." Jesus said: "How is that so? If what I do I do through the devil, explain why it is I am overthrowing the works of the devil. If I am a devil and if what I do is through the devil, then I wouldn't be working to hurt the works of the devil. I would not be doing what I am doing to destroy the works of the devil, but I would be working to destroy the works of God."

From that day forth they dared not ask him any questions.

I know there are various opinions held by men as to what they believe constitutes the sin against the Holy Ghost. There are those who think it could have been committed only by those who heard Jesus Christ speak and saw him in the flesh. If that be true then neither you nor I are in danger, for neither has ever seen Jesus in the flesh nor heard him. Another class think that it has been committed since the days of Jesus, but at extremely rare intervals; and still a third class think they have committed it and they spend their lives in gloom and dread and are perfectly useless to themselves and the community.

And yet I haven't the slightest doubt but that there are thousands that come under the head of my message, who are never gloomy, never depressed, never downcast; their conscience is at ease, their spirits are light and gay, they eat three meals a day and sleep as sound as a babe at night; nothing seems to disturb them, life is all pleasure and song.

WHAT IT IS

If you will lay aside any preconceived ideas or opinions which you may have had or still have as to what you imagine, think or believe constitutes the sin against the Holy Ghost, or the unpardonable sin, and if you will listen to me, for I have read every sermon I could ever get my hands upon the subject, and have listened to every man I have ever had an opportunity to hear preach, and have read everything the Bible has taught on the subject.

I do not say that my views on the subject are infallible, but I have wept and prayed and studied over it, and if time will permit and my strength will allow and your patience endure, I will try and ask and answer a few questions. What is it? Why will God not forgive it?

It is not swearing. If swearing were the unpardonable sin, lots of men in heaven would have to go to hell and there are multitudes on earth on their way to heaven who would have to go to hell. It is not drunkenness. There are multitudes in heaven that have crept and crawled out of the quagmires of filth and the cesspools of iniquity and drunkenness. Some of the brightest lights that ever blazed for God have been men that God saved from drunkenness.

It's not adultery. Jesus said to the woman committing adultery and caught in the very act: "Neither do I condemn thee; go and sin no more."

It isn't theft. He said to Zaccheus, "This day is salvation come upon thy house." Zaccheus had been a thief.

It's not murder. Men's hands have been red with blood and God has forgiven them. The Apostle Paul's hands were red with blood.

What is it? To me it is plain and simple. It is constant and continual, and final rejection of Jesus Christ as your Saviour. God's offer of mercy and salvation comes to you and you say, "No," and you push it aside. I do know that there is such a thing as the last call to every man or woman. God says that his spirit will not always strive with man, and when a man or woman says "No" as God's spirit strives for the last time it forever seals your doom.

It is no special form of sin, no one act. It might be swearing, it might be theft. Any one becomes unpardonable if God keeps calling on you to forsake that sin and you keep on refusing to forsake it, and if you don't then he will withdraw and let you alone and that sin will become unpardonable, for God won't ask you again to forsake it.

It is no one glaring act, but the constant repetition of the same thing. There will come a time when you commit that sin once too often. . . .

RESISTING THE TRUTH

By every known law of the mind, conversion must be effected by the influence of the truth on the mind. Every time you resist the truth the next time you hear it, it loses its force on your mind. And every time you hear a truth and withstand it, then you become stronger in your power to resist the truth. We all know this,

that each resistance strengthens you against the truth. When a man hears the truth and he resists it, the truth grows weaker and he grows stronger to resist it.

No matter what Jesus Christ did the Jews refused to believe. He had performed wonderful deeds but they wouldn't believe, so when Lazarus was dead, he said: "Lazarus, come forth," and then turned to the Jews and said: "Isn't that evidence enough that I am the Son of God?" and they cried: "Away with him." One day he was walking down the hot dusty road and he met a funeral procession. The mourners were bearing the body of a young man and his mother was weeping. He told them to place the coffin on the ground and said:

"Young man arise," and he arose. Then he asked the Pharisees: "Is that not proof enough that I am the Son of God, that I make the dead to arise?" and they cried: "Away with him." So no matter what Jesus did, the Jews refused to believe him. No matter what Jesus Christ says or does today, you'll refuse to accept, and continue to rush pell-mell to eternal damnation.

"TOO LATE"

Jesus Christ gives you just as much evidence today. Down in Indiana, my friend, Mrs. Robinson, was preaching. I don't remember the town, but I think it was Kokomo, and I remember the incident, and the last day she tried to get the leader of society there to give her heart to God. She preached and then went down in the aisle and talked to her. Then she went back to the platform and made her appeal from there. Again she went to the girl, but she still refused. As Mrs. Robinson turned to go she saw her borrow a pencil from her escort and write something in the back of a hymn book.

A few years afterward Mrs. Robinson went back to the town and was told the girl was dying. They told her the physicians had just held a consultation and said she could not live until night. Mrs. Robinson hurried to her home. The girl looked up, recognized her and said: "I didn't send for you. You came on your own account, and you're too late." To every appeal she would reply: "You're too late." Finally she said: "Go look in the hymn book in the church."

They hurried to the church and looked over the hymn books and found in the back of one her name

and address and these words, "I'll run the risk; I'll take my chance." That was the last call to her. Not any one sin is the unpardonable sin, but it may be that constant repetition, over and over again until God will say: "Take it and go to hell."

Who can commit it? I used to think that only the vile, the profane were the people who could commit it.

Whom did Jesus warn? The Pharisees. And who were they? The best men, morally, in Jerusalem.

Who can commit it? Any man or woman who says "No" to Jesus Christ. You may even defend the Bible. You may be the best man or woman, morally, in the world. Your name may be synonymous with virtue and purity, but let God try to get into your heart, let him try to get you to walk down the aisle and publicly acknowledge Jesus Christ, and your heart and lips are sealed like a bank vault, and God hasn't been able to pull you to your feet. And God won't keep on begging you to do it. . . .

DEATH-BED CONFESSIONS

I don't go much on these death-bed confessions. A death-bed confession is like burning a candle at both ends and then blowing the smoke in the face of Jesus. A deathbed confession is like drinking the cup of life and then offering the dregs to Christ. I think it is one of the most contemptible, miserable, low-down, unmanly and unwomanly things that you can do, to keep your life in your own control until the last moment and then try to creep into the kingdom on account of the long-suffering and mercy of Jesus Christ. I don't say that none is genuine. But there is only one on record in the Bible, and that was the first time the dying thief had ever heard of Christ, and he accepted at once. So your case is not analogous to this. You have wagon loads of sermons dumped into you, but it's a mighty hard thing to accept in the last moment. If you've lived without conviction, your friends ought not to get mad when the preacher preaches your funeral sermon, if he doesn't put you in the front row in heaven, with a harp in your hands and a crown on your head.

God can forgive sins but you have got to comply with his requirements. He is not willing that any shall perish, but he has a right to tell me and you what to do to be saved.

A doctor had been a practitioner for sixty years and he was asked how many Godless men he had seen show any trace of concern on their death-bed. He said he had kept track of three hundred and only three had shown any real concern. That is appalling to me. You ordinarily die as you have lived.

A minister was called to a house of shame to be with a dying girl in her last moment. He prayed and then looked at her face and saw no signs of hope of repentance. He was led to pray again and this time he was led to put in a verse of scripture, Isaiah 1:18: "Come now and let us reason together, saith the Lord: Though your sins be as scarlet, they shall be as white as snow; though they be red like crimson, they shall be as wool."

"Is that what the Bible says?" the girl asked. He said it was. "Would you let me see it?" and the minister pointed it out to her.

"Would you pray again and put in that verse?" the girl asked and as he started she called, "Stop! Let me put my finger on that verse." The minister prayed and when he looked again, he saw hope and pardon and peace in the girl's face. "I'm so glad God made that 'scarlet,'" she said, "for that means me."

All manner of sins God will forgive. Then tell me why you will not come when God says, "All manner of sin and blasphemy shall be forgiven unto men." Great heavens! I can't understand how you sit still.

But a man says: "Bill, will He forgive a murderer? My hands are red with blood, although no one knows it." Didn't I say he forgave Paul? . . .

POWER OF REVIVALS

Most people are converted at special revival services. I want to hurl this in the teeth, cram it down the throats of those who sneer at revival efforts—preachers included. Almost nine-tenths of the Christians at this meeting were converted at a revival. What does that show? It shows that if you are thirty and have not been converted, the chances are that if you are not converted at this revival you never will be converted.

If it weren't for revivals, just think of what hell would be like. Then think of any low-down, God-forsaken, dirty gang knocking a revival.

God says: "You can spurn my love and trample the blood under your feet, but if you seek my pardon I will forgive you." You might have been indifferent to the appeals of the minister, you might have been a thief, or an adulterer, or a blasphemer, or a scoffer, and all that, but God says: "I will forgive you." You might have been indifferent to the tears of poor wife and children and friends, but if you will seek God he will forgive you.

But when He came down and revealed himself as the Son of God through the Holy Spirit, if you sneer and say it is not true, your sin may become unpardonable. If you don't settle it here you never will settle it anywhere else.

I will close with a word of comfort and a word of warning. If you have a desire to be a Christian it is proof that the devil hasn't got you yet. That is the comfort. Now for the warning: If you have that desire thank God for it and yield to it. You may never have another chance.

QUESTIONS TO CONSIDER

1. How would you describe Sunday's view of sin and conversion?
2. Does Sunday's rhetoric seem similar or different to the rhetoric of previous religious movements, such as the First and Second Great Awakenings?

21.2 MARCUS GARVEY, "DECLARATION OF THE RIGHTS OF THE NEGRO PEOPLES OF THE WORLD" (1920)

Like W. E. B. DuBois (see Chapter 19, Reading 19.2), Marcus Garvey (1887–1940) was a strong supporter of Black Nationalism. The two men, however, differed on solutions to the problem of American racism. Born in Jamaica, Garvey spent much of his early life in Central America and the Caribbean. In the early twentieth century, Garvey emerged as a forceful proponent of Pan-Africanism, the idea that all descendants of Africa should find solidarity with each other. Along that line of thinking, Garvey promoted African American migration "back to Africa" in response to his disillusionment with American society. Garvey believed that only black separatism, especially separatism fostered by emigration from America, might solve African Americans' problems. In 1914, Garvey founded the Universal Negro Improvement Association (UNIA) in Jamaica. Over the next six years, the UNIA grew to include perhaps four million members. The organization even started the Black Star Line, a short-lived shipping line intended to transport first goods and then people to Africa. At the organization's 1920 meeting in Harlem, 25,000 delegates agreed on the following document, which laid out the problems faced by black people and a set of solutions to those problems. In 1927, after a politically motivated mail fraud trial, the United States deported Garvey to Jamaica. He would remain politically active for the rest of his life.

Be It Resolved, That the Negro people of the world, through their chosen representatives in convention assembled in Liberty Hall, in the City of New York and United States of America, from August 1 to August 31, in the year of Our Lord one thousand nine hundred and twenty, protest against the wrongs and injustices they are suffering at the hands of their white brethren, and state what they deem their fair and just rights, as well as the treatment they purpose *[propose?]* to demand of all men in the future.

We complain:

1. That nowhere in the world, with few exceptions, are black men accorded equal treatment with white men, although in the same situation and circumstances, but, on the contrary, are discriminated against and denied the common rights due to human beings for no other reason than their race and color.

We are not willingly accepted as guests in the public hotels and inns of the world for no other reason than our race and color.

2. In certain parts of the United States of America our race is denied the right of public trial accorded to other races when accused of crime, but are lynched and burned by mobs, and such brutal and inhuman treatment is even practiced upon our women.

3. That European nations have parcelled out among them and taken possession of nearly all of the continent of Africa, and the natives are compelled to surrender their lands to aliens and are treated in most instances like slaves.

Source: Robert A. Hill, ed., *The Marcus Garvey and Universal Negro Improvement Association Papers, Volume II* (Berkeley: University of California Press, 1983), 571–575.

4. In the southern portion of the United States of America, although citizens under the Federal Constitution, and in States almost equal to the whites in population and are qualified land owners and taxpayers, we are, nevertheless, denied all voice in the making and administration of the laws and are taxed without representation by the State governments, and at the same time compelled to do military service in defense of the country.

5. On the public conveyances and common carriers in the southern portion of the United States we are jim-crowed and compelled to accept separate and inferior accommodations and made to pay the same fare charged for first-class accommodations, and our families are often humiliated and insulted by drunken white men who habitually pass through the jim-crow cars going to the smoking car.

6. The physicians of our race are denied the right to attend their patients while in the public hospitals of the cities and States where they reside in certain parts of the United States.

Our children are forced to attend inferior separate schools for shorter terms than white children, and the public school funds are unequally divided, between the white and colored schools.

7. We are discriminated against and denied an equal chance to earn wages for the support of our families, and in many instances are refused admission into labor unions and nearly everywhere are paid smaller wages than white men.

8. In the Civil Service and departmental offices we are everywhere discriminated against and made to feel that to be a black man in Europe, America and the West Indies is equivalent to being an outcast and a leper among the races of men, no matter what the character attainments of the black men may be.

9. In the British and other West Indian islands and colonies Negroes are secretly and cunningly discriminated against and denied those fuller rights of government to which white citizens are appointed, nominated and elected.

10. That our people in those parts are forced to work for lower wages than the average standard of white men and are kept in conditions repugnant to good civilized tastes and customs.

11. That the many acts of injustices against members of our race before the courts of law in the respective islands and colonies are of such nature as to create disgust and disrespect for the white man's sense of justice.

12. Against all such inhuman, unchristian and uncivilized treatment we here and now emphatically protest, and invoke the condemnation of all mankind.

In order to encourage our race all over the world and to stimulate it to overcome the handicaps and difficulties surrounding it, and to push forward to a higher and grander destiny, we demand and insist on the following Declaration of Rights:

1. Be it known to all men that whereas all men are created equal and entitled to the rights of life, liberty and the pursuit of happiness, and because of this we, the duly elected representatives of the Negro peoples of the world, invoking the aid of the just and Almighty God, do declare all men, women and children of our blood throughout the world free denizens, and do claim them as free citizens of Africa, the Motherland of all Negroes.

[2.] That we believe in the supreme authority of our race in all things racial; that all things are created and given to man as a common possession; that there should be an equitable distribution and apportionment of all such things, and in consideration of the fact that as a race we are now deprived of those things that are morally and legally ours, we believed it right that all such things should be acquired and held by whatsoever means possible.

3. That we believe the Negro, like any other race, should be governed by the ethics of civilization, and therefore should not be deprived of any of those rights or privileges common to other human beings.

4. We declare that Negroes, wheresoever they form a community among themselves should be given the right to elect their own representatives to represent them in Legislatures, courts of law, or such institutions as may exercise control over that particular community.

5. We assert that the Negro is entitled to even-handed justice before all courts of law and equity in whatever country he may be found, and when this is denied him on account of his race or color such denial is an insult to the race as a whole and should be resented by the entire body of Negroes.

6. We declare it unfair and prejudicial to the rights of Negroes in communities where they exist in considerable

numbers to be tried by a judge and jury composed entirely of an alien race, but in all such cases members of our race are entitled to representation on the jury.

7. We believe that any law or practice that tends to deprive any African of his land or the privileges of free citizenship within his country is unjust and immoral, and no native should respect any such law or practice.

8. We declare taxation without representation unjust and tyran[n]ous, and there should be no obligation on the part of the Negro to obey the levy of a tax by any law-making body from which he is excluded and denied representation on account of his race and color.

9. We believe that any law especially directed against the Negro to his detriment and singling him out because of his race or color is unfair and immoral, and should not be respected.

10. We believe all men entitled to common human respect and that our race should in no way tolerate any insults that may be interpreted to mean disrespect to our race or color.

11. We deprecate the use of the term "nigger" as applied to Negroes, and demand that the word "Negro" be written with a capital "N."

12. We believe that the Negro should adopt every means to protect himself against barbarous practices inflicted upon him because of color.

13. We believe in the freedom of Africa for the Negro people of the world, and by the principle of Europe for the Europeans and Asia for the Asiatics, we also demand Africa for the Africans at home and abroad.

14. We believe in the inherent right of the Negro to possess himself of Africa and that his possession of same shall not be regarded as an infringement on any claim or purchase made by any race or nation,

15. We strongly condemn the cupidity of those nations of the world who, by open aggression or secret schemes, have seized the territories and inexhaustible natural wealth of Africa, and we place on record our most solemn determination to reclaim the treasures and possession of the vast continent of our forefathers.

16. We believe all men should live in peace one with the other, but when races and nations provoke the ire of other races and nations by attempting to infringe upon their rights[,] war becomes inevitable, and the attempt in any way to free one's self or protect one's rights or heritage becomes justifiable.

17. Whereas the lynching, by burning, hanging or any other means, of human beings is a barbarous practice and a shame and disgrace to civilization, we therefore declare any country guilty of such atrocities outside the pale of civilization.

18. We protest against the atrocious crime of whipping, flogging and overworking of the native tribes of Africa and Negroes everywhere. These are methods that should be abolished and all means should be taken to prevent a continuance of such brutal practices.

19. We protest against the atrocious practice of shaving the heads of Africans, especially of African women or individuals of Negro blood, when placed in prison as a punishment for crime by an alien race.

20. We protest against segregated districts, separate public conveyances, industrial discrimination, lynchings and limitations of political privileges of any Negro citizen in any part of the world on account of race, color or creed, and will exert our full influence and power against all such.

21. We protest against any punishment inflicted upon a Negro with severity, as against lighter punishment inflicted upon another of an alien race for like offense, as an act of prejudice and injustice, and should be resented by the entire race.

22. We protest against the system of education in any country where Negroes are denied the same privileges and advantages as other races.

23. We declare it inhuman and unfair to boycott Negroes from industries and labor in any part of the world.

24. We believe in the doctrine of the freedom of the press, and we therefore emphatically protest against the suppression of Negro newspapers and periodicals in various parts of the world, and call upon Negroes everywhere to employ all available means to prevent such suppression.

25. We further demand free speech universally for all men.

26. We hereby protest against the publication of scandalous and inflammatory articles by an alien press tending to create racial strife and the exhibition of picture films showing the Negro as a cannibal.

27. We believe in the self-determination of all peoples.

28. We declare for the freedom of religious worship.

29. With the help of Almighty God we declare ourselves the sworn protectors of the honor and virtue of our women and children, and pledge our lives for their protection and defense everywhere and under all circumstances from wrongs and outrages.

30. We demand the right of an unlimited and un-prejudiced education for ourselves and our posterity forever[.]

31. We declare that the teaching in any school by alien teachers to our boys and girls, that the alien race is superior to the Negro race, is an insult to the Negro people of the world.

32. Where Negroes form a part of the citizenry of any country, and pass the civil service examination of such country, we declare them entitled to the same consideration as other citizens as to appointments in such civil service.

33. We vigorously protest against the increasingly unfair and unjust treatment accorded Negro travelers on land and sea by the agents and employe[e]s of railroad and steamship companies, and insist that for equal fare we receive equal privileges with travelers of other races.

34. We declare it unjust for any country, State or nation to enact laws tending to hinder and obstruct the free immigration of Negroes on account of their race and color.

35. That the right of the Negro to travel unmolested throughout the world be not abridged by any person or persons, and all Negroes are called upon to give aid to a fellow Negro when thus molested.

36. We declare that all Negroes are entitled to the same right to travel over the world as other men.

37. We hereby demand that the governments of the world recognize our leader and his representatives chosen by the race to look after the welfare of our people under such governments.

38. We demand complete control of our social institutions without interference by any alien race or races.

39. That the colors, Red, Black and Green, be the colors of the Negro race.

40. Resolved, That the anthem "Ethiopia, Thou Land of Our Fathers etc.," shall be the anthem of the Negro race. (Copy anthem appended.)

QUESTIONS TO CONSIDER

1. What did the Declaration focus on especially?
2. What do you make of Pan-Africanism and the "Back to Africa" movement? Does it make sense to you as a strategy?

21.3 CLARENCE DARROW INTERROGATING WILLIAM JENNINGS BRYAN IN THE SCOPES MONKEY TRIAL (1925)

In 1925, the small town of Dayton, Tennessee, became the center of a national cultural controversy. A substitute high school teacher, John T. Scopes, was on trial for violating a Tennessee law that forbade the teaching of evolution in public schools. The initial case grew into a major, well-publicized event with the addition of two prominent lawyers: William Jennings Bryan for the prosecution and Clarence Darrow for the defense. Three decades previously, Bryan, a populist and religious fundamentalist, had given one of the most famous speeches in American history: "The Cross of Gold" (see Chapter 18, Reading 18.3). Darrow, a religious modernist, had gained acclaim for his high-profile defense work in a variety of civil liberties cases. In 1924, Darrow completed a twelve-hour closing argument in a successful attempt to save Nathan Leopold, Jr., and Richard Loeb, who had killed a boy in their neighborhood, from the death penalty. In Dayton, Darrow took up Scopes' defense, and in a surprise move on the seventh day of the trial, Darrow called Bryan, whom Darrow termed "a Bible expert," to the stand. Over the next two hours, the two men battled over the particulars of the Bible in a display of knowledge and wits that came to define the trial. Here, you will read an excerpt from Bryan's testimony. Prosecuting attorney Tom Stewart and defense attorney Arthur Hays also appear briefly. A jury eventually convicted Scopes and fined him $100, but in the years to come, fundamentalism increasingly took a lesser role in American cultural life.

BRYAN GOES ON WITNESS STAND.

Examination of W. J. Bryan by Clarence Darrow, of counsel for the defense:

Q—You have given considerable study to the Bible, haven't you, Mr. Bryan?

A—Yes, sir, I have tried to.

Q—Well, we all know you have, we are not going to dispute that at all. But you have written and published articles almost weekly, and sometimes have made interpretations of various things?

A—I would not say interpretations, Mr. Darrow, but comments on the lesson.

Q—If you comment to any extent these comments have been interpretations.

A—I presume that my discussion might be to some extent interpretations, but they have not been primarily intended as interpretations.

Q—But you have studied that question, of course?

A—Of what?

Q—Interpretation of the Bible.

A—On this particular question?

Q—Yes, sir.

A—Yes, sir.

Q—Then you have made a general study of it?

A—Yes, I have; I have studied the Bible for about fifty years, or sometime more than that, but of course, I have studied it more as I have become older than when I was but a boy.

Source: The World's Most Famous Court Trial: Tennessee Evolution Case (Cincinnati, OH: National Book Company, 1925), 264–304. Retrieved from *The Clarence Darrow Digital Collection,* http://moses.law.umn.edu/darrow/trials.php?tid=7 (Accessed June 12, 2018).

Q—Do you claim that everything in the Bible should be literally interpreted?

A—I believe everything in the Bible should be accepted as it is given illustratively. For instance: "Ye are the salt of the earth." I would not insist that man was actually salt, or that he had flesh of salt, but it is used in the sense of salt as saving God's people.

DID JONAH SWALLOW THE WHALE?

Q—But when you read that Jonah swallowed the whale—or that the whale swallowed Jonah—excuse me please—how do you literally interpret that?

A—When I read that a big fish swallowed Jonah—it does not say whale.

Q—Doesn't it? Are you sure?

A—That is my recollection of it. A big fish, and I believe it, and I believe in a God who can make a whale and can make a man and make both do what He pleases.

Q—Mr. Bryan, doesn't the New Testament say whale?

A—I am not sure. My impression is that it says fish; but it does not make so much difference; I merely called your attention to where it says fish—it does not say whale.

Q—But in the New Testament it says whale, doesn't it?

A—That may be true; I cannot remember in my own mind what I read about it.

Q—Now, you say, the big fish swallowed Jonah, and be there remained how long—three days—and then be spewed him upon the land. You believe that the big fish was made to swallow Jonah?

A—I am not prepared to say that; the Bible merely says it was done.

Q—You don't know whether it was the ordinary run of fish, or made for that purpose?

A—You may guess; you evolutionists guess.

Q—But when we do guess, we have a sense to guess right.

A—But do not do it often.

Q—You are not prepared to say whether that fish was made especially to swallow a man or not?

A—The Bible doesn't say, so I am not prepared to say.

Q—You don't know whether that was fixed up specially for the purpose?

A—No, the Bible doesn't say.

Q—But do you believe He made them—that He made such a fish and that it was big enough to swallow Jonah?

A—Yes, sir. Let me add: One miracle is just as easy to believe as another.

Q—It is for me.

A—It is for me.

Q—Just as hard?

A—It is hard to believe for you, but easy for me. A miracle is a thing performed beyond what man can perform. When you get beyond what man can do, you get within the realm of miracles; and it is just as easy to believe the miracle of Jonah as any other miracle in the Bible.

Q—Perfectly easy to believe that Jonah swallowed the whale?

A—If the Bible said so; the Bible doesn't make as extreme statements as evolutionists do.

Mr. Darrow—That may be question, Mr. Bryan, about some of those you have known?

A—The only thing is, you have a definition of fact that includes imagination.

Q—And you have a definition that excludes everything but imagination?

Gen. Stewart—I object to that as argumentative.

The Witness—You—

Mr. Darrow—The witness must not argue with me, either.

Q—Do you consider the story of Jonah and the whale a miracle?

A—I think it is.

DID THE SUN STAND STILL?

Q—Do you believe Joshua made the sun stand still?

A—I believe what the Bible says. I suppose you mean that the earth stood still?

Q—I don't know. I am talking about the Bible now.

A—I accept the Bible absolutely.

Q—The Bible says Joshua commanded the sun to stand still for the purpose of lengthening the day, doesn't it, and you believe it?

A—I do. . . .

WHAT ABOUT THE FLOOD?

Mr. Darrow—How long ago was the flood, Mr. Bryan?

A—Let me see Usher's calculation about it?

Mr. Darrow—Surely.

(Handing a Bible to the witness.)

A—I think this does not give it.

Q—It gives an account of Noah. Where is the one in evidence, I am quite certain it is there?

The Witness—Oh, I would put the estimate where it is, because I have no reason to vary it. But I would have to look at it to give you the exact date.

Q—I would, too. Do you remember what book the account is in?

A—Genesis.

Mr. Hays—Is that the one in evidence?

Mr. Neal—That will have it; that is King James' version.

Mr. Darrow—The one in evidence has it.

The Witness—It is given here, as 2348 years B. C.

Q—Well, 2348 years B. C. You believe that all the living things that were not contained in the ark were destroyed.

A—I think the fish may have lived.

Q—Outside of the fish?

A—I cannot say.

Q—You cannot say?

A—No, except that just as it is, I have no proof to the contrary.

Q—I am asking you whether you believe?

A—I do.

Q—That all living things outside of the fish were destroyed?

A—What I say about the fish is merely a matter of humor.

Q—I understand.

The Witness—Due to the fact a man wrote up here the other day to ask whether all the fish were destroyed, and the gentleman who received the letter told him the fish may have lived.

Q—I am referring to the fish, too?

A—I accept that, as the Bible gives it and I have never found any reason for denying, disputing, or rejecting it.

Q—Let us make it definite, 2,348 years?

A—I didn't say that. That is the time given there (indicating a Bible) but I don't pretend to say that is exact.

Q—You never figured it out, these generations, yourself?

A—No, sir; not myself.

Q—But the Bible you have offered in evidence, says 2,340, something, so that 4,200 years ago there was not a living thing on the earth, excepting the people on the ark and the animals of the ark and the fishes?

A—There have been living things before that.

Q—I mean at that time?

A—After that.

Q—Don't you know there are any number of civilizations that are traced back to more than 5,000 years?

A—I know we have people who trace things back according to the number of ciphers they have. But I am not satisfied they are accurate.

Q—You are not satisfied there is any civilization that can be traced back 5,000 years?

A—I would not want to say there is because I have no evidence of it that is satisfactory.

Q—Would you say there is not?

SCIENTISTS WILL HAVE TO GET CLOSER.

A—Well, so far as I know, but when the scientists differ, from 24,000,000 to 306,000,000 in their opinion, as to how long ago life came here, I want them nearer, to come nearer together before they demand of me to give up my belief in the Bible.

Q—Do you say that you do not believe that there were any civilizations on this earth that reach back beyond 5,000 years?

A—I am not satisfied by any evidence that I have seen. . . .

DARROW RELENTLESS ON QUESTION OF YEARS.

Q—You believe that all the various human races on the earth have come into being in the last 4,000 years or 4,200 years, whatever it is?

A—No, it would be more than that.

Q—1927?

A—Some time after creation, before the flood.

Q—1,927 added to it?

A—The flood is 2,300 and something, and creation, according to the estimate there, is further back than that.

Q—Then you don't understand me. If we don't get together on it, look at the book. This is the year of grace 1925, isn't it? Let us put down 1,925. Have you a pencil?

(One of the defense attorneys hands Mr. Darrow a pencil.)

The Witness—Add to that 4,004?

Mr. Darrow—Yes.

A—That is the date (referring to the Bible) given here on the first page, according to Bishop Usher, which I say I only accept because I have no reason to doubt it. In that page he gives it.

Q—1,925 plus 4,004 is 5,929 years. If a fallible person is right in his addition. Now, then, what do you subtract from that?

A—That is the beginning.

Q—I was talking about the flood.

A—2,348 on that, we said.

Q—Less than that?

A—No; subtract that from 4,000; it would be about 1,700 years?

Q—That is the same thing?

A—No; subtracted it is 2,300 and something before the beginning of the Christian era, about 1,700 years after the creation.

The Policeman—Let us have order.

Mr. Darrow—If I add 2,300 years, that is the beginning of the Christian era?

A—Yes, sir.

Q—That makes 4,262 years. If it is not correct, we can correct it.

A—According to the Bible there was a civilization before that, destroyed by the flood.

Q—Let me make this definite. You believe that every civilization on the earth and every living thing, except possibly the fishes, that came out of the ark were wiped out by the flood?

A—At that time.

Q—At that time. And then, whatever human beings, including all the tribes, that inhabited the world, and have inhabited the world, and who run their pedigree straight back, and all the animals, have come onto the earth since the flood?

A—Yes.

Q—Within 4,200 years. Do you know a scientific man on the face of the earth that believes any such thing?

A—I cannot say, but I know some scientific men who dispute entirely the antiquity of man as testified to by other scientific men.

Q—Oh, that does not answer the question. Do you know of a single scientific man on the face of the earth that believes any such thing as you stated, about the antiquity of man?

A—I don't think I have ever asked one the direct question.

Q—Quite important, isn't it?

A—Well, I don't know as it is.

Q—It might not be?

NO INTEREST IN REMOTE ANCESTORS.

A—If I had nothing else to do except speculate on what our remote ancestors were and what our remote descendants have been, but I have been more interested in Christians going on right now, to make it much more important than speculation on either the past or the future.

Q—You have never had any interest in the age of the various races and people and civilization and animals that exist upon the earth today? Is that right?

A—I have never felt a great deal of interest in the effort that has been made to dispute the Bible by the speculations of men, or the investigations of men.

Q—Are you the only human being on earth who knows what the Bible means?

Gen. Stewart—I object.

The Court—Sustained.

To which ruling of the court counsel for the defendant duly excepted.

Mr. Darrow—You do know that there are thousands of people who profess to be Christians who believe the earth is much more ancient and that the human race is much more ancient?

A—I think there may be.

Q—And you never have investigated to find out how long man has been on the earth?

A—I have never found it necessary.

Q—For any reason, whatever it is?

A—To examine every speculation; but if I had done it I never would have done anything else.

Q—I ask for a direct answer?

A—I do not expect to find out all those things, and I do not expect to find out about races.

Q—I didn't ask you that. Now, I ask you if you know if it was interesting enough, or important enough for you to try to find out about how old these ancient civilizations were?

A—No; I have not made a study of it.

Q—Don't you know that the ancient civilizations of China are 6,000 or 7,000 years old, at the very least?

A—No; but they would not run back beyond the creation, according to the Bible, 6,000 years.

Q—You don't know how old they are, is that right?

A—I don't know how old they are, but probably you do. (Laughter in the courtyard.) I think you would give the preference to anybody who opposed the Bible, and I give the preference to the Bible. . . .

NEVER INTERESTED IN PRIMITIVE PEOPLES.

Q—You have never in all your life made any attempt to find out about the other peoples of the earth—how old their civilizations are—how long they had existed on the earth, have you?

A—No, sir, I have been so well satisfied with the Christian religion that I have spent no time trying to find arguments against it.

Q—Were you afraid you might find some?

A—No, sir, I am not afraid now that you will show me any.

Q—You remember that man who said—I am not quoting literally—that one could not be content though he rose from the dead—you suppose you could be content?

A—Well, will you give the rest of it, Mr. Darrow?

Q—No.

A—Why not?

Q—I am not interested.

A—Why scrap the Bible—"they have Moses and the prophets"?

Q—Who has?

A—That is the rest of the quotation you didn't finish.

Q—And so you think if they have Moses and the prophets they don't need to find out anything else?

A—That was the answer that was made there.

Q—And you follow the same rule?

"ALL THE INFORMATION I NEED."

A—I have all the information I want to live by and to die by.

Q—And that's all you are interested in?

A—I am not looking for any more on religion.

Q—You don't care how old the earth is, how old man is and how long the animals have been here?

A—I am not so much interested in that.

Q—You have never made any investigation to find out?

A—No, sir, I have never. . . .

TOWER OF BABEL.

Q—You have heard of the Tower of Babel[,] haven't you?

A—Yes, sir.

Q—That tower was built under the ambition that they could build a tower up to heaven, wasn't it? And God saw what they were at and to prevent their getting into heaven he confused their tongues?

A—Something like that, I wouldn't say to prevent their getting into heaven. I don't think it is necessary to believe that God was afraid they would get to heaven—

Q—I mean that way?

A—I think it was a rebuke to them.

Q—A rebuke to them trying to go that way?

A—To build that tower for that purpose.

Q—Take that short cut?

A—That is your language, not mine.

Q—Now when was that?

A—Give us the Bible.

Q—Yes, we will have strict authority on it—scientific authority?

A—That was about 100 years before the flood, Mr. Darrow, according to this chronology. It is 2247—the date on one page is 2218 and on the other 2247 and it is described in here—

Q—That is the year 2247?

A—2218 B. C. is at the top of one page and 2247 at the other and there is nothing in here to indicate the change.

Q—Well, make it 2230 then?

A—All right, about.

Q—Then you add 1500 to that—

A—No, 1925.

Q—Add 1925 to that, that would be 4,155 years ago. Up to 4,155 years ago every human being on earth spoke the same language?

A—Yes, sir, I think that is the inference that could be drawn from that.

Q—All the different languages of the earth, dating from the Tower of Babel, is that right? Do you know how many languages are spoken on the face of the earth.

A—No, I know the Bible has been translated into 500 and no other book has been translated into anything like that many.

Q—That is interesting, if true? Do you know all the languages there are?

A—No, sir, I can't tell you. There may be many dialects besides that and some languages, but those are all the principal languages.

Q—There are a great many that are not principal languages?

A—Yes, sir.

Q—You haven't any idea how many there are?

A—No, sir.

Q—How many people have spoken all those various languages?

A—No, sir.

Q—And you say that all those languages of all the sons of men have come on the earth not over 4,150 years ago?

A—I have seen no evidence that would lead me to put it any further back than that.

Q—That is your belief anyway—that that was due to the confusion of tongues at the tower of Babel. Did you ever study philology at all?

A—No, I have never made a study of it—not in the sense in which you speak of it.

Q—You have used language all your life?

A—Well, hardly all my life—ever since I was about a year old.

Q—And good language, too, and you have never taken any pains to find anything about the origin of languages?

A—I have never studied it as science.

Q—Have you ever by any chance read Max Mueller?

A—No.

Q—The great German philologist?

A—No.

Q—Or any book on that subject?

A—I don't remember to have read a book on that subject, especially, but I have read extracts, of course, and articles on philology.

HOW OLD IS EARTH?

Q—Mr. Bryan, could you tell me how old the earth is?

A—No, sir, I couldn't

Q—Could you come anywhere near it?

A—I wouldn't attempt to. I could possibly come as near as the scientists do, but I had rather be more accurate before I give a guess.

Q—You don't think much of scientists, do you?

A—Yes, sir, I do, sir.

Q—Is there any scientists in the world you think much of?

A—I do.

Q—Who?

A—Well, I think the bulk of the scientists—

Q—I don't want that kind of an answer, Mr. Bryan, who are they?

A—I will give you George M. Price, for instance.

Q—Who is he?

A—Professor of geology in a college.

Q—Where?

A—He was out near Lincoln, Neb.

Q—How close to Lincoln[,] Neb.?

A—About three or four miles. He is now in a college out in California.

Q—Where is the college?

A—At Lodi.

Q—That is a small college?

A—I didn't know you had to judge a man by the size of the college—I thought you judged him by the size of the man.

Q—I thought the size of the college made some difference?

A—It might raise a presumption in the minds of some, but I think I would rather find out what be believed.

Q—You would rather find out whether his belief corresponds with your views or prejudices or whatever they are before you said how good he was?

A—Well, you know the word "prejudice" is—

Q—Well, I don't know?

A—Well, I don't know either, it is my guess.

Q—You mentioned Price because he is the only human being in the world so far as you know that signs his name as a geologist that believes like you do?

A—No, there is a man named Wright, who taught at Oberlin.

Q—I will get to Mr. Wright in a moment. Who publishes his book?

A—I can't tell you. I can get you the book.

Q—He publishes yours, doesn't he?

A—Yes, sir.

Gen. Stewart—Will you let me make an exception. I don't think it is pertinent about who publishes a book.

SAYS BRYAN QUOTES MONTEBANK.

Mr. Darrow—He has quoted a man that every scientist in this country knows is a mountebank and a pretender and not a geologist at all.

The Court—You can ask him about who publishes the book.

Q—Do you know anything about the college he is in?

A—No, I can't tell you.

Q—Do you know how old his book is?

A—No, sir, it a recent book.

Q—Do you know anything about his training?

A—No, I can't say on that.

Q—Do you know of any geologist on the face of the earth who ever recognized him?

A—I couldn't say.

Q—Do you think he is all right? How old does he say the earth is?

A—I am not sure that I would insist on some particular geologist that you picked out recognizing him before I would consider him worthy if he agreed with your views?

Q—You would consider him worthy if he agreed with your views?

A—Well, I think his argument is very good.

Q—How old does Mr. Price say the earth is?

A—I haven't examined the book in order to answer questions on it.

Q—Then you don't know anything about how old he says it is?

A—He speaks of the layers that are supposed to measure age and points out that they are not uniform and not always the same and that attempts to measure age by those layers where they are not in the order in which they are usually found makes it difficult to fix the exact age.

Q—Does he say anything whatever about the age of the earth?

A—I wouldn't be able to testify.

Q—You didn't get anything about the age from him?

A—Well, I know he disputes what you say and has very good evidence to dispute it—what some others say about the age.

Q—Where did you get your information about the age of the earth?

A—I am not attempting to give you information about the age of the earth.

WRIGHT OF OBERLIN?

Q—Then you say there was Mr. Wright, of Oberlin?

A—That was rather I think on the age of man than upon the age of the earth.

Q—There are two Mr. Wrights, of Oberlin?

A—I couldn't say.

Q—Both of them geologists. Do you know how long Mr. Wright says man has been on the earth?

A—Well, he gives the estimates of different people.

Q—Does he give any opinion of his own?

A—I think he does.

Q—What is it?

A—I am not sure.

Q—What is it?

A—It was based upon the last glacial age—that man has appeared since the last glacial age.

Q—Did he say there was no man on earth before the last glacial age?

A—I think he disputes the finding of any proof—where the proof is authentic—but I had rather read him than quote him. I don't like to run the risk of quoting from memory.

Q—You couldn't say then how long Mr. Wright places it?

A—I don't attempt to tell you.

Q—When was the last glacial age?

A—I wouldn't attempt to tell you that.

Q—Have you any idea?

A—I wouldn't want to fix it without looking at some of the figures.

Q—That was since the tower of Babel, wasn't it?

A—Well, I wouldn't want to fix it. I think it was before the time given in here, and that was only given as the possible appearance of man and not the actual.

Q—Have you any idea how far back the last glacial age was?

A—No, sir.

Q—Do you know whether it was more than 6,000 years ago?

A—I think it was more than 6,000 years.

Q—Have you any idea how old the earth is?

A—No.

BIBLE GIVES AGE OF EARTH?

Q—The book you have introduced in evidence tells you, doesn't it?

A—I don't think it does, Mr. Darrow.

Q—Let's see whether it does; is this the one?

A—That is the one, I think.

Q—It says B. C. 4004?

A—That is Bishop Usher's calculation.

Q—That is printed in the Bible you introduced?

A—Yes, sir.

Q—And numerous other Bibles?

A—Yes, sir.

Q—Printed in the Bible in general use in Tennessee?

A—I couldn't say.

Q—And Scofield's Bible?

A—I couldn't say about that.

Q—You have seen it somewhere else?

A—I think that is the chronology usually used.

Q—Does the Bible you have introduced for the jury's consideration say that?

A—Well, you will have to ask those who introduced that.

Q—You haven't practiced law for a long time, so I will ask you if that is the King James version that was introduced? That is your marking, and I assume it is?

A—I think that is the same one.

Mr. Darrow—There is no doubt about it, is there, gentlemen?

Mr. Stewart—That is the same one.

Q—Would you say that the earth was only 4,000 years old?

A—Oh, no; I think it is much older than that.

Q—How much?

A—I couldn't say.

Q—Do you say whether the Bible itself says it is older than that?

A—I don't think the Bible says itself whether it is older or not.

Q—Do you think the earth was made in six days?

BRYAN—"NOT SIX DAYS OF TWENTY-FOUR HOURS."

A—Not six days of twenty-four hours.

Q—Doesn't it say so?

A—No, sir.

Gen. Stewart—I want to interpose another objection. What is the purpose of this examination?

Mr. Bryan—The purpose is to cast ridicule on everybody who believes in the Bible, and I am perfectly willing that the world shall know that these gentlemen have no other purpose than ridiculing every Christian who believes in the Bible.

Mr. Darrow—We have the purpose of preventing bigots and ignoramuses from controlling the education of the United States and you know it, and that is all.

Mr. Bryan—I am glad to bring out that statement. I want the world to know that this evidence is not for the view Mr. Darrow and his associates have filed affidavits here stating, the purposes of which I understand it, is to show that the Bible story is not true.

Mr. Malone—Mr. Bryan seems anxious to get some evidence in the record that would tend to show that those affidavits are not true.

BRYAN WANTS WORLD TO KNOW HE IS NOT AFRAID.

Mr. Bryan—I am not trying to get anything into the record. I am simply trying to protect the word of God against the greatest atheist or agnostic in the United States. (Prolonged applause.) I want the papers to know I am not afraid to get on the stand in front of him and let him do his worst. I want the world to know. (Prolonged applause.)

Mr. Darrow—I wish I could get a picture of these clackers.

Gen. Stewart—I am not afraid of Mr. Bryan being perfectly able to take care of himself, but this examination cannot be a legal examination and it cannot be worth a thing in the world, and, your honor, I respectfully except to it, and call on your honor, in the name of all that is legal, to stop this examination and stop it here.

Mr. Hays—I rather sympathize with the general, but Mr. Bryan is produced as a witness because he is a student of the Bible and he presumably understands what the Bible means. He is one of the foremost students in the United States, and we hope to show Mr. Bryan, who is a student of the Bible, what the Bible really means in connection with evolution. Mr. Bryan has already stated that the world is not merely 6,000 years old and that is very helpful to us, and where your evidence is coming from, this Bible, which goes to the jury, is that the world started in 4004 B. C.

Mr. Bryan—You think the Bible says that?

Mr. Hays—The one you have taken in evidence says that.

Mr. Bryan—I don't concede that it does.

Mr. Hays—You know that that chronology is made up by adding together all of the ages of the people in the Bible, counting their ages; and now then, let us show the next stage from a Bible student, that these things are not to be taken literally, but that each man is entitled to his own interpretation.

Gen. Stewart—The court makes the interpretation.

Mr. Hays—But the court is entitled to information on what is the interpretation of an expert Bible student. . . .

BRYAN INSISTS ON BIBLE BEING QUOTED VERBATIM.

A—I believe the Bible as it is, and I do not permit you to put your language in the place of the language of the Almighty. You read that Bible and ask me questions, and I will answer them. I will not answer your questions in your language.

Q—I will read it to you from the Bible: "And the Lord God said unto the serpent, because thou hast done this, thou art cursed above all cattle, and above every beast of the field; upon thy belly shalt thou go and dust shalt thou eat all the days of thy life." Do you think that is why the serpent is compelled to crawl upon its belly?

A—I believe that.

Q—Have you any idea how the snake went before that time?

A—No, sir.

Q—Do you know whether he walked on his tail or not?

A—No, sir. I have no way to know. (Laughter in audience).

Q—Now, you refer to the cloud that was put in the heaven after the flood, the rainbow. Do you believe in that?

A—Read it.

Q—All right, Mr. Bryan, I will read it for you.

Mr. Bryan—Your honor, I think I can shorten this testimony. The only purpose Mr. Darrow has is to slur at the Bible, but I will answer his question. I will answer it all at once, and I have no objection in the world, I want the world to know that this man, who does not believe in a God, is trying to use a court in Tennessee—

Mr. Darrow—I object to that.

Mr. Bryan—(Continuing) to slur at it, and while it will require time, I am willing to take it.

Mr. Darrow—I object to your statement. I am exempting you on your fool ideas that no intelligent Christian on earth believes.

The Court—Court is adjourned until 9 o'clock tomorrow morning.

QUESTIONS TO CONSIDER

1. What was Darrow's legal strategy?
2. How does the two men's debate reveal a shift in American society?

21.4 EXCERPT FROM *THE AUTOBIOGRAPHY OF MARGARET SANGER* (1938)

Margaret Sanger (1879–1966) fought for a woman's right to have access to birth control. Born in Corning, New York, Sanger did not become a social activist until she was in her thirties and working as a nurse in a poor section of New York City. She became involved with the Industrial Workers of the World (see Chapter 19, Reading 19.4) and embraced the growing left-wing intellectual scene in the city. At the time, the Comstock Law forbade the dissemination of information about contraceptives, which led many women to try to self-induce abortions in desperation. Horrified by what she saw as a nurse, Sanger decided that giving women information about contraception was one way to uplift poorer people. In 1914, she began publishing *The Woman Rebel*, a monthly newsletter about contraception. Eventually, authorities arrested Sanger for violating the Comstock Law. In the following excerpt from her autobiography, Sanger recalls her early activism. In 1921, she founded the American Birth Control League. Later, she founded a series of birth control organizations that would eventually evolve into Planned Parenthood. She died in 1966, just one year after *Griswold v. Connecticut* legalized birth control in the United States.

I knew something must be done to rescue those women who were voiceless; someone had to express with white hot intensity the conviction that they must be empowered to decide for themselves when they should fulfill the supreme function of motherhood. They had to be made aware of how they were being shackled, and roused to mutiny. To this end I conceived the idea of a magazine to be called the *Woman Rebel*, dedicated to the interests of working women.

Often I had thought of Vashti as the first woman rebel in history. Once when her husband, King Ahasuerus, had been showing off to his people his fine linens, his pillars of marble, his beds of gold and silver, and all his riches, he had commanded that his beautiful Queen Vashti also be put on view. But she had declined to be exhibited as a possession or chattel. Because of her disobedience, which might set a very bad example to other wives, she had been cast aside and Ahasuerus had chosen a new bride, the meek and gentle Esther.

I wanted each woman to be a rebellious Vashti, not an Esther; was she to be merely a washboard with only one song, one song? Surely, she should be allowed to develop all her potentialities. Feminists were trying to free her from the new economic ideology but were doing nothing to free her from her biological subservience to man, which was the true cause of her enslavement.

Before gathering friends around me for that help which I must have in stirring women to sedition, before asking them to believe, I had to chart my own course. Should I bring the cause to the attention of the people by headlines and front pages? Should I follow my own compulsion regardless of extreme consequences?

I fully recognized I must refrain from acts which I could not carry through. So many movements had been issuing defiances without any ultimate goal, shooting off a popgun here, a popgun there, and finally shooting themselves to death. They had been too greatly resembling froth—too noisy with the screech of

Source: Margaret Sanger, *The Autobiography of Margaret Sanger* (New York: W. W. Norton, 1938). Retrieved from the Internet Archive website, https://archive.org/stream/margaretsangerau1938sang/margaretsangerau1938sang_djvu.txt. Reprinted here with permission of Alexander Sanger.

tin horns and other cheap instruments instead of the deeper sounds of an outraged, angry, serious people.

With as crystal a view as that which had come to me after the death of Mrs. Sachs when I had renounced nursing forever. I saw the path ahead in its civic, national, and even international direction—a panorama of things to be. Fired with this vision, I went into the lounge and wrote and wrote page after page until the hours of daylight.

Having settled the principles, I left the details to work themselves out. I realized that a price must be paid for honest thinking—a price for everything. Though I did not know exactly how I was to prepare myself, what turn events might take, or what I might be called upon to do, the future in its larger aspects has actually developed as I saw it that night.

The same thoughts kept repeating themselves over and over during the remainder of the otherwise uneventful voyage. As soon as possible after reaching New York, I rented an inexpensive little flat on Post Avenue near Dyckman Street, so far out on the upper end of Manhattan that even the Broadway subway trains managed to burrow their way into sunlight and fresh air. My dining room was my office, the table my desk.

A new movement was starting, and the baby had to have a name. It did not belong to Socialism nor was it in the labor field, and it had much more to it than just the prevention of conception. As a few companions were sitting with me one evening we debated in turn voluntary parenthood, voluntary motherhood, the new motherhood, constructive generation, and new generation. The terms already in use—Neo-Malthusianism, Family Limitation, and Conscious Generation seemed stuffy and lacked popular appeal.

The word control was good, but I did not like limitation—that was too limiting. I was not advocating a one-child or two-child system as in France, nor did I wholeheartedly agree with the English Neo-Malthusians whose concern was almost entirely with limitation for economic reasons. My idea of control was bigger and freer. I wanted family in it, yet family control did not sound right. We tried population control, race control, and birth rate control. Then someone suggested, "Drop the rate." Birth control was the answer; we knew we had it. Our work for that day was done and everybody picked up his hat and went home. The baby was named.

When I first announced that I was going to publish a magazine, "Where are you going to get the money?" was volleyed at me from all sides. I did not know, but I was certain of its coming somehow. Equally important was moral support. Those same young friends and I founded a little society, grandly titled the National Birth Control League, sought aid from enthusiasts for other causes, turning first to the Feminists because they seemed our natural allies. Armed with leaflets we went to Cooper Union to tell them that in the *Woman Rebel* they would have an opportunity to express their sentiments.

Charlotte Perkins Gilman, the Feminist leader, was trying to inspire women in this country to have a deeper meaning in their lives, which to her signified more than getting the vote. Nevertheless, at that time I struck no responsive chord from her or from such intelligent co-workers as Crystal Eastman, Marie Howe, or Henrietta Rodman. It seemed unbelievable they could be serious in occupying themselves with what I regarded as trivialities when mothers within a stone's throw of their meetings were dying shocking deaths.

Who cared whether a woman kept her Christian name—Mary Smith instead of Mrs. John Jones? Who cared whether she wore her wedding ring? Who cared about her demand for the right to work? Hundreds of thousands of laundresses, cloakmakers, scrub women, servants, telephone girls, shop workers would gladly have changed places with the Feminists in return for the right to have leisure, to be lazy a little now and then. When I suggested that the basis of Feminism might be the right to be a mother regardless of church or state, their inherited prejudices were instantly aroused. They were still subject to the age-old, masculine atmosphere compounded of protection and dominance.

Disappointed in that quarter I turned to the Socialists and trade unionists, trusting they would appreciate the importance of family limitation in the kind of civilization towards which they were stumbling. Notices were sent to *The Masses, Mother Earth, The Call, The Arm and Hammer, The Liberator,* all names echoing the spirit which had quickened them.

Shortly I had several hundred subscriptions to the *Woman Rebel,* paid up in advance at the rate of a dollar a year, the period for which I had made my plans. Proceeds were to go into a separate revolving account, scrupulously kept. Unlike so many ephemeral periodicals, mine was not to flare up and spark out before it had functioned, leaving its subscribers with only a few issues when they were entitled to more. Eventually we had a mailing list of about two thousand, but five, ten, even fifty copies often went in a bundle to be distributed without charge to some labor organization.

I was solely responsible for the magazine financially, legally, and morally; I was editor, manager, circulation department, bookkeeper, and I paid the printer's bill. But any cause that has not helpers is losing out. So many men and women secretaries, stenographers, clerks, used to come in of an evening that I could not find room for all. Some typed, some addressed envelopes, some went to libraries and looked up things for us to use, some wrote articles, though seldom signing their own names. Not one penny ever had to go for salaries, because service was given freely.

In March, 1914, appeared the first issue of the *Woman Rebel*, eight pages on cheap paper, copied from the French style, mailed first class in the city and expressed outside. My initial declaration of the right of the individual was the slogan "No Gods, No Masters." Gods, not God. I wanted that word to go beyond religion and also stop turning idols, heroes, leaders into gods.

I defined a woman's duty, "To look the world in the face with a go-to-hell look in the eyes; to have an idea; to speak and act in defiance of convention." It was a marvelous time to say what we wished. All America was a Hyde Park corner as far as criticism and challenging thought were concerned. We advocated direct action and took up the burning questions of the day. With a fine sense of irony we put anti-capitalist soapbox oratory in print. I do not know whether the financiers we denounced would have been tolerant or resentful of our onslaughts had they read them, or as full of passion for their cause as we for ours. Perhaps they too will have forgotten that emotion now.

My daily routine always started with looking over the pile of mail, and one morning my attention was caught by an unstamped official envelope from the New York Post Office. I tore it open.

Dear Madam, You are hereby notified that the Solicitor of the Post Office Department has decided that the *Woman Rebel* for March, 1914, is unmailable under Section 489, Postal Laws and Regulations.

E. M. Morgan, Postmaster.

I reread the letter. It was so unexpected that at first the significance did not sink in. I had given no contraceptive information; I had merely announced that I intended to do so. Then I began to realize that no mention was made of any special article or articles. I wrote Mr. Morgan and asked him to state what specifically had offended, thereby assisting me in my future course. His reply simply repeated that the March issue was unmailable.

I had anticipated objections from religious bodies, but believed with father, "Anything you want can be accomplished by putting a little piece of paper into the ballot box." Therefore, to have our insignificant magazine stopped by the big, strong United States Government seemed so ludicrous as almost to make us feel Important.

To the newspaper world this was news, but not one of the dailies picked it out as an infringement of a free press. The *Sun* carried a headline, "'WOMAN REBEL' BARRED FROM MAILS." And underneath the comment, "Too bad. The case should be reversed. They should be barred from her and spelled differently."

Many times I studied Section 211 of the Federal Statutes, under which the Post Office was acting. This penal clause of the Comstock Law had been left hanging in Washington like the dried shell of a tortoise. Its grip had even been tightened on the moral side; in case the word obscene should prove too vague, its definition had been enlarged to include the prevention of conception and the causing of abortion under one and the same heading. To me it was outrageous that information regarding motherhood, which was so generally called sacred, should be classed with pornography.

Nevertheless, I had not broken the law, because it did not prohibit discussion of contraception—merely giving advice. I harbored a burning desire to undermine that law. But if I continued publication I was making myself liable to a Federal indictment and a possible prison term of five years plus a fine of five thousand dollars. I had to choose between abandoning the *Woman Rebel*, changing its tone, or continuing as I had begun. Though I had no wish to become a martyr, with no hesitation I followed the last-named course.

I gathered our little group together. At first we assumed Comstock had stopped the entire issue before delivery, but apparently he had not, because only the A to M's which had been mailed in the local post office had been confiscated. We took a fresh lot downtown, slipped three into one chute, four in another, walked miles around the city so that no single box contained more than a few copies.

The same procedure had to be pursued in succeeding months. Sometimes daylight caught me, with one or more assistants, still tramping from the printer's and dropping the copies, piece by piece, into various boxes and chutes. I felt the Government was absurd and tyrannical to make us do this for no good purpose. I could not get used to its methods then. I have not yet, and probably never shall.

The *Woman Rebel* produced extraordinary results, striking vibrations that brought contacts, messages, inquiries, pamphlets, books, even some money. I corresponded with the leading Feminists of Europe—Ellen Key, then at the height of her fame, Olive Schreiner, Mrs. Pankhurst, Rosa Luxemburg, Adele Schreiber, Clara Zetkin, Roszika Schwimmer, Frau Maria Stritt. But I also heard from sources and groups I had hardly known existed—Theosophist, New Thought, Rosicrucian, Spiritualist, Mental Scientist. It was not alone from New York, but from the highways and byways of north, south, east, and west that inspiration came.

After the second number the focus had been birth control. Within six months we had received over ten thousand letters, arriving in accelerating volume. Most of them read, "Will your magazine give accurate and reliable information to prevent conception?" This I could not print. Realizing by now it was going to be a fairly big fight, I was careful not to break the law on such a trivial point. It would have been ridiculous to have a single letter reach the wrong destination; therefore, I sent no contraceptive facts through the mails.

However, I had no intention of giving up this primary purpose. I began sorting and arranging the material I had brought back from France, complete with formulas and drawings, to be issued in a pamphlet where I could treat the subject with more delicacy that in a magazine, writing it for women of extremely circumscribed vocabularies. A few hundred dollars were needed to finance publication of *Family Limitation,* as I named it, and I approached Theodore Schroeder, a lawyer of standing and an ardent advocate of free speech. He had been left a fund by a certain. Dr. Foote who had produced a book on *Borning Better Babies,* and I thought my pamphlet might qualify as a beneficiary.

Dr. Abraham Brill was just then bringing out a translation of Freud, in whom Schroeder was much interested. He asked whether I had been psychoanalyzed.

"What is psychoanalysis?"

He looked at me critically as from a great height. "You ought to be analyzed as to your motives. If, after six weeks, you still wish to publish this pamphlet, I'll pay for ten thousand copies."

"Well, do you think I won't want to go on?"

"I don't only think so. I'm quite sure of it."

"Then I won't be analyzed."

I took the manuscript to a printer well known for his liberal tendencies and courage. He read the contents page by page and said, "You'll never get this set up in any shop in New York. It's a Sing Sing job."

Every one of the twenty printers whom I tried to persuade was afraid to touch it. It was impossible ever, it seemed, to get into print the contents of that pamphlet.

Meanwhile, following the March issue the May and July numbers of the *Woman Rebel* had also been banned. In reply to each of the formal notices I inquired which particular article or articles had incurred disapproval, but could obtain no answer.

At that time I visualized the birth control movement as part of the fight for freedom of speech. How much would the postal authorities suppress? What were they really after? I was determined to prod and goad until some definite knowledge was obtained as to what was "obscene, lewd, and lascivious."

Theodore Schroeder and I used to meet once in a while at the Liberal Club, and he gave much sound advice—I could not go on with the *Woman Rebel* forever. Eventually the Post Office would wear me down by stopping the issues as fast as I printed them. He warned, "They won't do so and so unless you do thus and thus. If you do such and such, then you'll have to take the consequences." He was a good lawyer and an authority on the Constitution.

When my family learned that I might be getting in deep water a council was called just as when I had been a child. A verdict of nervous breakdown was openly decreed, but back in the minds of all was the unspoken dread that I must have become mentally unbalanced. They insisted father come to New York, where he had not been for forty years, to persuade me to go to a sanitarium.

For several days father and I talked over the contents of the *Woman Rebel*. In his fine, flowing language he expressed his hatred of it. He despised talk about revolution, and despaired of anyone who could discuss sex, blaming this on my nursing training, which, he intimated, had put me in possession of all the known secrets of the human body. He was not quite sure what birth control was, and my reasoning, which retraced the pattern of our old arguments, made no impression upon him.

Father would have nothing to do with the "queer people" who came to the house—people of whom no one had ever heard—turning up with articles on every possible subject and defying me to publish them in the name of free speech. I printed everything. For the August issue I accepted a philosophical essay on the theory of assassination, largely derived from Richard Carlile. It was vague, inane, and innocuous, and had no bearing on my policy except to taunt to Government to take action, because assassination also was included under Section 211.

Only a few weeks earlier, the war which Victor Dave had predicted had started its headlong progress. They very moment when most people were busy with geographies and atlases, trying to find out just where Sarajevo might be, the United States chose to sever diplomatic relations with me.

One morning I was startled by the peremptory, imperious, and incessant ringing of my bell. When I opened the door, I was confronted by two gentlemen.

"Will you come in?"

They followed me into my living room, scrutinized with amazement the velocipede and wagon, the woolly animals and toys stacked in the corner. One of them asked, "Are you the editor and publisher of a magazine entitled the *Woman Rebel?*"

When I confessed to it, he thrust a legal document into my hands. I tried to read it, threading my way slowly through the jungle of legal terminology. Perhaps the words became a bit blurred because of the slight trembling of my hands, but I managed to disentangle the crucial point of the message. I had been indicted—indicted on no less than nine counts—for alleged violation of the Federal Statutes. If found guilty on all, I might be liable to forty-five years in the penitentiary.

I looked at the two agents of the Department of Justice. They seemed nice and sensible. I invited them to sit down and started in to explain birth control. For three hours I presented to their imaginations some of the tragic stories of conscript motherhood. I forget now what I said, but at the end they agreed that such a law should not be on the statute books. Yet it was, and there was nothing to do about it but bring my case to court.

QUESTIONS TO CONSIDER

1. How did Sanger portray her work?
2. What can you glean about the time from Sanger's words?

21.5 MARGARET ONERHEIM, EXCERPT FROM *THREADS OF MEMORY* (1993)

Though the United States changed a great deal in the early twentieth century, life in rural America did not always change so fast. Many Americans still lived in rural locations. Of the 106 million Americans listed in the 1920 Census, for instance, the government identified around 50 million as "Rural Population" and about 30 million as "Farm Population." Margaret Onerheim fit the latter category. Born on a small farm in rural Iowa, Onerheim witnessed firsthand how America was changing. Her memoir *Threads of Memory,* from which the following document is excerpted, illustrates a divide between farm communities and town communities and the way in which such a divide affected Onerheim as a child.

MOVING IN

In the late winter of 1921, when I was three-and-a-half, my family moved to the farm of George Beal, my mother's paternal grandfather. I was somewhat prepared for the move because the week before, Mama, my eight-month-old brother Robert, and I had gone to call on Mama's cousin's wife, Mrs. Ralph Beal, in the house into which we would be moving. It seemed to be a social call, but I noticed that Mama looked speculatively around the rooms. On the way home she talked about the house, as much to herself as to me: "My little desk will fit in the northeast corner of the kitchen. I think my curtains will fit in the front room all right." The only other memory I have of the visit is seeing a child's potty chair in the ditch south of the driveway.

On moving day the air blew in cold as the friends who were helping us carried our furniture out of the house. In spite of a roaring fire Mama kept going in the kitchen stove, the house became chilled. The house got more and more empty, and I could see out the window that men were driving our livestock north toward the new place. I was excited, running from room to room and getting in Mama's way as she cleaned the house for the family who would be moving in. My brother,

Harry, a year older than I, was in and out of the house all day, keeping us abreast of the progress of the outside moving and chattering, "I helped Mr. Dailey move the tools in the machine shed, and it was a big job. I'm going to move to the new place with Pa when he drives the car there. When are you going to move, Mama?"

In late afternoon Mama, Robert, and I rode in the bed of the hayrack with the last load of furniture. The wheels of the wagons that had been going back and forth all day moving our belongings had cut ruts into the ice and dirty snow of the road, and the bright sun had caused some melting, making it sloppy underfoot. Mama sat in the back of the hayrack, her feet dangling over the end of the rack, holding her well-wrapped cut glass creamer and sugar bowl in her lap and keeping an eye on the basket packed with her other most-prized dishes, ready to reach out a hand and steady them if they seemed in danger of being jiggled too much.

Robert, a solemn little fellow, was swathed in blankets and propped up in our oval wicker clothes basket. His eyes darted from one to the other of us and to his surroundings as he struggled to free his arms. I made funny faces for him and pulled off my mittens to make finger pictures with my hands, but he was puckering

Source: Margaret Ott Onerheim, *Threads of Memory: A Memoir of the 1920s* (Ames: Iowa State University Press, 1993), 3–6, 96–113.

up to cry as the short trip ended. I looked to see, but the potty chair was gone from the ditch.

Although the trip was less than a quarter of a mile north, we moved from Butler County to Floyd County, Iowa. It was also a landmark move for Mama, from the house where she (and I) had been born, and where she had lived most of her life. She had told me stories of visiting her grandpa and her aunts and uncles many times in the house we now were moving into. From overhearing conversations with Papa, I understood that she didn't look forward to living in an older and less convenient house.

"Maybe we can make a few changes after we've lived there awhile," Pa consoled her.

One day before the move, while we were eating supper, Mama said, "I don't know if this stove is worth moving. See how uneven it baked this bread? Burned on one side and nearly raw on the other."

"If we need a new one, this would be a good time to get it," answered Pa. "What would a new one cost? A good one—it's no use buying anything but the best."

Mama had her answer ready. She brought out the Montgomery Ward catalog and opened it to the page she had marked.

"Go ahead and order it, if you're sure it's the one you want," Pa said, after he had read the description and looked at the picture. "We'll have it delivered the day we move."

Mama and I saw it for the first time burning brightly when we came into the house on moving day. It was called a "Copper Clad," and it had handsome chrome trim to brighten up the black iron top and sides. She just stood there and looked at it, and I did, too. I liked to act like Mama.

"Well, Dorothy, how does it suit you?" Pa asked her when he came in.

"I'll have no more excuse for burnt bread. Oh, Paul, it's so pretty. I'll always keep it looking nice like this."

I wove my way around the boxes and baskets packed full of things, in and out of the downstairs rooms. These rooms radiated from the kitchen like spokes from the hub of a wheel, an arrangement that fascinates me to this day.

Most of the kitchen things has been hastily unpacked, but one thing was missing. The little gray velveteen bear Grandpa Freem Beal had sent me for Christmas from California was not on the desk where it belonged. Mama assured me that it was packed away somewhere and that it would turn up.

We sat down to eat the meal that had been brought to us by friends who knew Mama would be tired after the busy day. Mama, Papa, Harry, and Robert were here with me, and I was content. . . .

YOU DON'T BELONG

One June evening Mama sat perusing our local paper, *The Recorder*. "I see there's going to be a celebration in town on Friday. They're going to have riders brought in, and exhibits showing all kinds of new things."

"Something else to separate us from our money, no doubt," Papa joked.

On the day of the celebration, Papa mentioned it at breakfast: "Do you want to go to the doings in town, Dorothy?"

"Oh, yes, let's do," Mama answered quickly. "The kids will enjoy the rides, and I'd like to see the exhibits. Helen says they're going, and Ellen. Others, too."

"I have hay down, but maybe it can wait. I'll come in early for dinner, and we'll see how the weather looks then."

When dinner time came, the urgency of haying was pushed back as the cloudless day promised good weather. Papa said we could go to town. We joined the throngs of people walking up and down the blocked-off main street, looking at exhibits and greeting friends.

The lilting music of the merry-go-round, its twinkling lights and horses in colors that never were, beckoned. Mama gave me a nickel to buy a ticket, and I hurried to climb on a gilt-trimmed blue horse with eager painted eyes and flaring nostrils. The frightening lurch as we started made me grab the shiny pole to which my horse was attached. After a few turns I could survey the crowds and wave to Dale in his baby buggy. I clucked my tongue and slapped the leather reins as if to urge on my horse to even greater speed. When the ride ended, I laughed because my legs didn't work right for a few steps.

Next we went into the big tent set up in the street between Buchholz's and Pooley's. On the sawdust-covered floor of the tent were groups of tables, forming booths for advertising and for selling things. I soon grew tired of looking in the murky light at roofing samples, bake sales, and needle work items being sold by the Ladies' Aid. Mama, who was talking to Genie Downs, said I could wander around by myself. It was safe enough, and I was so keyed up with excitement that I didn't feel the need to cling to an adult. I saw a group of girls, who seemed to be about my age, standing behind some tables in the corner. It looked like fun to stand there so importantly, chattering with each other and handing out papers to passersby. Still in my buoyant state, I walked behind the table and stood, too. At once two girls came over to me and scolded, "You can't stand here! You don't belong!"

Crestfallen, deflated, I walked away, deciding never to be so bold again. I couldn't help wondering why these girls, who seemed so much like me, belonged and I didn't. My fun was spoiled, and I stayed close to Mama for the rest of that colorless afternoon.

Several years later a promoter came to Greene and directed a big performance of variety acts by local people. By that time I knew several town girls from Sunday School. A group of them were chosen to do the "Highland Fling." No doubt they were chosen from town school classrooms, whereas I wasn't chosen because I went to country school. At various times the girls showed me the steps they were learning, hopping on one foot with the other foot bent at the knee, gracefully moving in different positions. It did look like such fun. I wondered if I could have learned to do the dance if I had been chosen. I thought I could have, but a lingering doubt remained that maybe I wasn't good enough to be chosen.

I often heard girls I knew at Sunday School talking about going to meetings of a church group they belonged to. I think they were "Mother's Jewels" and, when they were older, "King's Daughters." Occasionally someone would ask me if I were going to the meeting, as if it were a very ordinary question. I was embarrassed at not even knowing what they were talking about.

Eventually I was asked to attend. At the meeting I knew all the girls at least slightly, but they seemed like strangers as they played out their roles—taking part in the business meeting, discussing the religious lesson, handing around refreshments—in this setting so new

to me. They all knew what was expected of them, while I sat ill at ease, worrying that I might do the wrong thing or not do the right thing.

Because I wasn't asked again, I assumed I hadn't "made the grade," that I didn't belong. I wanted to be a part of the group but wouldn't risk embarrassment by asking about it. Maybe Mama sensed my ambivalent feelings and thought my hesitancy meant I didn't want to go. As an adult, I understand that girls my age were not only welcome to go but really were needed to perform the little missionary efforts of the group.

One summer every town girl (or so it seemed to me) wore strap sandals with buckles that slid over and hid the button fastener. The shoe clerk had shown them to me, saying, "These are the shoes all the girls are wearing this summer."

I tried them on, but my toes bumped against the ends of the shoes and hurt. As always when I bought shoes, the clerk said, "Oh, these are big enough. See how much room there is?"

The trouble was, they were too wide and too short, and I'd suffered through this poor fit too often before. He showed me some sandals with ribbon bows like a dancer's shoes. They felt much better, and I thought they were prettier. They were my choice.

The first time I wore them to Sunday School, I discovered that the clerk had been right. All the other girls were wearing the button style. They were a group belonging together, and once more I was the one who didn't fit in. I imagined that they looked at me with disdain, though not one girl ever mentioned that my feet weren't in step with the style that summer.

COUNTRY SCHOOL

Pleasant Grove #8 was the name of the rural school I attended for seven years. Harry started a year before I did, and immediately I thought it sounded interesting.

Mama sat rocking me by the window in the small north bedroom as he came sauntering home one day, banging his dinner pail against his knee. She called out to him, and he ran over to us.

"What did you learn in school today?" she asked.

"I learned a song about a pony," he answered, and he sang it to us.

Mama looked proud of her big boy, and I was impressed

The next fall I was old enough to start school. Mama got me a dinner pail, a new tin cup, two penny pencils, a box of Crayolas, and a Red Chief tablet. She packed a lunch for each of us, gave me the primer Harry had used, and sent me to school with my big brother.

When I got there, I hung back shyly until the big girls showed me around. They told me where to put my dinner pail and hang my cup, which toilet was for the girls, and how to play their games. Ring-Around the Rosy was fun, and Prisoner's Base. We played Pussy Wants a Corner inside the schoolhouse at recess when the weather was bad outside.

I liked the Victrola best. It had a big, fluted horn just like the ones pictured later in a Victrola ad with a dog sitting in front of the horn and the caption "His Master's Voice." The records were thick, ridged cylinders about five inches long, and they slipped over a rod on the top of the player. I had never seen a machine this old or had a chance to play records, to hear the quick, shrill sounds emerging from the speaker with a somewhat hollow sound, as though from a distance. The school had few records, but I was content to hear them again and again. My favorites were "Listen to the Mocking Bird," "School Days, School Days, Good Old Golden Rule Days," and especially the soothing melody and dreamy rhythm of "Swing Low, Sweet Chariot." The girls teased me gently about wanting to hear it so many times.

Mrs. Howe, our teacher, rang her big brass hand bell, and the pupils scurried to their seats. She took me to the smallest desk, right in front of Harry, and said that it would be mine. When we stood up to say the "Pledge of Allegiance," I moved my lips, but I didn't know the words. That night I had Harry repeat the pledge to me until I had learned it, so I wouldn't be embarrassed the next day.

My desk was a single one, but some were double, for two pupils to sit side by side. With only seven pupils enrolled the year I started to school, no one had to use those. I thought it would be fun to sit with a friend in such an arrangement. Each seat back was the front of the desk behind it. The inkwell at the top right corner didn't have any ink in it, so I put my pencil there. It fell right out, so I laid it in the little trough along the desk top, took my tablet and made marks in it, pretending to write the ABCs.

When the teacher had time, she brought me a picture to color. I tried to stay in the lines, but I'd never had a real picture to color before, only shapes like apples and bananas that Mama drew for me. I cut out the picture with Harry's scissors, and the teacher gave me a glob of paste on a piece of paper. When I finished pounding the picture into my tablet, the paste was gone. The first time I licked my fingers, I learned the childhood pleasure of eating library paste.

We pupils started in primary, corresponding to kindergarten. Harry was in first grade. I was eager to unlock the secrets of my primer. The first page read:

> Mama, see kitty.
> See kitty.
> See mama.
> See kitty, mama.

The teacher used phonics cards with the letter and a picture on the front for the pupil to see. On the back was a story the teacher read aloud as she held up the card. The letter "K" pictured a kitten. The story told about a kitten who got a fish bone caught in her throat, and she coughed with a kitten sound, "k-k-k."

We had only one reader each year. In second grade I finished mine early in the spring. The teacher asked Mama to buy me another one. The first story in the new book was about a little boy playing outside at dusk. The stars seemed so near to him that he got a stick and tried to knock one down. The second story was called "Leerie, the Lamplighter," about a child who watched out his window every evening when a man came with his ladder and torch to light the gas street lamps. I have never forgotten the joy, the excitement, and the power I felt when I realized that the world of adventure on the printed page was now mine. I am grateful to the teacher and to my mother for providing this book, which opened the world of reading for me. . . .

TOWN SCHOOL

In 1929, when Harry and I were in grades eight and seven, we started going to school in town. I am not sure why our parents decided to have us make this change, but I was in favor of it.

Although he was only thirteen, Harry drove us to school in a Model T pickup. No one needed a driver's license at that time, and he learned from our parents what he needed to know about driving. In rainy weather, when this little car drove through a puddle, muddy water splashed up through gaps in the floorboards. Years passed and cars improved before I could ride through a puddle without automatically lifting my feet.

Nadine, Hazel, and the others my age who had been in my Sunday School class were in Harry's grade, and I had a whole new set of friends in my class. The town students had been in first grade while we country students had taken a year in primary,

The best part of going to town school was the joy of having so many pupils in my class. I liked the feeling of belonging and made friends quickly. Dorothy lived in the country and brought her lunch as I did. We immediately became good friends. Dorothy's cousin Lucille, with whom I had often played, was in my class also. The girls' mothers were sisters, and their pictures, as well as that of their brother, Percy, were in Mama's Sunday School "Plus Ultra" picture. Mama said they had been good friends when they were children and their mothers had been friends, too. It made our friendship special, almost as if we were relatives. Dorothy and Lucille had many cousins around Greene. I envied them, as I had no cousins nearby. We decided I could call myself their cousin, and I felt as if I truly were.

Later that year Mr. Don Walter came to our school to start a band. One day the fifth and sixth graders came into our assembly room, and Mr. Walter demonstrated several band instruments for us. He arranged to meet with those who were interested in starting an instrument. My parents told me they could not afford to buy an instrument for me. They may have been influenced by my poor record as a piano player.

When Dorothy and several other friends filed out for practice the last period of the day, I longed to go along, to belong to that privileged group. Finally, the next year, my parents bought a cornet for me. Although I was always embarrassed by the cheap cardboard-like case the cornet came in, band was the highlight of the rest of my school years. Dorothy also played a cornet.

Our band uniforms consisted of a green cape, overseas-style cap, and white wash slacks with a green silk stripe down the sides of the legs. These stripes had to be taken off and sewed on again every time the pants were washed. Mama showed me how to take a small stitch on the right side and a long stitch underneath, and I grew quite expert at it.

When my country life broadened to include associations with town children, I had many cultural adjustments to make. None was harder for me than to decide what to call my father. The children in our family were taught to say "papa," but I soon realized that this was old-fashioned and that others my age said "daddy." By the time I started going to town school, I felt uncomfortable with either name. It was a problem I never really solved. The best I could do was to refer to "my dad" with my friends and to continue with "papa" at home.

Two activities I had not learned in country school were jacks and roller skating. Seventh-grade girls had almost outgrown playing jacks, but Dorothy and the other girls taught me how to bounce the little red rubber ball and pick up the jacks in variations of the game. Once I had learned how, I was satisfied to put my jacks away. Not so with roller skating. I swooped joyously along on the rough sidewalks at last, any noon hour that another girl would skate with me. A rink was opened downtown, and skating around and around its slick surface was a popular activity for young people of all ages. The metal wheels of the skates roared on the wooden floor as we skated, almost drowning out the musical accompaniment. To carry on a conversation, two people had to skate very close together. Many a courtship was furthered privately in this very public place. . . .

Learning new ways of doing lessons in a class with more twenty pupils was an interesting challenge. We often corrected each other's papers in class, and I was glad when we passed our papers forward so I would get Ralph's papers. He was Dorothy's brother, and his papers were so well done that they were easy to check.

Also new to me was the practice of going to another room for part of our classes. Our two junior high teachers alternated in using the rooms. After I got used to taking along everything I needed, I found it a nice break in the routine.

In eighth grade I got my first fountain pen, a bright green Palmer pen. I used this same pen until I was out of college, spoiling many a sheet of paper with the ink that dripped from it.

Also in eighth grade, the Kodak Company gave every girl who was twelve that year a nice little Brownie camera. It was the twelfth anniversary of some event in the life of Kodak. All my classmates got them and went around busily taking pictures. Alas, I was thirteen that year, and nothing could be done about that.

When we moved up to high school in ninth grade, our class size more than doubled because students from the rural schools joined us. I was pleased to become reacquainted with Ivan and Luverna, who had been in my grade in rural school at times in the lower grades.

It was satisfying to me to be an old hand in this school, and to help the new students make the adjustment from country school. At last I felt like one of the "in" group.

Because of various illnesses during my high school years, I was often out of school. When I missed school, I felt as if I slipped into a valley, and just as I climbed out, I was sick again. With the help of conscientious teachers, I made up all the work.

Being in the band gave me the recognition, the feeling of belonging, and the sense of achievement I had wanted all my life. When I put on the green and white uniform, I was one of a group, proud to play in the concerts, go to contests, and march in parades representing Greene High School.

QUESTIONS TO CONSIDER

1. How does Onerheim describe her life in the country and in town?
2. What can you glean about rural life from this excerpt?

21.6 A. PHILIP RANDOLPH, "THE NEGRO AND THE LABOR MOVEMENT" (1925) AND "A NEW CROWD—A NEW NEGRO" (1919)

Marcus Garvey (see Reading 21.2) believed that African Americans should migrate back to Africa in response to American racism, but A. Philip Randolph (1889–1979) decided to fight for African American rights in the United States. In many ways, Randolph laid the groundwork for the civil rights movement. In the 1910s, Randolph became enmeshed in the labor movement, which on a national level often excluded African Americans. In 1925, Randolph organized the Brotherhood of Sleeping Car Porters, the first mostly African American labor union. After a decade of struggle, Randolph helped the union to win a major new contract with the Pullman Company, the dominant producer and operator of sleeper railroad cars. In 1941, Randolph organized a potential march on Washington as a negotiating tactic to force President Franklin Delano Roosevelt to prohibit discrimination in the defense industry. The two documents that follow come from Randolph's voluminous public writings. The first discussed the relationship of African Americans to the national labor movement. In the second, Randolph demanded that a new group of African American leaders take power over activist movements.

THE NEGRO AND THE LABOR MOVEMENT

It is gratifying to note that there is now considerable interest manifest in the organization of the Negro workers. Doubtless the real reason is that the white unions are slowly but surely awakening to the serious necessity of unionizing the Negro worker in self-defense. They are beginning to realize that Negro labor is playing an increasingly larger and more significant role in American industry. Especially is this true in the East, West and North, where large numbers of Negro workers have migrated and are competing in the labor market with organized labor. It is this competition which has jolted the organized white workers out of their state of chronic indifference, apathy and unconcern.

Of course, even now nothing definite has been done in the interest of Negro labor by the organized labor movement. Some of its leaders such as Hugh Frayne, Thomas J. Curtis and Ernest Bohm, are members of the Trade Union Committee for Organizing Negro Workers, but it is not apparent that this committee has anything as yet save the moral good will of some of the local unions of New York City. In order for it to succeed in its organization work, however, it must be financed by the white organized workers. So far its financial backing has come from the American Fund for Public Service. It has made possible the employment of Frank R. Crosswaith as Secretary.

Of course, this work is not new or original. *The Messenger* has been the pioneer in the field advocating the organization of Negro labor. Now the *Crisis* is belatedly taking up the fight for the next three years, and the Negro press generally has become sympathetic and active in advising Negroes to organize into labor unions wherever their white brothers will accept them. We are glad to note that Negro editors are learning their economic lessons slowly but surely.

Let no Negro fail in his duty of advancing the cause of Negro labor without let or hindrance. The time is

Source: Andrew E. Kersten and David Lucander, eds., *For Jobs and Freedom: Selected Speeches and Writings of A. Philip Randolph* (Amherst: University of Massachusetts Press, 2004), 80–81, 122–124.

rotten ripe. Immigration from Europe has been materially cut, which means that the yearly supply of labor is much less than it formerly was. This gives the organized workers an advantage, greater bargaining power by virtue of this limited supply. It also gives the Negro worker a strategic position. It gives him power to exact a higher wage from capitalists, on the one hand, and to compel organized labor to let down the bars of discrimination against him, on the other. Thus it benefits him in two ways. And the Negro workers cannot rely upon anything but the force of necessity, the self-interests of the white unions, and the fear of Negro workers' competition, to give them a union card.

Another potent force in the organization of Negro labor is education and agitation. A certain course of action may be to a group's interest to take, but if it doesn't realize [this] it is not likely to act upon it. Thus the Negro press and the enlightened white labor press have a big task before them. But the task of Negro workers consists in more than merely deciding to organize. They must guard against being lured up blind alleys by irresponsible labor talkers who present them all sorts of wild, impossible dreams such as are advocated by the Communists. No labor movement in America among white or black workers can solve the industrial problems of the American workers, white or black, whose seat of control is outside of the country. This ought to be too obvious to require argument. The Communist movement in America is a menace to the American labor movement. It is a menace to the Negro workers. While healthy, intelligent, constructive criticism is valuable and necessary to the American labor movement, criticism which starts from the premise that the existing organized labor movement should be disrupted and destroyed must be resolutely opposed. . . . It ought to be patent now that the social history and psychology of the American workers will not yield to Communists' methods and tactics. Thus, instead of advancing, the Communists have set back and retarded the cause of labor in America. If such is true of the white worker it is as equally true of the Negro worker.

A NEW CROWD—A NEW NEGRO

Throughout the world among all peoples and classes, the clock of social progress is striking the high noon of the Old Crowd. And why? The reason lies in the inability of the Old Crowd to adapt itself to the changed conditions, to recognize and accept the consequences of the sudden, rapid and violent social changes that are shaking the world. In wild desperation, consternation and despair, the proud scions of regal pomp and authority, the prophets and high-priests of the old order, view the steady and menacing rise of the great working class. Yes, the Old Crowd is passing, and with it, its false, corrupt and wicked institutions of oppression and cruelty; its ancient prejudices and beliefs and its pious, hypocritical and venerated idols.

It's all like a dream! In Russia, one-hundred and eighty million of peasants and workmen—disinherited, writhing under the ruthless heel of the Czar for over three hundred years, awoke and revolted and drove their hateful oppressors from power. Here a New Crowd arose—the Bolsheviks, and expropriated their expropriators. They fashioned and established a new social machinery, the Soviet, to express the growing class consciousness of teaming millions, disillusioned and disenchanted. They also chose new leaders—Lenin and Trotsky—to invent and adopt scientific methods of social control; to marshal, organize and direct the revolutionary forces in constructive channels to build a New Russia. . . .

And the natural question arises: what does it all mean to the Negro? First it means that he, too, must scrap the Old Crowd. For not only is the Old Crowd useless, but like the vermiform appendix, it is decidedly injurious, it prevents all real progress. Before it is possible for the Negro to prosecute successfully a formidable offense for [fighting] injustice and [establishing] fair play, he must tear down his false leaders, just as the people of Europe are tearing down their false leaders. Of course, some of the Old Crowd mean well. But what matter is it that poison be administered to the sick intentionally or out of ignorance? The result is the same—death. And our indictment of the Old Crowd is that it lacks the knowledge of methods for the attainment of ends which it desires to achieve. For instance, the Old Crowd never counsels the Negro to organize and strike against low wages and long hours. It cannot see the advisability of the Negro, who is the most exploited of the American workers, supporting a workingman's political party.

The Old Crowd enjoins the Negro to be conservative, when he has nothing to conserve. Neither his life nor his property receives the protection of the government which conscripts his life to "make the world safe for democracy." The conservative in all lands are the wealthy and the ruling class. The Negro is in dire poverty, and he is no part of the ruling class.

But the question naturally arises: who is the Old Crowd? In the Negro schools and colleges the most typical reactionaries are Kelly Miller, [Robert Russa] Moton and William Pickens. In the press [W. E. B.] Du Bois, James Weldon Johnson, Fred R. Moore, T. Thomas Fortune, Roscoe Conkling Simmons and George Harris are compromising the case of the Negro. In politics Charles W. Anderson, W. H. Lewis, Ralph Tyler, Emmet Scott, George E. Haynes, and the entire old line palliating, me-to[o]-boss gang of Negro Republican politicians, are hopelessly ignorant and distressingly unwilling of their way.

In the church the old crowd still preaches that "the meek will inherit the earth," "if the enemy strikes you on one side of the face, turn the other," and "you may take all this world but give me Jesus." "Dry Bones," "The Three Hebrew Children in the Fiery Furnace" and "Jonah in the Belly of the Whale," constitute the subjects of the Old Crowd, for black men and women who are overworked and underpaid, lynched, Jim Crowed and disfranchised—a people who are yet languishing in the dungeons of ignorance and superstition. Such then is the Old Crowd. And this is not strange to the student of history, economics, and sociology.

A man will not oppose his benefactor. The Old Crowd of Negro leaders had been and is subsidized by the Old Crowd of White Americans—a group which viciously opposes every demand made by organized labor for an opportunity to live a better life. Now, if the Old Crowd of white people opposes every demand of white labor for economic justice, how can the Negro expect to get that which is denied the white working class? And it is well nigh that economic justice is at the basis of social and political equality. For instance, there is no organization of national prominence which ostensibly is working in the interest of the Negro which is not dominated by the Old Crowd of white people. And they are controlled by the white people because they receive their funds—their revenue—from it. It is, of course, a matter of common knowledge that Du Bois does not determine the policy of the National Association for the Advancement of Colored People; nor does [Eugene] Kinkle Jones or George E. Haynes control the National Urban League. The organizations are not responsible to the Negroes because Negroes do not maintain them.

This brings us to the question as to who shall assume the reins of leadership when the Old Crowd falls. As among all other peoples, the New Crowd must be composed of young men who are educated, radical and fearless. Young Negro Radicals must control the press, church, schools, politics and labor. The conditions for joining the New Crowd are: ability, radicalism and sincerity. The New Crowd views with much expectancy the revolutions ushering in a New World. The New Crowd is uncompromising. Its tactics are not defensive, but offensive. It would not send notes after a Negro is lynched. It would not appeal to white leaders. It would appeal to the plain working people everywhere. The New Crowd sees that the war came and the Negro fought, bled and died; that the war has ended, and he is not yet free.

The New Crowd would have no armistice with lynch-law; no truce with jim-crowism, and disfranchisement; no peace until the Negro receives complete social, economic and political justice. To this end the New Crowd would form an alliance with white radicals such as [the] I.W.W. [Industrial Workers of the World, or "Wobblies"], the Socialists and the Non-Partisan League, to build a new society—a society of equals, without class, race, caste or religious distinctions.

QUESTIONS TO CONSIDER

1. How would you describe Randolph's views?
2. Does Randolph seem more moderate or more radical than other African American leaders such as Garvey and DuBois?

CHAPTER 22

A GREAT DEPRESSION
AND A NEW DEAL, 1929–1940

22.1 JOHN CROWE RANSOM, EXCERPT FROM "RECONSTRUCTED BUT UNREGENERATE" (1930)

As more and more Americans moved away from rural places in the early twentieth century, some people wished to remind America of its agrarian roots. In the South, a collection of twelve male writers formed a group known as the Southern Agrarians to espouse the benefits of Southern rural culture. In 1930, the Southern Agrarians published *I'll Take My Stand*, a collection of twelve essays that collectively fought to defend Southern conservatism and religion in the face of Northern, anti-Southern sentiments. The following excerpt comes from the first essay in the book, "Reconstructed but Unregenerate," written by the poet John Crowe Ransom. In the essay, Ransom laid out the Southern Agrarians' main argument.

It is out of fashion in these days to look backward rather than forward. About the only American given to it is some unreconstructed Southerner, who persists in his regard for a certain terrain, a certain history, and a certain inherited way of living. He feels himself in the American scene as an anachronism, and knows he is felt by his neighbors as a reproach.

Of course he is a tolerably harmless reproach. He is like some quaint local character of eccentric but fixed principles who is thoroughly and almost pridefully accepted by the village as a rare exhibit in the antique kind. His position is secure from the interference of the police, but it is of a rather ambiguous dignity.

I wish now that he were not so entirely taken for granted, and that as a reproach he might bear a barb and inflict a sting. I wish that the whole force of my own generation in the South would get behind his principles and make them an ideal which the nation at large would have to reckon with. But first I will describe him in the light of the position he seems now to occupy actually before the public.

His fierce devotion is to a lost cause—though it grieves me that his contemporaries are so sure it is lost. They are so far from fearing him and his example that they even in the excess of confidence offer him a little honor, a little petting. As a Southerner I have observed

Source: John Crowe Ransom, "Reconstructed But Unregenerate," in *I'll Take My Stand* (Baton Rouge: Louisiana State University Press, 1960), 1–21. Reprinted here with permission of Louisiana State University Press.

this indulgence and I try to be grateful. Obviously it does not constitute a danger to the Republic; distinctly it is not treasonable. They are good enough to attribute a sort of glamour to the Southern life as it is defined for them in a popular tradition. They like to use the South as the nearest available locus for the scenes of their sentimental songs, and sometimes they send their daughters to the Southern seminaries. Not too much, of course, is to be made of this last gesture, for they do not expose to this hazard their sons, who in our still very masculine order will have to discharge the functions of citizenship, and who must accordingly be sternly educated in the principles of progress at progressive institutions of learning. But it does not seem to make so much difference what principles of a general character the young women acquire, since they are not likely to be impaired by principles in their peculiar functions, such as virtue and the domestic duties. And so, at suitable seasons, and on the main-line trains, one may see them in some numbers, flying south or flying north like migratory birds; and one may wonder to what extent their philosophy of life will be affected by two or three years in the South. One must remember that probably their parents have already made this calculation and are prepared to answer, Not much.

The Southerner must know, and in fact he does very well know, that his antique conservatism does not exert a great influence against the American progressivist doctrine. The Southern idea today is down, and the progressive or American idea is up. But the historian and the philosopher, who take views that are thought to be respectively longer and deeper than most, may very well reverse this order and find that the Southern idea rather than the American has in its favor the authority of example and the approval of theory. And some prophet may even find it possible to expect that it will yet rise again. . . .

And now the crisis in the South's decline has been reached.

Industrialism has arrived in the South. Already the local chambers of commerce exhibit the formidable data of Southern progress. A considerable party of Southern opinion, which might be called the New South party, is well pleased with the recent industrial accomplishments of the South and anxious for many

more. Southerners of another school, who might be said to compose an Old South party, are apprehensive lest the section become completely and uncritically devoted to the industrial ideal precisely as the other sections of the Union are. But reconstruction is actually under way. Tied politically and economically to the Union, her borders wholly violable, the South now sees very well that she can restore her prosperity only within the competition of an industrial system.

After the war the Southern plantations were often broken up into small farms. These have yielded less and less of a living, and it said that they will never yield a good living until once more they are integrated into large units. But these units will be industrial units, controlled by a board of directors or an executive rather than a squire, worked with machinery, and manned not by farmers living at home, but by "labor." Even so they will not, according to Mr. Henry Ford, support the population that wants to live on them. In the off seasons the laborers will have to work in factories, which henceforth are to be counted on as among the charming features of Southern landscape. The Southern problem is complicated, but at its center is the farmer's problem, and this problem is simply the most acute version of that general agrarian problem which inspires the despair of many thoughtful Americans today.

The agrarian discontent in America is deeply grounded in the love of the tiller for the soil, which is probably, it must be confessed, not peculiar to the Southern specimen, but one of the more ineradicable human attachments, be the tiller as progressive as he may. In proposing to wean men from this foolish attachment, industrialism sets itself against the most ancient and the most humane of all the modes of human livelihood. Do Mr. Hoover and the distinguished thinkers at Washington see how essential is the mutual hatred between the industrialists and the farmers, and how mortal is their conflict? The gentlemen at Washington are mostly preaching and legislating to secure the fabulous "blessings" of industrial progress; they are on the industrial side. The industrialists have a doctrine which is monstrous, but they are not monsters personally; they are forward-lookers with nice manners, and no American progressivist is against them. The farmers are boorish and inarticulate by comparison. Progressivism is against them in their fight, though their traditional status is still so strong that soft words are still spoken to them. All the solutions recommended for their difficulties are really enticements held out to them to become a little more cooperative, more mechanical, more mobile—in short, a little more industrialized. But the farmer who is not a mere laborer, even the farmer of the comparatively new places like Iowa and Nebraska, is necessarily among the more stable and less progressive elements of society. He refuses to mobilize himself and become a unit in the industrial army, because he does not approve of army life.

I will use some terms which are hardly in his vernacular. He identifies himself with a spot of ground, and this ground carries a good deal of meaning; it defines itself for him as nature. He would till it not too hurriedly and not too mechanically to observe in it the contingency and the infinitude of nature; and so his life acquires its philosophical and even its cosmic consciousness. A man can contemplate and explore, respect and love, an object as substantial as a farm or a native province. But he cannot contemplate nor explore, respect nor love, a mere turnover, such as an assemblage of "natural resources," a pile of money, a volume of produce, a market, or a credit system. It is into precisely these intangibles that industrialism would translate the farmer's farm. It means the dehumanization of his life.

However that may be, the South at last, looking defensively about her in all directions upon an industrial world, fingers the weapons of industrialism. There is one powerful voice in the South which, tired of a long status of disrepute, would see the South made at once into a section second to none in wealth, as that is statistically reckoned, and in progressiveness, as that might be estimated by the rapidity of the industrial turnover. This desire offends those who would still like to regard the South as, in the old sense, a home; but its expression is loud and insistent. The urban South, with its heavy importation of regular American ways and regular American citizens, has nearly capitulated to these novelties. It is the village South and the rural South which supply the resistance, and it is lucky for them that they represent a vast quantity of inertia.

Will the Southern establishment, the most substantial exhibit on this continent of a society of the European and historic order, be completely crumbled by the powerful acid of the Great Progressive Principle? Will there be no more looking backward but only looking forward? Is our New World to be dedicated forever to the doctrine of newness? . . .

QUESTIONS TO CONSIDER

1. How does Ransom defend his argument?
2. What does Ransom leave out in his discussion of Southern life?

22.2 EXCERPT FROM THE TENNESSEE VALLEY AUTHORITY ACT (1933)

Franklin Delano Roosevelt's New Deal aimed to use the power of the Federal government to ameliorate the worst effects of the Great Depression. The Tennessee Valley Authority was one extension of such power. The Tennessee Valley—mostly in Tennessee but encompassing parts of Kentucky, Georgia, Mississippi, Virginia, and North Carolina—was especially damaged by the Great Depression. Thirty percent of the region's population had malaria, and many families earned less than $100 per year. The region's farms suffered from erosion, after the Tennessee River flooded, and deforestation. The Tennessee Valley Authority (TVA) Act, which is excerpted in the following document, sought to remedy those problems. Under the Act, the TVA gained the power to teach the region's farmers better techniques, plant new trees, and build dams to prevent flooding. The corporation could also sell excess hydropower generated by power plants connected to the dams. Though the TVA displaced some 15,000 people in the process of damming parts of the river, it turned out to be a great success. The power plants introduced electricity into the region and lured new businesses there. Today, the TVA still exists as a federally owned corporation.

Be it enacted by the Senate and House of Representatives of the United States of America in Congress assembled, That for the purpose of maintaining and operating the properties now owned by the United States in the vicinity of Muscle Shoals, Alabama, in the interest of the national defense and for agriculture and industrial development, and to improve navigation in the Tennessee River and to control the destructive flood waters in the Tennessee River and Mississippi River Basins, there is hereby created a body corporate by the name of the "Tennessee Valley Authority" (hereinafter referred to as the "Corporation"). The board of directors first appointed shall be deemed the incorporators and the incorporation shall be held to have been effected from the date of the first meeting of the board. This Act may be cited as the "Tennessee Valley Authority Act of 1933."

Sec. 2. (a) The board of directors of the Corporation (hereinafter referred to as the "board") shall be composed of three members, to be appointed by the President, by and with the advice and consent of the Senate. In appointing the members of the board, the President shall designate the chairman. All other officials, agents, and employees shall be designated and selected by the board. . . .

(f) No director shall have financial interest in any public-utility corporation engaged in the business of distributing and selling power to the public nor in any corporation engaged in the manufacture, selling, or distribution of fixed nitrogen or fertilizer, or any ingredients thereof, nor shall any member have any interest in any business that may be adversely affected by the success of the Corporation as a producer of concentrated fertilizers or as a producer of electric power.

Source: "Transcript of Tennessee Valley Authority Act (1933)," https://www.ourdocuments.gov/doc.php?flash=false&doc=65& page=transcript (Accessed May 21, 2018).

(g) The board shall direct the exercise of all the powers of the Corporation.

(h) All members of the board shall be persons who profess a belief in the feasibility and wisdom of this Act. . . .

Sec. 4. Except as otherwise specifically provided in this Act, the Corporation—

(a) Shall have succession in its corporate name.

(b) May sue and be sued in its corporate name.

(c) May adopt and use a corporate seal, which shall be judicially noticed.

(d) May make contracts, as herein authorized.

(e) May adopt, amend, and repeal bylaws.

(f) May purchase or lease and hold such real and personal property as it deems necessary or convenient in the transaction of its business, and may dispose of any such personal property held by it.

The board shall select a treasurer and as many assistant treasurers as it deems proper, which treasurer and assistant treasurers shall give such bonds for the safe-keeping of the securities and moneys of the said Corporation as the board may require: Provided, That any member of said board may be removed from office at any time by a concurrent resolution of the Senate and the House of Representatives.

(g) Shall have such powers as may be necessary or appropriate for the exercise of the powers herein specifically conferred upon the Corporation.

(h) Shall have power in the name of the United States of America to exercise the right of eminent domain, and in the purchase of any real estate or the condemnation of real estate by condemnation proceedings, the title to such real estate shall be taken in the name of the United States of America, and thereupon all such real estate shall be entrusted to the Corporation as the agent of the United States to accomplish the purposes of this Act.

(i) Shall have power to acquire real estate for the construction of dams, reservoirs, transmission lines, power houses, and other structures, and navigation projects at any point along the Tennessee River, or any of its tributaries, and in the event that the owner or owners of such property shall fail and refuse to sell to the Corporation at a price deemed fair and reasonable by the board, then the Corporation may proceed to exercise the right of eminent domain, and to condemn all property that it deems necessary for carrying out the purposes of this Act, and all such condemnation proceedings shall be had pursuant to the provisions and requirements hereinafter specified, with reference to any and all condemnation proceedings.

(i) Shall have power to construct dams, reservoirs, power houses, power structures, transmission lines, navigation projects, and incidental works in the Tennessee River and its tributaries, and to unite the various power installations into one or more systems by transmission lines. . . .

Sec. 18. In order to enable and empower the Secretary of War, the Secretary of the Interior, or the board to carry out the authority hereby conferred, in the most economical and efficient manner, he or it is hereby authorized and empowered in the exercise of the powers of national defense in aid of navigation, and in the control of the flood waters of the Tennessee and Mississippi Rivers, constituting channels of interstate commerce, to exercise the right of eminent domain for all purposes of this Act, and to condemn all lands, easements, rights of way, and other area necessary in order to obtain a site for said Cove Creek Dam, and the flowage rights for the reservoir of water above said dam, and to negotiate and conclude contracts with States, counties, municipalities, and all State agencies and with railroads, railroad corporations, common carriers, and all public utility commissions and any other person, firm or corporation, for the relocation of railroad tracks, highways, highway bridges, mills, ferries, electric-light plants, and any and all other properties, enterprises, and projects whose removal may be necessary in order to carry out the provisions of this Act. When said Cove Creek Dam, transmission line, and power house shall have been completed, the possession, use, and control thereof shall be intrusted to the Corporation for use and operation in connection with the general Tennessee Valley project, and to promote flood control and navigation in the Tennessee River. . . .

Sec. 25. The Corporation may cause proceedings to be instituted for the acquisition by condemnation of any lands, easements, or rights of way which, in the opinion of the Corporation, are necessary to carry out the provisions of this Act. The proceedings shall be instituted in the United States district court for the district in which the land, easement, right of way, or other interest, or any part thereof, is located, and such court shall have full jurisdiction to divest the complete title to the property sought to be acquired out of all persons or claimants and vest the same in the United States in fee simple, and to enter a decree quieting the title thereto in the United States of America.

Upon the filing of a petition for condemnation and for the purpose of ascertaining the value of the property to be acquired, and assessing the compensation to be paid, the court shall appoint three commissioners who shall be disinterested persons and who shall take and subscribe an oath that they do not own any lands, or interest or easement in any lands, which it may be desirable for the United States to acquire in the furtherance of said project and such commissioners shall not be selected from the locality wherein the land sought to be condemned lies. Such commissioners shall receive a per diem of not to exceed $15 for their services, together with an additional amount of $5 per day for subsistence for time actually spent in performing their duties as commissioners.

It shall be the duty of such commissioners to examine into the value of the lands sought to be condemned, to conduct hearings and receive evidence, and generally to take such appropriate steps as may be proper for the determination of the value of the said lands sought to be condemned, and for such purpose the commissioners are authorized to administer oaths and subpoena witnesses, which said witnesses shall receive the same fees as are provided for witnesses in the Federal courts. The said commissioners shall thereupon file a report setting forth their conclusions as to the value of the said property sought to be condemned, making a separate award and valuation in the premises with respect to each separate parcel involved. Upon the filing of such award in court the clerk of said court shall give notice of the filing of such award to the parties to said proceeding, in manner and form as directed by the judge of said court.

Either or both parties may file exceptions to the award of said commissioners within twenty days from the date of the filing of said award in court. Exceptions filed to such award shall be heard before three Federal district judges unless the parties, in writing, in person, or by their attorneys, stipulate that the exceptions

may be heard before a lesser number of judges. On such hearing such judges shall pass de novo upon the proceedings had before the commissioners, may view the property, and may take additional evidence. Upon such hearings the said judges shall file their own award, fixing therein the value of the property sought to be condemned, regardless of the award previously made by the said commissioners.

At any time within thirty days from the filing of the decision of the district judges upon the hearing on exceptions to the award made by the commissioners, either party may appeal from such decision of the said judges to the circuit court of appeals, and the said circuit court of appeals shall upon the hearing on said appeal dispose of the same upon the record, without regard to the awards or findings theretofore made by the commissioners or the district judges, and such circuit court of appeals shall thereupon fix the value of the said property sought to be condemned.

Upon acceptance of an award by the owner of any property herein provided to be appropriated, and the payment of the money awarded or upon the failure of either party to file exceptions to the award of the commissioners within the time specified, or upon the award of the commissioners, and the payment of the money by the United States pursuant thereto, or the payment of the money awarded into the registry of the court by the Corporation, the title to said property and the right to the possession thereof shall pass to the United States, and the United States shall be entitled to a writ in the same proceeding to dispossess the former owner of said property, and all lessees, agents, and attorneys of such former owner, and to put the United States, by its corporate creature and agent, the Corporation, into possession of said property.

In the event of any property owned in Whole or in part by minors, or insane persons, or incompetent persons, or estates of deceased persons, then the legal representatives of such minors, insane persons, incompetent persons, or estates shall have power, by and with the consent and approval of the trial judge in whose court said matter is for determination, to consent to or reject the awards of the commissioners herein provided for, and in the event that there be no legal representatives, or that the legal representatives for such minors, insane persons, or incompetent persons shall fail or decline to act, then such trial judge may, upon motion, appoint a guardian ad litem to act for such minors, insane persons, or incompetent persons, and such guardian ad litem shall act to the full extent and to the same purpose and effect as his ward could act, if competent, and such guardian ad litem shall be deemed to have full power and authority to respond, to conduct, or to maintain any proceeding herein provided for affecting his said ward.

Sec. 26. The net proceeds derived by the board from the sale of power and any of the products manufactured by the Corporation, after deducting the cost of operation, maintenance, depreciation, amortization, and an amount deemed by the board as necessary to withhold as operating capital, or devoted by the board to new construction, shall be paid into the Treasury of the United States at the end of each calendar year.

Sec. 27. All appropriations necessary to carry out the provisions of this Act are hereby authorized. . . .

QUESTIONS TO CONSIDER

1. What did the Act specifically give the TVA the power to do? What was the Act most concerned with?
2. Does this seem like an overreach of Federal power to you?

22.3 UPTON SINCLAIR, EXCERPT FROM *I, GOVERNOR OF CALIFORNIA AND HOW I ENDED POVERTY* (1934)

There were a variety of reactions to the New Deal (for other reactions, see Readings 22.4 and 22.5). In California during the early 1930s, Upton Sinclair (1878–1968) decided to go far beyond the scope of the New Deal in his bid for the California governorship. Sinclair was a left-wing author best known for his 1906 *The Jungle*, a muckraking novel about the Chicago meatpacking industry. Sinclair moved to Southern California during the 1920s, where he twice lost Congressional elections on the Socialist Party ticket. In 1934, Sinclair ran in the Democratic primary for the California gubernatorial election. For the campaign, he created a comprehensive platform, End Poverty in California (EPIC). Under EPIC, California would forcibly seize unused factories and farms and hire the unemployed to work there. EPIC also would raise substantially taxes on the wealthy and expand California's pension system. Shockingly, Sinclair's radical agenda took hold. People came out in droves on primary day to support him, and Sinclair defeated World War I propaganda czar George Creel. In response, wealthy California elites from media and business industries smeared Sinclair at every turn, and he lost the general election to incumbent Frank Merriam. Sinclair wrote *I, Governor of California and How I Ended Poverty: A True Story of the Future* as a piece of advertising for his campaign. In it, he imagined a future in which he would gain victory and implement EPIC statewide. Here, you will read excerpts from the EPIC principles and from his final chapter, "Victory," in which he imagines the aftermath of EPIC.

THE TWELVE PRINCIPLES OF EPIC

1. God created the natural wealth of the earth for the use of all men, not of a few.
2. God created men to seek their own welfare, not that of masters.
3. Private ownership of tools, a basis of freedom when tools are simple, becomes a basis of enslavement when tools are complex.
4. Autocracy in industry cannot exist alongside democracy in government.
5. When some men live without working, other men are working without living.
6. The existence of luxury in the presence of poverty and destitution is contrary to good morals and sound public policy.
7. The present depression is one of abundance, not of scarcity.
8. The cause of the trouble is that a small class has the wealth, while the rest have the debts.
9. It is contrary to common sense that men should starve because they have raised too much food.
10. The destruction of food or other wealth, or the limitation of production, is economic insanity.
11. The remedy is to give the workers access to the means of production, and let them produce for themselves, not for others.
12. This change can be brought about by action of a majority of the people, and that is the American way.

Source: Upton Sinclair, *I, Governor of California and How I Ended Poverty: A True Story of the Future* (New York: Farrar & Rinehart, Inc., 1933), 10, 59–63.

CHAPTER VI: VICTORY

The process of EPIC was like that of a swiftly flowing river eating into a sand bank. Private industry began to crumble; and as quickly as any productive enterprise failed, it was made over into a public institution. Nothing could withstand the current of co-operation.

The Big Business men began to realize that it was no longer an advantage to gain enormous incomes, because the State income tax took so large a share of them, and when the owner died the State took so much of the balance. Land speculators found that a 10% tax on idle real estate spelled immediate ruin; they gave up their holdings, and the State took them over, and the colony laborers moved in and built new homes and social buildings, and the land colonists plowed and planted the soil. By the same method vacant lots in the cities were utilized for gardens under the supervision of the ever-vigilant CAL [California Authority for Land]. The workers, having plenty of money for homes, took up all the unused buildings, and CAP [California Authority for Production] soon had enormous jobs of new construction all over the State.

By midsummer, when the new crops began to come in, the system was flourishing. There was food for everybody, and word spread that California was paradise, and all over the United States caravans of automobiles were heading for the Golden State. Nobody worried, because it was known that each of these newcomers would bring a pair of arms and a head. CAL by now had plenty of land, and CAP was turning out building materials, and CAM [California Authority for Money] was no longer a speculative venture, but the one solid reality in a crumbling financial world. Twice a week the people of California listened while their Governor explained to them the fundamental economic fact that if you have land and natural resources, and if you apply labor to these, you produce wealth; then, if you own what you produce, you become able to pay your debts.

One by one the land colonies became self-supporting. After the first year they began paying off their bonds out of their sales of produce. When this process was completed, they would become free, self-governing institutions, democratically managed by their members, selling their own produce in the system, ordering their own supplies and erecting their own buildings. The State of California would exercise no further control over them, except to see that they conformed to the constitution for colonies laid down by CAL—that is, they must pay their bills, keep out of debt, and choose their managing committees at elections under the American system.

The opposition to EPIC began to collapse, with a suddenness which surprised everybody. The reason was the success of the colonies in planting crops, and the success of the factories in turning out goods. The California farmers knew how to farm, the workers knew how to work, and the managers knew how to manage. It became evident that there was going to be a publicly owned productive unit of enormous dimensions in the State. It also became apparent that the workers in the State-owned industries liked the idea, and could never be separated from it without a war. A great burden had been suddenly lifted off the backs of the people. The problem of the business cycle had been solved. Those who needed goods had the means to buy, therefore production and consumption balanced. It was useless to argue against that. That movement into EPIC became a tide.

Another reason for the dying away of opposition was that the opposers did not have so much money to spend. The graduated taxes were taking a large part of the wealth of the unproductive classes. The profit-takers were losing their customers, and they saw co-operation booming, and realized that the old system was doomed.

A third reason was the continuation of the crisis throughout the nation. The Federal Government was being compelled to carry out the EPIC plan on a larger scale, though without the name. The State governments were beginning to follow, and everybody realized that it was better for local affairs to be managed locally.

A fourth reason was the moral one. EPIC was right, and the right has a way of prevailing. There was prosperity for all inside the system. The people on the outside had many worries, and realized if they came inside, they would have none. There were jobs for all—even for those who had managed capitalist industries, because there was managing to be done in EPIC. The old-time parasites saw their dividends being pared, their money being taken for taxes. What was the use of trying to pile up wealth any more? It was better to sell out for what you could get.

And after all, what was the use of piling up millions which you could not leave to your family? The older people found that the young people were taking it gaily, not worrying about their lost fortunes, because EPIC was so interesting. It was no longer necessary to live on papa's money; and papa, for his part, began to reflect that it had not been entirely good to have the young growing up in idleness. Social ostentation, being no longer possible, was no longer necessary. The fashions were going out of fashion, because there were so few to pay attention. In short, the new principle won its way, that the production of the necessities of life must be a public service, democratically managed by the community.

In two years the victory was made complete. The great public service corporations, which had been buttressed behind the rate-fixing device, were humbled by the process of taxing them, which reduced the value of their securities. Finally the State of California took them over at physical cost, and thus the greatest source of corruption was gone from American public life. The old order crumbled like a dry-rotted log. Everybody came running, to get a desirable position on the bandwagon.

The people lost their fear of the State, for they discovered that it had become a new thing. It was no longer the incarnation of selfishness, an instrument of repression of exploiting classes. It became the people themselves, doing what they wanted done, with no one to prevent them. The sole question became, what was the most convenient and economical way to get a particular job done? Policemen laid down their clubs and took up tools.

It was interesting to see what became of the great capitalist newspapers, which had dominated the thought of America for a couple of generations. These papers were no longer making money, because there was no private business to provide them with advertising subsidies. Their owners were no longer able to maintain them, and the question arose, how should a community get its news? The problem was solved by the appointment of governing boards selected from various elements. Two members were named by the employees of the paper, two by the faculties of state universities, two were chosen by vote of the readers, and one was appointed by the Governor.

The same thing happened to the radio stations. They could no longer make money, because the advertisers of cigarettes and soaps and hair-tonics no longer subsidized them. They were socialized, and the trash was cut out of their programs.

By the end of the year 1938, the political situation had changed forever. The Republican party had sunk into harmless disuse. Nobody belonged to it, except the members of the Better America Federation and the Daughters of No More American Revolutions. The Democratic party had become a conservative organization, prepared to live forever on the deeds of its ancestors. The Socialist party was active and powerful, basing its campaign on a demand for the socialization of the luxury trades and the complete abolition of inheritance.

The Governor dedicated the last year of his administration to educating the people to the idea of generous endowments for all forms of scientific research and for the creative arts. He said: "We are winning new leisure; we shall very soon have more than was ever dreamed of in history. When our productive system is thoroughly organized and working at full speed, nobody will have to work more than two hours a day for the State. What are we going to do with the rest of our time? There are all kinds of important problems to be solved—of health, education, psychology, everything from astronomy to zoology. I hope you will make a beautiful and wise use of the opportunities you have won for yourselves."

The Governor made a last speech over the radio, saying that he had caused a careful investigation to be made throughout the State of California, and that the only poor person he had been able to find was a religious hermit who lived in a cave. Therefore he considered his job done, and he purposed to go home and write a novel.

ENVOI

Such, reader, is the story; and now, what shall I say to you? Shall I urge you to get busy and make it happen; and have you think, perhaps, that this is one more candidate, and one more political racket, although a new and entertaining one? Or shall I follow my own impulse, and say that this is book number forty-seven, and that I have number forty-eight, and in fact numbers forty-nine and fifty, all ready in my head, and can be quite happy writing them; that there was never a man who wanted less to hold a political office, or who could smile more cheerfully at defeat? And you, the reader, will go to see a ball game, or drive your family to the beach, or mend your shingle-roof, or your hog-pen, or whatever it may be, and all will be well.

But, alas, it won't be. For you will still be in poverty, or on the way to it; and our State will be drifting toward Fascism. So you will have to get your neighbors together and start a political fight; if not now, then very soon. And so I say to you, after thirty-eight years'

unremitting study of this problem, and after proving my knowledge of it by predicting in print, thirty years ago, everything that was going to happen—I say to you: This is your way out, and there is no other way, and you will have to take it. I have given you my best in this Book, and now it is up to you.

QUESTIONS TO CONSIDER

1. What stands out in "The Twelve Principles of EPIC"?
2. Why do you think Sinclair's campaign was so popular in Depression-era California?

22.4 HUEY LONG, "EVERY MAN A KING" (1934)

Like Upton Sinclair (see Reading 22.3), Huey Long (1893–1935) believed that the New Deal could be much more active. Nicknamed "The Kingfish," Long was the Governor of Louisiana from 1928 to 1932 and became a U.S. Senator in 1932. Long built a statewide support network through large public works projects. His gubernatorial administration built new schools, initiated a network of charity hospitals, and invested in highway construction. Notably, Long also demanded that each public employee who had a job in his administration give a portion of his or her salary to Long's political war chest. So powerful was Long in Louisiana that he continued to achieve legislative goals even after leaving the governorship. Long assumed his role in the Senate in the midst of the Great Depression. He initially supported Franklin Delano Roosevelt and the New Deal, but as the Depression deepened, Long began to support more radical measures to redistribute wealth in America. Eventually, he formulated a "Share Our Wealth" program, whereby the government would heavily tax the most wealthy, cap personal fortunes at $50 million, and redistribute the money gained so that every American could have a minimum annual income. The charismatic Long became a national figure at the time as he spread his ideas around the country. Some historians believe he planned to challenge FDR for the 1936 Democratic nomination for President. On September 8, 1935, however, the son of a political opponent assassinated Long in the Louisiana State Capitol building, and his "Share Our Wealth" movement fizzled after his death. In the following 1934 radio speech, Long introduced his "Share Our Wealth" plan.

"IT IS NECESSARY TO SCALE DOWN THE BIG FORTUNES"

Is that a right of life, when the young children of this country are being reared into a sphere which is more owned by 12 men than it is by 120 million people?

Ladies and gentlemen, I have only thirty minutes in which to speak to you this evening, and I, therefore, will not be able to discuss in detail so much as I can write when I have all of the time and space that is allowed me for the subjects, but I will undertake to sketch them very briefly without manuscript or preparation, so that you can understand them so well as I can tell them to you tonight.

I contend, my friends, that we have no difficult problem to solve in America, and that is the view of nearly everyone with whom I have discussed the matter here in Washington and elsewhere throughout the United States—that we have no very difficult problem to solve.

It is not the difficulty of the problem which we have; it is the fact that the rich people of this country—and by rich people I mean the super-rich—will not allow us to solve the problems, or rather the one little problem that is afflicting this country, because in order to cure all of our woes it is necessary to scale down the big fortunes, that we may scatter the wealth to be shared by all of the people.

We have a marvelous love for this government of ours; in fact, it is almost a religion, and it is well that it should be, because we have a splendid form of

Source: Huey P. Long, "Every Man a King," https://www.senate.gov/artandhistory/history/resources/pdf/EveryManKing.pdf (Accessed June 13, 2018).

government and we have a splendid set of laws. We have everything here that we need, except that we have neglected the fundamentals upon which the American government was principally predicated.

How many of you remember the first thing that the Declaration of Independence said? It said, "We hold these truths to be self-evident, that there are certain inalienable rights for the people, and among them are life, liberty, and the pursuit of happiness"; and it said, further, "We hold the view that all men are created equal."

Now, what did they mean by that? Did they mean, my friends, to say that all men were created equal and that that meant that any one man was born to inherit $10 billion and that another child was to be born to inherit nothing?

Did that mean, my friends, that someone would come into this world without having had an opportunity, of course, to have hit one lick of work, should be born with more than it and all of its children and children's children could ever dispose of, but that another one would have to be born into a life of starvation?

That was not the meaning of the Declaration of Independence when it said that all men are created equal or "That we hold that all men are created equal."

Nor was it the meaning of the Declaration of Independence when it said that they held that there were certain rights that were inalienable—the right of life, liberty, and the pursuit of happiness.

Is that right of life, my friends, when the young children of this country are being reared into a sphere which is more owned by 12 men than it is by 120 million people?

Is that, my friends, giving them a fair shake of the dice or anything like the inalienable right of life, liberty, and the pursuit of happiness, or anything resembling the fact that all people are created equal; when we have today in America thousands and hundreds of thousands and millions of children on the verge of starvation in a land that is overflowing with too much to eat and too much to wear?

I do not think you will contend that, and I do not think for a moment that they will contend it.

Now let us see if we cannot return this government to the Declaration of Independence and see if we are going to do anything regarding it. Why should we hesitate or why should we quibble or why should we quarrel with one another to find out what the difficulty is, when we know what the Lord told us what the difficulty is, and Moses wrote it out so a blind man could see it, then Jesus told us all about it, and it was later written in the Book of James, where everyone could read it?

I refer to the Scriptures, now, my friends, and give you what it says not for the purpose of convincing you of the wisdom of myself, not for the purpose, ladies and gentlemen, of convincing you of the fact that I am quoting the Scripture means that I am to be more believed than someone else; but I quote you the Scripture, or rather refer you to the Scripture, because whatever you see there you may rely upon will never be disproved so long as you or your children or anyone may live; and you may further depend upon the fact that not one historical fact that the Bible has ever contained has ever yet been disproved by any scientific discovery or by reason of anything that has been disclosed to man through his own individual mind or through the wisdom of the Lord which the Lord has allowed him to have.

"NOTHING SHOULD BE HELD PERMANENTLY BY ANY ONE PERSON"

But the Scripture says, ladies and gentlemen, that no country can survive, or for a country to survive it is necessary that we keep the wealth scattered among the people, that nothing should be held permanently by any one person, and that fifty years seems to be the year of jubilee in which all property would be scattered about and returned to the sources from which it originally came, and every seventh year debt should be remitted.

Those two things the Almighty said to be necessary—I should say He knew to be necessary, or else He would not have so prescribed that the property would be kept among the general run of the people, and that everyone would continue to share in it; so that no one man would get half of it and hand it down to a son, who takes half of what was left, and that son hand it down to another one, who would take half of what was left, until, like a snowball going downhill, all of the snow was off of the ground except what the snowball had.

I believe that was the judgment and the view and the law of the Lord, that we would have to distribute wealth ever so often, in order that there could not be people starving to death in a land of plenty, as there is in America today.

We have in America today more wealth, more goods, more food, more clothing, more houses than we have ever had. We have everything in abundance here.

We have the farm problem, my friends, because we have too much cotton, because we have too much wheat, and have too much corn, and too much potatoes.

We have a home-loan problem because we have too many houses, and yet nobody can buy them and live in them.

We have trouble, my friends, in the country, because we have too much money owing, the greatest indebtedness that has ever been given to civilization, where it has been shown that we are incapable of distributing the actual things that are here, because the people have not money enough to supply themselves with them, and because the greed of a few men is such that they think it is necessary that they own everything, and their pleasure consists in the starvation of the masses, and in their possessing things they cannot use, and their children cannot use, but who bask in the splendor of sunlight and wealth, casting darkness and despair and impressing it on everyone else.

"So, therefore," said the Lord, in effect, "if you see these things that now have occurred and exist in this and other countries, there must be a constant scattering of wealth in any country if this country is to survive."

"Then," said the Lord, in effect, "every seventh year there shall be a remission of debts; there will be no debts after seven years." That was the law.

Now, let us take America today. We have in America today, ladies and gentlemen, $272 billion of debt. Two hundred and seventy-two thousand millions of dollars of debts are owed by the various people of this country today. Why, my friends, that cannot be paid. It is not possible for that kind of debt to be paid.

The entire currency of the United States is only $6 billion. That is all of the money that we have got in America today. All the actual money you have got in all of your banks, all that you have got in the government treasury, is $6 billion; and if you took all that money and

paid it out today you would still owe $266 billion; and if you took all that money and paid again you would still owe $260 billion; and if you took it, my friends, 20 times and paid it you would still owe $150 billion.

You would have to have 45 times the entire money supply of the United States today to pay the debts of the people of America and then they would just have to start out from scratch, without a dime to go on with.

So, my friends, it is impossible to pay all of these debts, and you might as well find out that it cannot be done. The United States Supreme Court has definitely found out that it could not be done, because, in a Minnesota case, it held that when a state has postponed the evil day of collecting a debt it was a valid and constitutional exercise of legislative power.

"TEN MEN DOMINATE . . . AT LEAST 85 PERCENT OF THE ACTIVITIES THAT YOU OWN"

Now, ladies and gentlemen, if I may proceed to give you some other words that I think you can understand—I am not going to belabor you by quoting tonight—I am going to tell you what the wise men of all ages and all times, down even to the present day, have all said: that you must keep the wealth of the country scattered, and you must limit the amount that any one man can own. You cannot let any man own $300 billion or $400 billion. If you do, one man can own all of the wealth that the United States has in it.

Now, my friends, if you were off on an island where there were one hundred lunches, you could not let one man eat up the hundred lunches, or take the hundred lunches and not let anybody else eat any of them. If you did. There would not be anything else for the balance of the people to consume.

So, we have in America today, my friends, a condition by which about ten men dominate the means of activity in at least 85 percent of the activities that you own. They either own directly everything or they have got some kind of mortgage on it, with a very small percentage to be excepted. They own the banks, they own the steel mills, they own the railroads, they own the bonds, they own the mortgages, they own the stores, and they have chained the country from one end to the other until there is not any kind of business that a small, independent man could go into today and make a living, and there is not any kind of business that an independent man can go into and make any money to buy an automobile with; and they have finally and gradually and steadily eliminated everybody from the fields in which there is a living to be made, and still they have got little enough sense to think they ought to be able to get more business out of it anyway.

If you reduce a man to the point where he is starving to death and bleeding and dying, how do you expect that man to get hold of any money to spend with you? It is not possible.

Then, ladies and gentlemen, how do you expect people to live, when the wherewith cannot be had by the people? . . .

"THESE BIG-FORTUNE HOLDERS . . . OWN JUST AS MUCH AS THEY DID"

Both of these men, Mr. Hoover and Mr. Roosevelt, came out and said there had to be a decentralization of wealth, but neither one of them did anything about it. But, nevertheless, they recognized the principle. The fact that neither one of them ever did anything about it is their own problem that I am not undertaking to criticize; but had Mr. Hoover carried out what he says ought to be done, he would be retiring from the president's office, very probably three years from now, instead of one year ago; and had Mr. Roosevelt proceeded along the lines that he stated were necessary for the decentralization of wealth, he would have gone, my friends, a long way already, and within a few months he would have probably reached a solution of all of the problems that afflict this country today.

But I wish to warn now that nothing that has been done up to this date has taken one dime away from these big-fortune holders; they own just as much as they did, and probably a little bit more; they hold just as many of the debts of the common people as they ever held, and probably a little bit more; and unless we, my friends, are going to give the people of this country a fair shake of the dice, by which they will all get something out of the funds of this land, there is not a chance on the topside of this God's eternal earth by which we can rescue this country and rescue the people of this country.

It is necessary to save the government of the country, but is much more necessary to save the people of America. We love this country. We love this government. It is a religion, I say. It is a kind of religion people have read of when women, in the name of religion, would take their infant babes and throw them into the burning flame, where they would be instantly devoured by the all-consuming fire, in days gone by; and there probably are some people of the world even today, who, in the name of religion, throw their own babes to destruction; but in the name of our good government people today are seeing their own children hungry, tired, half naked, lifting their tear-dimmed eyes into the sad faces of their fathers and mothers, who cannot give them food and clothing they both needed, and which is necessary to sustain them, and that goes on day after day, and night after night, when day gets into darkness and blackness, knowing those children would arise in the morning without being fed, and probably go to bed at night without being fed.

Yet in the name of our government, and all alone, those people undertake and strive as hard as they can to keep a good government alive, and how long they can stand that no one knows. If I were in their place tonight, the place where millions are, I hope that I would have what I might say—I cannot give you the word to express the kind of fortitude they have; that is the word—I hope that I might have the fortitude to praise and honor my government that had allowed me here in this land, where there is too much to eat and too much to wear, to starve in order that a handful of men can have so much more than they can ever eat or they can ever wear.

"EVERY MAN A KING"

Now, we have organized a society, and we call it "Share Our Wealth Society," a society with the motto "every man a king."

Every man a king, so there would be no such thing as a man or woman who did not have the necessities of life, who would not be dependent upon the whims and caprices and *ipse dixit* of the financial martyrs for a living. What do we propose by this society? We propose to limit the wealth of big men in the country. There is an average of $15,000 in wealth to every family in America. That is right here today.

We do not propose to divide it up equally. We do not propose a division of wealth, but we propose to limit poverty that we will allow to be inflicted upon any man's family. We will not say we are going to try to guarantee any equality, or $15,000 to families. No; but we do say that one third of the average is low enough for any one family to hold, that there should be a guaranty of a family wealth of around $5,000; enough for a home, an automobile, a radio, and the ordinary conveniences, and the opportunity to educate their children; a fair share of the income of this land thereafter to that family so there will be no such thing as merely the select to have those things, and so there will be no such thing as a family living in poverty and distress.

We have to limit fortunes. Our present plan is that we will allow no one man to own more than $50 million. We think that with that limit we will be able to carry out the balance of the program. It may be necessary that we limit it to less than $50 million. It may be necessary, in working out of the plans, that no man's fortune would be more than $10 million or $15 million. But be that as it may, it will still be more than any one man, or any one man and his children and their children, will be able to spend in their lifetimes; and it is not necessary or reasonable to have wealth piled up beyond that point where we cannot prevent poverty among the masses.

Another thing we propose is old-age pension of $30 a month for everyone that is sixty years old. Now, we do not give this pension to a man making $1,000 a year, and we do not give it to him if he has $10,000 in property, but outside of that we do.

"WE WILL LIMIT HOURS OF WORK"

We will limit hours of work. There is not any necessity of having overproduction. I think all you have got to do, ladies and gentlemen, is just limit the hours of work to such an extent as people will work only so long as is necessary to produce enough for all of the people to have what they need. Why, ladies and gentlemen, let us say that all of these labor-saving devices reduce hours down to where you do not have to work but four hours a day; that is enough for these people, and then praise be the name of the Lord, if it gets that good. Let it be good and not a curse, and then we will have five hours a day and five days a week, or even less than that, and we might give a man a whole month off during a year, or give him two months; and we might do what other countries have seen fit to do, and what I did in Louisiana, by having schools by which adults could go back and learn the things that have been discovered since they went to school.

We will not have any trouble taking care of the agricultural situation. All you have to do is balance your production with your consumption. You simply have to abandon a particular crop that you have too much of, and all you have to do is store the surplus for the next year, and the government will take it over. When you have good crops in the area in which the crops that have been planted are sufficient for another year, put in your public works in the particular year when you do not need to raise any more, and by that means you get everybody employed. When the government has enough of any particular crop to take care of all the people, that will be all that is necessary; and in order to do all of this, our taxation is going to be to take the billion-dollar fortunes and strip them down to frying size, not to exceed $50 million, and if it is necessary to come to $10 million, we will come to $10 million. We have worked the proposition out to guarantee a limit upon property (and no man will own less than one third the average), and guarantee a reduction of fortunes and a reduction of hours to spread wealth throughout this country. We would care for the old people above sixty and take them away from this thriving industry and give them a chance to enjoy the necessities and live in ease, and thereby lift from the market the labor which would probably create a surplus of commodities.

Those are the things we propose to do. "Every man a king." Every man to eat when there is something to eat; all to wear something when there is something to wear. That makes us all a sovereign. . . .

QUESTIONS TO CONSIDER

1. How did Long defend his plan?
2. Why do you think Long was so popular at the time?

22.5 CHARLES COUGHLIN, EXCERPT FROM HIS SPEECH TO THE TOWNSENDITES (1936)

Similar to Upton Sinclair and Huey Long (see Readings 22.3 and 22.4, respectively), Charles Coughlin (1891–1979) believed that the New Deal should be more populist. A Roman Catholic priest to a church in Royal Oak, Michigan, Coughlin became a national figure with the advent of radio. During the 1930s, Coughlin's radio programs reached up to thirty million listeners nationwide. Like Long, Coughlin initially supported the New Deal but grew to believe that Franklin Delano Roosevelt was too comfortable with bankers, whom Coughlin blamed for the ravages of the Depression. Coughlin also blamed FDR for the increasing popularity of communism in America. Instead, Coughlin, and his National Union for Social Justice, wanted to guarantee Americans an income, nationalize certain industries, and redistribute wealth. He also wanted to reform banking. Coughlin gave the following speech to the Townsendites in 1936. Led by California physician Francis Townsend, the Townsendites proposed to pay every American over age 60 a guaranteed pension and to institute a two percent national sales tax to support the pensions. Townsend's ideals likely factored into the establishment of FDR's Social Security bill. In the speech, Coughlin attacked FDR at length. Coughlin became increasingly anti-Semitic during the 1930s and eventually supported Hitler's regime. Eventually, radio regulators forced Coughlin off the air, and he lived the rest of his life as a parish priest.

Mr. Chairman, Dr. Francis E. Townsend, Rev. Dr. Gerald Smith, ladies and gentlemen from every State in the Union:

It is my happy privilege to be here this morning on the invitation of Dr. Townsend. I feel that I will not be able to speak to you very lengthily because I have lost my voice somewhere between Virginia and Minnesota on a tour that I was making, speaking to the officers of the National Union for Social Justice, and thus I am inflicting this rasping sound upon you at your own displeasure. It is not my privilege to come here, ladies and gentlemen, to convince you, were it necessary to convince you, and I choose not to convince you of what resolutions you should pass at this convention.

It isn't my purpose even to endeavour to persuade you upon any future policy which you and your leaders will adopt. I come before you, however, to advise you of a few policies of the National Union for Social Justice that you may compare them, to tell you of some resolutions adopted by the National Union, in order that they may be safeguards to direct you either to follow along and examine or to reject them.

First of all, the National Union for Social Justice is not a political party, nor will it ever become one. It is true that we are interested in government, just the same as the United States Chamber of Commerce, just the same as the American Liberty League, just the same as the veterans of foreign wars, just the same as the bankers.

Nevertheless we are not a political party, but with our strength we are determined to influence good government, just as the major number of those whom I have mentioned are endeavouring to inflict bad government on us.

Source: "'Text of Father Coughlin's Address to Townsendites,' from *The New York Times,* July 17, 1936, p. 6," The Catholic University of America Archives, http://archives.lib.cua.edu/res/docs/education/politics/pdfs/24-coughlin-townsend-speech.pdf (Accessed June 13, 2018).

Government in this beloved nation of ours is represented by its three branches: the legislative branch, where the laws are made; the executive branch, where the laws are enforced, and the judicial branch, where the laws are adjudged to be in harmony with our Constitution before they can be enforced.

Naturally we have no quarrel with the Constitution of the United States, because it has been gotten under the past grand work established by both Democrats and Republicans. Ever since the founding fathers established our Constitution it appears that Congress has the right to coin and the right to regulate the value of money.

Both Democrats and Republicans have forfeited that right, until today the Federal Reserve Banks, like Congress, have the right to coin and regulate the value of money so that it causes 11,000,000 unemployed to tramp on our streets, so that it has put the farmers off their homesteads, so that it has made beggars of the millions of the aged heroes who with their hands have wrought this country into the beautiful land it is today.

The day has arrived when we must expel those who have forgotten our Constitution.

Thus, the National Union for Social Justice is not established upon any radical excursion into the wilderness of socialism, communism, and anarchism, nor on the other hand to those die-hard Tories and hoop-skirt politicians who profit in telling us in season and out of season that we must support the Roosevelts and the Landons of today, with their love of feasts on the banquet table of America for the money changers.

These principles of political change are the guiding star of the National Union for Social Justice, the Christian, the American, and the Constitutional.

Relative to our participation in politics: We have arrived at the conclusion that no candidate for Congress of the United States can receive the endorsement of the National Union unless while in Congress he has proven himself sympathetic to the principle of social justice, or if he is a new candidate, by his having pledged himself publicly to support the sixteen principles of social justice, regardless of the Democratic platform or the Republican platform.

The 1932 platform of the Democratic Party will take its place in the annals of American literature with the Gettysburg address of the great Lincoln. The

Inaugural address delivered on the streets of Washington on March 4, 1933[,] will be lived up to in practice at some future date and then we will have rendered complete the Gettysburg address of the emancipator, Lincoln. But the heart that conceived that platform and uttered that inaugural address has lacked that divine spark known to human children of the Lord, the spark of truthfulness and the spark of sincerity.

As far as the National Union is concerned, no candidate for Congress can campaign, go electioneering for, or support the great betrayer and liar, Franklin D. Roosevelt, he who promised to drive the money changers from the temple and succeeded in driving the farmers from their homesteads and the citizens from their homes in the cities.

He who promised to drive the money changers from the temple has built up the greatest debt in all history, $35,000,000,000, which he permitted the bankers the right, without restriction, to spend, and for which he contracted that you and your children shall repay with seventy billion hours of labor to farms, to factories or places of business.

Seven seconds to coin the money and seventy billion hours to pay it back! Is that driving the money changers from the temple?

He who advocated the doctrine of good neighborliness with his right hand, stretched out with the left to communistic Mexico where both Catholics and Protestants were assassinated for the mere act of holding up the cross. Is that good neighborliness?

For those two reasons which I have not time to amplify for you, the National Union for Social Justice will not endorse any candidate if he is a Democrat who openly advocates the re-election of the great betrayer, Franklin Delano Roosevelt. On the other hand, ladies and gentlemen, what is our stand for the Republicans?

I am cognizant of the history following the World War. I know of their Hardings and Coolidges, of their Hoovers and their gold standards, and I know that people were prostrate—how we, following the war, cancelled $14,000,000,000 of European war debts and repudiated $11,000,000,000 more of post-war debts simply to save the international bankers, simply to save the gold standard. I am forced to repudiate his philosophy and his platform as a return to the days of human slavery.

It is most significant, my friends, that the hand of Moscow backs the Communist leaders in America, and aims to pledge their support for Franklin Delano Roosevelt where communism stands.

Very likely in this assemblage this morning there are politicians who are thinking more of their jobs and their patronage than they do of Dr. Townsend and his principles.

Ladies and gentlemen, you have them here.

They raise their voices at the mention of democracy, but do they know the history of democracy in America? Study Andrew Jackson and his radical personal tax. Learn about the great fellow and his work. Who brought his ideas back and on what plank? Did Jackson succeed? Why, most certainly he did, because Jackson was a man of his word.

Jackson restored to Congress the right to coin and regulate the value of money, which Alexander Hamilton stole from Congress. Shortly after Jackson died those who still believed in his philosophy in their minds, but in whose hearts there wasn't the blood to carry their beliefs through, the Old World democracy, identified themselves with the thought of the international bankers until they sold you out as a mess of pottage.

Is this democracy? Or what is democracy today? Is it some fact of the mind that begins at the Mason and Dixon Line and ends at the Gulf, or is it a label for political patronage with the seal, sign and stamp of "Farleyism" smeared all over it?

On this platform or somewhere in this audience there is a candidate, a Democrat endorsed by the National Union for Congress. His name is Martin Sweeney (of Cleveland), and I am going to ask a public question of Martin Sweeney: "Although the National Union has endorsed you as a Democrat, are you aware that if you support Roosevelt you lose that endorsement?"

[Mr. Sweeney: "I have answered by my criticism of Roosevelt during the last four years. I know he is a double-crosser. I stand with the National Union."]

The same holds true from California to Maine. You can't be with us or against us at the same time.

Ladies and gentlemen, as I said before, we are wholly opposed to the Roosevelt taxes, dole, and to the farm propaganda that has been spread through this nation.

We are opposed, sympathetically, to poor Mr. Landon, the creature of three newspaper editors. He was never head of anything until these personas built him up out of nothing. Several months ago he wanted $300,000,000 of scrip money for taxes, and several months later he wanted to go back to the gold standard. He doesn't know whether he is going or coming.

There is only one avenue of escape for the downtrodden American people and that avenue lies not on the highway of the Democratic and Republican parties, for both are one, the left wing and the other right wing of the same bird of prey, the vulture; for the same thing, the banker.

Does democracy mean that we shall fail? Why should we pay men to work for less than living wages under the so-called WPA? Is that democracy?

Is it democracy for the President of this nation to assume power over Congress, to browbeat the Congress and to insist that his "must" legislation be passed? Is that democracy?

Is it democracy, I ask those who cling to the party of Andrew Jackson, to have our country filled with plutocrats or bureaucrats and their banks filled with unpayable debts, all to save the bankers? Is that democracy? I ask the Democrats from the South to examine the history, to learn your true Andrew Jackson, and to explore those Communists who have seized the party reins of the Democrats and who are flogging their party with destructional patronage.

I ask you to purge the man who claims to be a Democrat from the Democratic party, and I mean Franklin Double-Crossing Roosevelt.

Ladies and gentlemen, all those who are in favour of a free America from the double-crossing Democrats and from the gold-standard Republicans, stand up.

The time has come when the policies of the National Union must be fought for unto death, if necessary, in this land of ours where there is so much intelligence and executive ability.

And there is no escape from the ills which beset us by bringing them water of communism. We don't have to be Communists, nor do we have to be bureaucrats. We have been Americans, with the slogan "America for the Americans." Today it is my happy privilege to announce to America that the National Union is not amalgamated either with the Townsend movement or with the share-the-wealth movement.

We are keeping our identity, but just as theirs is a theory of opposing the Republicans, the Democrats, and the Communists with their Landon and Roosevelt and the gold standard, opposing them on this huge monopoly, there is Dr. Townsend, there is Rev. Dr. Gerald Smith. By those two leaders I stand four-square.

Ladies and gentlemen, you haven't come here to endorse any political party. You stultify yourselves if you endorse the Socialists, Roosevelt, and Landon. The principles of the National Union, the principles of Dr. Townsend, the principles of Dr. Gerald Smith have been incorporated in the new Union party.

You are not asked to endorse it. Your beloved leader endorses them, and how many of you will follow Dr. Townsend?

In the meantime, ladies and gentlemen, watch your own Judas Iscariots who are taking thirty dirty pieces of silver to sell you out. And thus I must leave for another speech this afternoon, and to tell you that I am willing to die in this struggle to liberate America from the money changers. God bless you.

QUESTIONS TO CONSIDER

1. On what basis did Coughlin attack FDR?
2. Why do you think Coughlin was so popular at the time?

CHAPTER 23

THE SECOND WORLD WAR, 1941–1945

23.1 TEXT OF EXECUTIVE ORDER 9066 (1942) AND EXCERPT FROM *KOREMATSU V. UNITED STATES* (1944)

The internment of Japanese Americans during World War II progressed from West Coast activism to Federal policy to U.S. Supreme Court validation of those policies. The following two documents show how the Roosevelt administration formulated its policy and how a Supreme Court majority ruled in the administration's favor. First, Executive Order 9066, signed in February 1942, just a few months after the Japanese attack on Pearl Harbor, laid the groundwork for Federal officials to forcibly intern the West Coast Japanese and Japanese American population. By June 1942, the government had removed over 110,000 people of Japanese ancestry or citizenship to inland concentration camps, where they were imprisoned until 1945 in often-brutal living conditions. Fred Korematsu, a Japanese-American citizen, refused to report to a relocation center and was arrested. The American Civil Liberties Union sued the government on his behalf. When the case progressed to the Supreme Court, a 6-3 majority ruled in favor of the Federal government's internment program. Here, you will read an excerpt from Hugo Black's majority opinion and Frank Murphy's dissent. In 1988, President Ronald Reagan formally apologized for internment, and the Federal government paid reparations of $20,000 to each surviving internee.

EXECUTIVE ORDER NO. 9066

Whereas the successful prosecution of the war requires every possible protection against espionage and against sabotage to national-defense material, national-defense premises, and national-defense utilities. . .

Now, therefore, by virtue of the authority vested in me as President of the United States, and Commander in Chief of the Army and Navy, I hereby authorize and direct the Secretary of War, and the Military Commanders whom he may from time to time designate,

Sources: "Transcript of Executive Order 9066: Resulting in the Relocation of Japanese (1942), https://www.ourdocuments.gov/doc.php?flash=false&doc=74&page=transcript (Accessed May 21, 2018); "Korematsu v. United States," https://cdn.loc.gov/service/ll/usrep/usrep323/usrep323214/usrep323214.pdf (Accessed June 13, 2018).

whenever he or any designated Commander deems such action necessary or desirable, to prescribe military areas in such places and of such extent as he or the appropriate Military Commander may determine, from which any or all persons may be excluded, and with respect to which, the right of any person to enter, remain in, or leave shall be subject to whatever restrictions the Secretary of War or the appropriate Military Commander may impose in his discretion. The Secretary of War is hereby authorized to provide for residents of any such area who are excluded therefrom, such transportation, food, shelter, and other accommodations as may be necessary, in the judgment of the Secretary of War or the said Military Commander, and until other arrangements are made, to accomplish the purpose of this order. The designation of military areas in any region or locality shall supersede designations of prohibited and restricted areas by the Attorney General under the Proclamations of December 7 and 8, 1941, and shall supersede the responsibility and authority of the Attorney General under the said Proclamations in respect of such prohibited and restricted areas.

I hereby further authorize and direct the Secretary of War and the said Military Commanders to take such other steps as he or the appropriate Military Commander may deem advisable to enforce compliance with the restrictions applicable to each Military area hereinabove authorized to be designated, including the use of Federal troops and other Federal Agencies, with authority to accept assistance of state and local agencies.

I hereby further authorize and direct all Executive Departments, independent establishments and other Federal Agencies, to assist the Secretary of War or the said Military Commanders in carrying out this Executive Order, including the furnishing of medical aid, hospitalization, food, clothing, transportation, use of land, shelter, and other supplies, equipment, utilities, facilities, and services.

This order shall not be construed as modifying or limiting in any way the authority heretofore granted under Executive Order No. 8972, dated December 12, 1941, nor shall it be construed as limiting or modifying the duty and responsibility of the Federal Bureau of Investigation, with respect to the investigation of alleged acts of sabotage or the duty and responsibility

of the Attorney General and the Department of Justice under the Proclamations of December 7 and 8, 1941, prescribing regulations for the conduct and control of alien enemies, except as such duty and responsibility is superseded by the designation of military areas hereunder.

Franklin D. Roosevelt
The White House,
February 19, 1942.

KOREMATSU V. UNITED STATES
MR. JUSTICE BLACK DELIVERED THE OPINION OF THE COURT.

The petitioner, an American citizen of Japanese descent, was convicted in a federal district court for remaining in San Leandro, California, a "Military Area," contrary to Civilian Exclusion Order No. 34 of the Commanding General of the Western Command, U. S. Army, which directed that after May 9, 1942, all persons of Japanese ancestry should be excluded from that area. No question was raised as to petitioner's loyalty to the United States. . . .

Exclusion Order No. 34, which the petitioner knowingly and admittedly violated, was one of a number of military orders and proclamations, all of which were substantially based upon Executive Order No. 9066, 7 Fed. Reg. 1407. That order, issued after we were at war with Japan, declared that "the successful prosecution of the war requires every possible protection against sabotage to national-defense material, national-defense premises, and national-defense utilities. . . ." . . .

. . . The power to exclude includes the power to do it by force if necessary. And any forcible measure must necessarily entail some degree of detention or restraint whatever method of removal is selected. But whichever view is taken, it results in holding that the order under which petitioner was convicted was valid.

It is said that we are dealing here with the case of imprisonment of a citizen in a concentration camp solely because of his ancestry, without evidence or inquiry concerning his loyalty and good disposition towards the United States. Our task would be simple, our duty clear, were this a case involving the imprisonment of a loyal citizen in a concentration camp because of racial prejudice. Regardless of the true nature of the assembly and relocation centers—and we deem it unjustifiable to call them concentration camps with all the ugly connotations that term implies—we are dealing specifically with nothing but an exclusion order. To cast this case into outlines of racial prejudice, without reference to the real military dangers which were presented, merely confuses the issue. Korematsu was not excluded from the Military Area because of hostility to him or his race. He *was* excluded because we are at war with the Japanese Empire, because the properly constituted military authorities feared an invasion of our West Coast and felt constrained to take proper security measures, because they decided that the military urgency of the situation demanded that all citizens of Japanese ancestry be segregated from the West Coast temporarily, and finally, because Congress, reposing its confidence in this time of war in our military leaders—as inevitably it must—determined that they should have the power to do just this. There was evidence of disloyalty on the part of some, the military authorities considered that the need for action was great, and time was short. We cannot—by availing ourselves of the calm perspective of hindsight—now say that at that time these actions were unjustified.

Affirmed.

MR. JUSTICE MURPHY, DISSENTING.

This exclusion of "all persons of Japanese ancestry, both alien and non-alien," from the Pacific Coast area on a plea of military necessity in the absence of martial law ought not to be approved. Such exclusion goes over "the very brink of constitutional power" and falls into the ugly abyss of racism.

In dealing with matters relating to the prosecution and progress of a war, we must accord great respect and consideration to the judgments of the military authorities who are on the scene and who have full knowledge of the military facts. The scope of their discretion must, as a matter of necessity and common sense, be wide. And their judgments ought not to be overruled lightly by those whose training and duties ill-equip them to deal intelligently with matters so vital to the physical security of the nation.

At the same time, however, it is essential that there be definite limits to military discretion, especially where martial law has not been declared. Individuals must not be left impoverished of their constitutional rights on a plea of military necessity that has neither substance nor support. Thus, like other claims conflicting with the asserted constitutional rights of the individual, the military claim must subject itself to the judicial process of having its reasonableness determined and its conflicts with other interests reconciled. "What are the allowable limits of military discretion, and whether or not they have been overstepped in a particular case, are judicial questions." *Sterling* v. *Constantin*, 287 U. S. 378, 401.

The judicial test of whether the Government, on a plea of military necessity, can validly deprive an individual of any of his constitutional rights is whether the deprivation is reasonably related to a public danger that is so "immediate, imminent, and impending" as not to admit of delay and not to permit the intervention of ordinary constitutional processes to alleviate the danger. . . . Civilian Exclusion Order No. 34, banishing from a prescribed area of the Pacific Coast "all persons of Japanese ancestry, both alien and non-alien," clearly does not meet that test. Being an obvious racial discrimination, the order deprives all those within its scope of the equal protection of the laws as guaranteed by the Fifth Amendment. It further deprives these individuals of their constitutional rights to live and work where they will, to establish a home where they choose and to move about freely. In excommunicating them without benefit of hearings, this order also deprives them of all their constitutional rights to procedural due process. Yet no reasonable relation to an "immediate, imminent, and impending" public danger is evident to support this racial restriction which is one of the most sweeping and complete deprivations of constitutional rights in the history of this nation in the absence of martial law.

It must be conceded that the military and naval situation in the spring of 1942 was such as to generate a very real fear of invasion of the Pacific Coast, accompanied by fears of sabotage and espionage in that area. The military command was therefore justified in adopting all reasonable means necessary to combat these dangers. In adjudging the military action taken in light of the then apparent dangers, we must not erect too high or too meticulous standards; it is necessary only that the action have some reasonable relation to the removal of the dangers of invasion, sabotage and espionage. But the exclusion, either temporarily or permanently, of all persons with Japanese blood in their veins has no such reasonable relation. And that relation is lacking because the exclusion order necessarily must rely for its reasonableness upon the assumption that *all* persons of Japanese ancestry may have a dangerous tendency to commit sabotage and espionage and to aid our Japanese enemy in other ways. It is difficult to believe that reason, logic or experience could be marshaled in support of such an assumption.

That this forced exclusion was the result in good measure of this erroneous assumption of racial guilt rather than bona fide military necessity is evidenced by the Commanding Genera's Final Report on the evacuation from the Pacific Coast area. In it he refers to all individuals of Japanese descent as "subversive," as belonging to "an enemy race" whose "racial strains are undiluted," and as constituting "over 112,000 potential enemies . . . at large today" along the Pacific Coast. In support of this blanket condemnation of all persons of Japanese descent, however, no reliable evidence is cited to show that such individuals were generally disloyal, or had generally so conducted themselves in this area as to constitute a special menace to defense installations or war industries, or had otherwise by their behavior furnished reasonable ground for their exclusion as a group.

Justification for the exclusion is sought, instead, mainly upon questionable racial and sociological grounds not ordinarily within the realm of expert military judgment, supplemented by certain semi-military conclusions drawn from an unwarranted use of circumstantial evidence. Individuals of Japanese ancestry are condemned because they are said to be "a large, unassimilated, tightly knit racial group, bound to an enemy nation by strong ties of race, culture, custom and religion." They are claimed to be given to "emperor worshipping ceremonies" and to "dual citizenship." Japanese language schools and allegedly pro-Japanese organizations are cited as evidence of possible group disloyalty, together with facts as to certain persons being educated and residing at length in Japan. It is intimated that many of these individuals deliberately resided "adjacent to strategic points," thus

enabling them "to carry into execution a tremendous program of sabotage on a mass scale should any considerable number of them have been inclined to do so." The need for protective custody is also asserted. The report refers without identity to "numerous incidents of violence" as well as to other admittedly unverified or cumulative incidents. From this, plus certain other events not shown to have been connected with the Japanese Americans, it is concluded that the "situation was fraught with danger to the Japanese population itself" and that the general public "was ready to take matters into its own hands." Finally, it is intimated, though not directly charged or proved, that persons of Japanese ancestry were responsible for three minor isolated shellings and bombings of the Pacific Coast area, as well as for unidentified radio transmissions and night signaling.

The main reasons relied upon by those responsible for the forced evacuation, therefore, do not prove a reasonable relation between the group characteristics of Japanese Americans and the dangers of invasion, sabotage and espionage. The reasons appear, instead, to be largely an accumulation of much of the misinformation, half-truths and insinuations that for years have been directed against Japanese Americans by people with racial and economic prejudices—the same people who have been among the foremost advocates of the evacuation. A military judgment based upon such racial and sociological considerations is not entitled to the great weight ordinarily given the judgments based upon strictly military considerations. Especially is this so when every charge relative to race, religion, culture, geographical location, and legal and economic status has been substantially discredited by independent studies made by experts in these matters.

The military necessity which is essential to the validity of the evacuation order thus resolves itself into a few intimations that certain individuals actively aided the enemy, from which it is inferred that the entire group of Japanese Americans could not be trusted to be or remain loyal to the United States. No one denies, of course, that there were some disloyal persons of Japanese descent on the Pacific Coast who did all in their power to aid their ancestral land. Similar disloyal activities have been engaged in by many persons of German, Italian and even more pioneer stock in our country. But to infer that examples of individual disloyalty prove group disloyalty and justify discriminatory action against the entire group is to deny that under our system of law individual guilt is the sole basis for deprivation of rights. Moreover, this inference, which is at the very heart of the evacuation orders, has been used in support of the abhorrent and despicable treatment of minority groups by the dictatorial tyrannies which this nation is now pledged to destroy. To give constitutional sanction to that inference in this case, however well-intentioned may have been the military command on the Pacific Coast, is to adopt one of the cruelest of the rationales used by our enemies to destroy the dignity of the individual and to encourage and open the door to discriminatory actions against other minority groups in the passions of tomorrow.

QUESTIONS TO CONSIDER

1. How did Roosevelt defend his reasoning in Executive Order 9066?
2. In *Korematsu v. United States,* how did Black and Murphy defend their arguments? Which do you find more persuasive?

23.2 JOINT CHIEFS OF STAFF MEMORANDUM ABOUT A POTENTIAL GROUND INVASION OF JAPAN (1945)

As World War II in Europe drew to a close, American leaders debated how to force Japan to surrender. One potential plan presented, "Operation Downfall," was to invade Japan in two waves. First, American military leaders planned to invade Kyushu, the southern island of Japan. Second, they would invade mainland Japan. In June 1945, American leaders gathered to secretly discuss the potential ground invasion. Nazi Germany had surrendered one month earlier, so they were now focused completely on the Pacific theater. Here, you will read the declassified minutes from their discussion. As it turned out, Operation Downfall never began, as President Harry Truman instead decided to use atomic weapons on Hiroshima and Nagasaki on August 6 and August 9, respectively. Japan surrendered on August 15, 1945.

THE PRESIDENT stated that he had called the meeting for the purpose of informing himself with respect to the details of the campaign against Japan set out in Admiral Leahy's memorandum to the Joint Chiefs of Staff of 14 June. He asked General Marshall if he would express his opinion.

GENERAL MARSHALL pointed out that the present situation with respect to operations against Japan was practically identical with the situation which had existed in connection with the operations proposed against Normandy. He then read, as an expression of his views, the following digest of a memorandum

Source: "Memorandum by the Secretary of the Joint Chiefs of Staff (McFarland)," *Foreign Relations of the United States: Diplomatic Papers, The Conference of Berlin (The Potsdam Conference), 1945, Volume I,* https://history.state.gov/historicaldocuments/frus1945Berlinv01/d598 (Accessed May 21, 2018).

prepared by the Joint Chiefs of Staff for presentation to the President (J. C. S. 1388):

Our air and sea power has already greatly reduced movement of Jap shipping south of Korea and should in the next few months cut it to a trickle if not choke it off entirely. Hence, there is no need for seizing further positions in order to block Japanese communications south of Korea.

General MacArthur and Admiral Nimitz are in agreement with the Chiefs of Staff in selecting 1 November as the target date to go into Kyushu because by that time:

a. If we press preparations we can be ready.
b. Our estimates are that our air action will have smashed practically every industrial target worth hitting in Japan as well as destroying huge areas in the Jap cities.
c. The Japanese Navy, if any still exists, will be completely powerless.
d. Our sea action and air power will have cut Jap reinforcement capabilities from the mainland to negligible proportions.

Important considerations bearing on the 1 November date rather than a later one are the weather and cutting to a minimum Jap time for preparation of defenses. If we delay much after the beginning of November the weather situation in the succeeding months may be such that the invasion of Japan, and hence the end of the war, will be delayed for up to 6 months.

An outstanding military point about attacking Korea is the difficult terrain and beach conditions which appear to make the only acceptable assault areas Fusan [Pusan] in the southeast corner and Keijo [Seoul], well up the western side. To get to Fusan, which is a strongly fortified area, we must move large and vulnerable assault forces past heavily fortified Japanese areas. The operation appears more difficult and costly than assault on Kyushu. Keijo appears an equally difficult and costly operation. After we have undertaken either one of them we still will not be as far forward as going into Kyushu.

The Kyushu operation is essential to a strategy of strangulation and appears to be the least costly worthwhile operation following Okinawa. The basic point is

that a lodgement in Kyushu is essential, both to tightening our strangle hold of blockade and bombardment on Japan, and to forcing capitulation by invasion of the Tokyo Plain.

We are bringing to bear against the Japanese every weapon and all the force we can employ and there is no reduction in our maximum possible application of bombardment and blockade, while at the same time we are pressing invasion preparations. It seems that if the Japanese are ever willing to capitulate short of complete military defeat in the field they will do it when faced by the completely hopeless prospect occasioned by (1) destruction already wrought by air bombardment and sea blockade, coupled with (2) a landing on Japan indicating the firmness of our resolution, and also perhaps coupled with (3) the entry or threat of entry of Russia into the war.

With reference to clean-up of the Asiatic mainland, our objective should be to get the Russians to deal with the Japs in Manchuria (and Korea if necessary) and to vitalize the Chinese to a point where, with assistance of American air power and some supplies, they can mop out their own country.

Casualties. Our experience in the Pacific War is so diverse as to casualties that it is considered wrong to give any estimate in numbers. Using various combinations of Pacific experience, the War Department staff reaches the conclusion that the cost of securing a worthwhile position in Korea would almost certainly be greater than the cost of the Kyushu operation. Points on the optimistic side of the Kyushu operation are that: General MacArthur has not yet accepted responsibility for going ashore where there would be disproportionate casualties. The nature of the objective area gives room for maneuver, both on the land and by sea. As to any discussion of specific operations, the following data are pertinent:

The record of General MacArthur's operations from 1 March 1944 through 1 May 1945 shows 13,742 U. S. killed compared to 310,165 Japanese killed, or a ratio of 22 to 1.

There is reason to believe that the first 30 days in Kyushu should not exceed the price we have paid for Luzon. It is a grim fact that there is not an easy, bloodless way to victory in war and it is the thankless task of the leaders to maintain their firm outward front which holds the resolution of their subordinates. Any irresolution in the leaders may result in costly weakening and indecision in the subordinates. . . .

An important point about Russian participation in the war is that the impact of Russian entry on the already hopeless Japanese may well be the decisive action levering them into capitulation at that time or shortly thereafter if we land in Japan.

In considering the matter of command and control in the Pacific war which the British wish to raise at the next conference, we must bear in mind the point that anything smacking of combined command in the Pacific might increase the difficulties with Russia and perhaps with China. Furthermore the obvious inefficiencies of combined command may directly result in increased cost in resources and American lives.

General Marshall said that he had asked General MacArthur's opinion on the proposed operation and had received from him the following telegram, which General Marshall then read:

"I believe the operation presents less hazards of excessive loss than any other that has been suggested and that its decisive effect will eventually save lives by eliminating wasteful operations of non-decisive character. I regard the operation as the most economical one in effort and lives that is possible. In this respect it must be remembered that the several preceding months will involve practically no losses in ground troops and that sooner or later a decisive ground attack must be made. The hazard and loss will be greatly lessened if an attack is launched from Siberia sufficiently ahead of our target date to commit the enemy to major combat. I most earnestly recommend no change in OLYMPIC. Additional subsidiary attacks will simply build up our final total casualties."

GENERAL MARSHALL said that it was his personal view that the operation against Kyushu was the only course to pursue. He felt that air power alone was not sufficient to put the Japanese out of the war. It was unable alone to put the Germans out. General Eaker and General Eisenhower both agreed to this. Against the Japanese, scattered through mountainous country, the problem would be much more difficult than it had been in Germany. He felt that this plan offered the only way the Japanese could be forced into a feeling of utter helplessness. The operation would be difficult

but not more so than the assault in Normandy. He was convinced that every individual moving to the Pacific should be indoctrinated with a firm determination to see it through.

ADMIRAL KING agreed with General Marshall's views and said that the more he studied the matter, the more he was impressed with the strategic location of Kyushu, which he considered the key to the success of any siege operations. He pointed out that within three months the effects of air power based on Okinawa will begin to be felt strongly in Japan. It seemed to him that Kyushu followed logically after Okinawa. It was a natural setup. It was his opinion that we should do Kyushu now, after which there would be time to judge the effect of possible operations by the Russians and the Chinese. The weather constituted quite a factor. So far as preparation was concerned, we must aim now for Tokyo Plain; otherwise we will never be able to accomplish it. If preparations do not go forward now, they cannot be arranged for later. Once started, however, they can always be stopped if desired.

GENERAL MARSHALL agreed that Kyushu was a necessity and pointed out that it constituted a landing in the Japanese homeland. Kyushu having been arranged for, the decision as to further action could be made later.

THE PRESIDENT inquired if a later decision would not depend on what the Russians agree to do. It was agreed that this would have considerable influence.

THE PRESIDENT then asked Admiral Leahy for his views of the situation.

ADMIRAL LEAHY recalled that the President had been interested in knowing what the price in casualties for Kyushu would be and whether or not that price could be paid. He pointed out that the troops on Okinawa had lost 35 percent in casualties. If this percentage were applied to the number of troops to be employed in Kyushu, he thought from the similarity of the fighting to be expected that this would give a good estimate of the casualties to be expected. He was interested therefore in finding out how many troops are to be used in Kyushu.

ADMIRAL KING called attention to what he considered an important difference in Okinawa and Kyushu. There had been only one way to go on Okinawa. This meant a straight frontal attack against a highly fortified position. On Kyushu, however, landings would be made on three fronts simultaneously and there would be much more room for maneuver. It was his opinion that a realistic casualty figure for Kyushu would lie somewhere between the number experienced by General MacArthur in the operations on Luzon and the Okinawa casualties.

GENERAL MARSHALL pointed out that the total assault troops for the Kyushu campaign were shown in the memorandum prepared for the President as 766,700. He said, in answer to the President's question as to what opposition could be expected on Kyushu, that it was estimated at eight Japanese divisions or about 350,000 troops. He said that divisions were still being raised in Japan and that reinforcement from other areas was possible but it was becoming increasingly difficult and painful.

THE PRESIDENT asked about the possibility of reinforcements for Kyushu moving south from the other Japanese islands.

GENERAL MARSHALL said that it was expected that all communications with Kyushu would be destroyed.

ADMIRAL KING described in some detail the land communications between the other Japanese islands and Kyushu and stated that as a result of operations already planned, the Japanese would have to depend on sea shipping for any reinforcement.

ADMIRAL LEAHY stressed the fact that Kyushu was an island. It was crossed by a mountain range, which would be difficult for either the Japanese or the Americans to cross. The Kyushu operation, in effect, contemplated the taking of another island from which to bring increased air power against Japan.

THE PRESIDENT expressed the view that it was practically creating another Okinawa closer to Japan, to which the Chiefs of Staff agreed.

THE PRESIDENT then asked General Eaker for his opinion of the operation as an air man.

GENERAL EAKER said that he agreed completely with the statements made by General Marshall in his digest of the memorandum prepared for the President. He had just received a cable in which General Arnold also expressed complete agreement. He stated that any blockade of Honshu was dependent upon airdromes on Kyushu; that the air plan contemplated employment of 40 groups of heavy bombers against Japan and that these could not be deployed without the use of

airfields on Kyushu. He said that those who advocated the use against Japan of air power alone overlooked the very impressive fact that air casualties are always much heavier when the air faces the enemy alone and that these casualties never fail to drop as soon as the ground forces come in. Present air casualties are averaging 2 percent per mission, about 30 percent per month. He wished to point out and to emphasize that delay favored only the enemy and he urged that there be no delay.

THE PRESIDENT said that as he understood it the Joint Chiefs of Staff, after weighing all the possibilities of the situation and considering all possible alternative plans were still of the unanimous opinion that the Kyushu operation was the best solution under the circumstances.

The Chiefs of Staff agreed that this was so.

THE PRESIDENT then asked the Secretary of War for his opinion.

MR. STIMSON agreed with the Chiefs of Staff that there was no other choice. He felt that he was personally responsible to the President more for political than for military considerations. It was his opinion that there was a large submerged class in Japan who do not favor the present war and whose full opinion and influence had never yet been felt. He felt sure that this submerged class would fight and fight tenaciously if attacked on their own ground. He was concerned that something should be done to arouse them and to develop any possible influence they might have before it became necessary to come to grips with them.

THE PRESIDENT stated that this possibility was being worked on all the time. He asked if the invasion of Japan by white men would not have the effect of more closely uniting the Japanese.

MR. STIMSON thought there was every prospect of this. He agreed with the plan proposed by the Joint Chiefs of Staff as being the best thing to do, but he still hoped for some fruitful accomplishment through other means.

THE PRESIDENT then asked for the views of the Secretary of the Navy.

MR. FORRESTAL pointed out that even if we wished to besiege Japan for a year or a year and a half, the capture of Kyushu would still be essential. Therefore, the sound decision is to proceed with the operation against

Kyushu. There will still be time thereafter to consider the main decision in the light of subsequent events.

Mr. McCloy said he felt that the time was propitious now to study closely all possible means of bringing out the influence of the submerged group in Japan which had been referred to by Mr. Stimson.

The President stated that one of his objectives in connection with the coming conference would be to get from Russia all the assistance in the war that was possible. To this end he wanted to know all the decisions that he would have to make in advance in order to occupy the strongest possible position in the discussions.

Admiral Leahy said that he could not agree with those who said to him that unless we obtain the unconditional surrender of the Japanese that we will have lost the war. He feared no menace from Japan in the foreseeable future, even if we were unsuccessful in forcing unconditional surrender. What he did fear was that our insistence on unconditional surrender would result only in making the Japanese desperate and thereby increase our casualty lists. He did not think that this was at all necessary.

The President stated that it was with that thought in mind that he had left the door open for Congress to take appropriate action with reference to unconditional surrender. However, he did not feel that he could take any action at this time to change public opinion on the matter.

The President said he considered the Kyushu plan all right from the military standpoint and, so far as he was concerned, the Joint Chiefs of Staff could go ahead with it; that we can do this operation and then decide as to the final action later.

The President reiterated that his main reason for this conference with the Chiefs of Staff was his desire to know definitely how far we could afford to go in the Japanese campaign. He had hoped that there was a possibility of preventing an Okinawa from one end of Japan to the other. He was clear on the situation now and was quite sure that the Joint Chiefs of Staff should proceed with the Kyushu operation.

With reference to operations in China, General Marshall expressed the opinion that we should not seek an over-all commander in China. The present situation in which the Generalissimo was supporting General Wedemeyer, acting as his Chief of Staff, was entirely satisfactory. The suggestion of the appointment of an over-all commander might cause some difficulty.

Admiral King said he wished to emphasize the point that, regardless of the desirability of the Russians entering the war, they were not indispensable and he did not think we should go so far as to beg them to come in. While the cost of defeating Japan would be greater, there was no question in his mind but that we could handle it alone. He thought that the realization of this fact should greatly strengthen the President's hand in the forthcoming conference.

The President and the Chiefs of Staff then discussed certain other matters.

QUESTIONS TO CONSIDER

1. What were the assembled leaders focused on most? What surprised you?
2. Does this change at all how you think about World War II?

23.3 J. ROBERT OPPENHEIMER, EXCERPT FROM "SPEECH TO THE ASSOCIATION OF LOS ALAMOS SCIENTISTS" (1945)

J. Robert Oppenheimer (1904–1967) was, to put it simply, "the father of the atomic bomb." In 1942, Army officials chose Oppenheimer, then a Professor of Theoretical Physics at the California Institute of Technology, to lead the Manhattan Project for the development of an atomic weapon. Though Oppenheimer was affiliated with a variety of left-wing and communist organizations, Army officials chose him based on his practical and theoretical knowledge. For the next three years, at the Los Alamos Laboratory in New Mexico, which the Army built for the project, Oppenheimer directed the work of over 6,000 people in a variety of fields. In July 1945, the scientists completed a successful nuclear test at Los Alamos, and President Harry Truman ordered the weapons used just a few weeks later. After his work became public knowledge, Oppenheimer became a public figure. He would later advocate for global organizations to limit nuclear proliferation. In November 1945, Oppenheimer gave the following speech to the Association of Los Alamos Scientists. In it, he speculated on the new world those scientists had ushered into existence through the creation of the atomic bomb.

. . . What has happened to us—it is really rather major, it is so major that I think in some ways one returns to the greatest developments of the twentieth century, to the discovery of relativity, and to the whole development of atomic theory and its interpretation in terms of complementarity, for analogy. These things, as you know, forced us to re-consider the relations between science and common sense. They forced on us the recognition that the fact that we were in the habit of talking a certain language and using certain concepts did not necessarily imply that there was anything in the real world to correspond to these. They forced us to be prepared for the inadequacy of the ways in which human beings attempted to deal with reality, for that reality. In some ways I think these virtues, which scientists quite reluctantly were forced to learn by the nature of the world they were studying, may be useful even today in preparing us for somewhat more radical views of what the issues are than would be natural or easy for people who had not been through this experience.

But the real impact of the creation of the atomic bomb and atomic weapons—to understand that one has to look further back, look, I think, to the times when physical science was growing in the days of the renaissance, and when the threat that science offered was felt so deeply throughout the Christian world. The analogy is, of course, not perfect. You may even wish to think of the days in the last century when the theories of evolution seemed a threat to the values by which men lived. The analogy is not perfect because there is nothing in atomic weapons—there is certainly nothing that we have done here or in the physics or chemistry that immediately preceded our work here—in which any revolutionary ideas were involved. I don't think that the conceptions of nuclear fission have strained any man's attempts to understand them, and I don't

Source: "Speech to the Association of Los Alamos Scientists," http://www.atomicarchive.com/Docs/ManhattanProject/Oppy-Farewell.shtml (Accessed June 13, 2018).

feel that any of us have really learned in a deep sense very much from following this up. It is in a quite different way. It is not an idea—it is a development and a reality—but it has in common with the early days of physical science the fact that the very existence of science is threatened, and its value is threatened. This is the point that I would like to speak a little about.

I think that it hardly needs to be said why the impact is so strong. There are three reasons: one is the extraordinary speed with which things which were right on the frontier of science were translated into terms where they affected many living people, and potentially all people. Another is the fact, quite accidental in many ways, and connected with the speed, that scientists themselves played such a large part, not merely in providing the foundation for atomic weapons, but in actually making them. In this we are certainly closer to it than any other group. The third is that the thing we made—partly because of the technical nature of the problem, partly because we worked hard, partly because we had good breaks—really arrived in the world with such a shattering reality and suddenness that there was no opportunity for the edges to be worn off.

In considering what the situation of science is, it may be helpful to think a little of what people said and felt of their motives in coming into this job. One always has to worry that what people say of their motives is not adequate. Many people said different things, and most of them, I think, had some validity. There was in the first place the great concern that our enemy might develop these weapons before we did, and the feeling—at least, in the early days, the very strong feeling—that without atomic weapons it might be very difficult, it might be an impossible, it might be an incredibly long thing to win the war. These things wore off a little as it became clear that the war would be won in any case. Some people, I think, were motivated by curiosity, and rightly so; and some by a sense of adventure, and rightly so. Others had more political arguments and said, "Well, we know that atomic weapons are in principle possible, and it is not right that the threat of their unrealized possibility should hang over the world. It is right that the world should know what can be done in their field and deal with it." And the people added to that that it was a time when all over the world men would be particularly ripe and

open for dealing with this problem because of the immediacy of the evils of war, because of the universal cry from everyone that one could not go through this thing again, even a war without atomic bombs. And there was finally, and I think rightly, the feeling that there was probably no place in the world where the development of atomic weapons would have a better chance of leading to a reasonable solution, and a smaller chance of leading to disaster, than within the United States. I believe all these things that people said are true, and I think I said them all myself at one time or another.

But when you come right down to it the reason that we did this job is because it was an organic necessity. If you are a scientist you cannot stop such a thing. If you are a scientist you believe that it is good to find out how the world works; that it is good to find out what the realities are; that it is good to turn over to mankind at large the greatest possible power to control the world and to deal with it according to its lights and its values.

There has been a lot of talk about the evil of secrecy, of concealment, of control, of security. Some of that talk has been on a rather low plane, limited really to saying that it is difficult or inconvenient to work in a world where you are not free to do what you want. I think that the talk has been justified, and that the almost unanimous resistance of scientists to the imposition of control and secrecy is a justified position, but I think that the reason for it may lie a little deeper. I think that it comes from the fact that secrecy strikes at the very root of what science is, and what it is for. It is not possible to be a scientist unless you believe that it is good to learn. It is not good to be a scientist, and it is not possible, unless you think that it is of the highest value to share your knowledge, to share it with anyone who is interested. It is not possible to be a scientist unless you believe that the knowledge of the world, and the power which this gives, is a thing which is of intrinsic value to humanity, and that you are using it to help in the spread of knowledge, and are willing to take the consequences. And, therefore, I think that this resistance which we feel and see all around us to anything which is an attempt to treat science of the future as though it were rather a dangerous thing, a thing that must be watched and managed, is resisted not because of its inconvenience—I think we are in a position where we must be willing to take any inconvenience—but resisted because it is based on a philosophy incompatible with that by which we live, and have learned to live in the past. . . .

. . . I think that these efforts to diffuse and weaken the nature of the crisis make it only more dangerous. I think it is for us to accept it as a very grave crisis, to realize that these atomic weapons which we have started to make are very terrible, that they involve a change, that they are not just a slight modification: to accept this, and to accept with it the necessity for those transformations in the world which will make it possible to integrate these developments into human life. As scientists I think we have perhaps a little greater ability to accept change, and accept radical change, because of our experiences in the pursuit of science. And that may help us—that, and the fact that we have lived with it—to be of some use in understanding these problems.

It is clear to me that wars have changed. It is clear to me that if these first bombs—the bomb that was dropped on Nagasaki—that if these can destroy ten square miles, then that is really quite something. It is clear to me that they are going to be very cheap if anyone wants to make them; it is clear to me that this is a situation where a quantitative change, and a change in which the advantage of aggression compared to defense—of attack compared to defense—is shifted, where this quantitative change has all the character of a change in quality, of a change in the nature of the world. . . . . .

Those are very far-reaching changes. They are changes in the relations between nations, not only in spirit, not only in law, but also in conception and feeling. I don't know which of these is prior; they must all work together, and only the gradual interaction of one on the other can make a reality. I don't agree with those who say the first step is to have a structure of international law. I don't agree with those who say the only thing is to have friendly feelings. All of these things will be involved. I think it is true to say that atomic weapons are a peril which affect everyone in the world, and in that sense a completely common problem, as common a problem as it was for the Allies to defeat the Nazis. I think that in order to handle this common problem there must be a complete sense of community

responsibility. I do not think that one may expect that people will contribute to the solution of the problem until they are aware of their ability to take part in the solution. I think that it is a field in which the implementation of such a common responsibility has certain decisive advantages. It is a new field, in which the position of vested interests in various parts of the world is very much less serious than in others. It is serious in this country, and that is one of our problems. It is a new field, in which the role of science has been so great that it is to my mind hardly thinkable that the international traditions of science, and the fraternity of scientists, should not play a constructive part. It is a new field, in which just the novelty and the special characteristics of the technical operations should enable one to establish a community of interest which might almost be regarded as a pilot plant for a new type of international collaboration. I speak of it as a pilot plant because it is quite clear that the control of atomic weapons cannot be in itself the unique end of such operation. The only unique end can be a world that is united, and a world in which war will not occur. But those things don't happen overnight, and in this field it would seem that one could get started, and get started without meeting those insuperable obstacles which history has so often placed in the way of any effort of cooperation. Now, this is not an easy thing, and the point I want to make, the one point I want to hammer home, is what an enormous change in spirit is involved. There are things which we hold very dear, and I think rightly hold very dear; I would say that the word democracy perhaps stood for some of them as well as any other word. There are many parts of the world in which there is no democracy. There are other things which we hold dear, and which we rightly should. And when I speak of a new spirit in international affairs I mean that even to these deepest of things which we cherish, and for which Americans have been willing to die—and certainly most of us would be willing to die—even in these deepest things, we realize that there is something more profound than that; namely, the common bond with other men everywhere. It is only if you do that that this makes sense; because if you approach the problem and say, "We know what is right and we would like to use the atomic bomb to persuade you to agree with us," then you are in a very weak position and you will not succeed, because under those conditions you will not succeed in delegating responsibility for the survival of men. It is a purely unilateral statement; you will find yourselves attempting by force of arms to prevent a disaster.

I want to express the utmost sympathy with the people who have to grapple with this problem and in the strongest terms to urge you not to underestimate its difficulty. I can think of an analogy, and I hope it is not a completely good analogy: in the days in the first half of the nineteenth century there were many people, mostly in the North, but some in the South, who thought that there was no evil on earth more degrading than human slavery, and nothing that they would more willingly devote their lives to than its eradication. Always when I was young I wondered why it was that when Lincoln was President he did not declare that the war against the South, when it broke out, was a war that slavery should be abolished, that this was the central point, the rallying point, of that war. Lincoln was severely criticized by many of the Abolitionists as you know, by many then called radicals, because he seemed to be waging a war which did not hit the thing that was most important. But Lincoln realized, and I have only in the last months come to appreciate the depth and wisdom of it, that beyond the issue of slavery was the issue of the community of the people of the country, and the issue of the Union. I hope that today this will not be an issue calling for war; but I wanted to remind you that in order to preserve the Union Lincoln had to subordinate the immediate problem of the eradication of slavery, and trust—and I think if he had had his way it would have gone so—to the conflict of these ideas in a united people to eradicate it. . . .

I think that we have no hope at all if we yield in our belief in the value of science, in the good that it can be to the world to know about reality, about nature, to attain a gradually greater and greater control of nature, to learn, to teach, to understand. I think that if we lose our faith in this we stop being scientists, we sell out our heritage, we lose what we have most of value for this time of crisis.

But there is another thing: we are not only scientists; we are men, too. We cannot forget our dependence on our fellow men. I mean not only our material dependence, without which no science would be possible, and without which we could not work; I mean also our deep moral dependence, in that the value of science must lie in the world of men, that all our roots lie there. These are the strongest bonds in the world, stronger than those even that bind us to one another, these are the deepest bonds—that bind us to our fellow men.

QUESTIONS TO CONSIDER

1. How did Oppenheimer feel about the world the atomic bomb had created?
2. What types of problems did he foresee in the future? Did he forecast accurately?

23.4 JOHN HERSEY, EXCERPT FROM "HIROSHIMA" (1946)

On August 6, 1945, the U.S. Air Force, on the orders of President Harry Truman, dropped an atomic bomb on the Japanese city of Hiroshima. An important Japanese industrial center, Hiroshima was also home to an important military headquarters. The damage was immediate and catastrophic. Thirty percent of the city's population—some 70,000 to 80,000 people were killed in the massive explosion. Another 70,000 were injured, and 4.7 square miles of Hiroshima were destroyed, including sixty-nine percent of the city's buildings. Hiroshima and Nagasaki, bombed three days later, are the only two cities in world history to be targeted by a nuclear weapon. In May 1946, *The New Yorker* writer John Hersey approached his editors and asked them to support a trip to Hiroshima to report on the damage there. The resulting work, "Hiroshima," is perhaps the most important piece ever published on the impact of nuclear weapons, a 31,000-word masterpiece that focused on six survivors. *The New Yorker* devoted the entire August 31st edition to Hersey's article. In the following excerpt, you will read portions from Hiroshima about the bombing and the resulting prevalent radiation sickness. Hersey later republished *Hiroshima* as a book.

A t exactly fifteen minutes past eight in the morning, on August 6, 1945, Japanese time, at the moment when the atomic bomb flashed above Hiroshima, Miss Toshiko Sasaki, a clerk in the personnel department of the East Asia Tin Works, had just sat down at her place in the plant office and was turning her head to speak to the girl at the next desk. At that same moment, Dr. Masakazu Fujii was settling down cross-legged to read the Osaka *Asahi* on the porch of his private hospital, overhanging one of the seven deltaic rivers which divide Hiroshima; Mrs. Hatsuyo Nakamura, a tailor's widow, stood by the window of her kitchen, watching a neighbor tearing down his house because it lay in the path of an air-raid-defense fire lane; Father Wilhelm Kleinsorge, a German priest of the Society of Jesus, reclined in his underwear on a cot on the top floor of his order's three-story mission house, reading a Jesuit magazine, *Stimmen der Zeit*; Dr. Terufumi Sasaki, a young member of the surgical staff of the city's large, modern Red Cross Hospital, walked along one of the hospital corridors with a blood specimen for a Wassermann test in his hand; and the Reverend Mr. Kiyoshi Tanimoto, pastor of the Hiroshima Methodist Church, paused at the door of a rich man's house in Koi, the city's western suburb, and prepared to unload a handcart full of things he had evacuated from town in fear of the massive B-29 raid which everyone expected Hiroshima to suffer. A hundred thousand people were killed by the atomic bomb, and these six were among the survivors. They still wonder why they lived when so many others died. Each of them counts many small items of chance or volition—a step taken in time, a decision to go indoors, catching one streetcar instead of the next—that spared him. And now each knows that in the act of survival he lived a dozen lives and saw more death than he ever thought he would see. At the time, none of them knew anything.

T he Reverend Mr. Tanimoto got up at five o'clock that morning. He was alone in the parsonage, because for some time his wife had been commuting with their year-old baby to spend nights with a friend in Ushida, a suburb to the north. Of all the important cities of Japan, only two, Kyoto and Hiroshima, had not been visited in strength by *B-san*, or Mr. B, as the Japanese, with a mixture of respect and unhappy familiarity, called the B-29; and Mr. Tanimoto, like all his neighbors and friends, was almost sick with anxiety. He had heard uncomfortably detailed accounts of mass raids on Kure, Iwakuni, Tokuyama, and other nearby towns; he was sure Hiroshima's turn would come soon. He had slept badly the night before, because there had been several air-raid warnings. Hiroshima had been getting such warnings almost every night for weeks, for at that time the B-29s were using Lake Biwa, northeast of Hiroshima, as a rendez-vous point, and no matter what city the Americans planned to hit, the Superfortresses streamed in over the coast near Hiroshima. The frequency of the warnings and the continued abstinence of Mr. B with respect to Hiroshima had made its citizens jittery; a rumor was going around that the Americans were saving something special for the city.

Mr. Tanimoto is a small man, quick to talk, laugh, and cry. He wears his black hair parted in the middle and rather long; the prominence of the frontal bones just above his eyebrows and the smallness of his mustache, mouth, and chin give him a strange, old-young look, boyish and yet wise, weak and yet fiery. He moves nervously and fast, but with a restraint which suggests that he is a cautious, thoughtful man. He showed, indeed, just those qualities in the uneasy days before the bomb fell. Besides having his wife spend the nights in Ushida, Mr. Tanimoto had been carrying all the portable things from his church, in the close-packed residential district called Nagaragawa, to a house that belonged to a rayon manufacturer in Koi, two miles from the center of town. They rayon man, a Mr. Matsui, has opened his then unoccupied estate to a large number of his friends and acquaintances, so that they might evacuate whatever they wished to a safe distance from the probable target area. Mr. Tanimoto had had no difficulty in moving chairs, hymnals, Bibles, altar gear, and church records by pushcart himself, but the organ console and an upright piano required some aid. A friend of his named Matsuo had, the day before, helped him get the piano out to Koi; in return, he had promised this day to assist Mr. Matsuo in hauling out a daughter's belongings. That is why he had risen so early.

Mr. Tanimoto cooked his own breakfast. He felt awfully tired. The effort of moving the piano the day before, a sleepless night, weeks of worry and unbalanced diet, the cares of his parish—all combined to make him feel hardly adequate to the new day's work. There was another thing, too: Mr. Tanimoto had studied theology at Emory College, in Atlanta, Georgia; he had graduated in 1940; he spoke excellent English; he dressed in American clothes; he had corresponded with many American friends right up to the time the war began; and among a people obsessed with a fear of being spied upon—perhaps almost obsessed himself— he found himself growing increasingly uneasy. The police had questioned him several times, and just a few days before, he had heard that an influential acquaintance, a Mr. Tanaka, a retired officer of the Toyo Kisen Kaisha steamship line, an anti-Christian, a man famous in Hiroshima for his showy philanthropies and notorious for his personal tyrannies, had been telling people that Tanimoto should not be trusted. In compensation, to show himself publicly a good Japanese, Mr. Tanimoto had taken on the chairmanship of his local *tonarigumi*, or Neighborhood Association, and to his other duties and concerns this position had added the business of organizing air-raid defense for about twenty families.

Before six o'clock that morning, Mr. Tanimoto started for Mr. Matsuo's house. There he found that their burden was to be a *tansu*, a large Japanese cabinet, full of clothing and household goods. The two men set out. The morning was perfectly clear and so warm that the day promised to be uncomfortable. A few minutes after they started, the air-raid siren went off—a minute-long blast that warned of approaching planes but indicated to the people of Hiroshima only a slight degree of danger, since it sounded every morning at this time, when an American weather plane came over. The two men pulled and pushed the handcart through the city streets. Hiroshima was a fan-shaped city, lying mostly on the six islands formed by the seven estuarial rivers that branch out from the Ota River; its main commercial and residential districts, covering about four square miles in the center of the city, contained three-quarters of its population, which had been reduced by several evacuation programs from a wartime peak of 380,000 to about 245,000. Factories and other residential districts, or suburbs, lay compactly around the edges of the city. To the south were the docks, an airport, and the island-studded Inland Sea. A rim of mountains runs around the other three sides of the delta. Mr. Tanimoto and Mr. Matsuo took their way through the shopping center, already full of people, and across two of the rivers to the sloping streets of Koi, and up them to the outskirts and foothills. As they started up a valley away from the tight-ranked houses, the all-clear sounded. (The Japanese radar operators, detecting only three planes, supposed that they comprised a reconnaissance.) Pushing the handcart up to the rayon man's house was tiring, and the men, after they had maneuvered their load into the driveway and to the front steps, paused to rest awhile. They stood with a wing of the house between them and the city. Like most homes in this part of Japan, the house consisted of a wooden frame and wooden walls supporting a heavy tile roof. Its front hall, packed with rolls of bedding and clothing, looked like a cool cave full of fat cushions. Opposite the house, to the right of the front door, there was a large, finicky rock garden. There was no sound of planes. The morning was still; the place was cool and pleasant.

Then a tremendous flash of light cut across the sky. Mr. Tanimoto has a distinct recollection that it travelled from east to west, from the city toward the hills. It seemed a sheet of sun. Both he and Mr. Matsuo reacted in terror—and both had time to react (for they were 3,500 yards, or two miles, from the center of the explosion). Mr. Matsuo dashed up the front steps into the house and dived among the bedrolls and buried himself there. Mr. Tanimoto took four or five steps and threw himself between two big rocks in the garden. He bellied up very hard against one of them. As his face was against the stone, he did not see what happened. He felt a sudden pressure, and then splinters and pieces of board and fragments of tile fell on him. He heard no roar. (Almost no one in Hiroshima recalls hearing any noise of the bomb. But a fisherman in his sampan on the Inland Sea near Tsuzu, the man with whom Mr. Tanimoto's mother-in-law and sister-in-law were living, saw the flash and heard a tremendous explosion; he was nearly twenty miles from Hiroshima,

but the thunder was greater than when the B-29s hit Iwakuni, only five miles away.)

When he dared, Mr. Tanimoto raised his head and saw that the rayon man's house had collapsed. He thought a bomb had fallen directly on it. Such clouds of dust had risen that there was a sort of twilight around. In panic, not thinking for the moment of Mr. Matsuo under the ruins, he dashed out into the street. He noticed as he ran that the concrete wall of the estate had fallen over—toward the house rather than away from it. In the street, the first thing he saw was a squad of soldiers who had been burrowing into the hillside opposite, making one of the thousands of dugouts in which the Japanese apparently intended to resist invasion, hill by hill, life for life; the soldiers were coming out of the hole, where they should have been safe, and blood was running from their heads, chests, and backs. They were silent and dazed.

Under what seemed to be a local dust cloud, the day grew darker and darker. . . .

By nightfall, ten thousand victims of the explosion had invaded the Red Cross Hospital, and Dr. Sasaki, worn out, was moving aimlessly and dully up and down the stinking corridors with wads of bandage and bottles of mercurochrome, still wearing the glasses he had taken from the wounded nurse, binding up the worst cuts as he came to them. Other doctors were putting compresses of saline solution on the worst burns. That was all they could do. After dark, they worked by the light of the city's fires and by candles the ten remaining nurses held for them. Dr. Sasaki had not looked outside the hospital all day; the scene inside was so terrible and so compelling that it had not occurred to him to ask any questions about what had happened beyond the windows and doors. Ceilings and partitions had fallen; plaster, dust, blood, and vomit were everywhere. Patients were dying by the hundreds, but there was nobody to carry away the corpses. Some of the hospital staff distributed biscuits and rice balls, but the charnel-house smell was so strong that few were hungry. By three o'clock the next morning, after nineteen straight hours of his gruesome work, Dr. Sasaki was incapable of dressing another wound. He and some other survivors of the hospital staff got straw mats and went outdoors—thousands of patients and hundreds of dead were in the yard and on the driveway—and hurried around behind the hospital and lay down in hiding to snatch some sleep. But within an hour wounded people had found them; a complaining circle formed around them: "Doctors! Help us! How can you sleep?" Dr. Sasaki got up again and went back to work. Early in the day, he thought for the first time of his mother at their country home in Mukaihara, thirty miles from town. He usually went home every night. He was afraid she would think he was dead. . . .

On August 18th, twelve days after the bomb burst, Father Kleinsorge set out on foot for Hiroshima from the Novitiate with his papier-mâché suitcase in his hand. He had begun to think that this bag, in which he kept his valuables, had a talismanic quality, because of the way he had found it after the explosion, standing handle-side up in the doorway of his room, while the desk under which he had previously hidden it was in splinters all over the floor. Now he was using it to carry the yen belonging to the Society of Jesus to the Hiroshima branch of the Yokohama Specie Bank, already reopened in its half-ruined building. On the whole, he felt quite well that morning. It is true that the minor cuts he had received had not healed in three or four days, as the rector of the Novitiate, who had examined them, had positively promised they would, but Father Kleinsorge had rested well for a week and considered that he was again ready for hard work. By now he was accustomed to the terrible scene through which he walked on his way into the city: the large rice field near the Novitiate, streaked with brown; the houses on the outskirts of the city, standing but decrepit, with broken windows and disheveled tiles; and then, quite suddenly, the beginning of the four square miles of reddish-brown scar, where nearly everything had been buffeted down and burned; range on range of collapsed city blocks, with here and there a crude sign erected on a pile of ashes and tiles ("Sister, where are you?" or "All safe and we live at Toyosaka"); naked trees and canted telephone poles; the few standing, gutted buildings only accentuating the horizontality of everything else (the Museum of Science and Industry, with its dome stripped to its steel frame, as if for an autopsy; the modern Chamber of Commerce Building, its tower as cold, rigid, and unassailable after the blow as before; the huge, low-lying,

camouflaged city hall; the row of dowdy banks, caricaturing a shaken economic system); and in the streets a macabre traffic—hundreds of crumpled bicycles, shells of streetcars and automobiles, all halted in mid-motion. The whole way, Father Kleinsorge was oppressed by the thought that all the damage he saw had been done in one instant by one bomb. By the time he reached the center of town, the day had become very hot. He walked to the Yokohama Bank, which was doing business in a temporary wooden stall on the ground floor of its building, deposited the money, went by the mission compound just to have another look at the wreckage, and then started back to the Novitiate. About halfway there, he began to have peculiar sensations. The more or less magical suitcase, now empty, suddenly seemed terribly heavy. His knees grew weak. He felt excruciatingly tired. With a considerable expenditure of spirit, he managed to reach the Novitiate. He did not think his weakness was worth mentioning to the other Jesuits. But a couple of days later, while attempting to say Mass, he had an onset of faintness and even after three attempts was unable to go through with the service, and the next morning the rector, who had examined Father Kleinsorge's apparently negligible but unhealed cuts daily, asked in surprise, "What have you done to your wounds?" They had suddenly opened wider and were swollen and inflamed.

As she dressed on the morning of August 20th, in the home of her sister-in-law in Kabe, not far from Nagatsuka, Mrs. Nakamura, who had suffered no cuts or burns at all, though she had been rather nauseated all though the week she and her children had spent as guests of Father Kleinsorge and the other Catholics at the Novitiate, began fixing her hair and noticed, after one stroke, that her comb carried with it a whole handful of hair; the second time, the same thing happened, so she stopped combing at once. But in the next three or four days, her hair kept falling out of its own accord, until she was quite bald. She began living indoors, practically in hiding. On August 26th, both she and her younger daughter, Myeko, woke up feeling extremely weak and tired, and they stayed on their bedrolls. Her son and other daughter, who had shared every experience with her during and after the bombing, felt fine.

At about the same time—he lost track of the days, so hard was he working to set up a temporary place of worship in a private house he had rented in the outskirts—Mr. Tanimoto fell suddenly ill with a general malaise, weariness, and feverishness, and he, too, took to his bedroll on the floor of the half-wrecked house of a friend in the suburb of Ushida.

These four did not realize it, but they were coming down with the strange, capricious disease which came later to be known as radiation sickness. . . .

. . . It would be impossible to say what horrors were embedded in the minds of the children who lived through the day of the bombing in Hiroshima. On the surface their recollections, months after the disaster, were of an exhilarating adventure. Toshio Nakamura, who was ten at the time of the bombing, was soon able to talk freely, even gaily, about the experience, and a few weeks before the anniversary he wrote the following matter-of-fact essay for his teacher at Nobori-cho Primary School: "The day before the bomb, I went for a swim. In the morning, I was eating peanuts. I saw a light. I was knocked to little sister's sleeping place. When we were saved, I could only see as far as the tram. My mother and I started to pack our things. The neighbors were walking around burned and bleeding. Hataya-*san* told me to run away with her. I said I wanted to wait for my mother. We went to the park. A whirlwind came. At night a gas tank burned and I saw the reflection in the river. We stayed in the park one night. Next day I went to Taiko Bridge and met my girl friends Kikuki and Murakami. They were looking for their mothers. But Kikuki's mother was wounded and Murakami's mother, alas, was dead."

QUESTIONS TO CONSIDER

1. What do you think of Hersey's micro focus on six survivors?
2. Does this change how you think about World War II?

23.5 STUDS TERKEL, EXCERPT FROM "THE GOOD WAR" (1984)

American author Studs Terkel is best known for his oral histories of major moments in American history. Initially employed by the Works Progress Administration's Federal Writers Project during the Great Depression, Terkel grew adept at weaving disparate narratives into a cohesive whole. His 1974 *Working* portrayed the lives of Americans through labor and later became a Broadway show. His oral history *Hard Times* illuminated the experience of the Great Depression for ordinary people. Terkel's most famous oral history, however, is *The Good War: An Oral History of World War II,* from which the following excerpt is drawn. Terkel won the 1985 Pulitzer Prize for General Non-Fiction for *The Good War,* which is divided into five major sections. In the following excerpt, you will read about the experiences of Eugene Sledge, a U.S. Marine who fought in the Pacific theater.

Half-hidden in the hilly greenery, toward the end of a winding country road, is the house he himself helped build. It is on the campus of the University of Montevallo, a forty-five-minute drive from Birmingham, Alabama.

On the wall near the fireplace—comforting on this unseasonably cool day—is a plaque with the familiar Guadalcanal patch: "Presented to Eugene B. Sledge. We, the men of K Co., 3rd Bn., 5th Reg., 1st Marine Div., do hereby proudly bestow this testimonial in expression of our great admiration and heartfelt appreciation to one extraordinary marine, who has honored his comrades in arms by unveiling to the world its exploits and heroism in his authorship of WITH THE OLD BREED AT PELELIU AND OKINAWA. *God love you, Sledgehammer. 1982." It is his remarkable memoir that led me to him.*

Small-boned, slim, gentle in demeanor, he is a professor of biology at the university. "My main interest is ornithology. I've been a bird-watcher since I was a kid in Mobile. Do you see irony in that? Interested in birds, nature, a combat marine in the front lines? People think of bird-watchers as not macho."

There was nothing macho about the war at all. We were a bunch of scared kids who had to do a job. People tell me I don't act like an ex-marine. How is an ex-marine supposed to act? They have some Hollywood stereotype in mind. No, I don't look like John Wayne. We were in it to get it over with, so we could go back home and do what we wanted to do with our lives.

I was nineteen, a replacement in June of 1944. Eighty percent of the division in the Guadalcanal campaign was less than twenty-one years of age. We were much younger than the general army units.

To me, there were two different wars. There was the war of the guy on the front lines. You don't come off until you are wounded or killed. Or, if lucky, relieved. Then there was the support personnel. In the Pacific, for every rifleman on the front lines there were nineteen people in the back. Their view of the war was different than mine. The man up front puts his life on the line day after day after day to the point of utter hopelessness.

The only thing that kept you going was your faith in your buddies. It wasn't just a case of friendship. I never heard of self-inflicted wounds out there. Fellows from other services said they saw this in Europe. Oh, there were plenty of times when I wished I had a million-dollar wound. (Laughs softly.) Like maybe shootin' a toe off. What was worse than death was the indignation of your buddies. You couldn't let 'em down. It was stronger than flag and country.

With the Japanese, the battle was all night long. Infiltratin' the lines, slippin' up and throwin' in grenades. Or runnin' in with a bayonet or saber. They were active all night. Your buddy would try to get a little catnap and you'd stay on watch. Then you'd switch off. It went on, day in and day out. A matter of simple survival. The only way you could get it over with was to kill them off before they killed you. The war I knew was totally savage.

The Japanese fought by a code they thought was right: *bushido.* The code of the warrior: no surrender. You don't really comprehend it until you get out there and fight people who are faced with an absolutely hopeless situation and will not give up. If you tried to help one of the Japanese, he'd usually detonate a grenade and kill himself as well as you. To be captured was a disgrace. To us, it was impossible, too, because we knew what happened in Bataan.

Toward the end of the Okinawa campaign, we found this emaciated Japanese in the bunk of what may have been a field hospital. We were on a patrol. There had been torrential rains for two weeks. The foxholes were filled with water. This Jap didn't have but a G-string on him. About ninety pounds. Pitiful. This buddy of mine picked him up and carried him out. Laid him out in the mud. There was no other place to put him.

We were sittin' on our helmets waitin' for the medical corpsman to check him out. He was very docile. We figured he couldn't get up. Suddenly he pulled a Japanese grenade out of his G-string. He jerked the pin out and hit it on his fist to pop open the cap. He was gonna make hamburger of me and my buddy and himself. I yelled, "Look out!" So my buddy said, "You son of a bitch, if that's how you feel about it—He pulled out his .45 and shot him right between the eyes.

This is what we were up against. I don't like violence, but there are times when you can't help it. I don't like to watch television shows with violence in them. I hate to see anything afraid. But 1 was afraid so much, day after day, that I got tired of being scared. I've seen guys go through three campaigns and get killed on Okinawa on the last day. You knew all you had was that particular moment you were living.

I got so tired of seein' guys get hit and banged up, the more I felt like takin' it out on the Japanese. The feeling grew and grew, and you became more callous. Have you ever read the poem by Wilfred Owen? The World War One poet? "Insensibility." (He shuts his eyes as he recalls snatches of the poem and interpolates) "Happy are the men who yet before they are killed/Can let their veins run cold. . . . And some cease feeling/Even themselves or for themselves. Dullness best solves/The tease and doubt of shelling." You see, the man who can go through combat and not be bothered by the deaths of others and escape what Owen calls Chance's strange arithmetic—he's the fortunate one. He doesn't suffer as much as the one who is sensitive to the deaths of his comrades. Owen says you can't compare this man to the old man at home, who is just callous and hardened to everything and has no compassion. The young man on the front line develops this insensitivity because it is the only way he can cope.

You developed an attitude of no mercy because they had no mercy on us. It was a no-quarter, savage kind of thing. At Peleliu, it was the first time I was close enough to see one of their faces. This Jap had been hit. One of my buddies was field-stripping him for souvenirs. I must admit it really bothered me, the guys dragging him around like a carcass. I was just horrified. This guy had been a human being. It didn't take me long to overcome that feeling. A lot of my buddies hit, the fatigue, the stress. After a while, the veneer of civilization wore pretty thin. . . .

We all had different kinds of mania. To me, the most horrible thing was to be under shellfire. You're absolutely helpless. The damn thing comes in like a freight train and there's a terrific crash. The ground shakes and all this shrapnel rippin' through the air.

I remember one afternoon on Half Moon Hill. The foxhole next to me had two boys in it. The next one to that had three. It was fairly quiet. We heard the shell come screeching over. They were firing it at us like a rifle. The shell passed no more than a foot over my head. Two foxholes down, a guy was sitting on his helmet drinking C-ration hot chocolate. It exploded in his foxhole. I saw this guy, Bill Leyden, go straight up in the air. The other two kids fell over backwards. Dead, of course. The two in the hole next to me were killed instantly.

Leyden was the only one who survived. Would you believe he gets only partial disability for shrapnel wounds? His record says nothing about concussion. He has seizures regularly. He was blown up in the air! If you don't call that concussion . . . The medics were too busy saving lives to fill out records.

Another kid got his leg blown off. He had been a lumberjack, about twenty-one. He was always telling me how good spruce Christmas trees smelled. He said, "Sledgehammer, you think I'm gonna lose my leg?" If you don't think that just tore my guts out . . . My God, there was his field shoe on the stretcher with this stump of his ankle stickin' out. The stretcher bearers just looked at each other and covered him with his poncho. He was dead.

It was raining like hell. We were knee-deep in mud. And I thought, What in the hell are we doin' on this nasty, stinkin' muddy ridge? What is this all about? You know what I mean? Wasted lives on a muddy slope.

People talk about Iwo Jima as the most glorious amphibious operation in history. I've had Iwo veterans tell me it was more similar to Peleliu than any other battle they read about. What in the hell was glorious about it?

QUESTIONS TO CONSIDER

1. What stands out in Sledge's remembrances?
2. Does this change the way you think about World War II? Why or why not?

CHAPTER 24

THE COLD WAR, 1945–1952

24.1 HARRY TRUMAN, "ADDRESS ON KOREA" (1950)

Just five years after the end of World War II, the United States became entangled in another international conflict. During the initial post-war era, the United States and the Soviet Union divided Korea into two territories: North Korea, supported by the USSR, and South Korea, supported by the United States. In June 1950, after a period of rising border tensions, North Korean forces, with the support of the USSR, invaded South Korea. North Korea quickly conquered much of South Korea, including its capital, Seoul. Two weeks later, President Harry Truman, whose administration was not prepared for the North Korean invasion, addressed America. In his speech, he defended sending American troops and ships into the region to protect South Korea, something he would term "a police action." The Korean War was the first substantial test of Truman's pledge to protect other nations against communism, often termed the "Truman Doctrine." On September 15, 1950, a major U.S. force led by General Douglas MacArthur landed at Inchon in northern South Korea and then liberated Seoul. Over the next month, the United States pushed far into North Korea, even reaching its capital, Pyongyang. However, a massive Chinese Army of almost 200,000 soldiers subsequently pushed U.S. forces back into South Korea and inflicted heavy damage when they tried to again push north. Over the next three years, the two sides essentially fought to a draw, and North and South Korea agreed to a truce in July 1953 that left the country divided with a neutral Demilitarized Zone between the two nations.

My fellow citizens:

At noon today I sent a message to the Congress about the situation in Korea. I want to talk to you tonight about that situation, and about what it means to the security of the United States and to our hopes for peace in the world.

Korea is a small country, thousands of miles away, but what is happening there is important to every American.

Source: "Harry Truman: Radio and Television Address to the American People on the Situation in Korea," http://www.presidency.ucsb.edu/ws/?pid=13561 (Accessed May 21, 2018).

On Sunday, June 25th, Communist forces attacked the Republic of Korea.

This attack has made it clear, beyond all doubt, that the international Communist movement is willing to use armed invasion to conquer independent nations. An act of aggression such as this creates a very real danger to the security of all free nations.

The attack upon Korea was an outright breach of the peace and a violation of the Charter of the United Nations. By their actions in Korea, Communist leaders have demonstrated their contempt for the basic moral principles on which the United Nations is founded. This is a direct challenge to the efforts of the free nations to build the kind of world in which men can live in freedom and peace.

This challenge has been presented squarely. We must meet it squarely.

It is important for all of us to understand the essential facts as to how the situation in Korea came about.

Before and during World War II, Korea was subject to Japanese rule. When the fighting stopped, it was agreed that troops of the Soviet Union would accept the surrender of the Japanese soldiers in the northern part of Korea, and that American forces would accept the surrender of the Japanese in the southern part. For this purpose, the 38th parallel was used as the dividing line.

Later, the United Nations sought to establish Korea as a free and independent nation. A commission was sent out to supervise a free election in the whole of Korea. However, this election was held only in the southern part of the country, because the Soviet Union refused to permit an election for this purpose to be held in the northern part. Indeed, the Soviet authorities even refused to permit the United Nations Commission to visit northern Korea.

Nevertheless, the United Nations decided to go ahead where it could. In August 1948 the Republic of Korea was established as a free and independent nation in that part of Korea south of the 38th parallel.

In December 1948, the Soviet Union stated that it had withdrawn its troops from northern Korea and that a local government had been established there. However, the Communist authorities never have permitted the United Nations observers to visit northern Korea to see what was going on behind that part of the Iron Curtain.

It was from that area, where the Communist authorities have been unwilling to let the outside world see what was going on, that the attack was launched against the Republic of Korea on June 25th. That attack came without provocation and without warning. It was an act of raw aggression, without a shadow of justification.

I repeat that it was an act of raw aggression. It had no justification whatever.

The Communist invasion was launched in great force, with planes, tanks, and artillery. The size of the attack, and the speed with which it was followed up, make it perfectly plain that it had been plotted long in advance.

As soon as word of the attack was received, Secretary of State Acheson called me at Independence, Mo., and informed me that, with my approval, he would ask for an immediate meeting of the United Nations Security Council. The Security Council met just 24 hours after the Communist invasion began.

One of the main reasons the Security Council was set up was to act in such cases as this—to stop outbreaks of aggression in a hurry before they develop into general conflicts. In this case the Council passed a resolution which called for the invaders of Korea to stop fighting, and to withdraw. The Council called on all members of the United Nations to help carry out this resolution. The Communist invaders ignored the action of the Security Council and kept fight on with their attack.

The Security Council then met again. It recommended that members of the United Nations help the Republic of Korea repel the attack and help restore peace and security in that area.

Fifty-two of the 59 countries which are members of the United Nations have given their support to the action taken by the Security Council to restore peace in Korea.

These actions by the United Nations and its members are of great importance. The free nations have now made it clear that lawless aggression will be met with force. The free nations have learned the fateful lesson of the 1930's. That lesson is that aggression must be met firmly. Appeasement leads only to further aggression and ultimately to war.

The principal effort to help the Koreans preserve their independence, and to help the United Nations restore peace, has been made by the United States. We have sent land, sea, and air forces to assist in these operations. We have done this because we know that what is at stake here is nothing less than our own national security and the peace of the world.

So far, two other nations—Australia and Great Britain—have sent planes to Korea; and six other nations—Australia, Canada, France, Great Britain, the Netherlands, and New Zealand—have made naval forces available.

Under the flag of the United Nations a unified command has been established for all forces of the members of the United Nations fighting in Korea. Gen. Douglas MacArthur is the commander of this combined force.

The prompt action of the United Nations to put down lawless aggression, and the prompt response to this action by free peoples all over the world, will stand as a landmark in mankind's long search for a rule of law among nations.

Only a few countries have failed to endorse the efforts of the United Nations to stop the fighting in Korea. The most important of these is the Soviet Union. The Soviet Union has boycotted the meetings of the United Nations Security Council. It has refused to support the actions of the United Nations with respect to Korea.

The United States requested the Soviet Government, 2 days after the fighting started, to use its influence with the North Koreans to have them withdraw. The Soviet Government refused.

The Soviet Government has said many times that it wants peace in the world, but its attitude toward this act of aggression against the Republic of Korea is in direct contradiction of its statements.

For our part, we shall continue to support the United Nations action to restore peace in the world.

We know that it will take a hard, tough fight to halt the invasion, and to drive the Communists back. The invaders have been provided with enough equipment and supplies for a long campaign. They overwhelmed the lightly armed defense forces of the Korean Republic in the first few days and drove southward.

Now, however, the Korean defenders have reorganized and are making a brave fight for their liberty, and an increasing number of American troops have joined them. Our forces have fought a skillful, rearguard delaying action, pending the arrival of reinforcements. Some of these reinforcements are now arriving; others are on the way from the United States. . . .

It is obvious that we must increase our military strength and preparedness immediately. There are three things we need to do.

First, we need to send more men, equipment, and supplies to General MacArthur.

Second, in view of the world situation, we need to build up our own Army, Navy, and Air Force over and above what is needed in Korea.

Third, we need to speed up our work with other countries in strengthening our common defenses.

To help meet these needs, I have already authorized increases in the size of our Armed Forces. These increases will come in part from volunteers, in part from Selective Service, and in part from the National Guard and the Reserves.

I have also ordered that military supplies and equipment be obtained at a faster rate.

The necessary increases in the size of our Armed Forces, and the additional equipment they must have, will cost about $10 billion, and I am asking the Congress to appropriate the amount required.

These funds will be used to train men and equip them with tanks, planes, guns, and ships, in order to build the strength we need to help assure peace in the world.

When we have worked out with other free countries an increased program for our common defense, I shall recommend to the Congress that additional funds be provided for this purpose. This is of great importance. The free nations face a worldwide threat. It must be met with a worldwide defense. The United States and other free nations can multiply their strength by joining with one another in a common effort to provide this defense. This is our best hope for peace.

The things we need to do to build up our military defense will require considerable adjustment in our domestic economy. We have a tremendously rich and productive economy, and it is expanding every year.

Our job now is to divert to defense purposes more of that tremendous productive capacity—more steel, more aluminum, more of a good many things.

Some of the additional production for military purposes can come from making fuller use of plants which are not operating at capacity. But many of our industries are already going full tilt, and until we can add new capacity, some of the resources we need for the national defense will have to be taken from civilian uses.

This requires us to take certain steps to make sure that we obtain the things we need for national defense, and at the same time guard against inflationary price rises.

The steps that are needed now must be taken promptly.

In the message which I sent to the Congress today, I described the economic measures which are required at this time.

First, we need laws which will insure prompt and adequate supplies for military and essential civilian use. I have therefore recommended that the Congress give the Government power to guide the flow of materials into essential uses, to restrict their use for nonessential purposes, and to prevent the accumulation of unnecessary inventories.

Second, we must adopt measures to prevent inflation and to keep our Government in a sound financial condition. One of the major causes of inflation is the excessive use of credit. I have recommended that the Congress authorize the Government to set limits on installment buying and to curb speculation in agricultural commodities. In the housing field, where Government credit is an important factor, I have already directed that credit restraints be applied, and I have recommended that the Congress authorize further controls.

As an additional safeguard against inflation, and to help finance our defense needs, it will be necessary to make substantial increases in taxes. This is a contribution to our national security that every one of us should stand ready to make. As soon as a balanced and fair tax program can be worked out, I shall lay it before the Congress. This tax program will have as a major aim the elimination of profiteering.

Third, we should increase the production of goods needed for national defense. We must plan to enlarge our defense production, not just for the immediate future, but for the next several years. This will be primarily a task for our businessmen and workers.

However, to help obtain the necessary increases, the Government should be authorized to provide certain types of financial assistance to private industry to increase defense production.

Our military needs are large, and to meet them will require hard work and steady effort. I know that we can produce what we need if each of us does his part—each man, each woman, each soldier, each civilian. This is a time for all of us to pitch in and work together.

I have been sorry to hear that some people have fallen victim to rumors in the last week or two, and have been buying up various things they have heard would be scarce. That is foolish—I say that is foolish, and it is selfish, very selfish, because hoarding results in entirely unnecessary local shortages.

Hoarding food is especially foolish. There is plenty of food in this country. I have read that there have been runs on sugar in some cities. That is perfectly ridiculous. We now have more sugar available than ever before. There are ample supplies of our other basic foods also.

Now, I sincerely hope that every American housewife will keep this in mind when she does her daily shopping.

If I had thought that we were actually threatened by shortages of essential consumer goods, I should have recommended that price control and rationing be immediately instituted. But there is no such threat. We have to fear only those shortages which we ourselves artificially create.

Every businessman who is trying to profiteer in time of national danger—and every person who is selfishly trying to get more than his neighbor—is doing just exactly the thing that any enemy of this country would want him to do.

If prices should rise unduly because of excessive buying or speculation, I know our people will want the Government to take action, and I will not hesitate to recommend rationing and price control.

We have the resources to meet our needs. Far more important, the American people are unified in their belief in democratic freedom. We are united in detesting Communist slavery.

We know that the cost of freedom is high. But we are determined to preserve our freedom—no matter what the cost.

I know that our people are willing to do their part to support our soldiers and sailors and airmen who are fighting in Korea. I know that our fighting men can count on each and every one of you.

Our country stands before the world as an example of how free men, under God, can build a community of neighbors, working together for the good of all.

That is the goal we seek not only for ourselves, but for all people. We believe that freedom and peace are essential if men are to live as our Creator intended us to live. It is this faith that has guided us in the past, and it is this faith that will fortify us in the stern days ahead.

QUESTIONS TO CONSIDER

1. How did Truman defend American intervention?
2. If you were living at the time, how would you have felt about the Korean War, as it began so quickly after World War II?

24.2 EXCERPT FROM "EMPLOYMENT OF HOMOSEXUALS AND OTHER SEX PERVERTS IN GOVERNMENT" (1950)

The "Red Scare," the Cold War–era persecution of Americans accused of communist sympathies, is relatively common knowledge in America. The "Lavender Scare," however, is less well known. In the 1950s, the United States Government tried to uncover evidence of homosexual employees and to oust them from government. The following 1950 document, produced by a U.S. Senate committee, sparked such anti-gay hysteria. Though the committee did not find evidence for any instances of gay Americans giving up state secrets, it still asserted homosexuals' susceptibility to blackmail. In 1953, the Eisenhower administration added "sexual perversion" to a list of factors that would invalidate a Federal job application. Many more employees were surveilled, and some 5,000 gay people were fired.

The primary objective of the subcommittee in this inquiry was to determine the extent of the employment of homosexuals and other sex perverts in Government; to consider reasons why their employment by the Government is undesirable; and to examine into the efficacy of the methods used in dealing with the problem. Because of the complex nature of the subject under investigation it was apparent that this investigation could not be confined to a mere personnel inquiry. Therefore, the subcommittee considered not only the security risk and other aspects of the employment of homosexuals, including the rules and procedures followed by Government agencies in handling these cases, but inquiries were also made into the basic medical, psychiatric, sociological and legal phases of the problem. A number of eminent physicians and psychiatrists, who are recognized authorities on this subject, were consulted and some of these authorities

Source: "Employment of Homosexuals and Other Sex Perverts in Government: Interim Report Submitted to the Committee on Expenditures in the Executive Departments by the Subcommittee on Investigations," 81st Congress, 2nd Session (Washington, D.C.: Government Printing Office, 1950), 1–10, 19–21.

testified before the subcommittee in executive session. In addition, numerous medical and sociological studies were reviewed. Information was also sought and obtained from law-enforcement officers, prosecutors, and other persons dealing with the legal and sociological aspects of the problem in 10 of the larger cities in the country.

The subcommittee, being well aware of the strong moral and social taboos attached to homosexuality and other forms of sex perversion, made every effort to protect individuals from unnecessary public ridicule and to prevent this inquiry from becoming a public spectacle. In carrying out this policy it was determined at the outset that all testimony would be taken by the subcommittee in executive session. Accordingly, all witness appearing before the subcommittee testified in executive hearings. In the conduct of this investigation the subcommittee tried to avoid the circus atmosphere which could attend an inquiry of this type and sought to make a thorough factual study of the problem at hand in an unbiased, objective manner.

It was determined that even among the experts there existed considerable difference of opinion concerning the many facets of homosexuality and other forms of sex perversion. Even the terms "sex pervert" and "homosexual" are given different connotations by the medical and psychiatric experts. For the purpose of this report the subcommittee has defined sex perverts as "those who engage in unnatural sexual acts" and homosexuals are perverts who may be broadly defined as "persons of either sex who as adults engage in sexual activities with persons of the same sex." In this inquiry the subcommittee is not concerned with so-called latent sex perverts, namely, those persons who knowingly or unknowingly have tendencies or inclinations toward homosexuality or other types of sex perversion, but who, by the exercise of self-restraint or for other reasons do not indulge in overt acts of perversion. This investigation in concerned only with those who engage in overt acts of homosexuality or other sex perversion.

The subcommittee found that most authorities agree on certain basic facts concerning sex perversion and it is felt that these facts should be considered in any discussion of the problem. Most authorities believe that sex deviation results from psychological rather than physical causes, and in many cases there are no outward characteristics or physical traits that are positive as identifying marks of sex perversion. Contrary to a common belief, all homosexual males do not have feminine mannerisms, nor do all female homosexuals display masculine characteristics in their dress or actions. The fact is that many male homosexuals are very masculine in their physical appearance and general demeanor, and many female homosexuals have every appearance of femininity in their outward behavior.

Generally speaking, the overt homosexual of both sexes can be divided into two general types; the active, aggressive or male type, and the submissive, passive or female type. The passive type of male homosexual, who often is effeminate in his mannerisms and appearance, is attracted to the masculine type of man and is friendly and congenial with women. On the other hand the active male homosexual often has a dislike for women. He exhibits no traces of femininity in his speech or mannerisms which would disclose his homosexuality. This active type is almost exclusively attracted to the passive type of homosexual or to young men or boys who are not necessarily homosexual but who are effeminate in general appearance or behavior. The active and passive type of female homosexual follow the same general patterns as their male counterparts. It is also a known fact that some perverts are bisexual. This type engages in normal heterosexual relationships as well as homosexual activities. These bisexual individuals are often married and have children, and except for their perverted activities they appear to lead normal lives.

Psychiatric physicians generally agree that indulgence in sexually perverted practices indicates a personality which has failed to reach sexual maturity. The authorities agree that most sex deviates respond to psychiatric treatment and can be cured if they have a genuine desire to be cured. However, many overt homosexuals have no real desire to abandon their way of life and in such cases cures are difficult, if not impossible. The subcommittee sincerely believes that persons afflicted with sexual desires which result in their engaging in overt acts of perversion should be considered as proper cases for medical and psychiatric treatment. However, sex perverts, like all other persons who by their overt acts violate moral codes and laws and the accepted standards of conduct, must be treated as transgressors and dealt with accordingly.

SEX PERVERTS AS GOVERNMENT EMPLOYEES

Those charged with the responsibility of operating the agencies of Government must insist that Government employees meet acceptable standards of personal conduct. In the opinion of this subcommittee homosexuals and other sex perverts are not proper persons to be employed in Government for two reasons; first, they are generally unsuitable, and second, they constitute security risks.

GENERAL UNSUITABILITY OF SEX PERVERTS

Overt acts of sex perversion, including acts of homosexuality, constitute a crime under our Federal, State, and municipal statutes and persons who commit such acts are law violators. Aside from the criminality and immorality involved in sex perversion such behavior is so contrary to the normal accepted standards of social behavior that persons who engage in such activity are looked upon as outcastes by society generally. The social stigma attached to sex perversion is so great that many perverts go to great lengths to conceal their perverted tendencies. This situation is evidenced by the fact that perverts are frequently victimized by blackmailers who threaten to expose their sexual deviations.

Law enforcement officers have informed the subcommittee that there are gangs of blackmailers who make a regular practice of preying upon the homosexual. The modus operandi in these homosexual blackmail cases usually follow the same general pattern. The victim, who is a homosexual, has managed to conceal his perverted activities and usually enjoys a good reputation in his community. The blackmailers, by one means or another, discover that the victim is addicted to homosexuality and under the threat of disclosure they extort money from him. These blackmailers often impersonate police officers in carrying out their blackmail schemes. Many cases have come to the attention of the police where highly respected individual have paid out substantial sums of money

to blackmailers over a long period of time rather than risk the disclosure of their homosexual activities. The police believe that this type of blackmail racket is much more extensive than is generally known, because they have found that most of the victims are very hesitant to bring the matter to the attention of the authorities.

In further considering the general suitability of perverts as Government employees, it is generally believed that those who engage in overt acts of perversion lack the emotional stability of normal persons. In addition there is an abundance of evidence to sustain the conclusion that indulgence in acts of sex perversion weakens the moral fiber of an individual to a degree that he is not suitable for a position of responsibility.

Most of the authorities agree and our investigation has shown that the presence of a sex pervert in a Government agency tends to have a corrosive influence upon his fellow employees. These perverts will frequently attempt to entice normal individuals to engage in perverted practices. This is particularly true in the case of young and impressionable people who might come under the influence of a pervert. Government officials have the responsibility of keeping this type of corrosive influence out of the agencies under their control. It is particularly important that the thousands of young men and women who are brought into Federal jobs not be subjected to that type of influence while in the service of the Government. One homosexual can pollute a Government office.

Another point to be considered in determining whether a sex pervert is suitable for Government employment is his tendency to gather other perverts about him. Eminent psychiatrists have informed the subcommittee that the homosexual is likely to seek his own kind because the pressures of society are such that he feels uncomfortable unless he is with his own kind. Due to this situation the homosexual tends to surround himself with other homosexuals, not only in his social, but in his business life. Under these circumstances if a homosexual attains a position in Government where he can influence the hiring of personnel, it is almost inevitable that he will attempt to place other homosexuals in Government jobs.

SEX PERVERTS AS SECURITY RISKS

The conclusion of the subcommittee that a homosexual or other sex pervert is a security risk is not based upon mere conjecture. That conclusion is predicated upon a careful review of the opinions of those best qualified to consider matters of security in Government, namely, the intelligence agencies of the Government. Testimony on this phase of the inquiry was taken from representatives of the Federal Bureau of the Central Intelligence Agency, and the intelligence services of the Army, Navy and Air Force. All of these agencies are in complete agreement that sex perverts in Government constitute security risks.

The lack of emotional stability which is found in most sex perverts and the weakness of their moral fiber, makes them susceptible to the blandishments of the foreign espionage agent. It is the experience of intelligence experts that perverts are vulnerable to interrogation by a skilled questioner and they seldom refuse to talk about themselves. Furthermore, most perverts tend to congregate at the same restaurants, night clubs, and bars, which places can be identified with comparative ease in any community, making it possible for a recruiting agent to develop clandestine relationships which can be used for espionage purposes.

As has been previously discussed in this report, the pervert is easy prey to the blackmailer. It follows that if blackmailers can extort money from a homosexual under the threat of disclosure, espionage agents can use the same type of pressure to extort confidential information or other material they might be seeking. . . .

EXTENT OF SEX PERVERSION IN GOVERNMENT

. . . In considering the extent of homosexuality in the Government, the subcommittee has confined itself, as far as it has been reasonably possible, to those cases where specific information has led to the conclusion that a person is a pervert, or at least a likely suspect. It is realized that there are bound to be some unknown perverts in Government, because in any organization as large as the Federal Government it is logical to assume that there will be perverts whose clandestine activities may never be discovered. However, it is expected that the number of perverts in Government can be kept to a minimum if the problem is handled properly.

The subcommittee has attempted to arrive at some idea as to the extent of sex perversion among Government employees by obtaining information form the personnel records of all Government agencies and the police records in the District of Columbia. Due to the manner in which personnel records are maintained it was found that any effort to obtain statistics from these records prior to January 1, 1947, would necessarily involve a prohibitive cost and that the fragmentary information obtained from such records prior to that date would be of little or no value to this investigation.

An individual check of the Federal agencies revealed that since January 1, 1947, the armed services and civilian agencies of Government have handled 4,954 cases involving charges of homosexuality or other types of sex perversion. It will be noted that the bulk of these cases are in the armed services as is indicated by the fact that that 4,380 of the known cases in Government involved military personnel and 574 involved civilian employees. However, in considering these statistics it is pointed out that the incidence of homosexuality and other forms of sex perversion is usually higher in military organizations or other groups where large numbers of men (or women) live and work in close confinement and are restricted in their normal social contacts. Furthermore it must be borne in mind in relation to the larger numerical figures of the military departments that the armed services are numerically several times larger than any civilian agency of government. Another important consideration in drawing conclusions from these statistics is the fact that the military services, unlike most other Government agencies, traditionally have been aggressive in ferreting out and removing sex perverts from their ranks and this is bound to make for a larger number of known cases in the services. . . .

METHODS USED TO PREVENT SEX PERVERTS FROM OBTAINING GOVERNMENT EMPLOYMENT AND TO REMOVE THEM FROM GOVERNMENT JOBS

. . . [I]n most of the sensitive agencies of the Government, including the Atomic Energy Commission, the State Department, and the FBI, all applicants are subjected to a full field investigation. Needless to say, this type of investigation should eliminate most sex perverts and other undesirables from positions in these agencies. However, it must be borne in mind that as a practical matter even the most elaborate and costly system of investigating applicants for Government positions will not prevent some sex perverts from finding their way into the Government service. Considering the fact that it is not practical to make a complete reemployment investigation of every government employee, it is believed that the present system of checking applicants is adequate; and, if the employing agencies will make it a standard policy to refuse employment to those persons who have a background of perversion, the number of such perverts who get into the Government service can be kept to a minimum.

On the other hand, the subcommittee has found that many civilian agencies of government have taken an entirely unrealistic view of the problem of sex perversion and have not taken adequate steps to get these people out of government. Known perverts and persons suspected of such activities have been retained in some Government agencies, or they have been allowed to leave one agency and obtain employment in another, notwithstanding the regulations of the Civil Service Commission and the rules of the agencies themselves. There are several reasons why this situation existed. In many cases the fault stemmed from the fact that personnel officers and other officials were acting in outright disregard of existing rules, and they handled the problem in accordance with their individual feelings or personal judgments in the matter. To further confuse the problem, there was considerable ignorance and wide difference of opinion among Government officials as to how personnel cases involving sex perverts should be handled. Some officials undoubtedly condoned the employment of homosexuals for one reason or another. This was particularly true in those instances where the perverted activities of the employee were carried on in such a manner as not to create public scandal or notoriety. Those who adopted that view based their conclusions on the false premise that what a Government employee did outside of the office on his own time, particularly if his actions did not involve his fellow employees or his work, was his own business. That conclusion may be true with regard to the normal behavior of employees in most types of Government work, but it does not apply to sex perversion or any other types of criminal activity or similar misconduct.

There also appears to have been a tendency in many Government agencies to adopt a head-in-the-sand attitude toward the problem of sex perversion. Some agencies tried to avoid the problem either by making no real effort to investigate charges of homosexuality or buy failing to take firm and positive steps to get known perverts out of Government and keep them out. In other cases some agencies did get rid of perverts, but in an apparent effort to conceal the fact that they had such persons in their employ, they eased out these perverts by one means or another in as quiet a manner as possible and circumvented the established rules with respect to the removal or dismissal of unsuitable personnel from Government positions. As a result of this situation a sex pervert would be forced out of one department and in many instances he would promptly obtain employment in another public agency. . . .

CONCLUSION

There is no place in the United States Government for persons who violate the laws or the accepted standards of morality, or who otherwise bring disrepute to the Federal services by infamous or scandalous personal conduct. Such persons are not suitable for Government positions and in the case of doubt the American people are entitled to have errors of judgment on the part of their officials, if there must be errors, resolved on the side of caution. It is the opinion of this subcommittee that those who engage in acts of homosexuality and other perverted sex activities are unsuitable for employment in the Federal government. This conclusion is based upon the fact that persons who indulge in such degraded activity are committing not only illegal and immoral acts, but they also constitute security risks in positions of public trust.

The subcommittee found that in the past many Government officials failed to take a realistic view of the problem of sex perversion in government with the result that a number of sex perverts were not discovered or removed from Government jobs, and in still other instances they were quietly eased out of one department and promptly found employment in another agency. This situation undoubtedly stemmed from the fact that there was a general disinclination on the part of many government officials to face squarely the problem of sex perversion among Federal employees and as a result they did not take the proper steps to solve the problem. The rules of the Civil Service Commission and the regulations of the agencies themselves prohibit the employment of sex perverts and these rules have been in effect for many years. Had the existing rules and regulation been enforced many of the perverts who were forced out of Government in recent months would have been long since removed from the Federal service.

It is quite apparent that as a direct result of this investigation officials throughout the Government have become much more alert to the problem of the employment of sex perverts in Government and in recent months they have removed a substantial number of these undesirables from public positions. This is evidenced by the fact that action has been taken in 382 sex perversion cases involving civilian employees of Government in the past 7 months, whereas action was taken in only 192 similar cases in the previous 3-year period from January 1, 1947, to April 1, 1950. However,

it appears to the subcommittee that some Government officials are not yet fully aware of the inherent dangers involved in the subcommittee that Government officials have the responsibility of exercising a high degree of diligence in the handling of the problem of sex perversion, and it is urged that they follow the recommendations of this subcommittee in that regard. . . .

Since the initiation of this investigation considerable progress has been made in removing homosexuals and similar undesirable employees from positions in the Government. However, it should be borne in mind that the public interest cannot be adequately protected unless responsible officials adopt and maintain a realistic and vigilant attitude toward the problem of sex perverts in the Government. To pussyfoot or to take half measures will allow some known perverts to remain in government and can result in the dismissal of innocent persons. . . .

QUESTIONS TO CONSIDER

1. How did the report make its case that homosexuals could not be trusted?
2. Why do you think the report gained such traction and influenced Federal policy to such a degree?

24.3 EXCERPT FROM THE ARMY-MCCARTHY HEARINGS TRANSCRIPT (1954)

Joseph McCarthy, a U.S. Senator from Wisconsin, became a national figure in the early 1950s through his accusations of widespread communist infiltration of the U.S. government. McCarthy had defeated Robert La Follette (see Chapter 19, Reading 19.6) in the 1946 Wisconsin Senate primary and began to look for an issue to latch onto in order to gain fame. In February 1950, at a public event in Wheeling, West Virginia, McCarthy claimed that he had a list of 205 State Department officials who were Community Party members. Three years later, with the Republican Party in control of the Senate, McCarthy used his committee chairmanship to carry out widespread investigations into communist activity in government. He also began to investigate the U.S. Army. The Army-McCarthy Hearings began in April 1954 and were nationally televised. During them, McCarthy and his chief counsel, Roy Cohn, tried their traditional method of badgering witnesses over long periods. In response, the Army asked Boston lawyer Joseph Welch to defend its policies. In a famous hearing on June 9th, from which the following document is excerpted, Welch interrupted McCarthy—who had begun attacking one of Welch's assistant attorneys, Fred Fisher—with the line "Have you no sense of decency?" Since the hearing was televised, Welch's criticism took hold, and McCarthy's career evaporated. He would die three years later of hepatitis exacerbated by alcoholism.

Mr. WELCH. I want to come back, Mr. Cohn, to the item that we were talking about this morning. I gathered, to sum it up a little, that as early as the spring, which must mean March or April, you knew about this situation of possible subversives and security risks, and even spies at Fort Monmouth, is that right?

Mr. COHN. Yes, sir.

Mr. WELCH. And I think you have used the word "disturbing," that you found it a disturbing situation?

Mr. COHN. Yes, sir.

Mr. WELCH. And you had, so to speak, only a sort of glimpse in it, you couldn't tell how big it was or how little it was, could you?

Mr. COHN. Not at the beginning, sir.

Mr. WELCH. And you probably knew enough about Fort Monmouth or found out quickly enough about Fort Monmouth, to know it was a sensitive place, didn't you?

Mr. COHN. Yes, sir.

Mr. WELCH. And I am sure the knowledge that you had was a source, Mr. Cohn, to one in your position, of some anxiety for the Nation's safety, wasn't it?

Mr. COHN. It was one situation among a number of serious situations; yes, sir.

Mr. WELCH. Well, I don't know how many worries you have, but I am sure that was, to you, a distributing and alarming situation.

Mr. COHN. Well, sir, it was certainly serious enough for me to want to check into it and see how many facts we could check out and—

Mr. WELCH. And stop it as soon as possible?

Mr. COHN. Well, it was a question of developing the —

Source: "Hearing Before the Special Subcommittee on Investigations of the Committee On Government Operations," 83rd Congress, 2nd Session (Washington D.C.: Government Printing Office, 1954), 2424–2430, https://www.senate.gov/artandhistory/history/resources/pdf/Volume5.pdf (Accessed June 14, 2018).

Mr. WELCH. But the thing that we have to do is stop it, isn't it?

Mr. COHN. Stop what, sir?

Mr. WELCH. Stop the risk.

Mr. COHN. Stop the risk, sir?

Mr. WELCH. Yes.

Mr. COHN. Yes, what we had to do was stop the risk and—

Mr. WELCH. That is right, get the people suspended or get them on trial or fire them or do something, that is right, isn't it?

Mr. COHN. Partly, sir.

Mr. WELCH. Sir?

Mr. COHN. Partly, sir.

Mr. WELCH. But it is primarily the thing, isn't it?

Mr. COHN. Well, the thing came up—

Mr. WELCH. Mr. Cohn, if I told you now that we had a bad situation at Monmouth, you would want to cure it by sundown, if you could, wouldn't you?

Mr. COHN. I am sure I couldn't, sir.

Mr. WELCH. But you would like to, if you could?

Mr. COHN. Sir—

Mr. WELCH. Isn't that right?

Mr. COHN. No, what I want—

Mr. WELCH. Answer me. That must be right. It has to be right.

Mr. COHN. What I would like to do and what can be done are two different things.

Mr. WELCH. Well, if you could be God and do anything you wished, you would cure it by sundown, wouldn't you?

Mr. COHN. Yes, sir.

Mr. WELCH. And you were that alarmed about Monmouth?

Mr. COHN. It doesn't go that way.

Mr. WELCH. I am just asking how it does go. When you find there are Communists and possible spies in a place like Monmouth, you must be alarmed, aren't you?

Mr. COHN. Now you have asked me how it goes, and I am going to tell you.

Mr. WELCH. No; I didn't ask you how it goes. I said aren't you alarmed when you find it is there?

Mr. COHN. Whenever I hear that people have been failing to act on FBI information about Communists, I do think it is alarming, I would like the Communists out, and I would like to be able to advise this committee of why people who have the responsibility for getting them out haven't carried out their responsibility.

Mr. WELCH. Yes, but what you want first of all, Mr. Cohn, and let's be fair with each other, what you want first of all, if it is within your power, is to get them out, isn't it?

Mr. COHN. I don't know if I draw a distinction as to what ought to come first, Mr. Welch.

Mr. WELCH. It certainly ranks terrifically high, doesn't it?

Mr. COHN. It was a situation that I thought should be developed, and we did develop it.

Mr. WELCH. When did you first meet Secretary Stevens?

Mr. COHN. I first met Secretary Stevens September 7 I believe it was.

Mr. WELCH. September 7? Where were you, sir?

Mr. COHN. Washington.

Mr. WELCH. Where in Washington?

Mr. COHN. I don't remember where I was when I met him. It was in this building, either at lunch or in a hearing room, something like that.

Mr. WELCH. And you knew that he was the new Secretary of the Army?

Mr. COHN. Yes; I did know he was the Secretary of the Army.

Mr. WELCH. And you must have had high hopes about him, didn't you?

Mr. COHN. I don't think I gave it too much thought, sir.

Mr. WELCH. Anybody wants the Secretary of the Army to do well, no matter what party he is from, do we not!

Mr. COHN. Surely, sir.

Mr. WELCH. And on September 7, when you met him, you had in your bosom this alarming situation about Monmouth, is that right?

Mr. COHN. Yes; I knew about Monmouth, then. Yes, sir.

Mr. WELCH. And you didn't tug at his lapel and say, "Mr. Secretary, I know something about Monmouth that won't let me sleep nights"? You didn't do it, did you?

Mr. COHN. I don't—as I testified, Mr. Welch, I don't know whether I talked to Mr. Stevens about it then or not. I know that on the 16th I did. Whether I talked to him on the 7th or not, is something I don't know.

Mr. WELCH. Don't you know that if you had really told him what yours fears were, and substantiated them to any extent, he could have jumped in the next day with suspensions?

Mr. COHN. No, sir.

Mr. WELCH. Did you then have any reason to doubt his fidelity?

Mr. COHN. No.

Mr. WELCH. Or his patriotism?

Mr. COHN. No.

Mr. WELCH. And yet, Mr. Cohn, you didn't tell him what you knew?

Mr. COHN. I don't know whether I did or not. I told him some of the things I knew, sir. I don't think I told him everything I knew on the first occasion. After the first 2 or 3 occasions, I think he had a pretty good idea of what we were working on.

Mr. WELCH. Mr. Cohn, tell me once more: Every time you learn of a Communist or a spy anywhere, is it your policy to get them out as fast as possible?

Mr. COHN. Surely, we want them out as fast as possible, sir.

Mr. WELCH. And whenever you learn of one from now on, Mr. Cohn, I beg of you, will you tell somebody about them quick?

Mr. COHN, Mr. Welch, with great respect, I work for the committee here. They know how we go about handling situations of Communist infiltration and failure to act on FBI information about Communist infiltration. If they are displeased with the speed with which I and the group of men who work with me proceed, if they are displeased with the order in which we move, I am sure they will give me appropriate instructions along those lines, and I will follow any which they give me.

Mr. WELCH. May I add my small voice, sir, and say whenever you know about a subversive or a Communist or a spy, please hurry. Will you remember those words?

Senator MCCARTHY. Mr. Chairman.

Mr. COHN. Mr. WELCH, I can assure you, sir, as far as I am concerned, and certainly as far as the chairman of this committee and the members, and the members of the staff, are concerned, we are a small group, but we proceed as expeditiously as is humanly possible to get out Communists and traitors and to bring to light the mechanism by which they have been permitted to remain where they were for so long a period of time.

Senator MCCARTHY. Mr. Chairman, in view of that question—

Senator MUNDT. Have you a point of order!

Senator MCCARTHY. Not exactly, Mr. Chairman, but in view of Mr. Welch's request that the information be given once we know of anyone who might be performing any work for the Communist Party, I think we should tell him that he has in his law firm a young man named Fisher whom he recommended, incidentally, to do work on this committee, who has been for a number of years a member of an organization which was named, oh, years and years ago, as the legal bulwark of the Communist Party. . . I certainly assume that Mr. Welch did not know of this young man at the time he recommended him as the assistant counsel for this committee, but he has such terror and such a great desire to know where anyone is located who may be serving the Communist cause, Mr. Welch, that I thought we should just call to your attention the fact that your Mr. Fisher, who is still in your law firm today, whom you asked to have down here looking over the secret and classified material, is a member of an organization, not named by me but named by various committees, named by the Attorney General, as I recall, and I think I quote this verbatim, as "the legal bulwark of the Communist Party." He belonged to that for a sizable number of years, according to his own admission, and he belonged to it long after it had been exposed as the legal arm of the Communist Party.

Knowing that, Mr. Welch, I just felt that I had a duty to respond to your urgent request that before sundown, when we know of anyone serving the Communist cause, we let the agency know. We are now letting you know that your man did belong to this organization for either 3 or 4 years, belonged to it long after he was out of law school.

I don't think you can find anyplace, anywhere, an organization which has done more to defend Communists—I am again quoting the report—to defend Communists, to defend espionage agents, and to aid the Communist cause, than the man whom you originally wanted down here at your right hand instead of Mr. St. Clair.

I have hesitated bringing that up, but I have been rather bored with your phony requests to Mr. Cohn here that he personally get every Communist out of government before sundown. Therefore, we will give you information about the young man in your own organization.

I am not asking you at this time to explain why you tried to foist him on this committee. Whether you knew he was a member of that Communist organization or not, I don't know. I assume you did not, Mr. Welch, because I get the impression that, while you are quite an actor, you play for a laugh, I don't think you have any conception of the danger of the Communist Party. I don't think you yourself would ever knowingly aid the Communist cause. I think you are unknowingly aiding it when you try to burlesque this hearing in which we are attempting to bring out the facts, however.

Mr. WELCH. Mr. Chairman.

Senator MUNDT. Mr. Welch, the Chair should say he has no recognition or no memory of Mr. Welch's recommending either Mr. Fisher anybody else as counsel for this committee.

I will recognize Mr. Welch.

Senator MCCARTHY. Mr. Chairman, I will give you the news story on that.

Mr. WELCH. Mr. Chairman, under these circumstances I must have something approaching a personal privilege.

Senator MUNDT. You may have it, sir. It will not be taken out of your time.

Mr. WELCH. Senator McCarthy, I did not know— Senator, sometimes you say "May I have your attention?"

Senator MCCARTHY. I am listening to you. I can listen with one ear.

Mr. WELCH. This time I want you to listen with both.

Senator MCCARTHY. Yes.

Mr. WELCH. Senator McCarthy, I think until this moment—

Senator MCCARTHY. Jim, will you get the news story to the effect that this man belonged to this Communist-front organization? Will you get the citations showing that this was the legal arm of the Communist Party, and the length of time that he belonged, and the fact that he was recommended by Mr. Welch? I think that should be in the record.

Mr. WELCH. You won't need anything in the record when I have finished telling you this.

Until this moment, Senator, I think I never really gaged your cruelty or your recklessness. Fred Fisher is a young man who went to the Harvard Law School and came into my firm and is starting what looks to be a brilliant career with us.

When I decided to work for this committee I asked Jim St. Clair, who sits on my right, to be my first assistant. I said to Jim, "Pick somebody in the firm who works under you that you would like." He chose Fred Fisher and they came down on an afternoon plane. That night, when he had taken a little stab at trying to see what the case was about, Fred Fisher and Jim St. Clair and I went to dinner together. I then said to these two young men, "Boys, I don't know anything about you except I have always liked you, but if there is anything funny in the life of either one of you that would hurt anybody in this case you speak up quick."

Fred Fisher said, "Mr. Welch, when I was in law school and for a period of months after, I belonged to the Lawyers Guild," as you have suggested, Senator. He went on to say, "I am secretary of the Young Republicans League in Newton with the son of Massachusetts' Governor, and I have the respect and admiration of my community and I am sure I have the respect and admiration of the 25 lawyers or so in Hale & Dorr."

I said, "Fred, I just don't think I am going to ask you to work on the case. If I do, one of these days that will come out and go over national television and it will just hurt like the dickens."

So, Senator, I asked him to go back to Boston.

Little did I dream you could be so reckless and so cruel as to do an injury to that lad. It is true he is still with Hale & Dorr. It is true that he will continue to be with Hale & Dorr. It is, I regret to say, equally true that I fear he shall always bear a scar needlessly inflicted by you. If it were in my power to forgive you for your reckless cruelty, I will do so. I like to think I am a gentleman, but your forgiveness will have to come from someone other than me.

Senator MCCARTHY. Mr. Chairman.

Senator MUNDT. Senator McCarthy?

Senator MCCARTHY. May I say that Mr. Welch talks about this being cruel and reckless. He was just baiting; he has been baiting Mr. Cohn here for hours, requesting that Mr. Cohn, before sundown, get out of any department of Government anyone who is serving the Communist cause.

I just give this man's record, and I want to say, Mr. Welch, that it has been labeled long before he became a member, as early as 1944—

Mr. WELCH. Senator, may we not drop this? We know he belonged to the Lawyers Guild, and Mr. Cohn nods his head at me. I did you, I think, no personal injury, Mr. Cohn.

Mr. COHN. No, sir.

Mr. WELCH. I meant to do you no personal injury, and if I did, I beg your pardon.

Let us not assassinate this lad further, Senator. You have done enough. Have you no sense of decency, sir, at long last? Have you left no sense of decency?

Senator MCCARTHY, I know this hurts you, Mr. Welch. But I may say, Mr. Chairman, on a point of personal privilege, and I would like to finish it—

Mr. WELCH. Senator, I think it hurts you, too, sir.

Senator MCCARTHY. I would like to finish this.

Mr. WELCH has been filibustering this hearing, he has been talking day after day about how he wants to get anyone tainted with communism out before sundown. I know Mr. Cohn would rather not have me go into this. I intend to, however, Mr. Welch talks about any sense of decency. If I say anything which is not the truth, then I would like to know about it.

> The foremost legal bulwark of the Communist Party, its front organizations, and controlled unions, and which, since its inception, has never failed to rally to the legal defense of the Communist Party, and individual members thereof, including known espionage agents.

Now, that is not the language of Senator McCarthy. That is the language of the Un-American Activities Committee. And I can go on with many more citations. It seems that Mr. Welch is pained so deeply he thinks it is improper for me to give the record, the Communist front record, of the man whom he wanted to foist upon this committee. But it doesn't pain him at all—there is no pain in his chest about the unfounded charges against Mr. Frank Carr; there is no pain there about the attempt to destroy the reputation and take the jobs away from the young men who were working in my committee.

And, Mr. WELCH, if I have said anything here which is untrue, then tell me. I have heard you and every one else talk so much about laying the truth upon the table that when I hear—and it is completely phony, Mr. Welch, I have listened to you for a long time— when you say "Now, before sundown, you must get these people out of Government," I want to have it very clear, very clear that you were not so serious about that when you tried to recommend this man for this committee.

And may I say, Mr. Welch, in fairness to you, I have reason to believe that you did not know about his Communist-front record at the time you recommended him. I don't think you would have recommended him to the committee if you knew that.

I think it is entirely possible you learned that after you recommended him.

Senator MUNDT. The Chair would like to say again that he does not believe that Mr. Welch recommended Mr. Fisher as counsel for this committee, because he has through his office all the recommendations that were made. He does not recall any that came from Mr. Welch, and that would include Mr. Fisher.

Senator MCCARTHY. Let me ask Mr. Welch. You brought him down, did you not, to act as your assistant?

Mr. WELCH. Mr. McCarthy, I will not discuss this with you further. You have sat within 6 feet of me, and could have asked me about Fred Fisher. You have brought it out. If there is a God in heaven, it will do neither you nor your cause any good.

QUESTIONS TO CONSIDER

1. How would you describe McCarthy's interrogation style?

2. Why do you think Welch's retort became so famous and had such an effect?

24.4 BRETT HARVEY, EXCERPT FROM *THE FIFTIES* (2002)

The 1950s were a complicated time for women in America. Many women had taken jobs on the home front during World War II but did not remain employed after the war. The decade was also a time of consumerism, nascent feminist attitudes, and changing ideas related to gender relations. In the following excerpt from Brett Harvey's oral history *The Fifties* is a recollection from Marion Samuels, who became a nurse over the objections of her husband in the early 1950s. As you will read, Samuels found the 1950s to be transformative for her.

"I always wanted to be a nurse. Don't know why, that's just what I wanted to be. Of course, I also expected to be married and have a family. There wasn't any place nearby where I could go to nursing school, so I went to a small liberal arts college for a year, but I didn't like it too much. Then Pearl Harbor came and everyone was going to work, so I decided I would, too. I went down with a boyfriend of mine to this ammunition plant near Louisville, Kentucky. They wouldn't accept him, but they took me because I'd had a year of college chemistry.

"This was during gas rationing and we were supposed to share rides, so I used to ride to work with a bunch of older fellows. They were all very nice to me, very gentlemanly. I worked in a lab where we were testing cellulose, I remember. There were a few other women working there and the men in the lab were nice to us, too. It was wartime, you know, and there was this feeling of everyone doing unusual things and pulling together.

"After about a year I decided to see if I could go to nursing school and I applied to Case Western in Cleveland. It so happened that was when they started the Cadet Nurse Corps, which paid for your education. I had just enough money saved from working at the plant to get to Cleveland and start out, and then the CNC paid the tuition and gave us a small stipend. And uniforms, we had very nice uniforms. That was all there was to being in the Corps—you just went to school." . . .

"In 1952, when my daughter was five and my son was three, the local hospital called and asked me if I was willing to work. They were very shorthanded and said I could have any hours I wanted. I said I'd love to. We lived right behind the hospital, so it couldn't have been more convenient. I could look out the window and see my own backyard. And if the children needed me I could be home in a minute. And I had my mother-in-law to watch the children.

"My husband did have a hard time with it for a while. He felt I shouldn't work because it looked as if he couldn't take care of me. It helped that the hospital just begged me to come because they were so desperate for nurses. Later on I had an offer from a big hospital in Dayton, a good offer, but my husband opposed that. He felt it would take me too far away from the children. So I didn't pursue it.

"I worked part-time, about four or five hours a day at first. Later on, I worked the three to eleven shift. Jim's mom would come in from the farm and do her shopping and I would pick her up and bring her home and she'd cook dinner for the family and put the children to bed." . . .

Source: Brett Harvey, *The Fifties: A Women's Oral History* (New York: Harper Collins, 2002), 130–132.

"I didn't really think what I was doing was all that unusual. Most of my friends were staying home with their children, but I can't say anyone was critical about me working, at least not to my face. After all, they'd be playing bridge or playing golf and I wasn't spending any more time at the hospital. I just preferred nursing to bridge or golf. Working may have come more naturally to me because my own mother worked. I thought it was kind of nice for the kids and kind of nice for my mother-in-law, too. And to tell you the truth, I thought it made me a better person to get away from them some and to have other experiences."

QUESTIONS TO CONSIDER

1. Why did Samuels think entering the workforce was important to her?
2. Does this change how you think about the 1950s? Why or why not?

CHAPTER 25

THE CONSUMER SOCIETY, 1945–1961

25.1 HO CHI MINH, "DECLARATION OF INDEPENDENCE OF THE DEMOCRATIC REPUBLIC OF VIETNAM" (1945)

In 1945, Ho Chi Minh announced Vietnamese independence. Minh had lived a cosmopolitan life before becoming a revolutionary leader. From 1911 to 1917, Minh traveled the world while working on steamships. He visited France, lived in New York City for a period, and then traveled to the United Kingdom. Later, he spent time in the Soviet Union and in the People's Republic of China. In 1941, Minh traveled back to Vietnam to fight for Vietnamese independence from its French colonizers and Japanese occupiers. He based the following document on the American Declaration of Independence. Afterward, he failed to secure a peace agreement with French leaders and again declared war against them. For the next nine years, Minh fought another war for independence, until he secured the division of Vietnam in 1954, with North Vietnam as a communist nation. There, Minh brutally repressed any dissent and courted the support of the Soviet Union and China. Later, Minh led North Vietnam against South Vietnam and the United States during the Vietnam War. He died in 1969, four years before the United States formally withdrew its forces and North Vietnam took control over the whole country.

All men are created equal; they are endowed by their Creator with certain unalienable Rights; among these are Life, Liberty, and the pursuit of Happiness.

This immortal statement was made in the Declaration of Independence of the United States of America in 1776. In a broader sense, this means: All the peoples on the earth are equal from birth, all the peoples have a right to live, to be happy and free.

The Declaration of the French Revolution made in 1791 on the Rights of Man and the Citizen also states: "All men are born free and with equal rights, and must always remain free and have equal rights."

Source: Bernard B. Fall, ed., *Ho Chi Minh On Revolution: Selected Writings, 1920–1966* (New York: Frederick A. Praeger, 1967), 143–145.

Those are undeniable truths.

Nevertheless, for more than eighty years, the French imperialists, abusing the standard of Liberty, Equality, and Fraternity, have violated our Fatherland and oppressed our fellow citizens. They have acted contrary to the ideals of humanity and justice.

In the field of politics, they have deprived our people of every democratic liberty.

They have enforced inhuman laws; they have set up three distinct political regimes in the North, the Center, and the South of Viet-Nam in order to wreck our national unity and prevent our people from being united.

They have built more prisons than schools. They have mercilessly slain our patriots; they have drowned our uprisings in rivers of blood.

They have fettered public opinion; they have practiced obscurantism against our people.

To weaken our race they have forced us to use opium and alcohol.

In the field of economics, they have fleeced us to the backbone, impoverished our people and devastated our land.

They have robbed us of our rice fields, our mines, our forests, and our raw materials. They have monopolized the issuing of bank notes and the export trade.

They have invented numerous unjustifiable taxes and reduced our people, especially our peasantry, to a state of extreme poverty.

They have hampered the prospering of our national bourgeoisie; they have mercilessly exploited our workers.

In the autumn of 1940, when the Japanese fascists violated Indochina's territory to establish new bases in their fight against the Allies, the French imperialists went down on their bended knees and handed over our country to them.

Thus, from that date, our people were subjected to the double yoke of the French and the Japanese. Their sufferings and miseries increased. The result was that, from the end of last year to the beginning of this year, from Quang Tri Province to the North of Viet-Nam, more than two million of our fellow citizens died from starvation. On March 9 [1945], the French troops were disarmed by the Japanese. The French colonialists either fled or surrendered, showing that not only were they incapable of "protecting" us, but that, in the span of five years, they had twice sold our country to the Japanese.

On several occasions before March 9, the Viet Minh League urged the French to ally themselves with it against the Japanese. Instead of agreeing to this proposal, the French colonialists so intensified their terrorist activities against the Viet Minh members that before fleeing they massacred a great number of our political prisoners detained at Yen Bay and Cao Bang.

Notwithstanding all this, our fellow citizens have always manifested toward the French a tolerant and humane attitude. Even after the Japanese *Putsch* of March, 1945, the Viet Minh League helped many Frenchmen to cross the frontier, rescued some of them from Japanese jails, and protected French lives and property.

From the autumn of 1940, our country had in fact ceased to be a French colony and had become a Japanese possession.

After the Japanese had surrendered to the Allies, our whole people rose to regain our national sovereignty and to found the Democratic Republic of Viet-Nam.

The truth is that we have wrested our independence from the Japanese and not from the French.

The French have fled, the Japanese have capitulated, Emperor Bao Dai has abdicated. Our people have broken the chains which for nearly a century have fettered them and have won independence for the Fatherland. Our people at the same time have overthrown the monarchic regime that has reigned supreme for dozens of centuries. In its place has been established the present Democratic Republic.

For these reasons, we, members of the Provisional Government, representing the whole Vietnamese people, declare that from now on we break off all relations of a colonial character with France; we repeal all the international obligation that France has so far subscribed to on behalf of Viet-Nam, and we abolish all the special rights the French have unlawfully acquired in our Fatherland.

The whole Vietnamese people, animated by a common purpose, are determined to fight to the bitter end against any attempt by the French colonialists to reconquer their country.

We are convinced that the Allied nations, which at Teheran and San Francisco have acknowledged the principles of self-determination and equality of nations, will not refuse to acknowledge the independence of Viet-Nam.

A people who have courageously opposed French domination for more than eighty years, a people who have fought side by side with the Allies against the fascists during these last years, such a people must be free and independent.

For these reasons, we, members of the Provisional Government of the Democratic Republic of Viet-Nam, solemnly declare to the world that Viet-Nam has the right to be a free and independent country—and in fact it is so already. The entire Vietnamese people are determined to mobilize all their physical and mental strength, to sacrifice their lives and property in order to safeguard their independence and liberty.

QUESTIONS TO CONSIDER

1. How did Minh portray Vietnam's history?
2. How did he use the American Declaration of Independence to his advantage?

25.2 ALLEN GINSBERG, "AMERICA" (1956)

American poet Allen Ginsberg (1926–1997) was a foundational member of the Beat Generation during the 1950s. The Beat authors, part of a growing counterculture during the time, emphasized new narrative methods, anti-materialism, drug use, and sexual freedom. Other well-known Beat authors included Jack Kerouac and William Burroughs. In the 1950s, Ginsberg moved to San Francisco and became a member of the growing literary scene there. In 1956, he published *Howl and Other Poems*. The poem "Howl" came to define the counterculture during that decade. Another poem in the collection, however, "America," more directly took aim at the consumer society Ginsberg saw around him and the nation's global engagements. The collection was later temporarily banned on allegations that it was obscene.

America I've given you all and now I'm nothing.
America two dollars and twentyseven cents
    January 17, 1956.
I can't stand my own mind.
America when will we end the human war?
Go fuck yourself with your atom bomb.
I don't feel good don't bother me.
I won't write my poem till I'm in my right mind.
America when will you be angelic?
When will you take off your clothes?
When will you look at yourself through the grave?

When will you be worthy of your million
    Trotskyites?
America why are your libraries full of tears?
America when will you send your eggs to India?
I'm sick of your insane demands.
When can I go into the supermarket and buy
    what I need with my good looks?
America after all it is you and I who are perfect
    not the next world.
Your machinery is too much for me.
You made me want to be a saint.

There must be some other way to settle this
argument.
Burroughs is in Tangiers I don't think he'll come
back it's sinister.
Are you being sinister or is this some form of
practical joke?
I'm trying to come to the point.
I refuse to give up my obsession.
America stop pushing I know what I'm doing.
America the plum blossoms are falling.
I haven't read the newspapers for months, every-
day somebody goes on trial for murder.
America I feel sentimental about the Wobblies.
America I used to be a communist when I was a
kid I'm not sorry.
I smoke marijuana every chance I get.
I sit in my house for days on end and stare at the
roses in the closet,
When I go to Chinatown I get drunk and never
get laid.
My mind is made up there's going to be trouble.
You should have seen my reading Marx.
My psychoanalyst thinks I'm perfectly right.
I won't say the Lord's Prayer.
I have mystical visions and cosmic vibrations.
America I still haven't told you what you
    did to Uncle Max after he came over from
    Russia.

I'm addressing you.
Are you going to let your emotional life be run by
Time Magazine?
I'm obsessed by Time Magazine.
I read it every week.
Its cover stares at me every time I slink past the
corner candystore.
I read it in the basement of the Berkeley Public
Library.
It's always telling me about responsibility.
Business-men are serious. Movie producers
are serious. Everybody's serious but me.
It occurs to me that I am America.
I am talking to myself again.

Asia is rising against me.
I haven't got a chinaman's chance.
I'd better consider my national resources.

My national resources consist of two joints of marijuana millions of genitals an unpublishable
private literature that goes 1400 miles an hour
and twenty-five-thousand mental institutions.
I say nothing about my prisons nor the millions
of underprivileged who live in my flowerpots
under the light of five hundred suns.
I have abolished the whorehouses of France,
Tangiers is the next to go.
My ambitions is to be President despite the fact
that I'm a Catholic.

America how can I write a holy litany in your silly
mood?
I will continue like Henry Ford my strophes are as
individual as his automobiles more so they're
all different sexes.
America I will sell you strophes $2500 apiece
$500 down on your old strophe
America free Tom Mooney
America save the Spanish Loyalists
America Sacco & Vanzetti must not die
America I am the Scottsboro boys.
America when I was seven momma took me to
Communist Cell meetings they sold us gar-
banzos a handful per ticket a ticket costs a
nickel and the speeches were free everybody
was angelic and sentimental about the work-
ers it was all so sincere you have no idea what
a good thing the party was in 1835 Scott
Nearing was a grand old man a real mensch
Mother Bloor made me cry I once saw Israel
Amter plain. Everybody must have been a spy.
America you don't really want to go to war.
America it's them bad Russians.
Them Russians them Russians and them China-
men. And them Russians.
The Russia wants to eat us alive. The Russia's
power mad. She wants to take our cars from
out our garages.
Her wants to grab Chicago. Her needs a Red
Readers' Digest. Her wants our auto plants
in Siberia. Him big bureaucracy running
fillingstations.
That no good. Ugh. Him make Indians learn read.
Him need big back niggers. Hah. Her make us
all work sixteen hours a day. Help.

America this is quite serious.
America this is the impression I get from looking
    in the television set.
America is this correct?
I'd better get right down to the job.
It's true I don't want to join the Army or
    turn lathes in precision parts factories,
    I'm nearsighted and psychopathic anyway.

America I'm putting my queer shoulder to the
    wheel.

QUESTIONS TO CONSIDER

1. How did Ginsberg portray America?
2. Does this poem change the way you think about the 1950s? Why or why not?

25.3 DWIGHT D. EISENHOWER, "FAREWELL ADDRESS" (1961)

President Dwight D. Eisenhower (1890–1969) had a formative impact on twentieth-century American history. During World War II, Eisenhower attained the rank of five-star general and Supreme Allied Commander. He managed the invasions of North Africa, Sicily, France, and Germany. After the war, Eisenhower served as President of Columbia University. In 1952, he entered the presidential race as a Republican and swept to victory over Adlai Stevenson, and against Stevenson again in his 1956 re-election bid. As President, Eisenhower was relatively successful. A moderate Republican, he expanded highway infrastructure spending and educational spending. The economy boomed during the vast majority of his tenure. In terms of foreign policy, Eisenhower worked to contain Soviet influence and supported coups in Iran and Guatemala against regimes he believed were too close to Soviet influence. As he exited office in 1961, Eisenhower gave a farewell address to the nation. The speech has become famous for his prescient warnings about a "military-industrial complex" in the Cold War world.

My fellow Americans:

Three days from now, after half a century in the service of our country, I shall lay down the responsibilities of office as, in traditional and solemn ceremony, the authority of the Presidency is vested in my successor.

This evening I come to you with a message of leave-taking and farewell, and to share a few final thoughts with you, my countrymen.

Like every other citizen, I wish the new President, and all who will labor with him, Godspeed. I pray that the coming years will be blessed with peace and prosperity for all.

I

Our people expect their President and the Congress to find essential agreement on issues of great moment, the wise resolution of which will better shape the future of the Nation.

My own relations with the Congress, which began on a remote and tenuous basis when, long ago, a

Source: "Transcript of President Dwight D. Eisenhower's Farewell Address (1961)," https://www.ourdocuments.gov/doc.php?flash=false&doc=90&page=transcript (Accessed May 21, 2018).

member of the Senate appointed me to West Point, have since ranged to the intimate during the war and immediate post-war period, and, finally, to the mutually interdependent during these past eight years.

In this final relationship, the Congress and the Administration have, on most vital issues, cooperated well, to serve the national good rather than mere partisanship, and so have assured that the business of the Nation should go forward. So, my official relationship with the Congress ends in a feeling, on my part, of gratitude that we have been able to do so much together.

II

We now stand ten years past the midpoint of a century that has witnessed four major wars among great nations. Three of these involved our own country. Despite these holocausts America is today the strongest, the most influential and most productive nation in the world. Understandably proud of this pre-eminence, we yet realize that America's leadership and prestige depend, not merely upon our unmatched material progress, riches and military strength, but on how we use our power in the interests of world peace and human betterment.

III

Throughout America's adventure in free government, our basic purposes have been to keep the peace; to foster progress in human achievement, and to enhance liberty, dignity and integrity among people and among nations. To strive for less would be unworthy of a free and religious people. Any failure traceable to arrogance, or our lack of comprehension or readiness to sacrifice would inflict upon us grievous hurt both at home and abroad.

Progress toward these noble goals is persistently threatened by the conflict now engulfing the world. It commands our whole attention, absorbs our very beings. We face a hostile ideology—global in scope, atheistic in character, ruthless in purpose, and insidious in method. Unhappily the danger it poses promises to be of indefinite duration. To meet it successfully, there is called for, not so much the emotional and transitory sacrifices of crisis, but rather those which enable us to carry forward steadily, surely,

and without complaint the burdens of a prolonged and complex struggle—with liberty at stake. Only thus shall we remain, despite every provocation, on our charted course toward permanent peace and human betterment.

Crises there will continue to be. In meeting them, whether foreign or domestic, great or small, there is a recurring temptation to feel that some spectacular and costly action could become the miraculous solution to all current difficulties. A huge increase in newer elements of our defense; development of unrealistic programs to cure every ill in agriculture; a dramatic expansion in basic and applied research—these and many other possibilities, each possibly promising in itself, may be suggested as the only way to the road we which to travel.

But each proposal must be weighed in the light of a broader consideration: the need to maintain balance in and among national programs—balance between the private and the public economy, balance between cost and hoped for advantage—balance between the clearly necessary and the comfortably desirable; balance between our essential requirements as a nation and the duties imposed by the nation upon the individual; balance between action of the moment and the national welfare of the future. Good judgment seeks balance and progress; lack of it eventually finds imbalance and frustration.

The record of many decades stands as proof that our people and their government have, in the main, understood these truths and have responded to them well, in the face of stress and threat. But threats, new in kind or degree, constantly arise. I mention two only.

IV

A vital element in keeping the peace is our military establishment. Our arms must be mighty, ready for instant action, so that no potential aggressor may be tempted to risk his own destruction.

Our military organization today bears little relation to that known by any of my predecessors in peace time, or indeed by the fighting men of World War II or Korea.

Until the latest of our world conflicts, the United States had no armaments industry. American makers of plowshares could, with time and as required, make swords as well. But now we can no longer risk emergency improvisation of national defense; we have been compelled to create a permanent armaments industry of vast proportions. Added to this, three and a half million men and women are directly engaged in the defense establishment. We annually spend on military security more than the net income of all United State corporations.

This conjunction of an immense military establishment and a large arms industry is new in the American experience. The total influence—economic, political, even spiritual—is felt in every city, every state house, every office of the Federal government. We recognize the imperative need for this development. Yet we must not fail to comprehend its grave implications. Our toil, resources and livelihood are all involved; so is the very structure of our society.

In the councils of government, we must guard against the acquisition of unwarranted influence, whether sought or unsought, by the military-industrial complex. The potential for the disastrous rise of misplaced power exists and will persist.

We must never let the weight of this combination endanger our liberties or democratic processes. We should take nothing for granted. Only an alert and knowledgeable citizenry can compel the proper meshing of huge industrial and military machinery of defense with our peaceful methods and goals, so that security and liberty may prosper together.

Akin to, and largely responsible for the sweeping changes in our industrial-military posture, has been the technological revolution during recent decades.

In this revolution, research has become central; it also becomes more formalized, complex, and costly. A steadily increasing share is conducted for, by, or at the direction of, the Federal government.

Today, the solitary inventor, tinkering in his shop, has been over shadowed by task forces of scientists in laboratories and testing fields. In the same fashion, the free university, historically the fountainhead of free ideas and scientific discovery, has experienced a revolution in the conduct of research. Partly because of the huge costs involved, a government contract becomes virtually a substitute for intellectual curiosity. For every old blackboard there are now hundreds of new electronic computers.

The prospect of domination of the nation's scholars by Federal employment, project allocations, and the power of money is ever present and is gravely to be regarded.

Yet, in holding scientific research and discovery in respect, as we should, we must also be alert to the equal and opposite danger that public policy could itself become the captive of a scientific-technological elite.

It is the task of statesmanship to mold, to balance, and to integrate these and other forces, new and old, within the principles of our democratic system-ever aiming toward the supreme goals of our free society.

V

Another factor in maintaining balance involves the element of time. As we peer into society's future, we—you and I, and our government—must avoid the impulse to live only for today, plundering, for our own ease and convenience, the precious resources of tomorrow. We cannot mortgage the material assets of our grandchildren without risking the loss also of their political and spiritual heritage. We want democracy to survive for all generations to come, not to become the insolvent phantom of tomorrow.

VI

Down the long lane of the history yet to be written America knows that this world of ours, ever growing smaller, must avoid becoming a community of dreadful fear and hate, and be, instead, a proud confederation of mutual trust and respect.

Such a confederation must be one of equals. The weakest must come to the conference table with the same confidence as do we, protected as we are by our moral, economic, and military strength. That table, though scarred by many past frustrations, cannot be abandoned for the certain agony of the battlefield.

Disarmament, with mutual honor and confidence, is a continuing imperative. Together we must learn how to compose difference, not with arms, but with intellect and decent purpose. Because this need is so sharp and apparent I confess that I lay down my official responsibilities in this field with a definite sense of disappointment. As one who has witnessed the horror and the lingering sadness of war—as one who knows that another war could utterly destroy this civilization which has been so slowly and painfully built over thousands of years—I wish I could say tonight that a lasting peace is in sight.

Happily, I can say that war has been avoided. Steady progress toward our ultimate goal has been made. But, so much remains to be done. As a private citizen, I shall never cease to do what little I can to help the world advance along that road.

VII

So—in this my last good night to you as your President—I thank you for the many opportunities you have given me for public service in war and peace. I trust that in that service you find some things worthy; as for the rest of it, I know you will find ways to improve performance in the future.

You and I—my fellow citizens—need to be strong in our faith that all nations, under God, will reach the goal of peace with justice. May we be ever unswerving in devotion to principle, confident but humble with power, diligent in pursuit of the Nation's great goals.

To all the peoples of the world, I once more give expression to America's prayerful and continuing inspiration:

We pray that peoples of all faiths, all races, all nations, may have their great human needs satisfied; that those now denied opportunity shall come to enjoy it to the full; that all who yearn for freedom may experience its spiritual blessings; that those who have freedom will understand, also, its heavy responsibilities; that all who are insensitive to the needs of others will learn charity; that the scourges of poverty, disease and ignorance will be made to disappear from the earth, and that, in the goodness of time, all peoples will come to live together in a peace guaranteed by the binding force of mutual respect and love.

QUESTIONS TO CONSIDER

1. What did Eisenhower mean by a "military-industrial complex"?
2. How did Eisenhower suggest American political leaders should act in the future? What did he fear?

CHAPTER 26

THE TABLE OF DEMOCRACY, 1960–1968

26.1 BARRY GOLDWATER, EXCERPT FROM *THE CONSCIENCE OF A CONSERVATIVE* (1960)

Well before the conservative revolution led to great gains for Republicans during the 1980s and 1990s, Barry Goldwater (1909–1998) laid out its major intellectual tenets. Born in Phoenix, Arizona, Goldwater flew supplies for the U.S. Air Force during World War II. After the war, Goldwater returned to Arizona and entered politics as a conservative Republican and opponent of the New Deal. In the 1952 Senate election, Goldwater upset incumbent Democrat Ernest McFarland, and he again defeated McFarland in 1958. As a Senator, Goldwater often opposed the Eisenhower administration for its moderation, even though Eisenhower was also a Republican. In 1964, Goldwater entered the presidential election and won the Republican nomination, though he handily lost the general election to Lyndon Baines Johnson, who portrayed Goldwater as an extremist that could not be trusted with America's nuclear weapons. Nevertheless, Goldwater remained a formidable part of the American conservative movement. Goldwater published *The Conscience of a Conservative* in 1960 in preparation for the 1964 campaign. Ghostwritten by a former speechwriter, the book laid out Goldwater's beliefs on a variety of issues and made him a national political figure. The excerpt you will read introduced the general tenets of his conservatism.

I HAVE BEEN much concerned that so many people today with Conservative instincts feel compelled to apologize for them. Or if not to apologize directly, to qualify their commitment in a way that amounts to breast-beating. "Republican candidates," Vice President Nixon has said, "should be economic conservatives, but conservatives with a heart." President Eisenhower announced during his first term, "I am

Source: Barry Goldwater, *The Conscience of a Conservative* (Shepherdsville, KY: Victor Publishing Company Inc., 1960), 1–14. Retrieved from the Hathi Trust website, https://babel.hathitrust.org/cgi/pt?id=mdp.39015046344738;view=1up;seq=5 (Accessed June 14, 2018).

conservative when it comes to economic problems but liberal when it comes to human problems." Still other Republican leaders have insisted on calling themselves "progressive" Conservatives.* These formulations are tantamount to an admission that Conservatism is a narrow, mechanistic *economic* theory that may work very well as a bookkeeper's guide, but cannot be relied upon as a comprehensive political philosophy.

The same judgment, though in the form of an attack rather than an admission, is advanced by the radical camp. "We liberals," they say, "are interested in *people*. Our concern is with human beings, while you Conservatives are preoccupied with the preservation of economic privilege and status." Take them a step further, and the Liberals will turn the accusations into a class argument: it is the little people that concern us, not the "malefactors of great wealth."

Such statements, from friend and foe alike, do great injustice to the Conservative point of view. Conservatism is *not* an economic theory, though it has economic implications. The shoe is precisely on the other foot: it is Socialism that subordinates all other considerations to man's material well-being. It is Conservatism that puts material things in their proper place—that has a structured view of the human being and of human society, in which economics plays only a subsidiary role.

The root difference between the Conservatives and the Liberals of today is that Conservatives take account of the *whole* man, while the Liberals tend to look only at the material side of man's nature. The Conservative believes that man is, in part, an economic, an animal creature; but that he is also a spiritual creature with spiritual needs and spiritual desires. What is more, these needs and desires reflect the *superior* side of man's nature, and thus take precedence over his economic wants. Conservatism therefore looks upon the enhancement of man's spiritual nature as the primary concern of political philosophy. Liberals, on the other hand,—in the name of a concern for "human beings"—regard the satisfaction of economic wants as the dominant mission of society. They are, moreover,

in a hurry. So that their characteristic approach is to harness the society's political and economic forces into a collective effort to *compel* "progress." In this approach, I believe they fight against Nature!

Surely the first obligation of a political thinker is to understand the nature of man. The Conservative does not claim special powers of perception on this point, but he does claim a familiarity with the accumulated wisdom and experience of history, and he is not too proud to learn from the great minds of the past.

The first thing he has learned about man is that each member of the species is a unique creature. Man's most sacred possession is his individual soul—which has an immortal side, but also a mortal one. The mortal side establishes his absolute differentness from every other human being. *Only a philosophy that takes into account the essential difference between men, and, accordingly, makes provision for developing the different potentialities of each man can claim to be in accord with Nature.* We have heard much in our time about "the common man." It is a concept that pays little attention to the history of a nation that grew great through the initiative and ambition of uncommon men. The Conservative knows that to regard man as part of an undifferentiated mass is to consign him to ultimate slavery.

Secondly, the Conservative has learned that the economic and spiritual aspects of man's nature are inextricably intertwined. He cannot be economically free, or even economically efficient, if he is enslaved politically; conversely, man's political freedom is illusory if he is dependent for his economic needs on the State.

The Conservative realizes, thirdly, that man's development, in both its spiritual and material aspects, is not something that can be directed by outside forces. Every man, for his individual good and for the good of his society, is responsible for his *own* development. The choices that govern his life are choices that *he* must make: they cannot be made by any other human being, or by a collectivity of human beings. If the Conservative is less anxious than his Liberal brethren to increase Social Security "benefits," it is because he is more anxious than his Liberal brethren that people

---

* This is a strange label indeed: it implies that "ordinary" Conservatism is opposed to progress. Have we forgotten that America made its greatest progress when Conservative principles were honored and preserved?

be free throughout their lives to spend their earnings when and as they see fit.

So it is that Conservatism, throughout history, has regarded man neither as a potential pawn of other men, nor as a part of a general collectivity in which the sacredness and the separate identity of individual human beings are ignored. Throughout history, true Conservatism has been at war equally with autocrats and with "democratic" Jacobins. The true Conservative was sympathetic with the plight of the hapless peasant under the tyranny of the French monarchy. And he was equally revolted at the attempt to solve that problem by a mob tyranny that paraded under the banner of egalitarianism. The con-science of the Conservative is pricked by *anyone* who would debase the dignity of the individual human being. Today, therefore, he is at odds with dictators who rule by terror, and equally with those gentler collectivists who ask our permission to play God with the human race.

With this view of the nature of man, it is understandable that the Conservative looks upon politics as the art of achieving the maximum amount of freedom for individuals that is consistent with the maintenance of social order. The Conservative is the first to understand that the practice of freedom requires the establishment of order: it is impossible for one man to be free if another is able to deny him the exercise of his freedom. But the Conservative also recognizes that the political power on which order is based is a self-aggrandizing force; that its appetite grows with eating. He knows that the utmost vigilance and care are require to keep political power within its proper bounds.

In our day, order is pretty well taken care of. The delicate balance that ideally exists between freedom and order has long since tipped against freedom practically everywhere on earth. In some countries, freedom is altogether down and order holds absolute sway. In our country the trend is less far advanced, but it is well along and gathering momentum every day. Thus, for the American Conservative, there is no difficulty in identifying the day's overriding political challenge: it is *to preserve and extend freedom.* As he surveys the various attitudes and institutions and laws that currently prevail in America, many questions will occur to him, but the Conservative's first concern will always be: *Are we maximizing freedom?*

QUESTIONS TO CONSIDER

1. How did Goldwater define his conservatism? Does the definition make sense to you?
2. Why do you think the book made Goldwater into such a national figure?

26.2 MICHAEL HARRINGTON, EXCERPT FROM *THE OTHER AMERICA* (1962)

President Lyndon Baines Johnson's Great Society propagated as one of its main ideals a "War on Poverty." Much of the impetus for the "War on Poverty" likely came from Michael Harrington's 1962 book *The Other America*. Harrington, who would later found the Democratic Socialists of America, identified the kind of poverty that was not readily apparent to contemporary observers—the lives of the rural poor, for instance—in an effort to bring light to the plight of the poor. In the excerpt presented here, Harrington introduced "an invisible land" and the people who live there. After its publication, *The Other America* became a seminal sociological work that propelled Harrington to national acclaim.

There is a familiar America. It is celebrated in speeches and advertised on television and in the magazines. It has the highest mass standard of living the world has ever known.

In the 1950's this America worried about itself, yet even its anxieties were products of abundance. The title of a brilliant book was widely misinterpreted, and the familiar America began to call itself "the affluent society." There was introspection of the emotional suffering taking place in the suburbs. In all this, there was an implicit assumption that the basic grinding economic problems had been solved in the United States. In this theory the nation's problems were no longer a matter of basic human needs, of food, shelter, and clothing. Now they were seen as qualitative, a question of learning to live decently amid luxury.

While this discussion was carried on, there existed another America. In it dwelt somewhere between 40,000,000 and 50,000,000 citizens of this land. They were poor. They still are.

To be sure, the other America is not impoverished in the same sense as those poor nations where millions cling to hunger as a defense against starvation. This country has escaped such extremes. That does not change the fact that tens of millions of Americans are, at this very moment, maimed in body and spirit, existing at levels beneath those necessary for human decency. If these people are not starving, they are hungry, and sometimes fat with hunger, for that is what cheap foods do. They are without adequate housing and education and medical care.

The Government has documented what this means to the bodies of the poor, and the figures will be cited throughout this book. But even more basic, this poverty twists and deforms the spirit. The American poor are pessimistic and defeated, and they are victimized by mental suffering to a degree known in Suburbia. . . .

There are perennial reasons that make the other America an invisible land.

Poverty is often off the beaten track. It always has been. The ordinary tourist never left the main highway, and today he rides interstate turnpikes. He does not go into the valleys of Pennsylvania where the towns look like movie sets of Wales in the thirties. He does not see the company houses in rows, the rutted road (the poor always have bad roads whether they live in the city, in town, or on farms), and everything is black and dirty. And even if he were to pass through such a place by accident, the tourist would not meet the unemployed men in the bar or the women coming home a runaway sweatshop.

Then, too, beauty and myths are perennial masks of poverty. The traveler comes to the Appalachians in the lovely season. Or perhaps he looks at a run-down

Source: Michael Harrington, *The Other America: Poverty in the United States* (New York: The Macmillan Company, 1964), 1–6.

mountain house and, remembering Rousseau rather than seeing with his eyes, decides that "those people" are truly fortunate to be living the way they are and that they are lucky to be exempt from the strains and tensions of the middle class. The only problem is that "those people," the quaint inhabitants of those hills, are undereducated, underprivileged, lack medical care, and are in the process of being forced from the land into a life in the cities, where they are misfits.

These are normal and obvious causes of the invisibility of the poor. They operated a generation ago; they will be functioning a generation hence. It is more important to understand that the very development of American society is creating a new kind of blindness about poverty. The poor are increasingly slipping out of the very experience and consciousness of the nation.

If the middle class never did like ugliness and poverty, it was at least aware of them. "Across the tracks" was not a very long way to go. There were forays into the slums at Christmas time; there were charitable organizations that brought contact with the poor. Occasionally, almost everyone passed through the Negro ghetto or the blocks of tenements, if only to get downtown to work or to entertainment.

Now the American city has been transformed. The poor still inhabit the miserable housing in the central area, but are increasingly isolated from contact with, or sight of, anybody else. Middle-class women coming in from suburbia on a rare trip may catch the merest glimpse of the other America on the way to an evening at the theater, but their children are segregated in suburban schools. The business or professional man may drive along the fringes of slums in a car or bus, but it is not an important experience to him. The failures, the unskilled, the disabled, the aged, and the minorities are right there, across the tracks, where they always been. But hardly anyone else is.

In short, the very development of the American city has removed poverty from the living, emotional experience of millions upon millions of middle-class American. Living out in the suburbs, it is easy to assume that ours is, indeed, an affluent society.

This new segregation of poverty is compounded by a well-meaning ignorance. A good many concerned and sympathetic Americans are aware that there is much discussion of urban renewal. Suddenly, driving through the city, they notice that a familiar slum has been torn down and that there are towering, modern buildings where once there had been tenements or hovels. There is a warm feeling of satisfaction, of pride in the way things are working out: the poor, it is obvious, are being taken care of.

The irony in this (as the chapter on housing will document) is that the truth is nearly the exact opposite to the impression. The total impact of the various housing programs in postwar America has been to squeeze more and more people into existing slums. More often than not, the modern apartment in a towering building rent at $40 a room or more. For, during the past decade and a half, there has been more subsidization of middle- and upper-income housing than there been of housing for the poor.

Clothes make the poor invisible too: America has the best-dressed poverty the world has ever known. For a variety of reason, the benefits of mass production have been spread much more evenly in this area than in many others. It is much easier in the United States to be decently dressed than it is to be decently housed, fed, or doctored. Even people with terribly depressed incomes can look prosperous.

This is an extremely important factor in defining our emotional and existential ignorance of poverty. In Detroit the existence of social classes became much more difficult to discern the day the companies put lockers in the plants. From that moment on, one did not see men in work clothes on the way to the factory, but citizens in slacks and white shirts. This process has been magnified with the poor throughout the country. There are tens of thousands of Americans in the big cities who are wearing shoes, perhaps even a stylishly cut suit or dress, and yet are hungry. It is not a matter of planning, though it almost seems as if the affluent society had given out costumes to the poor so that they would not offend the rest of society with the sight of rags.

Then, many of the poor are the wrong age to be seen. A god number of them (over 8,000,000) are sixty-five years of age or better; an even larger number are under eighteen. The aged members of the other America are often sick, and they cannot move. Another group of them live out their lives in loneliness and frustration: they sit in rented rooms, or else they stay close to a house in a neighborhood that has completely changed from the old days. Indeed, one of the worst aspects of poverty among the aged is that these people are out of sight and out of mind, and alone.

They young are somewhat more visible, yet they too stay close to their neighborhoods. Sometimes they advertise poverty through a lurid tabloid story about a gang killing. But generally they do not disturb the quiet streets of the middle class.

And finally, the poor are politically invisible. It is one of the cruelest ironies of social life in advanced countries that the dispossessed at the bottom of society are unable to speak for themselves. The people of other America do not, by far and large, belong to unions, to fraternal organizational, or to political parties. They are without lobbies of their own; they put forward no legislative program. As a group, they are atomized. They have no face; they have no voice.

QUESTIONS TO CONSIDER

1. How does Harrington try to convince his readers of the problem's prevalence?
2. Do you find his argument effective? Why do you think it influenced policy?

26.3 GEORGE WALLACE, "SEGREGATION FOREVER" SPEECH (1963)

There were a variety of responses to the civil rights movement (see also Readings 26.4 and 26.5). In Alabama, for instance, George Wallace (1919–1988) raged against desegregation movements and urged Southerners to defend their Confederate heritage. Born in Alabama, Wallace received his education from the University of Alabama. After a failed run for governor in 1958, Wallace reemerged in the 1962 election as a hardline segregation supporter. After winning the election, he gave the following speech at his inauguration. The speech became infamous for Wallace's support of "segregation now . . . segregation tomorrow . . . segregation forever." Later that year, Wallace stood "In the Schoolhouse Door," in front of an auditorium at the University of Alabama, in an effort to stop the university's forced desegregation by Federal troops. Wallace would eventually serve for a combined sixteen years as the Governor of Alabama and run for President unsuccessfully four times. In the 1968 election, Wallace won almost ten million votes nationwide and the electoral votes from five states as a pro-segregation, third-party candidate, making him the last third-party candidate to win electoral votes in a presidential election.

This is the day of my Inauguration as Governor of the State of Alabama. And on this day I feel a deep obligation to renew my pledges, my covenants with you. . .the people of this great state.

General Robert E. Lee said that "duty" is the most sublime word in the English language and I have come, increasingly, to realize what he meant. I SHALL do my duty to you, God helping. . .to every man, to

Source: "The Inaugural Address of Governor George C. Wallace," January 19, 1963, Alabama Department of Archives and History, http://digital.archives.alabama.gov/cdm/ref/collection/voices/id/2952 (Accessed June 14, 2018).

every woman. . .yes, and to every child in the State. I shall fulfill my duty toward honesty and economy in our State government so that no man shall have a part of his livelihood cheated and no child shall have a bit of his future stolen away.

[. . .]

Today I have stood, where once Jefferson Davis stood, and took an oath to my people. It is very appropriate then that from this Cradle of the Confederacy, this very Heart of the Great Anglo-Saxon Southland, that today we sound the drum for freedom as have our generations of forebears before us done, time and again down through history. Let us rise to the call of freedom-loving blood that is in us and send our answer to the tyranny that clanks its chains upon the South. In the name of the greatest people that have ever trod this earth, I draw the line in the dust and toss the gauntlet before the feet of tyranny. . .and I say. . .segregation now . . .segregation tomorrow. . .segregation forever.

The Washington, D.C.[,] school riot report is disgusting and revealing. We will not sacrifice our children to any such type school system—and you can write that down. The federal troops in Mississippi could better be used guarding the safety of the citizens of Washington, D.C., where it is even unsafe to walk or go to a ball game—and that is the nation's capitol. I was safer in a B-29 bomber over Japan during the war in an air raid, than the people of Washington are walking in the White House neighborhood. A closer example is Atlanta. The city officials fawn for political reasons over school integration and THEN build barricades to stop residential integration—what hypocrisy!

Let us send this message back to Washington by our representatives who are with us today . . .that from this day we are standing up, and the heel of tyranny does not fit the neck of an upright man. . .that we intend to take the offensive and carry our fight for freedom across this nation, wielding the balance of power we know we possess in the Southland. . .that WE, not the insipid bloc voters of some sections. .will determine in the next election who shall sit in the White House of these United States. . . .that from this day. . .from this hour. . .from this minute. . .we give the word of a race of honor that we will tolerate their boot in our face no longer. . . .and let those certain judges put that in their opium pipes of power and smoke it for what it is worth.

Here me, Southerners! You son and daughters who have moved north and west throughout this nation. . . .we call on you from your native soil to join with us in national support and vote. . and we know. . .wherever you are. .away from the hearths of the Southland. . .that you will respond, for though you may live in the fartherest reaches of this vast country. . .your heart has never left Dixieland.

And you native sons and daughters of old New England's rock-ribbed patriotism . . . and you sturdy natives of the great Mid-West . . and you descendants of the far West flaming spirit of pioneer freedom. .we invite you to come and be with us. .for you are of the Southern mind. .and the Southern spirit. .and the Southern philosophy. . .you are Southerners too and brothers with us in our fight.

What I have said about segregation goes double this day. . .and what I have said to or about some federal judges goes TRIPLE this day.

[. . .]

Not so long ago men stood in marvel and awe at the cities, the buildings, the schools, the autobahns that the government of Hitler's Germany had built. . .just as centuries before they stood in wonder at Rome's building. . .but it could not stand. . .for the system that built it had rotted the souls of the builders. . .and in turn. . .rotted the foundation of what God meant that men should be. Today that same system on an international scale is sweeping the world. It is the "changing world" of which we are told. . .it is called "new" and "liberal." It is as old as the oldest dictator. It is degenerate and decadent. As the national racism of Hitler's Germany persecuted a <u>national</u> minority to the whim of a national majority. . .so the <u>international</u> racism of the liberals seek to persecute the <u>international</u> white minority to the whim of the <u>international</u> colored majority. . .so that we are footballed about according to the favor of the Afro-Asian bloc. But the Belgian survivors of the Congo cannot present their case to a war crimes commission. . .nor the Portuguese of Angola. . .nor the survivors of Castro. . .nor the citizens of Oxford, Mississippi.

It is this theory of international power politic that led a group of men on the Supreme Court for the first time in American history to issue an edict, based not on legal precedent, but upon a volume, the editor of which has said our Constitution is outdated and must be changed and the writers of which, some had admittedly belonged to as many as half a hundred communist-front organizations. It is this theory that led this same group of men to briefly bare the ungodly core of that philosophy in forbidding little school children to say a prayer. And we find the evidence of that ungodliness even in the removal of the words "in God we trust" from some of our dollars, which was placed there as like evidence by our founding fathers as the faith upon which this system of government was built. It is the spirit of power thirst that caused a President in Washington to take up Caesar's pen and with one stroke of it, make a law. A Law which the law making body of Congress refused to pass. . .a law that tells us that we can or cannot buy or sell our very homes, except by his conditions. . .and except at HIS discretion. It is the spirit of power thirst that led that same President to launch a full offensive of twenty-five thousand troops against a university. . .of all places. . .in his own country. . .and against his own people, when this nation maintains only six thousand troops in the beleaguered city of Berlin. We have witnessed such acts of "might makes right" over the world as men yielded to the temptation to play God. . .but we have never before witnessed it in America. We reject such acts as free men. We do not defy, for there is nothing to defy. . .since as free men we do not recognize any government right to give freedom. . .or deny freedom. No government erected by man has that right. As Thomas Jefferson has said, "The God who gave us life, gave us liberty at the same time; no King holds the right of liberty in his hands." Nor does any ruler in American government.

We intend, quite simply, to practice the free heritage as bequeathed to us as sons of free fathers. We intend to re-vitalize the truly new and progressive form of government that is less than two hundred years old. . .a government first founded in this nation simply and purely on faith. . .that there is a personal God who rewards good and punishes evil. . .that hard work will receive its just desserts. . .that ambition and ingenuity and incentiveness. . .and profit of such. .are admirable traits and goals. .that the individual is encouraged in his spiritual growth and from that growth arrives at a character that enhances his

charity toward others and from that character and that charity so is influenced business, and labor and farmer and government. We intend to renew our faith as God-fearing men. . .not government-fearing men nor any other kind of fearing-men. We intend to roll up our sleeves and pitch in to develop this full bounty God has given us. . .to live full and useful lives and in absolute freedom from all fear. Then can we enjoy the full richness of the Great American Dream.

We have placed this sign, "In God We Trust," upon our State Capitol on this Inauguration Day as physical evidence of determination to renew the faith of our fathers and to practice the free heritage they bequeathed to us. We do this with the clear and solemn knowledge that such physical evidence is evidently a direct violation of the logic of that Supreme Court in Washington, D.C., and if they or their spokesmen in this state wish to term this defiance. . .I say. . .then let them make the most of it.

[. . .]

The true brotherhood of America, of respecting the separateness of others. .and uniting in effort. .has been so twisted and distorted from its original concept that there is small wonder that communism is winning the world.

We invite the negro citizens of Alabama to work with us from his separate racial station. .as we will work with him. .to develop, to grow in individual freedom and enrichment. We want jobs and a good future for BOTH our races. We want to help the physically and mentally sick of BOTH races. .the tubercular and the infirm. This is the basic heritage of my religion, of which I make full practice. . . .for we are all the handiwork of God.

But we warn those, of any group, who would follow the false doctrine of communistic amalgamation that we will not surrender our system of government. . .our freedom of race and religion. For that freedom was won at a hard price, and if it require a hard price to keep it. .we are able. .and quite willing to pay it.

The liberal's theory that poverty, discrimination and lack of opportunity is the cause of communism is a false theory. . .if it were true the South would have been the biggest single communist bloc in the western hemisphere long ago. . .for after the great War Between the States, our people faced a desolate land of burned universities, destroyed crops and homes, with manpower depleted and crippled, and even the mule, which was required to work the land, was so scarce that whole communities shared one animal to make the spring plowing. There were no government hand-outs, no Marshall Plan aid, no coddling to make sure that <u>our</u> people would not suffer; instead the South was set upon by the vulturous carpetbagger and federal troops, all loyal Southerners were denied the vote at the point of bayonet, so that the infamous, illegal 14th Amendment might be passed. There was no money, no food and no hope of either. But our grandfathers bent their knee only in church and bowed their head only to God.

Not for one single instant did they ever consider the easy way of federal dictatorship and amalgamation in return for fat bellies. They fought. They dug sweet roots from the ground with their bare hands and boiled them in the old iron pots. . . .they gathered poke salad from the woods and acorns form the ground. They fought. They followed no false doctrine. . .they knew what they wanted. .and they fought for freedom! They came up from their knees in the greatest display of sheer nerve, grit and guts that has ever been set down in the pages of written history. . .and they won! The great writer, Rudyard Kipling, wrote of them, that: "There in the Southland of the United States of America, lives the greatest fighting breed of man. . .in all the world!"

And that is why today, I stand ashamed of the fat, well-fed whiners who say that it is inevitable. . .that our cause is lost. I am ashamed of them. . .and I am ashamed <u>for</u> them. They do not represent the people of the Southland.

And may we take note of one other fact, with all the trouble with communists that some sections of this country have. . .there are not enough native communists in the South to fill up a telephone booth. . .and THAT is a matter of public FBI record.

We remind all within hearing of this Southland that a <u>Southerner</u>, Peyton Randolph, presided over the Continental Congress in our nation's beginning. . .that a <u>Southerner</u>, Thomas Jefferson, wrote the Declaration of Independence, that a <u>Southerner</u>, George Washington, is the Father of our Country. . .that a <u>Southerner</u>, James Madison, authored our Constitution, that a <u>Southerner</u>, George Mason, authored the Bill of Rights and it was a Southerner who said, "Give me liberty. . . . .or give me death," Patrick Henry.

Southerners played a most magnificent part in erecting this great divinely inspired system of freedom. .and as God is our witness, Southerners will save it.

Let us, as Alabamians, grasp the hand of destiny and walk out of the shadow of fear. . .and fill our divine destination. Let us not simply defend. .but let us assume the leadership of the fight and carry our leadership across this nation. God has placed us herein this crisis. . .let us not fail in this. .our most historical moment.

[. . .]

QUESTIONS TO CONSIDER

1. How did Wallace deploy ideals of Southern heritage in the speech?
2. Why do you think Wallace was such a popular Southern politician?

26.4 BENJAMIN MAYS, EULOGY FOR MARTIN LUTHER KING, JR. (1968)

On April 3, 1968, as Martin Luther King, Jr., relaxed at the Lorraine Motel in Memphis, Tennessee, where had gone to support striking African American sanitary workers, James Earl Ray assassinated him. Race riots broke out throughout the country on news of King's death. King's funeral was held on April 7th, in the midst of a tumultuous period in American history. At the funeral, only one person gave a eulogy: Morehouse College President Benjamin Mays, who had taught King at Morehouse and served as his mentor. Mays' eulogy remains a deeply personal recollection of Martin Luther King in the raw days after his assassination.

To be honored by being requested to give the Eulogy at the funeral of Dr. Martin Luther King, Jr., is like being asked to eulogize a deceased son—so close and so precious was he to me. Our friendship goes back to his student days at Morehouse College. It is not an easy task; nevertheless, I accept it, with a sad heart, and with full knowledge of my inadequacy to do justice to this man. It was *my desire* that if I pre-deceased Dr. King he would pay tribute to me on my final day. It was *his wish* that if he pre-deceased me I would deliver the homily at his funeral. Fate has decreed that I eulogize him. I wish it might have been otherwise, for, after all, I am three score years and ten and Martin Luther is dead at thirty-nine.

Although there are some who rejoice in his death, there are millions across the length and breadth of this world who are smitten with grief that this friend of mankind—all mankind—has been cut down in the flower of his youth. So multitudes here and in foreign lands, queens, kings, heads of governments, the clergy of the world, and the common man everywhere are praying that God will be with the family, the American people, and the President of the United States in this tragic hour. We hope that this universal concern will bring comfort to the family—for grief is like a heavy load: when shared it is easier to bear. We come today to help the family carry the load.

We have assembled here from every section of this great nation and from other parts of the world to give thanks to God that he gave to America, at this moment in history, Martin Luther King, Jr. Truly God is no respecter of persons. How strange! God called the grandson of a slave on his father's side, and the grandson of a man born during the Civil War on his mother's side, and said to him: *Martin Luther, speak to America about war and peace; about social justice and racial discrimination; about its obligation to the poor, and about nonviolence as a way of perfecting social change in a world of brutality and war.*

Here was a man who believed with all of his might that the pursuit of violence at any time is ethically and morally wrong; that God and the moral weight of the universe are against it; that violence is self-defeating; and that only love and forgiveness can break the vicious circle of revenge. He believed that nonviolence would prove effective in the abolition of injustice in politics, in economics, in education, and in race relations. He was convinced also that people could not be moved to abolish voluntarily the inhumanity of man to man by mere persuasion and pleading, but that they could be moved to do so by dramatizing the evil through massive nonviolent resistance. He believed that nonviolent direct action was necessary to supplement the nonviolent victories won in the federal courts. He believed that the nonviolent approach to

Source: Benjamin E. Mays, *Born to Rebel: An Autobiography* (Athens: University of Georgia Press, 2003), 357–360. Reprinted here with permission of University of Georgia Press.

solving social problems would ultimately prove to be redemptive.

Out of this conviction, history records the marches in Montgomery, Birmingham, Selma, Chicago, and other cities. He gave people an ethical and moral way to engage in activities designed to perfect social change without bloodshed and violence; and when violence did erupt it was that which is potential in any protest which aims to uproot deeply entrenched wrongs. No reasonable person would deny that the activities and the personality of Martin Luther King, Jr., contributed largely to the success of the student sit-in movements in abolishing segregation in downtown establishments; and that his activities contributed mightily to the passage of the Civil Rights legislation of 1964 and 1965.

Martin Luther King, Jr., believed in a united America. He believed that the walls of separation brought on by legal and de facto segregation, and discrimination based on race and color, could be eradicated. As he said in his Washington Monument address: *"I have a dream!"*

He had faith in his country. He died striving to desegregate and integrate America to the end that this great nation of ours, born in revolution and blood, conceived in liberty and dedicated to the proposition that all men are created free and equal, will truly become the lighthouse of freedom where none will be denied because his skin is black and none favored because his eyes are blue; where our nation will be militarily strong but perpetually at peace; economically secure but just; learned but wise; where the poorest—the garbage collectors—will have bread enough and to spare; where no one will be poorly housed; each educated up to his capacity; and where the richest will understand the meaning of empathy. *This* was his dream, and the end toward which he strove. As he and his followers so often sang: *"We shall overcome someday; black and white together."*

Let it be thoroughly understood that our deceased brother did not embrace nonviolence out of fear or cowardice. Moral courage was one of his noblest virtues. As Mahatma Gandhi challenged the British Empire without a sword and won, Martin Luther King, Jr., challenged the interracial wrongs of his country without a gun. And he had the faith to believe that he would win the battle for social justice. I make bold to assert that it took more courage for King to practice nonviolence than it took for his assassin to fire the fatal shot. The assassin is a coward: he committed his dastardly deed and fled. When Martin Luther disobeyed an unjust law, he accepted the consequences of his actions. He never ran away and he never begged for mercy. He returned to the Birmingham jail to serve his time.

Perhaps he was more courageous than soldiers who fight and die on the battlefield. There is an element of compulsion in their dying. But when Martin Luther faced death again and again, and finally embraced it, there was no pressure. He was acting on an inner compulsion that drove him on. More courageous than those who advocate violence as a way out, for they carry weapons of destruction for defense. But Martin Luther faced the dogs, the police, jail, heavy criticism, and finally death, and he never carried a gun, not even a knife, to defend himself. He had only his faith in a just God to rely on; and the belief that "thrice is he armed that hath his quarrel just." The faith that Browning writes about when he said: "One who never turned his back, but marched breast forward, / Never doubted clouds would break, / Never dreamed, though right were worsted, wrong would triumph, / Held we fall to rise, are baffled to fight better, / Sleep to wake."

Coupled with moral courage was Martin Luther King, Jr.'s capacity to love people. Though deeply committed to a program of freedom for Negroes, he had love and concern for all kinds of people. He drew no distinction between the high and the low; none between the rich and the poor. He believed especially that he was sent to champion the cause of the man farthest down. He would probably say that *if death had to come, I am sure there was no greater cause to die for than fighting to get a just wage for garbage collectors.* He was supra-class, and supra-culture. He belonged to the world and mankind. Now he belongs to posterity.

But there is a dichotomy in all this. This man was loved by some and hated by others. If any man knew the meaning of suffering, King knew. House bombed; living day by day for thirteen years under constant threats of death; maliciously accused of being a Communist; falsely accused of being insincere and seeking the limelight for his own glory; stabbed by a member of his own race; slugged in a hotel lobby; jailed thirty times; occasionally deeply hurt because friends betrayed him—and yet this man had no bitterness in his heart; no rancor in his soul; no revenge in his mind; and he went up and down the length and breadth of this world preaching nonviolence and the redemptive power of love. He believed with all of his heart, mind and soul that the way to peace and brotherhood is through nonviolence, love, and suffering. He was severely criticized for his opposition to the war in Vietnam. It must be said, however, that one could hardly expect a prophet of Dr. King's commitments to advocate nonviolence at home and violence in Vietnam. Nonviolence to King was total commitment not only in solving the problems of race in the United States but the problems of the world.

Surely this man was called of God to do this work. If Amos and Micah were prophets in the eighth century, B.C., Martin Luther King, Jr., was a prophet in the twentieth century. If Isaiah was called of God to prophesy in his day, Martin Luther was called of God to prophesy in his time. If Hosea was sent to preach love and forgiveness centuries ago, Martin Luther was sent to expound the doctrine of nonviolence and forgiveness in the third quarter of the twentieth century. If Jesus was called to preach the Gospel to the poor, Martin Luther King, Jr., fits that designation. If a prophet is one who does not seek popular causes to espouse, but rather the causes he thinks are right, Martin Luther qualified on that score.

No! He was not ahead of his time. No man is ahead of his time. Every man is within his star, each in his time. Each man must respond to the call of God in his lifetime and not in somebody else's time. Jesus had to respond to the call of God in the first century, A.D., and not in the twentieth century. He had but one life to live. He couldn't wait. How long do you think Jesus would have had to wait for the constituted authorities to accept him? Twenty-five years? A hundred years? A thousand? He died at thirty-three. He couldn't wait. Paul, Galileo, Copernicus, Martin Luther, the Protestant reformer, Gandhi, and Nehru couldn't wait for another time. They had to act in their lifetimes. No man is ahead of his time. Abraham, leaving the country in obedience to God's call; Moses leading a rebellious people to the Promised Land; Jesus dying on a cross; Galileo on his knees recanting; Lincoln dying of an assassin's bullet; Woodrow Wilson crusading for a League of Nations; Martin Luther King, Jr., dying fighting for justice for garbage collectors—none of these men were ahead of their time. With them the time was always ripe to do that which was right and that which needed to be done.

Too bad, you say, that Martin Luther King, Jr., died so young. I feel that way, too. But, as I have said many times before, it isn't how long one lives, but how well. It's what one accomplishes for mankind that matters. Jesus died at thirty-three; Joan of Arc at nineteen; Byron and Burns at thirty-six; Keats at twenty-six; and Marlowe at twenty-nine; Shelley at thirty; Dunbar before thirty-five; John Fitzgerald Kennedy at forty-six; William Rainey Harper at forty-nine; and Martin Luther King, Jr.[,] at thirty-nine.

We all pray that the assassin will be apprehended and brought to justice. But, make no mistake, the American people are in part responsible for Martin Luther King, Jr.'s death. The assassin heard enough condemnation of King and of Negroes to feel that he had public support. He knew that millions hated King.

The Memphis officials must bear some of the guilt for Martin Luther's assassination. The strike should have been settled several weeks ago. The lowest paid men in our society should not have to strike for a more just wage. A century after Emancipation, and after the enactment of the 13th, 14th, and 15th Amendments, it should not have been necessary for Martin Luther King, Jr., to stage marches in Montgomery, Birmingham, and Selma, and to go to jail thirty times trying to achieve for his people those rights which people of lighter hue get by virtue of their being born white. We, too, are guilty of murder. It is time for the American people to repent and make democracy equally applicable to all Americans. What can we do? We, not the assassin, represent America at its best. *We* have the power—not the prejudiced, not the assassin—to make things right.

If we love Martin Luther King, Jr., and respect him, as this crowd surely testifies, let us see to it that he did not die in vain; let us see to it that we do not dishonor his name by trying to solve our problems through rioting in the streets. Violence was foreign to his nature. He warned that continued riots could produce a Fascist state. But let us see to it also that the conditions that cause riots are promptly removed, as the President of the United States is trying to get us to do. Let black and white alike search their hearts; and if there be prejudice in our hearts against any racial or ethnic group, let us exterminate it and let us pray, as Martin Luther King, Jr., would pray if he could: *Father, forgive them for they know not what they do.* If we do this, Martin Luther King, Jr., will have died a redemptive death from which all mankind will benefit. . . .

I close by saying to you what Martin Luther King, Jr., believed: *If physical death was the price he had to pay to rid America of prejudice and injustice, nothing could be more redemptive.* And to paraphrase the words of the immortal John Fitzgerald Kennedy, Martin Luther King, Jr.'s unfinished work on earth must truly be our own.

QUESTIONS TO CONSIDER

1. How did Mays portray King?
2. Which lessons did he ask listeners to draw from King's death?

CHAPTER 27

LIVING WITH LESS, 1968–1980

27.1 DANIEL PATRICK MOYNIHAN, EXCERPT FROM "THE NEGRO FAMILY: THE CASE FOR NATIONAL ACTION" (1965)

In the midst of the civil rights movement, Assistant Secretary of Labor Daniel Patrick Moynihan called for governmental intervention to ameliorate perceived issues in African American families. Moynihan, who worked in the Johnson administration, set out to explore how the "War on Poverty" might alleviate problems in the African American community. The report singled out the decline of traditional nuclear families as the source of African American problems. He called for significant programs to improve the lives of black men, which, in turn, would foster improved family structures. "The Negro Family" remains a controversial report; many African American leaders accused Moynihan of being patronizing and even racist. Regardless, Moynihan's work likely influenced the development of Great Society programs.

The United States is approaching a new crisis in race relations.

In the decade that began with the school desegregation decision of the Supreme Court, and ended with the passage of the Civil Rights Act of 1964, the demand of Negro Americans for full recognition of their civil rights was finally met.

The effort, no matter how savage and brutal, of some State and local governments to thwart the exercise of those rights is doomed. The nation will not put up with it—least of all the Negroes. The present moment will pass. In the meantime, a new period is beginning.

In this new period the expectations of the Negro Americans will go beyond civil rights. Being Americans, they will now expect that in the near future equal opportunities for them as a group will produce roughly equal results, as compared with other groups. This is not going to happen. Nor will it happen for generations to come unless a new and special effort is made.

There are two reasons. First, the racist virus in the American blood stream still afflicts us: Negroes

Source: "The Negro Family: The Case for National Action," Office of Policy Planning and Research, U.S. Department of Labor, March 1965, https://web.stanford.edu/~mrosenfe/Moynihan%27s%20The%20Negro%20Family.pdf (Accessed June 15, 2018).

will encounter serious personal prejudice for at least another generation. Second, three centuries of sometimes unimaginable mistreatment have taken their toll on the Negro people. The harsh fact is that as a group, at the present time, in terms of ability to win out in the competitions of American life, they are not equal to most of those groups with which they will be competing. Individually, Negro Americans reach the highest peaks of achievement. But collectively, in the spectrum of American ethnic and religious and regional groups, where some get plenty and some get none, where some send eighty percent of their children to college and others pull them out of school at the 8th grade, Negroes are among the weakest.

The most difficult fact for white Americans to understand is that in these terms the circumstances of the Negro American community in recent years has probably been getting *worse, not better.*

Indices of dollars of income, standards of living, and years of education deceive. The gap between the Negro and most other groups in American society is widening.

The fundamental problem, in which this is most clearly the case, is that of family structure. The evidence—not final, but powerfully persuasive—is that the Negro family in the urban ghettos is crumbling. A middle-class group has managed to save itself, but for vast numbers of the unskilled, poorly educated city working class the fabric of conventional social relationships has all but disintegrated. There are indications that the situation may have been arrested in the past few years, but the general post-war trend is unmistakable. So long as this situation persists, the cycle of poverty and disadvantage will continue to repeat itself.

The thesis of this paper is that these events, in combination, confront the nation with a new kind of problem. Measures that have worked in the past, or would for most groups in the present, will not work here. A national effort is required that will give a unity of purpose to the many activities of the Federal government is this area, directed to a new kind of national goal: the establishment of a stable Negro family structure.

This would be a new departure for Federal policy. And a difficult one. But it almost certainly offers the only possibility of resolving in our time what is, after all, the nation's oldest, and most intransigent, and

now its most dangerous social problem. What Gunnar Myrdal said in *An American Dilemma* remains true today: *"America is free to choose whether the Negro shall remain her liability or become her opportunity."* . . .

THE NEGRO AMERICAN FAMILY

At the heart of the deterioration of the fabric of Negro society is the deterioration of the Negro family.

It is the fundamental source of the weakness of the Negro Community at the present time.

There is probably no single fact of Negro American life so little understood by whites The Negro situation is commonly perceived by whites in terms of the visible manifestations of discrimination and poverty, in part because Negro protest is directed against such obstacles, and in part, no doubt, because these are facts which involve the actions and attitudes of the white community as well. It is more difficult, however, for whites to perceive the effect that three centuries of exploitation have had on the fabric of Negro society itself. Here the consequences of the historic injustices done to Negro Americans are silent and hidden from view. But here is where the true injury has occurred: unless this damage is repaired, all the effort to end discrimination and poverty and injustice will come to little.

The role of the family in shaping character and ability is so pervasive as to be easily overlooked. The family is the basic social unit of American life; it is the basic socializing unit. By and large, adult conduct in society is learned as a child.

As fundamental insight of psychoanalytic theory, for example, is that the child learns a way of looking at life in his early years through which all later experience is viewed and which profoundly shapes his adult conduct.

It may be hazarded that the reason family structure does not loom larger in public discussion of social issues is that people tend to assume that the nature of family life is about the same throughout American society. The mass media and the development of suburbia have created an image of the American family as a highly standardized phenomenon. It is therefore easy to assume that whatever it is that makes for differences among individuals or groups of individuals, it is not a different family structure.

There is much truth to this; as with any other nation, Americans are producing a recognizable family system. But that process is not completed by any means. There are still, for example, important differences in family patterns surviving from the age of the great European migration to the United States, and these variations account for notable differences in the progress and assimilation of various ethnic and religious groups. A number of immigrant groups were characterized by unusually strong family bonds; these groups have characteristically progressed more rapidly than others.

But there is one truly great discontinuity in family structures in the United States at the present time: that between the white world in general and that of the Negro American.

The white family has achieved a high degree of stability and is maintaining that stability.

By contrast, the family structure of lower class Negroes is highly unstable, and in many urban centers is approaching complete break-down.

N.b. There is considerable evidence that the Negro community is in fact dividing between a stable middle-class group that is steadily growing stronger and more successful, and an increasingly disorganized and disadvantaged lower-class group. There are indications, for example, that the middle-class Negro family puts a higher premium on family stability and the conserving of family resources than does the white middle-class family. The discussion of this paper is not, obviously, directed to the first group excepting as it is affected by the experiences of the second—an important exception.

Nearly a Quarter of Urban Negro Marriages Are Dissolved.

Nearly a quarter of Negro women living in cities who have ever married are divorced, separated, or are living apart from their husbands.

The rates are highest in the urban Northeast where 26 percent of Negro women ever married are either divorced, separated, or have their husbands absent.

On the urban frontier, the proportion of husbands absent is even higher. In New York City in 1960, it was 30.2 percent, *not* including divorces. . . .

Nearly One-Quarter of Negro Births Are Now Illegitimate.

Both white and Negro illegitimacy rates have been increasing, although from dramatically different bases. The white rate was 2 percent in 1940; it was 3.07 percent in 1963. In that period, the Negro rate went from 16.8 percent to 23.6 percent.

The number of illegitimate children per 1,000 live births increased by 11 among whites in the period 1940-63, but by 68 among nonwhites. There are, of course, limits to the dependability of these statistics. There are almost certainly a considerable number of Negro children who, although technically illegitimate, are in fact the offspring of stable unions. On the other hand, it may be assumed that many births that are in fact illegitimate are recorded otherwise. Probably the two opposite effects cancel each other out.

On the urban frontier, the nonwhite illegitimacy rates are usually higher than the national average, and the increase of late has been drastic.

In the District of Columbia, the illegitimacy rate for nonwhites grew from 21.8 percent in 1950, to 29.5 percent in 1964.

A similar picture of disintegrating Negro marriages emerges from the divorce statistics. Divorces have increased of late for both whites and nonwhites, but at a much greater rate for the latter. In 1940 both groups had a divorce rate of 2.2 percent, but the nonwhite rate had reached 5.1 percent—40 percent greater than the formerly equal white rate.

Almost One-Fourth of Negro Families Are Headed by Females.

As a direct result of this high rate of divorce, separation, and desertion, a very large percent of Negro families are headed by females. While the percentage of such families among whites has been dropping since 1940, it has been rising among Negroes.

The percent of nonwhite families headed by a female is more than double the percent for whites. Fatherless nonwhite families increased by a sixth between 1950 and 1960, but held constant for white families.

It has been estimated that only a minority of Negro children reach the age of 18 having lived all their lives with both their parents. . . .

A 1960 study of Aid to Dependent Children in Cook Country, III. stated:

> The 'typical' ADC mother in Cook Country was married and had children by her husband, who deserted; his whereabouts are unknown, and he does not contribute to the support of his children. She is not free to remarry and had an illegitimate child since her husband left. (Almost 90 percent of the ADC families are Negro.)

The steady expansion of this welfare program, as of public assistance programs in general, can be taken as a measure of the steady disintegration of the Negro family structure over the past generation in the United States. . . .

THE TANGLE OF PATHOLOGY

That the Negro American has survived at all is extraordinary—a lesser people might simply have died out, as indeed others have. That the Negro community has not only survived, but in this political generation has entered national affairs as a moderate, humane, and constructive national force is the highest testament to the healing powers of the democratic ideal and the creative vitality of the Negro people.

But it may not be supposed that the Negro American community has not paid a fearful price for the incredible mistreatment to which it has been subjected over the past three centuries.

In essence, the Negro community has been forced into a matriarchal structure which, because it is so out of line with the rest of the American society, seriously retards the progress of the group as a whole, and imposes a crushing burden on the Negro male and, in consequence, on a great many Negro women as well.

There is, presumably, no special reason why a society in which males are dominant in family relationships is to be preferred to a matriarchal arrangement. However, it is clearly a disadvantage for a minority group to be operating on one principle, while the great majority of the population, and the one with the most advantage to begin with, is operating on another. This is the present situation of the Negro. Ours is a society which presumes male leadership in private and public affairs. The arrangements of society facilitate such leadership and reward it. A subculture, such as that of the Negro American, in which this is not the pattern, is placed at a distinct disadvantage.

Here an earlier word of caution should be repeated. There is much evidence that a considerable number of Negro families have managed to break out of the tangle pathology and to establish themselves as stable, effective units, living according to patterns of American society in general. E. Franklin Frazier has suggested that the middle-class Negro American family is, if anything, more patriarchal and protective of its children than the general run of such families. Given equal opportunities, the children of these families will perform as well or better than their white peers. They need no help from anyone, and ask none. . . .

In a word, most Negro youth are in *danger* of being caught up in the tangle of pathology that affects their world, and probably a majority are so entrapped. Many of those who escape do so for one generation only: as things now are, their children may have to run the gauntlet all over again. That is not the least vicious aspect of the world that white America has made for the Negro.

Obviously, not every instance of social pathology afflicting the Negro community can be traced to the weakness of family structure. If, for example, organized crime in the Negro community were not largely controlled by whites, there would be more capital accumulation among Negroes, and therefore probably more Negro business enterprises. If it were not for the hostility and fear many whites exhibit towards Negroes, they in turn would be less afflicted by hostility and fear and so on. There is no one Negro community. There is no one Negro problem. There is no one solution. Nonetheless, at the center of the tangle of pathology is the weakness of the family structure. Once or twice removed, it will be found to be the principal source of most of the aberrant, inadequate, or anti-social behavior that did not establish, but now serves to perpetuate the cycle of poverty and deprivation.

It was by destroying the Negro family under slavery that white America broke the will of the Negro people. Although that will has reasserted itself in our time, it is a resurgence doomed to frustration unless the viability of the Negro family is restored.

Matriarchy

A fundamental fact of Negro American family life is the often reversed roles of husband and wife.

Robert O. Blood, Jr.[,] and Donald M. Wolfe, in a study of Detroit families, note that "Negro husbands have unusually low power," and while this is characteristic of all low income families, the pattern pervades the Negro social structure: "the cumulative result of discrimination in jobs . . ., the segregated housing, and the poor schooling of Negro men." In 44 percent of the Negro families studied, the wife was dominant, as against 20 percent of white wives. "Whereas the majority of white families are equalitarian, the largest percentage of Negro families are dominated by the wife."

The matriarchal pattern of so many Negro families reinforces itself over the generations. This process begins with education. Although the gap appears to be closing at the moment, for a long while, Negro females were better educated than Negro males, and this remains true today for the Negro population as a whole. . . .

There is much evidence that Negro females are better students than their male counterparts.

Daniel Thompson of Dillard University, in a private communication on January 9, 1965, writes:

> As low as is the aspirational level among lower class Negro girls, it is considerably higher than among the boys. For example, I have examined the honor rolls in Negro high schools for about 10 years. As a rule, from 75 to 90 percent of all Negro honor students are girls.

Dr. Thompson reports that 70 percent of all applications for the National Achievement Scholarship Program financed by the Ford Foundation for outstanding Negro high school graduates are girls, despite special efforts by high school principals to submit the names of boys. . . .

The testimony to the effects of these patterns in Negro family structure is widespread, and hardly to be doubted. . . .

> Robin M. Williams, Jr. in a study of Elmira, New York:

> Only 57 percent of Negro adults reported themselves as married—spouse present, as compared with 78 percent of native white American gentiles, 91 percent of Italian-American, and 96percent of Jewish informants. Of the 93 unmarried Negro youths interviewed, 22 percent did not have their mother living in the home with them, and 42 percent reported that their father was not living in their home. One-third of the youths did not know their father's present occupation , and two thirds of a s ample of 150 Negro adults did not know what the occupation of their father's father had been. Forty percent of the youths said that they had brothers and sisters living in other communities: another 40 percent reported relatives living in their home who were not parents, siblings , or grandparent.

The Failure of Youth

Williams' account of Negro youth growing up with little knowledge of their fathers, less of their fathers' occupations, still less of family occupational traditions, is in sharp contrast to the experience of the white child.

The white family, despite many variants, remains a powerful agency not only for transmitting property from one generation to the next, but also for transmitting no less valuable contracts with the world of education and work. In an earlier age, the Carpenters, Wainwrights, Weavers, Mercers, Farmers, Smiths acquired their names as well as their trades from their fathers and grandfathers. Children today still learn the patterns of work from their fathers even though they may no longer go into the same jobs.

White children without fathers at least perceive all about them the pattern of men working.

Negro children without fathers flounder—and fail.

Delinquency and Crime

The combined impact of poverty, failure, and isolation among Negro youth has had the predictable outcome in a disastrous delinquency and crime rate.

In a typical pattern of discrimination, Negro children in all public and private orphanages are a smaller proportion of all children than their proportion of the population although their needs are clearly greater.

On the other hand Negroes represent a third of all youth in training schools for juvenile delinquents.

Children in Homes for Dependent and Neglected Children, 1960

	Number	Percent
White	64,807	88.4
Negro	6,140	8.4
Other races	2,359	3.2
All races	73,306	100.0

Source: 1960 Census, Inmates of Institutions, PC (2) 3A, table 31, p. 44.

It is probable that at present, a majority of the crimes against the person, such as rape, murder, and aggravated assault are committed by Negroes. There is, of course, no absolute evidence; inference can only be made from arrest and prison population statistics. The data that follow unquestionably are biased against Negroes, who are arraigned much more casually than are whites, but it may be doubted that the bias is great enough to affect the general proportions.

Number of arrests in 1963

	White	Negro
Offences charged total	31,988	38,549
Murder and nonnegligent manslaughter	2,288	2,948
Forcible rape	4,402	3,935
Aggravated assault	25,298	31,666

Source: Crime in the United States (Federal Bureau of Investigation, 1963) table 25, p. 111.

Again on the urban frontier the ratio is worse: 3 out of every 5 arrests for these crimes were of Negroes.

In Chicago in 1963, three-quarters of the persons arrested for such crimes were Negro; in Detroit, the same proportions held.

In 1960, 37 percent of all persons in Federal and State prisons were Negro. In that year, 56 percent of the homicide and 57 percent of the assault offenders committed to State institutions were Negro. . . .

The overwhelming number of offenses committed by Negroes are directed toward other Negroes: the cost of crime to the Negro community is a combination of that to the criminal and to the victim. . . .

The Armed Forces

The ultimate mark of inadequate preparation for life is the failure rate on the Armed Forces mental test. The Armed Forces Qualification Test is not quite a mental test, nor yet an education test. It is a test of ability to perform at an acceptable level of competence. It roughly measures ability that ought to be found in an average 7th or 8th grade student. A grown young man who cannot pass this test is in trouble.

Fifty-six percent of Negroes fail it.

This is a rate almost four times that of the whites.

The Army, Navy, Air Force, and Marines conduct by far the largest and most important education and training activities of the Federal Government, as well as provide the largest single source of employment in the nation.

Military service is disruptive in some respects. For those comparatively few who are killed or wounded in combat, or otherwise, the personal sacrifice is inestimable. But on balance service in the Armed Forces over the past quarter-century has worked greatly to the advantage of those involved. The training and experience of military duty itself is unique; the advantages that have generally followed in the form of the G.I. Bill, mortgage guarantees, Federal life insurance, Civil Service preference, veterans hospitals, and veterans pensions are singular, to say the least.

Although service in the Armed Forces is at least nominally a duty of all male citizens coming of age, it is clear that the present system does not enable Negroes to serve in anything like their proportionate numbers. This is not a question of discrimination. Induction into the Armed Forces is based on a variety of objective tests and standards, but these tests nonetheless have the effect of keeping the number of Negroes disproportionately small.

In 1963 the United States Commission on Civil Rights reported that "A decade ago, Negroes constituted 8 percent of the Armed Forces. Today . . . they continue to constitute 8 percent of the Armed Forces."

In 1964 Negroes constituted 11.8 percent of the population, but probably remain at 8 percent of the Armed Forces. . . .

The significance of Negro under-representation in the Armed Forces is greater than might at first be supposed. If Negroes were represented in the same proportions in the military as they are in the population, would number 300,000 plus. This would be over 100,000 more than at present (using 1964 strength figures). If the more than 100,000 unemployed Negro men were to have gone into the military the Negro male unemployment rate would have been 7.0 percent in 1964 instead of 9.1 percent.

In 1963 the Civil Rights Commission commented on the occupational aspect of military service for Negroes. "Negro enlisted men enjoy relatively better opportunities in the Armed Forces than in the civilian economy in every clerical, technical, and skilled field for which the data permit comparison."

There is, however, an even more important issue involved in military service for Negroes. Service in the United States Armed Forces is the *only* experience open to the Negro American in which he is truly treated as an equal: not as a Negro equal to a white, but as one man equal to any other man in a world where the category "Negro" and "white" do not exist. If this is a statement of the ideal rather than reality, it is an ideal that is close to realization. In food, dress, housing, pay, work—the Negro in the Armed Forces *is* equal and is treated that way.

There is another special quality about military service for Negro men: it is an utterly masculine world. Given the strains of the disorganized and matrifocal family life in which so many Negro youth come of age, the Armed Forces are a dramatic and desperately needed change: a world away from women, a world run by strong men of unquestioned authority, where discipline, if harsh, is nonetheless orderly and predictable, and where rewards, if limited, are granted on the basis of performance.

The theme of a current Army recruiting message states it as clearly as can be: "In the U.S. Army you get to know what it means to feel like a man."

At the recent Civil Rights Commission hearings in Mississippi a witness testified that his Army service was in fact "the only time I ever felt like a man."

QUESTIONS TO CONSIDER

1. What favors did Moynihan blame for problems in "The Negro Family"?
2. If you were to criticize the report, how would you do so?

27.2 AMERICAN INDIAN MOVEMENT, "THE ALCATRAZ PROCLAMATION" (1969) AND "TRAIL OF BROKEN TREATIES" EXCERPTS (1972)

The American Indian Movement (AIM) grew out of the "Rights Revolution" of the 1960s. In 1968, a group of Native American activists gathered in Minneapolis, Minnesota, to found AIM as an advocacy organization. Primarily, AIM leaders hoped to stop Federal assimilation policies, which, they charged, robbed Native Americans of their culture and sovereignty. The following two documents attest to AIM's activism. In November 1969, a group of 89 AIM supporters occupied the former Federal prison on Alcatraz Island in the San Francisco Bay. The group, which grew to include almost 400 people at its height, stayed there until June 1971, when Federal officers forcibly removed the remaining protesters. Their stay, however, had illuminated problems in Federal Native American policy. In 1972, AIM issued the "Trail of Broken Treaties" position paper to further highlight the group's demands. Collectively, the two documents indicate how AIM used Native American history and rights rhetoric in their campaigns.

THE ALCATRAZ PROCLAMATION

Fellow citizens, we are asking you to join with us in our attempt to better the lives of all Indian people.

We are on Alcatraz Island to make known to the world that we have a right to use our land for our own benefit.

In a proclamation of November 20, 1969, we told the government of the United States that we are here "to create a meaningful use for our Great Spirit's Land."

We, the native Americans, reclaim the land known as Alcatraz Island in the name of all American Indians by right of discovery.

We wish to be fair and honorable in our dealings with the Caucasian inhabitants of this land, and hereby offer the following treaty:

We will purchase said Alcatraz Island for twenty-four dollars in glass beads and red cloth, a precedent set by the white man's purchase of a similar island

about 300 years ago. We know that $24 in trade goods for these 16 acres is more than was paid when Manhattan Island was sold, but we know that land values have risen over the years. Our offer of $1.24 per acre is greater than the $0.47 per acre the white men are now paying the California Indians for their lands.

We will give to the inhabitants of this island a portion of the land for their own to be held in trust . . . by the Bureau of Caucasian Affairs . . . in perpetuity for as long as the sun shall rise and the rivers go down to the sea. We will further guide the inhabitants in the proper way of living. We will offer them our religion, our education, our life-ways in order to help them achieve our level of civilization and thus raise them and all their white brothers up from their savage and unhappy state. We offer this treaty in good faith and wish to be fair and honorable in our dealings with all white men.

Sources: "The Alcatraz Proclamation to the Great White Father and His People," University of North Dakota Native Media Center, https://arts-sciences.und.edu/native-media-center/_files/docs/1950-1970/1969alcatrazproclamation.pdf (Accessed June 15, 2018); "The Trail of Broken Treaties: 20-Point Position Paper," American Indian Movement Grand Governing Council, https://www.aimovement.org/ggc/trailofbrokentreaties.html (Accessed May 21, 2018).

We feel that this so-called Alcatraz Island is more than suitable for an Indian reservation, as determined by the white man's own standards. By this, we mean that this place resembles most Indian reservations in that:

1. It is isolated from modern facilities, and without adequate means of transportation.
2. It has no fresh running water.
3. It has inadequate sanitation facilities.
4. There are no oil or mineral rights.
5. There is no industry and so unemployment is very great.
6. There are no health-care facilities.
7. The soil is rocky and non-productive, and the land does not support game.
8. There are no educational facilities.
9. The population has always exceeded the land base.
10. The population has always been held as prisoners and kept dependent upon others.

Further, it would be fitting and symbolic that ships from all over the world, entering the Golden Gate, would first see Indian land, and thus be reminded of the true history of this nation. This tiny island would be a symbol of the great lands once ruled by free and noble Indians.

What use will we make of this land?

Since the San Francisco Indian Center burned down, there is no place for Indians to assemble and carry on tribal life here in the white man's city. Therefore, we plan to develop on this island several Indian institutions:

1. A Center for Native American Studies will be developed which will educate them to the skills and knowledge relevant to improve the lives and spirits of all Indian peoples. Attached to this center will be travelling universities, managed by Indians, which will go to the Indian Reservations, learning those necessary and relevant materials now about.

2. An American Indian Spiritual Center, which will practice our ancient tribal religious and sacred healing ceremonies. Our cultural arts will be featured and our young people trained in music, dance, and healing rituals.

3. An Indian Center of Ecology, which will train and support our young people in scientific research and practice to restore our lands and waters to their pure and natural state. We will work to de-pollute the air and

waters of the Bay Area. We will seek to restore fish and animal life to the area and to revitalize sea-life which has been threatened by the white man's way. We will set up facilities to desalt sea water for human benefit.

4. A Great Indian Training School will be developed to teach our people how to make a living in the world, improve our standard of living, and to end hunger and unemployment among all our people. This training school will include a center for Indian arts and crafts, and an Indian restaurant serving native foods, which will restore Indian culinary arts. This center will display Indian arts and offer Indian foods to the public, so that all may know of the beauty and spirit of the traditional Indian ways.

Some of the present buildings will be taken over to develop an American Indian Museum which will depict our native food and other cultural contributions we have given to the world. Another part of the museum will present some of the things the white man has given to the Indians in return for the land and life he took: disease, alcohol, poverty, and cultural decimation (as symbolized by old tin cans, barbed wire, rubber tires, plastic containers, etc.). Part of the museum will remain a dungeon to symbolize both those Indian captives who were incarcerated for challenging white authority and those who were imprisoned on reservations. The museum will show the noble and tragic events of Indian history, including the broken treaties, the documentary of the Trail of Tears, the Massacre of Wounded Knee, as well as the victory over Yellow-Hair Custer and his army.

In the name of all Indians, therefore, we reclaim this island for our Indian nations, for all these reasons. We feel this claim is just and proper, and that this land should rightfully be granted to us for as long as the rivers run and the sun shall shine.

We hold the rock!

"THE TRAIL OF BROKEN TREATIES": FOR RENEWAL OF CONTRACTS[,] RECONSTRUCTION OF INDIAN COMMUNITIES & SECURING AN INDIAN FUTURE IN AMERICA!

1. RESTORATION OF CONSTITUTIONAL TREATY-MAKING AUTHORITY:

The U.S. President should propose by executive message, and the Congress should consider and enact legislation, to repeal the provision in the 1871 Indian Appropriations Act which withdrew federal recognition from Indian Tribes and Nations as political entities, which could be contracted by treaties with the United States, in order that the President may resume the exercise of his full constitutional authority for acting in the matters of Indian Affairs—and in order that Indian Nations may represent their own interests in the manner and method envisioned and provided in the Federal Constitution.

2. ESTABLISHMENT OF TREATY COMMISSION TO MAKE NEW TREATIES:

The President should impanel and the Congress establish, with next year, a Treaty Commission to contract a security and assistance treaty of treaties, with Indian people to negotiate a national commitment to the future of Indian people for the last quarter of the Twentieth Century. Authority should be granted to allow tribes to contract by separate and individual treaty, multi-tribal or regional groupings or national collective, respecting general or limited subject matter[,] and provide that no provisions of existing treaty agreements may be withdrawn or in any manner affected without the explicit consent and agreement of any particularly related Indian Nation.

3. AN ADDRESS TO THE AMERICAN PEOPLE & JOINT SESSSIONS OF CONGRESS:

The President and the leadership of Congress should make a commitment now and next January to request and arrange for four Native Americans—selected by Indian people at a future date—and the President of the United States and any designated U.S. Senators and Representatives to address a joint session of Congress and the American people through national communications media regarding the Indian future within the American Nation, and relationships between the Federal Government and Indian Nations—on or before June 2, 1974, the first half century anniversary of the 1924 "Indian Citizenship Act."

4. COMMISSION TO REVIEW TREATY COMMITMENTS & VIOLATIONS:

The President should immediately create a multilateral, Indian and non-Indian Commission to review domestic treaty commitments and complaints of chronic violations and to recommend or act for corrective actions including the imposition of mandatory sanctions or interim restraints upon violative activities, and including formulation of legislation designed to protect the jeopardized Indian rights and eliminate the unending patterns of prohibitively complex lawsuits and legal defenses—which habitually have produced indecisive and intermittent results, only too frequently forming guidelines for more court battles, or additional challenges and attacks against Indian rights. (Indians have paid attorneys and lawyers more than $40,000,000 since 1962. Yet many Indian people are virtually imprisoned in the nation's courtrooms in being forced constantly to defend their rights, while many tribes are forced to maintain a multitude of suits in numerous jurisdictions relating to the same or a single issue, or a few similar issues. There is less need for more attorney assurances than there is for institution of protections that reduce violations and minimize the possibilities for attacks upon Indian rights). . . .

10. LAND REFORM AND RESTORATION OF A 110-MILLION ACRE NATIVE LAND BASE:

The next Congress and Administration should commit themselves and effect a national commitment implemented by statutes or executive and administrative actions, to restore a permanent non-diminishing Native American land base of not less than 110-million acres by July 4, 1976. This land base and its separate parts, should be vested with the recognized rights and conditions of being perpetually non-taxable except by autonomous and sovereign Indian authority, and should never again be permitted to be alienated from Native American or Indian ownership and control.

A. Priorities in Restoration of the Native American Line Base:

When Congress acted to delimit the President's authority and the Indian Nations' powers for making treaties in 1871, approximately 135,000,000 acres of land and territory had been secured to Indian ownership against cession or relinquishment. This acreage did not include the 1867 treaty-secured recognition of land title and rights of Alaskan Natives, nor millions of acres otherwise retained by Indians in what were to become "unrelated" treaties of Indian land cession as in California; nor other land areas authorized to be set aside for Indian Nations contracted by, but never benefiting from their treaties. When the Congress, in 1887, under the General Allotment Act and other measures of the period and "single system of legislation," delegated treaty-assigned Presidential responsibilities to the Secretary of the Interior and his Commissioner of Indian Affairs and agents in the Bureau of Indian Affairs, relating to the government of Indian relations under the treaties for the 135 million acres, collectively held, immediately became subject to loss. The 1887 Act provided for the sale of "surplus" Indian lands—and contained a formula for the assignment or allocation of land tracts to Indian individuals, dependent partly on family size, which would have allowed an average-sized allotment of 135 acres to one million Indians—at a time when the number of tribally-related Indians was less than a quarter million or fewer than 200,000. The Interior Department efficiently managed the loss of 100-million acres of Indian land, and its transfer to non-Indian ownership (frequently by homestead, not direct purchase) in little more than the next quarter century. When Congress prohibited further allotments to Indian individuals, by its 1934 Indian Reorganization Act, it effectively determined that future generations of Indian people would be "land-less Indians" except by heirship and inheritance. (110-million acres, including 40-million acres in Alaska, would approximate an average 135 acres multiplied by .8 million Native Americans, a number indicated by the 1970 U.S. Census. Simple justice would seem to demand that priorities in restorations of land bases be granted to those Indian Nations who are land-less by fault of unratified or unfulfilled treaty provisions; Indian Nations, land-less because of congressional and administrative actions reflective of criminal abuse of trust responsibilities; and other groupings of land-less Indians, particularly of the land-less generations, including many urban Indians and non-reservation Indian people—many of whom have been forced to pay in forms of deprivation, loss of rights and entitlements, and other extreme costs upon their lives, an "emigration-migration-education-training" tax for their unfulfilled pursuit of opportunity in America—a "tax" as unwarranted and unjustified as it is unprecedented in the history of human rights mature nations possessed of a modern conscience. . . .

13. RESUME FEDERAL PROTECTIVE JURISDICTION FOR OFFENSES AGAINST INDIANS:

[. . .]

A. Establishment of a National Federal Indian Grand Jury:

The Congress should establish a special national grand jury consisting solely of Indian members selected in part by the President and in part by Indian people, having a continuous life, and equipped with its own investigative and legal staff, and presided over by competent judicial officers, while vested with prescribed authorities of indictments to be prosecuted in the federal and Indian court systems. This grand jury should be granted jurisdiction to act in the bringing of indictments on basis of evidence and probable cause within any federal judicial district where a crime of violence has been committed against an Indian and resulting in an Indian's death, or resulting in bodily injury and involving lethal weapons or aggressive force, when finding reason to be not satisfied with handling or disposition of a case or incident by local authorities, and operating consistent with federal constitutional standards respecting rights of an accused. More broadly and generally, the grand jury should be granted broad authority to monitor the enforcement of law under Titles 18, 25, and 42, respecting Indian jurisdiction and civil rights protections; the administration of law enforcement; confinement facilities and juvenile detention centers, and judicial systems in Indian country; corrupt practices or violations of law in the administration of federal Indian agencies or of federally-funded programs for Indian people—including administration by tribal officials or tribal governmental units—and federal employees, and issue special reports bringing indictments when warranted, directed toward elimination of wrong-doing, wrongful administration or practices; and improvement recommendations for-systems to ensure proper services and benefits to communities, or Indian people. . . .

18. PROTECTION OF INDIANS' RELIGIOUS FREEDOM AND CULTURAL INTEGRITY:

The Congress shall proclaim its insistence that the religious freedom and cultural integrity of Indian people shall be respected and protected throughout the United States, and provide that Indian religion and culture, even in regenerating or renaissance or developing stages, or when manifested in the personal character and treatment of one's own body, shall not be interfered with, disrespected, or denied. (No Indian shall be forced to cut their hair by any institution or public agency or official, including military authorities or prison regulation, for example.) It should be an insistence by Congress that implies strict penalty for its violation. . . .

QUESTIONS TO CONSIDER

1. What types of injustices do both documents highlight?
2. Do you find the two documents convincing?

27.3 JOHN KERRY, STATEMENT ON BEHALF OF THE VIETNAM VETERANS AGAINST THE WAR (1971)

American involvement in Vietnam evolved from a campaign to support French forces, to a limited conflict, to a major ground war paired with a massive bombing campaign. By the mid-1960s, American involvement in Vietnam became controversial in the United States, and the anti-war movement grew in power during the late 1960s. Sometimes, protests exploded into violence. On May 4, 1970, the National Guard killed four protesting students on the campus of Kent State University, and on May 15, 1970, police killed two Jackson State University students during a Vietnam War protest. Escalating domestic turmoil led Congress to hold hearings on the Vietnam War. During a Senate Foreign Relations Committee hearing on April 22, 1970, Vietnam veteran John Kerry spoke on behalf of the Vietnam Veterans Against the War. Kerry's eloquent statements against the war were especially effective given his distinguished service; he won three Purple Heart Medals and a Silver Star Medal while leading a Swift Boat during the War. Kerry later served for twenty-eight years as a U.S. Senator from Massachusetts and was the 2004 Democratic nominee for President. U.S. forces formally withdraw from Vietnam in March 1973.

M r. PELL. Mr. President, the distinguished Senator from Arkansas (Mr. FULBRIGHT) is absent today by necessity. He has prepared, however, a statement concerning the testimony of Mr. John F. Kerry before the Committee on Foreign Relations, which Senator FULBRIGHT so ably chairs. I ask unanimous consent that this statement, together with its attachments, be printed at this point in the RECORD.

Source: John Kerry Testimony to the Senate Foreign Relations Committee, *Congressional Record*, 92nd Congress, 1st Session (April 22, 1971): 11738–11739.

I am very glad to be doing this, as I know and admire John Kerry and consider immensely eloquent his testimony concerning our ill-advised Indochina war.

There being no objection, the material was ordered to be printed in the RECORD, as follows:

STATEMENT BY MR. FULBRIGHT

Mr. President, yesterday Mr. John F. Kerry, representing the Vietnam Veterans Against the War, made a very eloquent statement before the Senate Committee on Foreign Relations. In due course the full hearing will be printed and available to the Senate and the public. In the meantime, however, I ask unanimous consent that Mr. Kerry's opening statement be printed in the RECORD.

In addition, Mr. President, I ask unanimous consent that the profile of Mr. Kerry which appeared in this morning's New York Times also be included in the RECORD.

STATEMENT OF MR. JOHN KERRY, REPRESENTING THE VIETNAM VETERANS AGAINST THE WAR

Mr. KERRY. Thank you very much, Senator Fulbright, Senator Javits, Senator Symington, Senator Pell. I would like to say for the record, and also for the men behind me who are also wearing the uniform and their medals, that my sitting here is really symbolic. I am not here as John Kerry. I am here as one member of the group of 1,000, which is a small representation of a very much larger group of veterans in this country, and were it possible for all of them to sit at this country, and were it possible for all of them to sit at this table they would be here and have the same kind of testimony.

I would simply like to speak in very general terms. I apologize if my statement is general because I received notification yesterday you would hear me and I am afraid that because of the court injunction I was up most of the night and haven't had a great deal of time to prepare for this hearing.

I would like to talk on behalf of all those veterans and say that several months ago in Detroit we had an investigation at which over 150 honorably discharged, and many very highly decorated, veterans testified to war crimes committed in Southeast Asia. These were not isolated incidents but crimes committed on a day to day basis with the full awareness of officers at all levels of command.

It is impossible to describe to you exactly what did happen in Detroit—the emotions in the room and the feelings of the men who were reliving their experiences in Vietnam. They relived the absolute horror of what this country, in a sense, made them do.

They told stories that at times they had personally raped, cut off ears, cut of heads, taped wires from portable telephones to human genitals and turned up the power, cut off limbs, blown up bodies, randomly shot at civilians, razed villages in fashion reminiscent of Genghis Khan, shot cattle and dogs for fun, poisoned food stocks, and generally ravaged the countryside of South Vietnam in addition to the normal ravage of war and the normal and very particular ravaging which is done by the applied bombing power of this country.

We call this investigation the Winter Soldier Investigation. The term Winter Soldier is a play on words of Thomas Paine's in 1776 when he spoke of the Sunshine Patriot and summer time soldiers who deserted at Valley Forge because the going was rough.

We who have come here to Washington have come here because we feel we have to be winter soldiers now. We could come back to this country, we could be quiet, we could hold our silence, we could not tell what went on in Vietnam, but we feel because of what threatens this country, not the reds, but the crimes which we are committing that threaten it, that we have to speak out.

I would like to talk to you a little bit about what the result is of the feelings these men carry with them after coming back from Vietnam. The country doesn't know it yet but it has created a monster, a monster in the form of millions of men who have been taught to deal and to trade in violence and who are given the chance to die for the biggest nothing in history; men who have returned with a sense of anger and a sense of betrayal which no one has yet grasped.

As a veteran and one who feels this anger I would like to talk about it. We are angry because we feel we have been used in the worst fashion by the administration of this country.

In 1970 at West Point Vice President Agnew said "some glamorize the criminal misfits of society while our best men die in Asian rice paddies to preserve the freedom which most of those misfits abuse," and this was used as a rallying point for our effort in Vietnam.

But for us, as boys in Asia who the country was supposed to support, his statement is a terrible distortion from which we can only draw a very deep sense of revulsion, and hence the anger of some of the men who are here in Washington today. It is a distortion because we in no way consider ourselves the best men of this country; because those he calls misfits were standing up for us in a way that nobody else in this country dared to; because so many who have died would have returned to this country to join the misfits in their efforts to ask for an immediate withdrawal from South Vietnam; because so many of those best men have returned as quadriplegics and amputees—and they lie forgotten in Veterans Administration Hospitals in this country which fly the flag which so many have chosen as their own personal symbol—and we cannot consider ourselves America's best men when we are ashamed of and hated for what we were called on to do in Southeast Asia.

In our opinion, and from our experience, there is nothing in South Vietnam which could happen that realistically threatens the United States of America. And to attempt to justify the loss of one American life in Vietnam, Cambodia or Laos by linking such loss to the preservation of freedom, which those misfits supposedly abuse, is to us the height of criminal hypocrisy, and it is that kind of hypocrisy which we feel has torn this country apart.

We are probably much more angry than that, but I don't want to go into the foreign policy aspects because I am outclassed here. I know that all of you talk about every possible alternative to getting out of Vietnam. We understand that. We know you have considered the seriousness of the aspects to the utmost level and I am not going to try to dwell on that. But I want to relate to you the feeling that many of the men who have returned to this country express because we are probably angriest about all that we were told about Vietnam and about the mystical war again communism.

We found that not only was it a civil war, an effort by a people who had for years been seeking their liberation from any colonial influence whatsoever, but also we found that the Vietnamese whom he had enthusiastically molded after our own image were hard put to take up the fight against the threat we were supposedly saving them from.

We found most people didn't even know the difference between communism and democracy. They only wanted to work in rice paddies without helicopters strafing them and bombs with napalm burning their villages and tearing that country apart. They wanted everything to do with the war, particularly with this foreign presence of the United States of America, to leave them alone in peace, and they practiced the art of survival by siding with whichever military force was present at a particular time, be it Viet Cong, North Vietnamese or American.

We found also that all too often American men were dying in those rice paddies for want of support from their allies. We saw first hand how monies from American taxes were used for a corrupt dictatorial regime. We saw that many people in this country had a one-sided idea of who was kept free by our flag, and blacks provided the highest percentage of casualties. We saw Vietnam ravaged equally by American bombs and search and destroy missions, as well as by Viet Cong terrorism, and yet we listened while this country tried to blame all of the havoc on the Viet Cong.

We rationalized destroying villages in order to save them. We saw America lose her sense of morality as she accepted very coolly a My Lai and refused to give up the image of American soldiers who hand out chocolate bars and chewing gum.

We learned the meaning of free fire zones, shooting anything that moves, and we watched while America placed a cheapness on the lives of orientals.

We watched the United States falsification of body counts, in fact the glorification of body counts. We listened while month after month we were told the back of the enemy was about to break. We fought using weapons against "oriental human beings." We fought using weapons against those people which I do not believe this country would dream of using were we fighting in the European theater. We watched while men charged up hills because a general said that hill has to be taken, and after losing one platoon or two platoons they marched away to leave the hill for re-occupation by the North Vietnamese. We watched pride allow the most unimportant battles to be blown into extravaganzas, because we couldn't lose, and we couldn't retreat, and because it didn't matter how many American bodies were lost to prove that point, and so there were Hamburger Hills and Khe Sahns and Hill 81s and Fire Base 6s, and so many others.

Now we are told that the men who fought there must watch quietly while American lives are lost so that we can exercise the incredible arrogance of Vietnamizing the Vietnamese.

Each day to facilitate the process by which the United States washes her hands of Vietnam someone has to give up his life so that the United States doesn't have to admit something that the entire world already knows, so that we can't say that we have made a mistake. Someone has to die so that President Nixon won't be, and these are his words, "the first President to lose a war."

We are asking Americans to think about that because how do you ask a man to be the last man to die in Vietnam? How do you ask a man to be the last man to die for a mistake? But we are trying to do that, and we are doing it with thousands of rationalizations, and if you read carefully the President's last speech to the people of this country, you can see that he says, and says clearly, "but the issue, gentlemen, the issue, is communism, and the question is whether or not we will leave that country to the communists or whether or not we will try to give it hope to be a free people." But the point is they are not a free people now under us. They are not a free people. And we cannot fight communism all over the world. I think we should have learned that lesson by now.

But the problem of veterans goes beyond this personal problem, because you think about a poster in this country with a picture of Uncle Sam and the picture says "I want you." And a young man comes out of high school and says, "that is fine, I am going to serve my country," and he goes to Vietnam and he shoots and he kills and he does his job. Or maybe he doesn't kill. Maybe he just goes and he comes back, and when he gets back to this country he finds that he isn't really wanted, because the largest corps of unemployed in the country—it varies depending on who you get it from, the Veterans Administration says 15 percent and various other sources 22 percent—but the largest corps of unemployed in this country are veterans of this war, and of those veterans 33 percent of the unemployed

are black. That means one out of every ten of the nation's unemployed is a veteran of Vietnam.

The hospitals across the country won't, or can't meet their demands. It is not a question of not trying; they haven't got the appropriations. A man recently died after he had a tracheotomy in California, not because of the operation but because there weren't enough personnel to clean the mucus out of his tube and he suffocated to death.

Another young man just died in a New York VA Hospital the other day. A friend of mine was lying in a bed two beds away and tried to help him but he couldn't. He rang a bell and there was nobody there to service that man and so he died of convulsions.

I understand 57 percent of all those entering the VA hospitals talk about suicide. Some 27 percent have tried, and they try because they come back to this country and they have to face what they did in Vietnam, and then they come back and find the indifference of a country that doesn't really care.

Suddenly we are faced with a very sickening situation in this country, because there is no moral indignation and, if there is, it comes from people who are almost exhausted by their past indignations, and I know that many of them are sitting in front of me. The country seems to have lain down and shrugged of something as serious as Laos, just as we calmly shrugged off the loss of 700,000 lives in Pakistan, the so-called greatest disaster of all times.

But we are here as veterans to say we think we are in the midst of the greatest disaster off all times now because they are still dying over there—not just Americans, but Vietnamese—and we are rationalizing leaving that country so that those people can go on killing each other for years to come.

Americans seem to have accepted the idea that the war is winding down, at least for Americans, and they have also allowed the bodies which were once used by a President for statistics to prove that we were winning that war, to be used as evidence against a man who followed orders and who interpreted those orders no differently than hundreds of other men in Vietnam.

We veterans can only look with amazement on the fact that this country has been unable to see there is absolutely no difference between ground troops and a helicopter crew, and yet people have accepted a differentiation fed them by the administration.

No ground troops are in Laos so it is all right to kill Laotians by remote control. But believe me the helicopter crews fill the same kind of damage on the Vietnamese and Laotian countryside as anybody else, and the President is talking about allowing that to go on for many years to come. One can only ask if we will really be satisfied only when the troops march into Hanoi.

We are asking here in Washington for some action: action from the Congress of the United States of America which has the power to raise and maintain armies, and which by the Constitution also has the power to declare war.

We have come here, not to the President, because we believe that this body can be responsive to the will of the people, and we believe that the will of the people says that we should be out of Vietnam now.

We are here in Washington also to say that the problem of this war is not just a question of war and diplomacy. If is part and parcel of everything that we are trying as human beings to communicate to people in this country—the question of racism, which is rampant in the military, and so many other questions such as the use of weapons; the hypocrisy in our taking umbrage in the Geneva Conventions and using that as justification for a continuation of this war when we are more guilty than any other body of violations of those Geneva Conventions; in the use of free fire zones, harassment interdiction fire, search and destroy missions, the bombings, the torture of prisoners, the killing of prisoners, all accepted policy by many units in South Vietnam. That is what we are trying to say. It is part and parcel of everything.

An American Indian friend of mine who lives in the Indian Nation of Alcatraz put it to me very succinctly. He told me how as a boy on an Indian reservation he had watched television and he used to cheer the cowboys when they came in and shot the Indians, and then suddenly one day he stopped in Vietnam and he said "my God, I am doing to these people the very same thing that was done to my people," and he stopped. And that is what we are trying to say, that we think this thing has to end.

We are also here to ask, and we are here to ask vehemently, where are the leaders of our country? Where is the leadership? We are here to ask where are McNamara, Rostow, Bundy, Gilpatric and so many others? Where are they now that we, the men whom they sent off to war, have returned? These are commanders who have deserted their troops, and there is no more serious crime in the law of war. The Army says they never leave their wounded. The Marines say they never leave even their dead. These men have left all the casualties and retreated behind a pious shield of public rectitude. They have left the real stuff of their reputations bleaching behind them in the sun in this country.

Finally, this administration has done us the ultimate dishonor. They have attempted to disown us and the sacrifices we made for this country. In their blindness and fear they have tried to deny that we are veterans or that we served in Nam. We do not need their testimony. Our own scars and stumps of limbs are witness enough for others and for ourselves.

We wish that a merciful God could wipe away our own memories of that service as easily as this administration has wiped away their memories of us. But all that they have done and all that they can do by this denial is to make more clear than ever our own determination to undertake one last mission—to search out and destroy the last vestige of this barbaric war, to pacify our own hearts, to conquer the hate and the fear that have driven this country these last ten years and more, so when 30 years from now our brothers go down the street without a leg, without an arm, or a face, and small boys ask why, we will be able to say "Vietnam" and not mean a desert, not a filthy obscene memory, but mean instead the place where America finally turned and where soldiers like us helped it in the turning.

Thank you.

QUESTIONS TO CONSIDER

1. Why did Kerry oppose the war?
2. If you were watching Kerry give his testimony, would he have persuaded you to oppose the War?

27.4 RICHARD NIXON, RESIGNATION SPEECH (1974)

The Watergate saga that had engulfed the presidency of Richard Nixon (1913–1994) drew to a dramatic close on August 8, 1974, when Nixon announced his resignation. Congress had formally drawn up articles of impeachment against him, and his political support had vanished. Three days previously, the U.S. Supreme Court had forced Nixon to release the audio tapes of Oval Office conversations he had with his staff, including discussions about forcing the FBI to end its investigation. Nixon's public resignation speech took a subdued tone, as he reviewed the new revelations in the scandal and summarized the state of the world.

Good evening:

This is the 37th time I have spoken to you from this office, where so many decisions have been made that shaped the history of this Nation. Each time I have done so to discuss with you some matter that I believe affected the national interest.

In all the decisions I have made in my public life, I have always tried to do what was best for the Nation. Throughout the long and difficult period of Watergate, I have felt it was my duty to persevere, to make every possible effort to complete the term of office to which you elected me.

In the past few days, however, it has become evident to me that I no longer have a strong enough political base in the Congress to justify continuing that effort. As long as there was such a base, I felt strongly that it was necessary to see the constitutional process through to its conclusion, that to do otherwise would be unfaithful to the spirit of that deliberately difficult process and a dangerously destabilizing precedent for the future.

But with the disappearance of that base, I now believe that the constitutional purpose has been served, and there is no longer a need for the process to be prolonged.

I would have preferred to carry through to the finish, whatever the personal agony it would have involved, and my family unanimously urged me to do so. But the interests of the Nation must always come before any personal considerations.

From the discussions I have had with Congressional and other leaders, I have concluded that because of the Watergate matter, I might not have the support of the Congress that I would consider necessary to back the very difficult decisions and carry out the duties of this office in the way the interests of the Nation will require.

I have never been a quitter. To leave office before my term is completed is abhorrent to every instinct in my body. But as President, I must put the interests of America first. America needs a full-time President and a full-time Congress, particularly at this time with the problems we face at home and abroad.

To continue to fight through the months ahead for my personal vindication would almost totally absorb the time and attention of both the President and the Congress in a period when our entire focus should be on the great issues of peace abroad and prosperity without inflation at home.

Therefore, I shall resign the Presidency effective at noon tomorrow. Vice President Ford will be sworn in as President at that hour in this office.

As I recall the high hopes for America with which we began this second term, I feel a great sadness that I

Source: "Richard Nixon: Address to the Nation Announcing Decision to Resign the Office of President of the United States," http://www.presidency.ucsb.edu/ws/index.php?pid=4324 (Accessed May 21, 2018).

will not be here in this office working on your behalf to achieve those hopes in the next 2 1/2 years. But in turning over direction of the Government to Vice President Ford, I know, as I told the Nation when I nominated him for that office 10 months ago, that the leadership of America will be in good hands.

In passing this office to the Vice President, I also do so with the profound sense of the weight of responsibility that will fall on his shoulders tomorrow and, therefore, of the understanding, the patience, the cooperation he will need from all Americans.

As he assumes that responsibility, he will deserve the help and the support of all of us. As we look to the future, the first essential is to begin healing the wounds of this Nation, to put the bitterness and divisions of the recent past behind us and to rediscover those shared ideals that lie at the heart of our strength and unity as a great and as a free people.

By taking this action, I hope that I will have hastened the start of that process of healing which is so desperately needed in America.

I regret deeply any injuries that may have been done in the course of the events that led to this decision. I would say only that if some of my judgments were wrong—and some were wrong—they were made in what I believed at the time to be the best interest of the Nation.

To those who have stood with me during these past difficult months—to my family, my friends, to many others who joined in supporting my cause because they believed it was right—I will be eternally grateful for your support.

And to those who have not felt able to give me your support, let me say I leave with no bitterness toward those who have opposed me, because all of us, in the final analysis, have been concerned with the good of the country, however our judgments might differ.

So, let us all now join together in affirming that common commitment and in helping our new President succeed for the benefit of all Americans.

I shall leave this office with regret at not completing my term, but with gratitude for the privilege of serving as your President for the past 5 1/2 years. These years have been a momentous time in the history of our Nation and the world. They have been a time of achievement in which we can all be proud, achievements that represent the shared efforts of the Administration, the Congress, and the people.

But the challenges ahead are equally great, and they, too, will require the support and the efforts of the Congress and the people working in cooperation with the new Administration.

We have ended America's longest war, but in the work of securing a lasting peace in the world, the goals ahead are even more far-reaching and more difficult. We must complete a structure of peace so that it will be said of this generation, our generation of Americans, by the people of all nations, not only that we ended one war but that we prevented future wars.

We have unlocked the doors that for a quarter of a century stood between the United States and the People's Republic of China.

We must now ensure that the one quarter of the world's people who live in the People's Republic of China will be and remain not our enemies, but our friends.

In the Middle East, 100 million people in the Arab countries, many of whom have considered us their enemy for nearly 20 years, now look on us as their friends. We must continue to build on that friendship so that peace can settle at last over the Middle East and so that the cradle of civilization will not become its grave.

Together with the Soviet Union, we have made the crucial breakthroughs that have begun the process of limiting nuclear arms. But we must set as our goal not just limiting but reducing and, finally, destroying these terrible weapons so that they cannot destroy civilization and so that the threat of nuclear war will no longer hang over the world and the people.

We have opened the new relation with the Soviet Union. We must continue to develop and expand that new relationship so that the two strongest nations of the world will live together in cooperation, rather than confrontation.

Around the world in Asia, in Africa, in Latin America, in the Middle East—there are millions of people who live in terrible poverty, even starvation. We must keep as our goal turning away from production for war and expanding production for peace so that people everywhere on this Earth can at last look forward in their children's time, if not in our own time, to having the necessities for a decent life.

Here in America, we are fortunate that most of our people have not only the blessings of liberty but also the means to live full and good and, by the world's standards, even abundant lives. We must press on, however, toward a goal, not only of more and better jobs but of full opportunity for every American and of what we are striving so hard right now to achieve, prosperity without inflation.

For more than a quarter of a century in public life, I have shared in the turbulent history of this era. I have fought for what I believed in. I have tried, to the best of my ability, to discharge those duties and meet those responsibilities that were entrusted to me.

Sometimes I have succeeded and sometimes I have failed, but always I have taken heart from what Theodore Roosevelt once said about the man in the arena, "whose face is marred by dust and sweat and blood, who strives valiantly, who errs and comes short again and again because there is not effort without error and shortcoming, but who does actually strive to do the deed, who knows the great enthusiasms, the great devotions, who spends himself in a worthy cause, who at the best knows in the end the triumphs of high achievements and who at the worst, if he fails, at least fails while daring greatly"

I pledge to you tonight that as long as I have a breath of life in my body, I shall continue in that spirit. I shall continue to work for the great causes to which I have been dedicated throughout my years as a Congressman, a Senator, Vice President, and President, the cause of peace, not just for America but among all nations—prosperity, justice, and opportunity for all of our people.

There is one cause above all to which I have been devoted and to which I shall always be devoted for as long as I live.

When I first took the oath of office as President 5 1/2 years ago, I made this sacred commitment: to "consecrate my office, my energies, and all the wisdom I can summon to the cause of peace among nations."

I have done my very best in all the days since to be true to that pledge. As a result of these efforts, I am confident that the world is a safer place today, not only for the people of America but for the people of all nations, and that all of our children have a better chance than before of living in peace rather than dying in war.

This, more than anything, is what I hoped to achieve when I sought the Presidency. This, more than anything, is what I hope will be my legacy to you, to our country, as I leave the Presidency.

To have served in this office is to have felt a very personal sense of kinship with each and every American. In leaving it, I do so with this prayer: May God's grace be with you in all the days ahead.

QUESTIONS TO CONSIDER

1. What did Nixon especially highlight in his final speech as President?
2. How would you characterize his tone toward the Watergate investigation?

27.5 GERALD FORD, "REMARKS ON TAKING THE OATH OF OFFICE" (1974)

The day after Richard Nixon announced his resignation (see Reading 27.4), new President Gerald Ford (1913–2006) addressed the nation. Ford was the first person to become Vice President and then President without being elected to either position. He became Vice President after Richard Nixon's previous Vice President, Spiro Agnew, resigned due to tax evasion charges. As House Majority Leader, Ford was next in the line of succession. After Nixon resigned during the Watergate investigation, Ford assumed the Presidency. In his first speech, Ford, who had previously served as Congressman from Michigan for thirteen terms, tried to reassure the nation as to its stability. Just months later, however, Ford officially pardoned Nixon, an action that permanently damaged his presidency. In the 1974 midterm elections, Ford's Republican Party lost 49 House seats. In the 1976 Presidential election, Democrat Jimmy Carter defeated Ford, which ended Ford's political career.

Mr. Chief Justice, my dear friends, my fellow Americans:

The oath that I have taken is the same oath that was taken by George Washington and by every President under the Constitution. But I assume the Presidency under extraordinary circumstances never before experienced by Americans. This is an hour of history that troubles our minds and hurts our hearts.

Therefore, I feel it is my first duty to make an unprecedented compact with my countrymen. Not an inaugural address, not a fireside chat, not a campaign speech—just a little straight talk among friends. And I intend it to be the first of many.

I am acutely aware that you have not elected me as your President by your ballots, and so I ask you to confirm me as your President with your prayers. And I hope that such prayers will also be the first of many.

If you have not chosen me by secret ballot, neither have I gained office by any secret promises. I have not campaigned either for the Presidency or the Vice Presidency. I have not subscribed to any partisan platform.

I am indebted to no man, and only to one woman—my dear wife—as I begin this very difficult job.

I have not sought this enormous responsibility, but I will not shirk it. Those who nominated and confirmed me as Vice President were my friends and are my friends. They were of both parties, elected by all the people and acting under the Constitution in their name. It is only fitting then that I should pledge to them and to you that I will be the President of all the people.

Thomas Jefferson said the people are the only sure reliance for the preservation of our liberty. And down the years, Abraham Lincoln renewed this American article of faith asking, "Is there any better way or equal hope in the world?"

I intend, on Monday next, to request of the Speaker of the House of Representatives and the President pro tempore of the Senate the privilege of appearing before the Congress to share with my former colleagues and with you, the American people, my views on the priority business of the Nation and to solicit your views and their views. And may I say to the Speaker and

Source: "Gerald Ford: Remarks on Taking the Oath of Office," http://www.presidency.ucsb.edu/ws/?pid=4409 (Accessed May 21, 2018).

the others, if I could meet with you right after these remarks, I would appreciate it.

Even though this is late in an election year, there is no way we can go forward except together and no way anybody can win except by serving the people's urgent needs. We cannot stand still or slip backwards. We must go forward now together.

To the peoples and the governments of all friendly nations, and I hope that could encompass the whole world, I pledge an uninterrupted and sincere search for peace. America will remain strong and united, but its strength will remain dedicated to the safety and sanity of the entire family of man, as well as to our own precious freedom.

I believe that truth is the glue that holds government together, not only our Government but civilization itself. That bond, though strained, is unbroken at home and abroad.

In all my public and private acts as your President, I expect to follow my instincts of openness and candor with full confidence that honesty is always the best policy in the end.

My fellow Americans, our long national nightmare is over.

Our Constitution works; our great Republic is a government of laws and not of men. Here the people rule. But there is a higher Power, by whatever name we honor Him, who ordains not only righteousness but love, not only justice but mercy.

As we bind up the internal wounds of Watergate, more painful and more poisonous than those of foreign wars, let us restore the golden rule to our political process, and let brotherly love purge our hearts of suspicion and of hate.

In the beginning, I asked you to pray for me. Before closing, I ask again for your prayers, for Richard Nixon and for his family. May our former President, who brought peace to millions, find it for himself. May God bless and comfort his wonderful wife and daughters, whose love and loyalty will forever be a shining legacy to all who bear the lonely burdens of the White House.

I can only guess at those burdens, although I have witnessed at close hand the tragedies that befell three Presidents and the lesser trials of others.

With all the strength and all the good sense I have gained from life, with all the confidence my family, my friends, and my dedicated staff impart to me, and with the good will of countless Americans I have encountered in recent visits to 40 States, I now solemnly reaffirm my promise I made to you last December 6: to uphold the Constitution, to do what is right as God gives me to see the right, and to do the very best I can for America.

God helping me, I will not let you down.

Thank you.

QUESTIONS TO CONSIDER

1. What tone did Ford strike in his address?
2. Would you have found Ford's words reassuring if you were watching the speech at the time?

27.6 CESAR CHAVEZ, ADDRESS TO THE COMMONWEALTH CLUB OF CALIFORNIA (1984)

Cesar Chavez (1927–1993) brought the rhetoric of the Rights Revolution to farm workers in the American Southwest. In 1962, Chavez co-founded the National Farm Workers Association (later renamed the United Farm Workers) and began organizing various groups of laborers who had not traditionally received support from labor unions. In 1970, the United Farm Workers organized the Salad Bowl strike, the largest farm laborer strike in American history, which eventually gained farm workers the right to collectively bargain. During the strikes he led, Chavez often fasted to further publicize the laborers' message. He gave the following speech to the Commonwealth Club of California in 1984. In it, he reviewed the past and speculated on future activism. Chavez died in 1993, but the United Farm Workers remains a major labor union today.

Twenty-one years ago last September, on a lonely, stretch of railroad track paralleling U.S. Highway 101 near Salinas, 32 Bracero farm workers lost their lives in a tragic accident.

The Braceros had been imported from Mexico to work on California farms. They died when their bus, which was converted from a flatbed truck, drove in front of a freight train.

Conversion of the bus had not been approved by any government agency. The driver had "tunnel" vision.

Most of the bodies lay unidentified for days. No one, including the grower who employed the workers even knew their names.

Today, thousands of farm workers live under savage conditions—beneath trees and amid garbage and human excrement—near tomato fields in San Diego County—tomato fields which use the most modern farm technology.

Vicious rats gnaw on them as they sleep. They walk miles to buy food at inflated prices and they carry in water from irrigation pumps.

Child labor is still common in many farm areas.

As much as 30 per cent of Northern California's garlic harvesters are under-aged children. Kids as young as six years old have voted in state-conducted union elections since they qualified as workers.

Some 800,000 under-aged children work with their families harvesting crops across America.

Babies born to migrant workers suffer 25 percent higher infant mortality than the rest of the population.

Malnutrition among migrant worker children is 10 times higher than the national rate.

Farm workers' average life expectancy is still 49 years—compared to 73 years for the average American.

All my life, I have been driven by one dream, one goal, one vision: To overthrow a farm labor system in this nation which treats farm workers as if they were not important human beings.

Farm workers are not agricultural implements—they are not beasts of burden to be used and discarded.

That dream was born in my youth. It was nurtured in my early days of organizing. It has flourished. It has been attacked.

Source: "Address by Cesar Chavez," California Department of Education, http://chavez.cde.ca.gov/ModelCurriculum/Teachers/Lessons/Resources/Documents/Commonwealth_Club_SanFrancisco_11-9-84.pdf (Accessed June 15, 2018).

I'm not very different from anyone else who has ever tried to accomplish something with his life. My motivation comes from my personal life—from watching what my mother and father went through when I was growing up—from what we experienced as migrant farm workers in California.

That dream, that vision grew from my own experience with racism—with hope—with the desire to be treated fairly and to see my people treated as human beings and not as chattel.

It grew from anger and rage—emotions I felt 40 years ago when people of my color were denied the right to see a movie or eat at a restaurant in many parts of California.

It grew from the frustration and humiliation I felt as a boy who couldn't understand how the growers could abuse and exploit farm workers when there were so many of us and so few of them.

Later, in the '50s, I experienced a different kind of exploitation. In San Jose, in Los Angeles and in other urban communities, we, the Mexican American people, were dominated by a majority that was Anglo.

I began to realize what other minority people had discovered: That the only answer—the only hope was in organizing.

More of us had to become citizens. We had to register to vote. And people like me had to develop the skills it would take to organize, to educate, to help empower the Chicano people.

I spent many years—before we founded the union—learning how to work with people.

We experienced some successes in voter registration in politics in battling racial discrimination—successes in an era when Black Americans were just beginning to assert their civil rights and when political awareness among Hispanics was almost non-existent.

But deep in my heart, I knew I could never be happy unless I tried organizing the farm workers. I didn't know if I would succeed. But I had to try.

All Hispanics—urban and rural, young and old—are connected to the farm workers' experience. We had all lived through the fields or our parents had. We shared that common humiliation.

How could we progress as a people, even if we lived in the cities, while the farm workers—men and women of our color—were condemned to a life without pride?

How could we progress as a people while the farm workers—who symbolized our history in this land—were denied self-respect?

How could our people believe that their children could become lawyers and doctors and judges and business people while this shame, this injustice was permitted to continue?

Those who attack our union often say, "It's not really a union. It's something else—a social movement. A civil rights movement. It's something dangerous."

They're half right.

The United Farm Workers is first and foremost a union. A union like any other. A union that either produces for its members on the bread and butter issues or doesn't survive.

But the UFW has always been something more than a union. Although it's never been dangerous if you believe in the Bill of Rights.

The UFW was the beginning! We attacked that historical source of shame and infamy that our people in this country lived with.

We attacked that injustice not by complaining; not by seeking hand-outs; not by becoming soldiers in the War on Poverty.

We organized! . . .

The very fact of our existence forces an entire industry—unionized and non-unionized—to spend millions of dollars year after year on improved wages—on improved working conditions—on benefits for workers.

If we're so weak and unsuccessful, why do the growers continue to fight us with such passion?

Because so long as we continue to exist, farm workers will benefit from our existence even if they don't work under union contract.

It doesn't really matter whether we have 100,000 members or 500,000 members. In truth, hundreds of thousands of farm workers in California—and in other states—are better off today because of our work.

And Hispanics across California and the nation, who don't work in agriculture, are better off today because of what the farm workers taught people—about organization—about pride and strength—about seizing control over their own lives.

Tens of thousands of the children and grandchildren of farm workers—and the children and grandchildren of poor Hispanics—are moving out of the fields and out of the barrios—and into the professions—and into business—and into politics.

And that movement cannot be reversed!

Our union will forever exist as an empowering force among Chicanos in the Southwest.

And that means our power and our influence will grow and not diminish. . . .

South of the Sacramento River in California, Hispanics now make up more than 25 percent of the population.

That figure will top 30 percent by the year 2000.

There are 1.1 million Spanish-surnamed registered voters in California; 85 percent are Democrats; only 13 percent are Republicans.

In 1975, there were 200 Hispanic elected officials at all levels of government.

In 1984, there are over 400 elected judges, city council members, mayors and legislators.

In light of these trends, it is absurd to believe or suggest that we are going to go back in time as a union or as a people!

The growers often try to blame the union for their problems to lay their sins off on us—sins for which they only have themselves to blame.

The growers only have themselves to blame as they begin to reap the harvest from decades of environmental damage they have brought upon the land—The pesticides, the herbicides, the soil fumigants, the fertilizers, the salt deposits from thoughtless irrigation—The ravages from years of unrestrained poisoning of our soil and water.

Thousands of acres of land in California have already been irrevocably damaged by this wanton abuse of nature. Thousands more will be lost unless growers understand that dumping more poisons on the soil won't solve their problems—on the short term or the long term.

Health authorities in many San Joaquin Valley towns already warn young children and pregnant women not to drink the water because of nitrates from fertilizers which have contaminated the groundwater.

The growers only have themselves to blame for an increasing demand by consumers for higher quality food—food that isn't tainted by toxics—food that doesn't result from plant mutations or chemicals which produce red, luscious-looking tomatoes—that tastes like alfalfa.

The growers are making the same mistake American automakers made in the '60s and '70s when they refused to produce small economical cars and opened the door to increased foreign competition.

Growers only have themselves to blame for increasing attacks on their publicly-financed hand-outs and government welfare: Water subsidies; mechanization research; huge subsidies for not growing crops.

These special privileges came into being before the Supreme Court's one-person, one-vote decision at a time when rural lawmakers dominated the Legislature and the Congress.

Soon, those hand-outs could be in jeopardy—as government searches for more revenue and as urban taxpayers take a closer look at farm programs—and who they benefit.

The growers only have themselves to blame for the humiliation they have brought upon succeeding waves of immigrant groups which have sweated and sacrificed for 100 years to make this industry rich.

For generations, they have subjugated entire races of dark-skinned farm workers.

These are the sins of the growers—not the farm workers.

We didn't poison the land.

We didn't open the door to imported produce.

We didn't covet billions of dollars in government handouts.

We didn't abuse and exploit the people who work the land.

Today, the growers are like a punch-drunk old boxer who doesn't know he's past his prime.

The times are changing. The political and social environment has changed.

The chickens are coming home to roost and the time to account for past sins is approaching.

Like the other immigrant groups, the day will come when we win the economic and political rewards which are in keeping with our numbers in society.

The day will come when the politicians do the right thing by our people out of political necessity and not out of charity or idealism.

That day may not come this year.

That day may not come during this decade.

But it will come, someday!

And when that day comes, we shall see the fulfillment of that passage from the Book of Matthew in the New Testament, "That the last shall be first and the first shall be last."

And on that day, our nation shall fulfill its creed and that fulfillment shall enrich us all.

Thank you very much.

QUESTIONS TO CONSIDER

1. How did Chavez characterize the past?
2. Do you think he was optimistic about future activism?

CHAPTER 28

THE TRIUMPH OF CONSERVATISM, 1980–1991

28.1 PHYLLIS SCHLAFLY, "WHAT'S WRONG WITH 'EQUAL RIGHTS' FOR WOMEN?" (1972)

In the 1970s, Phyllis Schlafly (1924–2016) emerged as one of the foremost opponents of feminism and women's rights. Her arguments, of course, gain special attention because Schlafly was a woman. Schlafly had first gained attention for her support of Barry Goldwater's 1964 Presidential campaign. Later, she became a public opponent of the Equal Rights Amendment (ERA), which Congress ratified in 1972 but has never received the necessary thirty-eight state ratifications. In the following essay, "What's Wrong with Equal Rights for Women?" Schlafly laid out her opposition to the amendment and to feminism more broadly. Schlafly remain an important conservative activist as CEO of a conservative political interest organization, Eagle Forum.

Of all the classes of people who ever lived, the American woman is the most privileged. We have the most rights and rewards, and the fewest duties. Our unique status is the result of a fortunate combination of circumstances.

1) We have the immense good fortune to live in a civilization which respects the family as the basic unit of society. This respect is part and parcel of our laws and our customs. It is based on the fact of life—which no legislation or agitation can erase—that women have babies and men don't.

If you don't like this fundamental difference, you will have to take up your complaint with God because He created us this way. The fact that women, not men, have babies is not the fault of selfish and domineering men, or of the establishment, or of any clique of conspirators who want to oppress women. It's simply the way God made us.

Our Judeo-Christian civilization has developed the law and custom that, since women must bear the physical consequences of the sex act, men must be required to bear the other consequences and pay in other ways.

These laws and customs decree that a man must carry his share by physical protection and financial support of his children and of the woman who bears his children, and also by a code of behavior which benefits and protects both the woman and the children.

THE GREATEST ACHIEVEMENT OF WOMEN'S RIGHTS

This is accomplished by the institution of the family. Our respect for the family as the basic unit of society, which is ingrained in the laws and customs of our Judeo-Christian civilization, is the greatest single achievement in the entire history of women's rights. It assures a woman the most precious and important right of all—the right to keep her own baby and to be supported and protected in the enjoyment of watching her baby grow and develop.

The institution of the family is advantageous for women for many reasons. After all, what do we want out of life? To love and be loved? Mankind has not discovered a better nest for a lifetime of reciprocal love. A sense of achievement? A man may search 30 to 40 years for accomplishment in his profession. A woman can enjoy real achievement when she is young—by having a baby. She can have the satisfaction of doing a job well—and being recognized for it. Do we want financial security? We are fortunate to have the great legacy of Moses, the Ten Commandments, especially this one: "Honor thy father and thy mother that thy days may be long upon the land." Children are a woman's best social security—her best guarantee of social benefits such as old age pension, unemployment compensation, workman's compensation, and sick leave. The family gives a woman the physical, financial and emotional security of the home—for all her life.

THE FINANCIAL BENEFITS OF CHIVALRY

2) The second reason why American women are a privileged group is that we are the beneficiaries of a tradition of special respect for women which dates from the Christian Age of Chivalry. The honor and respect paid to Mary, the Mother of Christ, resulted in all women, in effect, being put on a pedestal. This respect for women is not just the lip service that politicians pay to "God, Motherhood, and the Flag." It is not—as some youthful agitators seem to think—just a matter of opening doors for women, seeing that they are seated first, carrying their bundles, and helping them in and out of automobiles. Such good manners are merely the superficial evidences of a total attitude toward women which expresses itself in many more tangible ways, such as money. In other civilizations, such as the African and the American Indian, the men strut around wearing feathers and beads and hunting and fishing (great sport for men!), while the women do all the hard, tiresome drudgery including the tilling of the soil (if any is done), the hewing of wood, the making of fires, the carrying of water, as well as the cooking, sewing and caring for babies. This is not the American way because we were lucky enough to inherit the traditions of the Age of Chivalry. In America, a man's first significant purchase is a diamond for his bride, and the largest financial investment of his life is a home for her to live in. American husbands work hours of overtime to buy a fur piece or other finery to keep their wives in fashion, and to pay premiums on their life insurance policies to provide for her comfort when she is a widow (benefits in which he can never share). In the states which follow the English common law, a wife has a dower right in her husband's real estate which he cannot take away from her during life or by his will. A man cannot dispose of his real estate without his wife's signature. Any sale is subject to her 1/3 interest. Women fare even better in the states which follow the Spanish and French community-property laws, such as California, Arizona, Texas and Louisiana. The basic philosophy of the Spanish/French law is that a wife's work in the home is just as valuable as a husband's work at his job. Therefore, in community-property states, a wife owns one-half of all the property and income her husband earns during their marriage, and he cannot take it away from her. In Illinois, as a result of agitation by "equal rights" fanatics, the real-estate dower laws were repealed as of January 1, 1972. This means that in Illinois a husband can now sell the family home, spend the money on his girlfriend or gamble it away, and his faithful wife of 30 years can no longer stop him. "Equal rights" fanatics have also deprived women in Illinois and in some other states of most of their basic common-law rights to recover damages

for breach of promise to marry, seduction, criminal conversation, and alienation of affections.

THE REAL LIBERATION OF WOMEN

3) The third reason why American women are so well off is that the great American free enterprise system has produced remarkable inventors who have lifted the backbreaking "women's work" from our shoulders. In other countries and in other eras, it was truly said that "Man may work from sun to sun, but woman's work is never done." Other women have labored every waking hour—preparing food on wood-burning stoves, making flour, baking bread in stone ovens, spinning yarn, making clothes, making soap, doing the laundry by hand, heating irons, making candles for light and fires for warmth, and trying to nurse their babies through illnesses without medical care.

The real liberation of women from the backbreaking drudgery of centuries is the American free enterprise system which stimulated inventive geniuses to pursue their talents—and we all reap the profits. The great heroes of women's liberation are not the straggly-haired women on television talk shows and picket lines, but Thomas Edison who brought the miracle of electricity to our homes to give light and to run all those labor- saving devices—the equivalent, perhaps, of a half-dozen household servants for every middle-class American woman. Or Elias Howe who gave us the sewing machine which resulted in such an abundance of readymade clothing. Or Clarence Birdseye who invented the process for freezing foods. Or Henry Ford, who mass-produced the automobile so that it is within the price-range of every American, man or woman. A major occupation of women in other countries is doing their daily shopping for food, which requires carrying their own containers and standing in line at dozens of small shops. They buy only small portions because they can't carry very much and have no refrigerator or freezer to keep a surplus anyway. Our American free enterprise system has given us the gigantic food and packaging industry and beautiful supermarkets, which provide an endless variety of foods, prepackaged for easy carrying and a minimum of waiting. In America, women have the freedom from the slavery of standing in line for daily food. Thus, household duties have

been reduced to only a few hours a day, leaving the American woman with plenty of time to moonlight. She can take a full[-] or part-time paying job, or she can indulge to her heart's content in a tremendous selection of interesting educational or cultural or home-making activities.

THE FRAUD OF THE EQUAL RIGHTS AMENDMENT

In the last couple of years, a noisy movement has sprung up agitating for "women's rights." Suddenly, everywhere we are afflicted with aggressive females on television talk shows yapping about how mistreated American women are, suggesting that marriage has put us in some kind of "slavery," that housework is menial and degrading, and—perish the thought—that women are discriminated against. New "women's liberation" organizations are popping up, agitating and demonstrating, serving demands on public officials, getting wide press coverage always, and purporting to speak for some 100,000,000 American women. It's time to set the record straight. The claim that American women are downtrodden and unfairly treated is the fraud of the century. The truth is that American women never had it so good. Why should we lower ourselves to "equal rights" when we already have the status of special privilege? The proposed Equal Rights Amendment states: "Equality of rights under the law shall not be denied or abridged by the United States or by any state on account of sex." So what's wrong with that? Well, here are a few examples of what's wrong with it. This Amendment will absolutely and positively make women subject to the draft. Why any woman would support such a ridiculous and un-American proposal as this is beyond comprehension. Why any Congressman who had any regard for his wife, sister or daughter would support such a proposition is just as hard to understand. Foxholes are bad enough for men, but they certainly are not the place for women—and we should reject any proposal which would put them there in the name of "equal rights." It is amusing to watch the semantic chicanery of the advocates of the Equal Rights Amendment when confronted with this issue of the draft. They evade, they sidestep, they try to muddy up the issue, but they cannot deny that the Equal Rights Amendment will positively make women subject to the draft. Congresswoman Margaret Heckler's answer to this question was, Don't worry, it will take two years for the Equal Rights Amendment to go into effect, and we can rely on President Nixon to end the Vietnam War before then! Literature distributed by Equal Rights Amendment supporters confirms that "under the Amendment a draft law which applied to men would apply also to women." The Equal Rights literature argues that this would be good for women so they can achieve their "equal rights" in securing veterans' benefits. Another bad effect of the Equal Rights Amendment is that it will abolish a woman's right to child support and alimony, and substitute what the women's libbers think is a more "equal" policy, that "such decisions should be within the discretion of the Court and should be made on the economic situation and need of the parties in the case." Under present American laws, the man is always required to support his wife and each child he caused to be brought into the world. Why should women abandon these good laws—by trading them for something so nebulous and uncertain as the "discretion of the Court"? The law now requires a husband to support his wife as best as his financial situation permits, but a wife is not required to support her husband (unless he is about to become a public charge). A husband cannot demand that his wife go to work to help pay for family expenses. He has the duty of financial support under our laws and customs. Why should we abandon these mandatory wife-support and child-support laws so that a wife would have an "equal" obligation to take a job? By law and custom in America, in case of divorce, the mother always is given custody of her children unless there is overwhelming evidence of mistreatment, neglect or bad character. This is our special privilege because of the high rank that is placed on motherhood in our society. Do women really want to give up this special privilege and lower themselves to "equal rights", so that the mother gets one child and the father gets the other? I think not. . . .

WHAT "WOMEN'S LIB" REALLY MEANS

Many women are under the mistaken impression that "women's lib" means more job employment opportunities for women, equal pay for equal work,

appointments of women to high positions, admitting more women to medical schools, and other desirable objectives which all women favor. We all support these purposes, as well as any necessary legislation which would bring them about. But all this is only a sweet syrup which covers the deadly poison masquerading as "women's lib." The women's libbers are radicals who are waging a total assault on the family, on marriage, and on children. Don't take my word for it—read their own literature and prove to yourself what these characters are trying to do. The most pretentious of the women's liberation magazines is called *Ms.*, and subtitled "The New Magazine for Women," with Gloria Steinem listed as president and secretary. Reading the Spring 1972 issue of *Ms.* gives a good understanding of women's lib, and the people who promote it. It is anti-family, anti-children, and pro-abortion. It is a series of sharp-tongued, high-pitched whining complaints by unmarried women. They view the home as a prison, and the wife and mother as a slave. To these women's libbers, marriage means dirty dishes and dirty laundry. One article lauds a woman's refusal to carry up the family laundry as "an act of extreme courage." Another tells how satisfying it is to be a lesbian (page 117). The women's libbers don't understand that most women want to be wife, mother and homemaker—and are happy in that role. The women's libbers actively resent the mother who stays at home with her children and likes it that way. The principal purpose of *Ms.*'s shrill tirade is to sow seeds of discontent among happy, married women so that all women can be unhappy in some new sisterhood of frustrated togetherness. Obviously intrigued by the 170 clauses of exemptions from marital duties given to Jackie Kennedy, and the special burdens imposed on Aristotle Onassis, in the pre-marriage contract they signed, *Ms.* recommends two women's lib marriage contracts. The "Utopian marriage contract" has a clause on "sexual rights and freedoms" which approves "arrangements such as having Tuesdays off from one another," and the husband giving "his consent to abortion in advance." The "Shulmans' marriage agreement" includes such petty provisions as "wife strips beds, husband remakes them," and "Husband does dishes on Tuesday, Thursday and Sunday. Wife does Monday, Wednesday and Saturday, Friday is split . . ." If the baby cries in the night, the chore of "handling" the baby is assigned as follows: "Husband does Tuesday, Thursday and Sunday. Wife does Monday, Wednesday and Saturday, Friday is split . . ." Presumably, if the baby cries for his mother on Tuesday night, he would be informed that the marriage contract prohibits her from answering. Of course, it is possible, in such a loveless home, that the baby would never call for his mother at all. Who put up the money to launch this 130-page slick-paper assault on the family and motherhood? A count of the advertisements in *Ms.* shows that the principal financial backer is the liquor industry. There are 26 liquor ads in this one initial issue. Of these, 13 are expensive full-page color ads, as opposed to only 18 full-page ads from all other sources combined, most of which are in the cheaper black-and-white.

Another women's lib magazine, called *Women*, tells the American woman that she is a prisoner in the "solitary confinement" and "isolation" of marriage. The magazine promises that it will provide women with "escape from isolation . . . release from boredom," and that it will "break the barriers . . . that separate wife, mistress and secretary . . . heterosexual women and homosexual women."

These women's libbers do, indeed, intend to "break the barriers" of the Ten Commandments and the sanctity of the family. It hasn't occurred to them that a woman's best "escape from isolation and boredom" is—not a magazine subscription to boost her "stifled ego"—but a husband and children who love her. The first issue of *Women* contains 68 pages of such proposals as "The BITCH Manifesto," which promotes the line that "Bitch is Beautiful and that we have nothing to lose. Nothing whatsoever." Another article promotes an organization called W.I.T.C.H. (Women's International Terrorist Conspiracy from Hell), "an action arm of Women's Liberation." In intellectual circles, a New York University professor named Warren T. Farrell has provided the rationale for why men should support women's lib. When his speech to the American Political Science Association Convention is stripped of its egghead verbiage, his argument is that men should eagerly look forward to the day when they can enjoy free sex and not have to pay for it. The husband will no longer be "saddled with the tremendous

guilt feelings" when he leaves his wife with nothing after she has given him her best years. If a husband loses his job, he will no longer feel compelled to take any job to support his family. A husband can go "out with the boys" to have a drink without feeling guilty. Alimony will be eliminated.

WOMEN'S LIBBERS DO NOT SPEAK FOR US

The "women's lib" movement is not an honest effort to secure better jobs for women who want or need to work outside the home. This is just the superficial sweet-talk to win broad support for a radical "movement." Women's lib is a total assault on the role of the American woman as wife and mother, and on the family as the basic unit of society. Women's libbers are trying to make wives and mothers unhappy with their career, make them feel that they are "second-class citizens" and "abject slaves." Women's libbers are promoting free sex instead of the "slavery" of marriage. They are promoting Federal "day-care centers" for babies instead of homes. They are promoting abortions instead of families.

Why should we trade in our special privileges and honored status for the alleged advantage of working in an office or assembly line? Most women would rather cuddle a baby than a typewriter or factory machine. Most women find that it is easier to get along with a husband than a foreman or office manager. Offices and factories require many more menial and repetitious chores than washing dishes and ironing shirts. Women's libbers do not speak for the majority of American women. American women do not want to be liberated from husbands and children. We do not want to trade our birthright of the special privileges of American women—for the mess of pottage called the Equal Rights Amendment. Modern technology and opportunity have not discovered any nobler or more satisfying or more creative career for a woman than marriage and motherhood. The wonderful advantage that American women have is that we can have all the rewards of that number-one career, and still moonlight with a second one to suit our intellectual, cultural or financial tastes or needs. And why should the men acquiesce in a system which gives preferential rights and lighter duties to women? In return, the men get the pearl of great price: a happy home, a faithful wife, and children they adore.

If the women's libbers want to reject marriage and motherhood, it's a free country and that is their choice. But let's not permit these women's libbers to get away with pretending to speak for the rest of us. Let's not permit this tiny minority to degrade the role that most women prefer. Let's not let these women's libbers deprive wives and mothers of the rights we now possess.

Tell your Senators NOW that you want them to vote NO on the Equal Rights Amendment. Tell your television and radio stations that you want equal time to present the case FOR marriage and motherhood.

QUESTIONS TO CONSIDER

1. How did Schlafly defend her opposition to equal rights for women?
2. Do you find the argument persuasive?

28.2 SUPREME COURT, EXCERPT FROM MAJORITY AND DISSENTING OPINIONS IN *ROE V. WADE* (1973)

In 1973, the U.S. Supreme Court issued a decision in *Roe v. Wade*, one of the most controversial decisions in the Court's twentieth-century history. *Roe v. Wade* came eight years after *Griswold v. Connecticut*, in which the Court ruled that states could not ban contraceptive use. *Roe* revolved around the ability of a woman to receive an abortion in Texas, a state that allowed abortion only in the case of a mother's life being in danger. On January 22, 1973, the Court ruled in a 7-2 decision that the Texas statue was unconstitutional. Here, you will read excerpts from Harry Blackmun's majority opinion and William Rehnquist's dissent. In 1992's *Planned Parenthood v. Casey*, the Court upheld a woman's right to an abortion but ruled that states could regulate first-trimester abortions as long as their regulations did not place an "undue burden" on the woman.

MR. JUSTICE BLACKMUN, DELIVERED THE OPINION OF THE COURT.

This Texas federal appeal and its Georgia companion, *Doe v. Bolton, post,* p. 179, present constitutional challenges to state criminal abortion legislation. The Texas statutes under attack here are typical of those that have been in effect in many States for approximately a century. The Georgia statues, in contrast, have a modern cast and are a legislative product that, to an extent at

least, obviously reflects the influences of recent attitudinal change, of advancing medical knowledge and techniques, and of new thinking about an old issue.

We forthwith knowledge our awareness of the sensitive and emotional nature of the abortion controversy, of the vigorous opposing views, even among physicians, and of the deep and seemingly absolute convictions that the subject inspires. One's philosophy, one's experiences, one's exposure to the raw edges

Source: "U.S. Reports: *Roe v. Wade,* 410 U.S. 113 (1973)," https://awpc.cattcenter.iastate.edu/2016/02/02/whats-wrong-with-equal-rights-for-women-1972/ (Accessed June 15, 2018).

of human existence, one's religious training, one's attitudes toward life and family and their values, and the moral standards one establishes and seeks to observe are all likely to influence and to color one's thinking and conclusions about abortion.

In addition, population growth, pollution, poverty, and racial overtones tend to complicate and not to simplify the problem.

Our task, of course, is to resolve the issue by constitutional measurement, free of emotion and of predilection. We seek earnestly to do this, and, because we do, we have injured into, and in this opinion place some emphasis upon, medical and medical-legal history and what that history reveals about man's attitudes toward the abortion procedure over the centuries. We bear in mind, too, Mr. Justice Holmes' admonition in his now-vindicated dissent in *Lochner* v. *New York*, 198 U. S. 45, 76 (1905):

> "[The Constitution] is made for people of fundamentally differing views, and the accident of our finding certain opinions natural and familiar or novel and even shocking ought not to conclude our judgment upon the question whether statutes embodying them conflict with the Constitution of the United States." . . .

Jane Roe, a single woman who was residing in Dallas County, Texas, instituted this federal action in March 1970 against the District Attorney of the county. She sought a declaratory judgment that the Texas criminal abortion statutes were unconstitutional on their face, and an injuction restraining the defendant from enforcing the statutes.

Roe alleged that she was unmarried and pregnant; that she wished to terminate her pregnancy by an abortion "performed by a competent, licensed physician, under safe, clinical conditions"; that she was unable to get a "legal" abortion in Texas because her life did not appear to be threatened by the continuation of her pregnancy; and that she could not afford to travel to another jurisdiction in order to secure a legal abortion under safe conditions. She claimed that the Texas statutes were unconstitutionally vague and that they abridged her right of personal privacy, protected by the First, Fourth, Fifth, Ninth, and Fourteenth Amendments. By an amendment to her complaint Roe purported to sue "on behalf of herself and all other women" similarly situated. . . .

John and Mary Doe, a married couple, filed a companion complaint to that of Roe. They also name the District Attorney as defendant, claimed the constitutional deprivations, and sought declaratory and injunctive relief. The Does alleged that they were a childless couple; that Mrs. Doe was suffering from a "neural-chemical" disorder; that her physician had "advised her to avoid pregnancy until such time as her condition has materially improved" (although a pregnancy at the present time would not present "a serious risk" to her life); that, pursuant to medical advice, she had discontinued use of birth control pills; and that if she should become pregnant, she would want to terminate the pregnancy by an abortion performed by a competent, licensed physician under safe, clinical conditions. By an amendment to their complaint, the Does purported to sue "on behalf of themselves and all couples similarly situated." . . .

The Constitution does not explicitly mention any right of privacy. In a line of decisions, however, going back perhaps as far as *Union Pacific R. Co.* v. *Botsford*, 141 U. S. 250, 251 (1891), the Court has recognized that a right of personal privacy, or a guarantee of certain areas or zones of privacy, does exist under the Constitution. . . .

This right of privacy, whether it be founded in the Fourteenth Amendment's concept of personal liberty and restrictions upon state action, as we feel it is, or, as the District Court determined, in the Ninth Amendment's reservation of rights to the people, is broad enough to encompass a woman's decision whether or not to terminate her pregnancy. The detriment that the State would impose upon the pregnant woman by denying this choice altogether is apparent. Specific and direct harm medically diagnosable even in early pregnancy may be involved. Maternity, or additional offspring, may force upon the woman a distressful life and future. Psychological harm may be imminent. Mental and physical health may be taxed by child care. There is also the distress, for all concerned, associated with the unwanted child, and there is the problem of bringing a child into a family already unable, psychologically and otherwise, to care for it. In other cases, as in this one, the additional difficulties and continuing stigma of unwed motherhood may be involved. All these are factors the woman and her responsible physician necessarily will consider in consultation.

On the basis of elements such as these, appellant and some *amici* argue that the woman's right is absolute and that she is entitled to terminate her pregnancy at whatever time, in whatever way, and for whatever reason she alone chooses. With this we do not agree. Appellant's arguments that Texas either has no valid interest at all in regulating the abortion decision, or no interest strong enough to support any limitation upon the woman's sole determination, are unpersuasive. The Court's decisions recognizing a right of privacy also acknowledge that some state regulation in areas protected by that right is appropriate. As noted above, a State may properly assert important interests in safeguarding health, in maintaining medical standards, and in protecting potential life. At some point in pregnancy, these respective interests become sufficiently compelling to sustain regulation of the factors that govern the abortion decision. The privacy right involved, therefore, cannot be said to be absolute. . . .

We, therefore, conclude that the right of personal privacy includes the abortion decision, but that this right is not unqualified and must be considered against important state interests in regulation. . . .

In view of all this, we do not agree that, by adopting one theory of life, Texas may override the rights of the pregnant woman that are at stake. We repeat, however, that the State does have an important and legitimate interest in preserving and protecting the health of the pregnant woman, whether she be a resident of the State or a nonresident who seeks medical consultation and treatment there, and that it has still another important and legitimate interest in protecting the potentiality of human life. These interests are separate and distinct. Each grows in substantiality as the woman approaches term and, at a point during pregnancy, each becomes "compelling."

With respect to the State's important and legitimate interest in the health of the mother, the "compelling" point, in the light of present medical knowledge, is at approximately the end of the first trimester. This is so because of the now-established medical fact, referred to above at 149, that until the end of the first trimester mortality in abortion may be less than mortality in normal childbirth. It follows that, from and after this point, a State may regulate the abortion procedure to

the extent that the regulation reasonably relates to the preservation and protection of maternal health. Examples of permissible state regulation in this area are requirements as to the qualifications of the person who is to perform the abortion; as to the licensure of that person; as to the facility in which the procedure is to be performed, that is, whether it must be a hospital or may be a clinic or some other place of less-than-hospital status; as to the licensing of the facility; and the like.

This means, on the other hand, that, for the period of pregnancy prior to this "compelling" point, the attending physician, in consultation with his patient, is free to determine, without regulation by the State, that, in his medical judgment, the patient's pregnancy should be terminated. If that decision is reached, the judgment may be effectuated by an abortion free of interference by the State.

With respect to the State's important and legitimate interest in potential life, the "compelling" point is at viability. This is so because the fetus the presumably has the capability of meaningful life outside the mother's womb. State regulation protective of fetal life after viability thus has both logical and biological justifications. If the State is interested in protecting fetal life after viability, it may go so far as to proscribe abortion during that period, except when it is necessary to preserve the life or health of the mother. . . .

To summarize and to repeat:

1. A state criminal abortion statute of the current Texas type, that excepts from criminality only a *life-saving* procedure on behalf of the mother, without regard to pregnancy stage and without recognition of the other interests involved, is violative of the Due Process Clause of the Fourteenth Amendment.

(a) For the stage prior to approximately the end of the first trimester, the abortion decision and its effectuation must be left to the medical judgment of the pregnant woman's attending physician.

(b) For the stage subsequent to approximately the end of the first trimester, the State, in promoting its interest in the health of the mother, may, if it chooses, regulate the abortion procedure in ways that are reasonably related to maternal health.

(c) For the stage subsequent to viability, the State in promoting its interest in the potentiality of human life may, if it chooses, regulate, and even proscribe, abortion except where it is necessary, in appropriate medical judgment, for the preservation of the life or health of the mother.

2. The State may define the term "physician," as it has been employed in the preceding paragraphs of this . . . of this opinion, to mean only a physician currently licensed by the State, and may proscribe any abortion by a person who is not a physician as so defined.

In *Doe* v. *Bolton, post,* p. 179, procedural requirements contained in one of the modern abortion statutes are considered. That opinion and this one, of course, are to be read together.

This holding, we feel, is consistent with the relative weights of the respective interests involved, with the lessons and examples of medical and legal history, with the lenity of the common law, and with the demands of the profound problems of the present day. The decision vindicates the right of the physician to administer medical treatment according to his professional judgment up to the points where important state interests provide compelling justifications for intervention. Up to those points, the abortion decision in all its aspects is inherently, and primarily, a medical decision, and basic responsibility for it must rest with the physician. If an individual practitioner abuses the privilege of exercising proper medical judgment, the usual remedies, judicial and intra-professional, are available. . . .

MR. JUSTICE REHNQUIST, DISSENTING.

The Court's opinion brings to the decision of this troubling question both extensive historical fact and a wealth of legal scholarship. While the opinion thus commands my respect, I find myself nonetheless in fundamental disagreement with those parts of it that invalidate the Texas statue in question, and therefore dissent. . . .

Even if there were a plaintiff in this case capable of litigating the issue which the Court decides, I would reach a conclusion opposite to that reached by the Court. I have difficulty in concluding, as the Court does, that the right of "privacy" is involved in this case. Texas, by the statute here challenged, bars the performance of a medical abortion by a licensed physician on a plaintiff such as Roe. A transaction resulting in an operation such as this is not "private" in the ordinary usage of that word. Nor is the "privacy" that the Court finds here even a distant relative of the freedom from searches and seizures protected by the Fourth Amendment to the Constitution, which the Court has referred to as embodying a right to privacy. . . .

If the Court means by the term "privacy" no more than that the claim of a person to be free from unwanted state regulation of consensual transactions may be a form of "liberty" protected by the Fourteenth Amendment, there is no doubt that similar claims have been upheld in our earlier decisions on the basis of that liberty. I agree with the statement of MR. JUSTICE STEWARD in his concurring opinion that the "liberty," against deprivation of which without due process the Fourteenth Amendment protects, embraces more than the rights found in the Bill of Rights. But that liberty is not guaranteed absolutely against deprivation, only against deprivation without due process of law. . . .

To reach its result, the Court necessarily has had to find within the scope of the Fourteenth Amendment a right that was apparently completely unknown to the drafters of the Amendment. . . .

There apparently was no question concerning the validity of this provision or of any of the other state statutes when the Fourteenth Amendment was adopted. The only conclusion possible from this history is that drafters did not intend to have the Fourteenth Amendment withdraw from the States the power of legislate with respect to this matter. . . .

QUESTIONS TO CONSIDER

1. How did each justice defend his argument?
2. Which argument do you find more persuasive?

28.3 GLORIA STEINEM, "IF MEN COULD MENSTRUATE" (1978)

On the opposite end of the spectrum from Phyllis Schlafly (see Reading 28.1) was the activism of Gloria Steinem. Steinem began writing on gender issues for various magazines in the early 1960s. In 1963, she published an explosive article on her experience working as a Playboy Bunny at the New York Playboy Club. Steinem, who herself had had an abortion earlier in her life, became involved in the pro-choice movement during the late 1960s and moved from there into the broader feminist movement. In 1972, she was one of the co-founders of the feminist *Ms.* magazine, which still exists today. In 1978, Steinem published the following article, "If Men Could Menstruate," a satirical piece that highlighted gender inequities, *Cosmopolitan*. Steinem remains a prominent feminist writer and activist today and travels around the world in support of women's rights.

Living in India made me understand that a white minority of the world has spent centuries conning us into thinking a white skin makes people superior, even though the only thing it really does is make them more subject to ultraviolet rays and wrinkles.

Reading Freud made me just as skeptical about penis envy. The power of giving birth makes "womb envy" more logical, and an organ as external and unprotected as the penis makes men very vulnerable indeed.

But listening recently to a woman describe the unexpected arrival of her menstrual period (a red stain had spread on her dress as she argued heatedly on the public stage) still made me cringe with embarrassment. That is, until she explained that, when finally informed in whispers of the obvious event, she had said to the all-male audience, "and you should be *proud* to have a menstruating woman on your stage. It's probably the first real thing that's happened to this group in years!"

Laughter. Relief. She had turned a negative into a positive. Somehow her story merged with India and Freud to make me finally understand the power of positive thinking. Whatever a "superior" group has will be used to justify its superiority, and whatever an "inferior" group has will be used to justify its plight. Black men were given poorly paid jobs because they were said to be "stronger" than white men, while all women were relegated to poorly paid jobs because they were said to be "weaker." As the little boy said when asked if he wanted to be a lawyer like his mother, "Oh no, that's women's work." Logic has nothing to do with oppression.

So what would happen if suddenly, magically, men could menstruate and women could not?

Clearly, menstruation would become an enviable, boast-worthy, masculine event:

Men would brag about how long and how much.

Young boys would talk about it as the envied beginning of manhood. Gifts, religious ceremonies, family dinners, and stag parties would mark the day.

To prevent monthly work loss among the powerful, Congress would fund a National Institute of Dysmenorrhea. Doctors would research little about heart attacks, from which men were hormonally protected, but everything about cramps.

Sanitary supplies would be federally funded and free. Of course, some men would still pay for the prestige of such commercial brands as Paul Newman Tampons, Muhammad Ali's Rope-a-Dope Pads, John

Source: Gloria Steinem, *Outrageous Acts and Everyday Rebellions* (New York: Holt, Rinehart and Winston, 1983), 337–340. Reprinted here with permission of Gloria Steinem and East Toledo Productions.

Wayne Maxi Pads, and Joe Namath Jock Shields—"For Those Light Bachelor Days."

Statistical surveys would show that men did better in sports and won more Olympic medals during their periods.

Generals, right-wing politicians, and religious fundamentalists would cite menstruation ("*men*-struation") as proof that only men could serve God and country in combat ("You have to give blood to take blood"), occupy high political office ("Can women be properly fierce without a monthly cycle governed by the planet Mars?"), be priests, ministers, God Himself ("He gave this blood for our sins"), or rabbis ("Without a monthly purge of impurities, women are unclean").

Male liberals or radicals, however, would insist that women are equal, just different; and that any woman could join their ranks if only she were willing to recognize the primacy of menstrual right ("Everything else is a single issue") or self-inflict a major wound every month ("You *must* give blood for the revolution").

Street guys would invent slang ("He's a three-pad man") and "give fives" on the corner with some exchange like, "Man, you lookin' *good!*'

"Yeah, man, I'm on the rag!"

TV shows would treat the subject openly. (Happy Days: Richie and Potsie try to convince Fonzie that he is still "The Fonz," though he has missed two periods in a row. *Hill Street Blues:* The whole precinct hits the same cycle.) So would newspapers. (SUMMER SHARK SCARE THREATENS MENSTRUATING MEN. JUDGE CITES MONTHLIES IN PARDONING RAPIST.) And so would movies. (Newman and Redford in *Blood Brother!*)

Men would convince women that sex was more pleasurable at "that time of the month." Lesbians would be said to fear blood and therefore life itself, though all they needed was a good menstruating man.

Medical schools would limit women's entry ("they might faint at the sight of blood").

Of course, intellectuals would offer the most moral and logical arguments. Without that biological gift for measuring the cycles of the moon and planets, how could a woman master any discipline that demanded a sense of time, space, mathematic—or the ability to measure anything at all? In philosophy and religion, how could women compensate for being disconnected from the rhythm of the universe? Or for their lack of symbolic death and resurrection every month?

Menopause would be celebrated as a positive event, the symbol that men had accumulated enough years of cyclical wisdom to need no more.

Liberal males in every field would try to be kind. The fact that "these people" have no gift for measuring life, the liberals would explain, should be punishment enough.

And how would women be trained to react? One can imagine right-wing women agreeing to all these arguments with a staunch and smiling masochism. ("The ERA would force housewives to wound themselves every month": Phyllis Schlafly. "Your husband's blood is as sacred as that of Jesus—and so sexy, too!": Marabel Morgan.) Reformers and Queen Bees would adjust their lives to the cycles of the men around them. Feminists would explain endlessly that men, too, needed to be liberated from the false idea of Martian aggressiveness, just as women needed to escape the bonds of "menses-envy." Radical feminists would add that the oppression of the nonmenstrual was the pattern for all other oppressions. ("Vampires were our first freedom fighters!") Cultural feminists would exalt a female bloodless imagery in art and literature. Socialist feminists would insist that, once capitalism and imperialism were overthrown, women would menstruate, too. ("If women aren't yet menstruating in Russia," they would explain, "it's only because true socialism can't exist within capitalist encirclement.")

In short, we would discover, as we should already guess, that logic is in the eye of the logician. (For instance, here's an idea for theorists and logicians: If women are supposed to be less rational and more emotional at the beginning of our menstrual cycle when the female hormone is at its lowest level, then why isn't it logical to say that, in those few days, women behave the most like the way men behave all month long? I leave further improvisations up to you.)

The truth is that, if men could menstruate, the power justifications would go on and on.

If we let them.

QUESTIONS TO CONSIDER

1. What is Steinem's major argument?
2. Do you find the argument convincing?

28.4 EXCERPTS FROM THE CARTER-REAGAN PRESIDENTIAL ELECTION DEBATE (1980)

The 1980 Presidential election came at a tumultuous moment for America domestically and abroad. The United States had experienced a major energy crisis from 1977 to 1979, during which oil prices shot up and political leaders asked Americans to conserve fuel. The domestic economy also suffered during the energy crisis, as inflation rose and growth slowed. In July 1979, President Jimmy Carter gave a speech bemoaning the "crisis of confidence" in America, which came to be known as his "malaise" speech. Internationally, the Carter administration could not resolve the Iran Hostage Crisis, in which 52 Americans were imprisoned in the U.S. embassy in Tehran after the Iranian Revolution. Carter's opponent in the 1980 election was Ronald Reagan, a former actor and former Governor of California. In contrast to Carter, Reagan often projected a sense of optimism in the future of America. One of Reagan's campaign commercials, "Morning in America," predicted American renewal if Reagan were elected. On October 28, 1980, just one week before the election, the two men held their only debate in Cleveland, Ohio. The debate became famous for Reagan's retort "There you go again" in response to Carter's attacks on his record. One week later, Reagan beat Carter in a landslide, signaling the beginning of a conservative era in American politics.

THE NATION'S ECONOMY

MR. ELLIS. Mr. President, when you were elected in 1976, the Consumer Price Index stood at 4.8 percent. It now stands at more than 12 percent. Perhaps more significantly, the Nation's broader, underlying inflation rate has gone up from 7 to 9 percent. Now, a part of that was due to external factors beyond U.S. control, notably the more than doubling of oil prices by OPEC last year.

Because the United States remains vulnerable to such external shocks, can inflation in fact be controlled? If so, what measures would you pursue in a second term?

THE PRESIDENT. Again it's important to put the situation into perspective. In 1974 we had a so-called oil shock, wherein the price of OPEC oil was raised to an extraordinary degree. We had an even worse oil shock in 1979. In 1974 we had the worst recession, the deepest and most penetrating recession since the Second World War. The recession that resulted this time was the briefest we've had since the Second World War.

In addition, we've brought down inflation. Earlier this year, the first quarter, we did have a very severe inflation pressure, brought about by the OPEC price increase. It averaged about 18 percent the first quarter of this year. The second quarter, we had dropped it down to about 13 percent. The most recent figures, the last 3 months, or the third quarter of this year, the inflation rate is 7 percent—still too high, but it illustrates very vividly that in addition to providing an enormous number of jobs—9 million new jobs in the last 3 1/2 years—that the inflationary threat is still urgent on us.

I noticed that Governor Reagan recently mentioned the Reagan-Kemp-Roth proposal, which his own running mate, George Bush, described as voodoo economics, and said that it would result in a 30-percent inflation rate. And *Business Week*, which is

Source: "Presidential Debate in Cleveland," http://www.presidency.ucsb.edu/ws/index.php?pid=29408 (Accessed May 21, 2018).

not a Democratic publication, said that this Reagan-Kemp-Roth proposal—and I quote them, I think—was completely irresponsible and would result in inflationary pressures which would destroy this Nation.

So, our proposals are very sound and very carefully considered to stimulate jobs, to improve the industrial complex of this country, to create tools for American workers, and at the same time would be anti-inflationary in nature. So, to add 9 million new jobs, to control inflation, and to plan for the future with the energy policy now intact as a foundation is our plan for the years ahead. . . .

MR. SMITH. Now, the same question goes to Governor Reagan. . . .

GOVERNOR REAGAN. Mr. Ellis, I think this idea that has been spawned here in our country, that inflation somehow came upon us like a plague and therefore it's uncontrollable and no one can do anything about it, is entirely spurious, and it's dangerous to say this to the people. When Mr. Carter became President, inflation was 4.8 percent, as you said. It had been cut in two by President Gerald Ford. It is now running at 12.7 percent.

President Carter also has spoken of the new jobs created. Well, we always, with the normal growth in our country and increase in population, increase the number of jobs. But that can't hide the fact that there are 8 million men and women out of work in America today, and 2 million of those lost their jobs in just the last few months. Mr. Carter had also promised that he would not use unemployment as a tool to fight against inflation. And yet, his 1980 economic message stated that we would reduce productivity and gross national product and increase unemployment in order to get a handle on inflation, because in January, at the beginning of the year, it was more than 18 percent.

Since then, he has blamed to the people for inflation, OPEC, he's blamed the Federal Reserve System, he has blamed the lack of productivity of the American people, he has then accused the people of living too well and that we must share in scarcity, we must sacrifice and get used to doing with less. We don't have inflation because the people are living too well. We have inflation because the Government is living too well.

And the last statement, just a few days ago, was a speech to the effect that we have inflation because Government revenues have not kept pace with Government spending. I see my time is running out here. I'll have to get this down very fast.

Yes, you can lick inflation by increasing productivity and by decreasing the cost of Government to the place that we have balanced budgets and are no longer grinding out printing press money, flooding the market with it because the Government is spending more than it takes in. And my economic plan calls for that.

The President's economic plan calls for increasing the taxes to the point that we finally take so much money away from the people that we can balance the budget in that way. But we'll have a very poor nation and a very unsound economy if we follow that path. . . .

INTERNATIONAL TERRORISM

MS. WALTERS. Mr. President, the eyes of the country tonight are on the hostages in Iran. I realize this is a sensitive area, but the question of how we respond to acts of terrorism goes beyond this current crisis. Other countries have policies that determine how they will respond. Israel, for example, considers hostages like soldiers and will not negotiate with terrorists.

For the future, Mr. President, the country has the right to know, do you have a policy for dealing with terrorism wherever it might happen, and what have we learned from this experience in Iran that might cause us to do things differently if this or something similar happens again?

THE PRESIDENT. Barbara, one of the blights on this world is the threat and the activities of terrorists. At one of the recent economic summit conferences between myself and the other leaders of the Western world, we committed ourselves to take strong action against terrorism. Airplane hijacking was one of the elements of that commitment. There is no doubt that we have seen in recent years, in recent months, additional acts of violence against Jews in France and, of course, against those who live in Israel by the PLO and other terrorist organizations.

Ultimately, the most serious terrorist threat is if one of those radical nations, who believe in terrorism as a policy, should have atomic weapons. Both I and all my predecessors have had a deep commitment to controlling the proliferation of nuclear weapons in countries like Libya or Iraq. We have even alienated some of our closest trade partners, because we have insisted upon the control of the spread of nuclear weapons to those potentially terrorist countries.

When Governor Reagan has been asked about that, he makes a very disturbing comment that nonproliferation, or the control of the spread of nuclear weapons, is none of our business. And when he was asked specifically, recently, about Iraq, he said there's nothing we can do about it.

This ultimate terrorist threat is the most fearsome of all, and it's part of a pattern where our country must stand firm to control terrorism of all kinds. . . .

I have been accused lately of having a secret plan with regard to the hostages. Now, this comes from an answer that I've made at least 50 times during this campaign to the press. The question would be, "Have you any ideas of what you would do if you were there?" And I said, well, yes. And I think that anyone that's seeking this position, as well as other people, probably, have thought to themselves, "What about this, what about that?" These are just ideas of what I would think of if I were in that position and had access to the information, in which I would know all the options that were open to me. I have never answered the question, however. Second—the one that says, "Well, tell me, what are some of those ideas?" First of all, I would be fearful that I might say something that was presently under way or in negotiations, and thus expose it and endanger the hostages. And sometimes, I think some of my ideas might involve quiet diplomacy, where you don't say in advance or say to anyone what it is you're thinking of doing.

Your question is difficult to answer, because, in the situation right now, no one wants to say anything that would inadvertently delay, in any way, the return of those hostages if there is a chance of their coming home soon, or that might cause them harm.

What I do think should be done, once they are safely here with their families and that tragedy is over—and we've endured this humiliation for just lacking 1 week of a year now—then, I think, it is time for us to have a complete investigation as to the diplomatic efforts that were made in the beginning, why they have

been there so long, and when they come home, what did we have to do in order to bring that about, what arrangements were made? And I would suggest that Congress should hold such an investigation.

In the meantime, I'm going to continue praying that they'll come home. . . .

SOCIAL SECURITY

MR. HILLIARD. Governor Reagan, wage earners in this country—especially the young—are supporting a social security system that continues to affect their income drastically. The system is fostering a struggle between the young and the old, and is drifting the country toward a polarization of these two groups. How much longer can the young wage earner expect to bear the ever-increasing burden of the social security system?

GOVERNOR REAGAN. The social security system was based on a false premise, with regard to how fast the number of workers would increase and how fast the number of retirees would increase. It is actuarially out of balance, and this first became evident about 16 years ago, and some of us were voicing warnings then. Now, it is trillions of dollars out of balance, and the only answer that has come so far is the biggest single tax increase in our Nation's history, the payroll tax increase for social security, which will only put a Band-aid on this and postpone the day of reckoning by a few years at most. . . .

THE PRESIDENT. As long as there's a Democratic President in the White House, we will have a strong and viable social security system, free of the threat of bankruptcy. Although Governor Reagan has changed his position lately, on four different occasions he has advocated making social security a voluntary system, which would, in effect, very quickly bankrupt it. I noticed also in the *Wall Street Journal* earlier this week that a preliminary report of his task force advocates making social security more sound by reducing the adjustments in social security for the retired people to compensate for the impact of inflation. These kinds of approaches are very dangerous to the security and the well-being, and the peace of mind of the retired people of this country and those approaching retirement age. . . .

MR. SMITH. Governor Reagan.

GOVERNOR REAGAN. Well, that just isn't true. It has, as I said, delayed the actuarial imbalance falling on us for just a few years with that increase in taxes. And I don't believe we can go on increasing the tax, because the problem for the young people today is that they're paying in far more than they can ever expect to get out.

Now, again this statement that somehow I wanted to destroy it, and I just changed my tune, that I am for voluntary social security, which would mean the ruin of it. Mr. President, the voluntary thing that I suggested many years ago was that a young man, orphaned and raised by an aunt who died, his aunt was ineligible for social security insurance, because she was not his mother. And I suggested that if this is an insurance program, certainly the person who's paying in should be able to name his own beneficiaries. And that's the closest I've ever come to anything voluntary with social security. I, too, am pledged to a social security program that will reassure these senior citizens of ours they're going to continue to get their money.

These are some changes I'd like to make. I would like to make a change that discriminates in the regulations against a wife who works and finds that she then is faced with a choice between her husband's benefits, if he dies first, or what she has paid in; but it does not recognize that she has also been paying in herself, and she is entitled to more than she presently can get. I'd like to change that.

MR. SMITH. President Carter's rebuttal now.

THE PRESIDENT. Fine. These constant suggestions that the basic social security system should be changed does cause concern and consternation among the aged of our country. It's obvious that we should have a commitment to them, that social security benefits should not be taxed, and that there would be no peremptory change in the standards by which social security payments are made to the retired people. We also need to continue to index the social security payments so that if inflation rises, the social security payments would rise a commensurate degree to let the buying power of the social security check continue intact.

In the past, the relationship between social security and Medicare has been very important to provide some modicum of aid for senior citizens in the retention of health benefits. Governor Reagan, as a matter of fact, began his political career campaigning around this Nation against Medicare. Now we have an opportunity to move toward national health insurance, with an emphasis on the prevention of disease; an emphasis on outpatient care, not inpatient care; an emphasis on hospital cost containment to hold down the cost of hospital care for those who are ill; an emphasis on catastrophic health insurance, so that if a family is threatened with being wiped out economically because of a very high medical bill, then the insurance would help pay for it. These are the kind of elements of a national health insurance, important to the American people. Governor Reagan, again, typically is against such a proposal.

MR. SMITH. Governor.

GOVERNOR REAGAN. There you go again. [Laughter]

When I opposed Medicare, there was another piece of legislation meeting the same problem before the Congress. I happened to favor the other piece of legislation and thought that it would be better for the senior citizens and provide better care than the one that was finally passed. I was not opposing the principle of providing care for them. I was opposing one piece of legislation as versus another.

There is something else about social security—of course, that doesn't come out of the payroll tax; it comes out of the general fund—that something should be done about. I think it's disgraceful that the Disability Insurance Fund in social security finds checks going every month to tens of thousands of people who are locked up in our institutions for crime or for mental illness, and they are receiving disability checks from social security every month while a State institution provides for all of their needs and their care. . . .

QUESTIONS TO CONSIDER

1. What did the two men especially highlight?
2. Which candidate would have appealed to you more if you were watching the debate?

28.5 JESSE JACKSON, ADDRESS TO THE DEMOCRATIC NATIONAL CONVENTION (1988)

The American activist, minister, and politician Jesse Jackson has had a long and varied career. He worked for Martin Luther King, Jr.'s Southern Christian Leadership Conference during the civil rights movement, and he continued working for the organization until 1971, when he left to form People United to Save Humanity (Operation PUSH). In 1984, Jackson decided to move into politics and founded the Rainbow Coalition, a political civil rights organization, for his run for the Democratic nomination. He finished a surprising third place in the primary that year and decided to run again for the Democratic nomination in 1988. That time, Jackson surprised political commentators and nearly won the primary, being narrowly defeated by Michael Dukakis, who went on to lose the election to George H. W. Bush. Jackson gave the following address at the 1988 Democratic National Convention. In it, he asked Americans to join together and defended the role of government in American society. Today, Jackson continues to be a major political activist.

Thank you. Thank you. Thank you.

Tonight, we pause and give praise and honor to God for being good enough to allow us to be at this place, at this time. When I look out at this convention, I see the face of America: Red, Yellow, Brown, Black and White. We are all precious in God's sight—the real rainbow coalition.

(Applause) . . .

My right and my privilege to stand here before you has been won, won in my lifetime, by the blood and the sweat of the innocent.

Twenty-four years ago, the late Fannie Lou Hamer and Aaron Henry—who sits here tonight from Mississippi—were locked out into the streets in Atlantic City; the head of the Mississippi Freedom Democratic Party.

But tonight, a Black and White delegation from Mississippi is headed by Ed Cole, a Black man from Mississippi; 24 years later. (Applause)

Many were lost in the struggle for the right to vote: Jimmy Lee Jackson, a young student, gave his life; Viola Liuzzo, a White mother from Detroit, called nigger lover, had her brains blown out at point blank range; [Michael] Schwerner, [Andrew] Goodman and [James] Chaney—two Jews and a Black—found in a common grave, bodies riddled with bullets in Mississippi; the four darling little girls in a church in Birmingham, Alabama. They died that we might have a right to live.

Dr. Martin Luther King Jr. lies only a few miles from us tonight. Tonight he must feel good as he looks down upon us. We sit here together, a rainbow, a coalition—the sons and daughters of slavemasters and the sons and daughters of slaves, sitting together around a common table, to decide the direction of our party and our country. His heart would be full tonight.

As a testament to the struggles of those who have gone before; as a legacy for those who will come after; as a tribute to the endurance, the patience, the courage of our forefathers and mothers; as an assurance that their prayers are being answered, their work has not been in vain, and hope is eternal; tomorrow night my name will go into nomination for the Presidency of the United States of America.

Source: "Address by The Reverend Jesse Louis Jackson," https://www.pbs.org/wgbh/pages/frontline/jesse/speeches/jesse88speech.html (Accessed May 21, 2018). Copyright © Jesse L. Jackson Sr. All rights reserved. Reprinted here with permission.

We meet tonight at the crossroads, a point of decision. Shall we expand, be inclusive, find unity and power; or suffer division and impotence?

We've come to Atlanta, the cradle of the old South, the crucible of the new South. Tonight, there is a sense of celebration, because we are moved, fundamentally moved from racial battlegrounds by law, to economic common ground. Tomorrow we will challenge to move to higher ground.

Common ground! Think of Jerusalem, the intersection where many trails met. A small village that became the birthplace for three religions—Judaism, Christianity and Islam. Why was this village so blessed? Because it provided a crossroads where different people met, different cultures, different civilizations could meet and find common ground. When people come together, flowers always flourish—the air is rich with the aroma of a new spring.

Take New York, the dynamic metropolis. What makes New York so special? It's the invitation of the Statue of Liberty, "Give me your tired, your poor, your huddled masses who yearn to breathe free." Not restricted to English only. (Applause) Many people, many cultures, many languages—with one thing in common, they yearn to breathe free. Common ground!

Tonight in Atlanta, for the first time in this century, we convene in the South; a state where Governors once stood in school house doors; where Julian Bond was denied a seat in the State Legislature because of his conscientious objection to the Vietnam War; a city that, through its five Black Universities, has graduated more black students than any city in the world. (Applause) Atlanta, now a modern intersection of the new South.

Common ground! That's the challenge of our party tonight. Left wing. Right wing.

Progress will not come through boundless liberalism nor static conservatism, but at the critical mass of mutual survivalIt takes two wings to fly. Whether you're a hawk or a dove, you're just a bird living in the same environment, in the same world. . . .

When we divide, we cannot win. We must find common ground as the basis for survival and development and change, and growth. (Applause) . . .

. . . Politics can be a moral arena where people come together to find common ground.

We find common ground at the plant gate that closes on workers without notice. We find common ground at the farm auction, where a good farmer loses his or her land to bad loans or diminishing markets. Common ground at the school yard where teachers cannot get adequate pay, and students cannot get a scholarship, and can't make a loan. Common ground at the hospital admitting room, where somebody tonight is dying because they cannot afford to go upstairs to a bed that's empty waiting for someone with insurance to get sick. We are a better nation than that. We must do better. (Applause)

Common ground. What is leadership if not present help in a time of crisis? So I met you at the point of challenge. In Jay, Maine, where paper workers were striking for fair wages; in Greenville, Iowa, where family farmers struggle for a fair price; in Cleveland, Ohio, where working women seek comparable worth; in McFarland, California, where the children of Hispanic farm workers may be dying from poisoned land, dying in clusters with cancer; in an AIDS hospice in Houston, Texas, where the sick support one another, too often rejected by their own parents and friends.

Common ground. America is not a blanket woven from one thread, one color, one cloth. When I was a child growing up in Greenville, South Carolina[,] my grandmama could not afford a blanket, she didn't complain and we did not freeze. Instead she took pieces of old cloth—patches, wool, silk, gabardine, crocker sack—only patches, barely good enough to wipe off your shoes with. But they didn't stay that way very long. With sturdy hands and a strong cord, she sewed them together into a quilt, a thing of beauty and power and culture. Now, Democrats, we must build such a quilt.

Farmers, you seek fair prices and you are right—but you cannot stand alone. Your patch is not big enough. Workers, you fight for fair wages, you are right—but your patch of labor is not big enough. Women, you seek comparable worth and pay equity, you are right—but your patch is not big enough. (Applause)

Women, mothers, who seek Head Start, and day care and prenatal care on the front side of life, relevant jail care and welfare on the back side of life—you are right—but your patch is not big enough. Students, you seek scholarships, you are right—but your patch is not big enough. Blacks and Hispanics, when we fight for civil rights, we are right—but our patch is not big enough.

Gays and lesbians, when you fight against discrimination and a cure for AIDS, you are right—but your patch is not big enough. Conservatives and progressives, when you fight for what you believe, right wing, left wing, hawk, dove, you are right from your point of view, but your point of view is not enough.

But don't despair. Be as wise as my grandmama. Pull the patches and the pieces together, bound by a common thread. When we form a great quilt of unity and common ground, we'll have the power to bring about health care and housing and jobs and education and hope to our Nation. (Standing ovation)

We, the people, can win!

We stand at the end of a long dark night of reaction. We stand tonight united in the commitment to a new direction. For almost eight years we've been led by those who view social good coming from private interest, who view public life as a means to increase private wealth. They have been prepared to sacrifice the common good of the many to satisfy the private interests and the wealth of a few.

We believe in a government that's a tool of our democracy in service to the public, not an instrument of the aristocracy in search of private wealth. We believe in government with the consent of the governed, "of, for and by the people." We must now emerge into a new day with a new direction.

Reaganomics. Based on the belief that the rich had too little money and the poor had too much. That's classic Reaganomics. They believe that the poor had too much money and the rich had too little money so they engaged in reverse Robin Hood—took from the poor and gave to the rich, paid for by the middle class. We cannot stand four more years of Reaganomics in any version, in any disguise. (Applause)

How do I document that case? Seven years later, the richest 1 percent of our society pays 20 percent less in taxes. The poorest 10 percent pay 20 percent more. Reaganomics. . . .

If an issue is morally right, it will eventually be political. It may be political and never be right. Fanny Lou Hamer didn't have the most votes in Atlantic City, but her principles have outlasted the life of every delegate who voted to lock her out. Rosa Parks did not have the most votes, but she was morally right. Dr. King didn't have the most votes about the Vietnam War, but he was morally right. If we are principled first, our politics will fall in place. "Jesse, why do you take these big bold initiatives?" A poem by an unknown author went something like this: "We mastered the air, we conquered the sea, annihilated distance and prolonged life, but we're not wise enough to live on this earth without war and without hate."

As for Jesse Jackson: "I'm tired of sailing my little boat, far inside the harbor bar. I want to go out where the big ships float, out on the deep where the great ones are. And should my frail craft prove too slight for waves that sweep those billows o'er, I'd rather go down in the stirring fight than drowse to death at the sheltered shore."

We've got to go out, my friends, where the big boats are. (Applause)

And then for our children. Young America, hold your head high now. We can win. We must not lose to the drugs, and violence, premature pregnancy, suicide, cynicism, pessimism and despair. We can win. Wherever you are tonight, now I challenge you to hope and to dream. Don't submerge your dreams. Exercise above all else, even on drugs, dream of the day you are drug free. Even in the gutter, dream of the day that you will be up on your feet again.

You must never stop dreaming. Face reality, yes, but don't stop with the way things are. Dream of things as they ought to be. Dream. Face pain, but love, hope, faith and dreams will help you rise above the pain. Use hope and imagination as weapons of survival and progress, but you keep on dreaming, young America. Dream of peace. Peace is rational and reasonable. War is irrational in this age, and unwinnable.

Dream of teachers who teach for life and not for a living. Dream of doctors who are concerned more about public health than private wealth. Dream of lawyers more concerned about justice than a judgeship. Dream of preachers who are concerned more about prophecy than profiteering. Dream on the high road with sound values.

And then America, as we go forth to September, October, November and then beyond, America must never surrender to a high moral challenge.

Do not surrender to drugs. The best drug policy is a "no first use." Don't surrender with needles and cynicism. (Applause) Let's have "no first use" on the one hand, or clinics on the other. Never surrender, young America. Go forward.

America must never surrender to malnutrition. We can feed the hungry and clothe the naked. We must never surrender. We must go forward.

We must never surrender to inequality. Women cannot compromise ERA or comparable worth. Women are making 60 cents on the dollar to what a man makes. Women cannot buy meat cheaper. Women cannot buy bread cheaper. Women cannot buy mil k cheaper. Women deserve to get paid for the work that you do. (Applause) It's right and it's fair. (Applause)

Don't surrender, my friends. Those who have AIDS tonight, you deserve our compassion. Even with AIDS you must not surrender.

In your wheelchairs. I see you sitting here tonight in those wheelchairs. I've stayed with you. I've reached out to you across our Nation. Don't you give up. I know it's tough sometimes. People look down on you. It took you a little more effort to get here tonight. And no one should look down on you, but sometimes mean people do. The only justification we have for looking down on someone is that we're going to stop and pick them up.

But even in your wheelchairs, don't you give up. We cannot forget 50 years ago when our backs were against the wall, Roosevelt was in a wheelchair. I would rather have Roosevelt in a wheelchair than Reagan and Bush on a horse. (Applause) Don't you surrender and don't you give up. Don't surrender and don't give up!

Why can I challenge you this way? "Jesse Jackson, you don't understand my situation. You be on television. You don't understand. I see you with the big people. You don't understand my situation."

I understand. You see me on TV, but you don't know the me that makes me, me. They wonder, "Why does Jesse run?" because they see me running for the White House. They don't see the house I'm running from. (Applause)

I have a story. I wasn't always on television. Writers were not always outside my door. When I was

born late one afternoon, October 8th, in Greenville, South Carolina, no writers asked my mother her name. Nobody chose to write down our address. My mama was not supposed to make it, and I was not supposed to make it. You see, I was born of a teen-age mother, who was born of a teen-age mother.

I understand. I know abandonment, and people being mean to you, and saying you're nothing and nobody and can never be anything.

I understand. Jesse Jackson is my third name. I'm adopted. When I had no name, my grandmother gave me her name. My name was Jesse Burns until I was 12. So I wouldn't have a blank space, she gave me a name to hold me over. I understand when nobody knows your name. I understand when you have no name.

I understand. I wasn't born in the hospital. Mama didn't have insurance. I was born in the bed at [the] house. I really do understand. Born in a three-room house, bathroom in the backyard, slop jar by the bed, no hot and cold running water.

I understand. Wallpaper used for decoration? No. For a windbreaker. I understand. I'm a working person's person. That's why I understand you whether you're Black or White.

I understand work. I was not born with a silver spoon in my mouth. I had a shovel programmed for my hand.

My mother, a working woman. So many of the days she went to work early, with runs in her stockings. She knew better, but she wore runs in her stockings so that my brother and I could have matching socks and not be laughed at at school. I understand.

At 3 o'clock on Thanksgiving Day, we couldn't eat turkey because momma was preparing somebody else's turkey at 3 o'clock. We had to play football to entertain ourselves. And then around 6 o'clock she would get off the Alta Vista bus and we would bring up the leftovers and eat our turkey—leftovers, the carcass, the cranberries—around 8 o'clock at night. I really do understand.

Every one of these funny labels they put on you, those of you who are watching this broadcast tonight in the projects, on the corners, I understand. Call you outcast, low down, you can't make it, you're nothing, you're from nobody, subclass, underclass; when you see Jesse Jackson, when my name goes in nomination, your name goes in nomination. (Applause)

I was born in the slum, but the slum was not born in me. (Applause) And it wasn't born in you, and you can make it. (Applause)

Wherever you are tonight, you can make it. Hold your head high, stick your chest out. You can make it. It gets dark sometimes, but the morning comes. Don't you surrender. Suffering breeds character, character breeds faith. In the end faith will not disappoint.

You must not surrender. You may or may not get there but just know that you're qualified. And you hold on, and hold out. We must never surrender. America will get better and better.

Keep hope alive. (Applause) Keep hope alive. (Applause) Keep hope alive. On tomorrow night and beyond, keep hope alive! (Applause)

I love you very much. (Applause) I love you very much. (Standing ovation and spontaneous demonstration)

QUESTIONS TO CONSIDER

1. How did Jackson defend his argument?
2. Do you find the argument persuasive?

CHAPTER 29

THE GLOBALIZED NATION, 1989–2001

29.1 MICHAEL C. SEKORA, WARNING TO CONGRESS ABOUT THE IMPACT OF GLOBALIZATION (1991)

In the 1980s and early 1990s, certain American commentators became worried about the nation's competitiveness in the global economy and globalization's impact on U.S. industries. American productivity was relatively low during the period, so some people feared what the future might hold. In 1991, the House Subcommittee on Technology and Competiveness held a hearing on "Globalization of Manufacturing: Implications for U.S. Competitiveness." Michael C. Sekora, a former Defense Intelligence Agency employee who left government to start an advising firm for U.S. corporations dealing with globalization, was one of the hearing's witnesses. In Sekora's statement, he broadcast strong views about the need for greater governmental intervention to retain American competitiveness in the changing global economic landscape.

Thank you, Mr. Chairman, I appreciate this opportunity to appear before you today to discuss the globalization of manufacturing and R&D. This is an issue which plays a key role in the present and future economic health of the United States. I am encouraged by the Subcommittee's actions to address this issue, and would like to provide my support to the effort in any manner the Subcommittee deems appropriate.

I am not as well known as the other gentlemen on the two panels, so let me start out by briefly explaining where I gained my experience with the issue being addressed today.

In 1983, as an official of the Defense Intelligence Agency, I initiated and directed the Socrates Project to address lagging U.S. competitiveness. Project Socrates was designed to provide the United States with a strategic level science and technology planning capability which would enable the country to effectively acquire and utilize worldwide S&T to achieve a significant competitive advantage. Project Socrates was designed by examining the methods used by our most successful commercial adversaries to gain their competitive advantage.

In 1990, I resigned as the Project Socrates director and formed a corporation, Technology Strategic

Source: Michael Sekora testimony to the Subcommittee on Technology and Competitiveness of the Committee on Science, Space and Technology, 102nd Congress, 1st Session (Washington D.C.: U.S. Government Printing Office, 1991), 99–101.

Planning, Inc., to provide strategic level S&T planning directly to U.S. corporations. My comments today will be based upon my experience both from the Federal side, as past director of Project Socrates, and from the private side, as president of TSP Inc.

The key to the globalization of manufacturing issue is not the physical location in which the manufacturing occurs. The key is the location of those who control the technology which is required to execute the manufacturing. In order to assure our current competitive position while also maintaining the technology and skill base required for future growth and development, control of this technology must reside within the United States.

The world is rapidly evolving to the point where the most valuable resource is becoming the technology commodity. The technology commodity together with the natural resources, for example, people, are what enables a company to produce the product or provide the services to satisfy their client's needs which, in turn, results in generating the economic commodity for the company—the money. In the past, the natural resources were viewed as the most valuable resources. But now the technology commodity has begun to evolve to the point where with the proper technology a company can satisfy their client's needs from a variety of natural resources, therefore negating the power of the natural resource. Control of the technology commodity is rapidly becoming the key to competitiveness today and in the future.

The globalization of manufacturing issue is a problem for the U.S because of two key facts. First, our European and Japanese adversaries have realized for years that the technology commodity is the most valuable resource and have planned and continue to plan accordingly. Second, the U.S corporations and Government, for the most part, do not view technology as a commodity let alone a valuable resource. As a result, the U.S. decisionmakers do not base their planning on the technology commodity and do not comprehend a foreign organization's planning that is based on it.

So the real issue is not as simple as whether the globalization of manufacturing is good or bad. Rather, the issue is multi-faceted with the key part being the effective utilization and control of the worldwide technology commodity. To effectively utilize and control the worldwide technology commodity the organizations' decisionmakers must engage in strategic level S&T planning.

Strategic level S&T planning is the ability of an organization to effectively acquire and utilize worldwide S&T to achieve their objectives. It is based on the premise that every S&T in the world is simultaneously a potential threat and simultaneously a potential resource and it is up to the company's planners to try to dictate whether each S&T becomes a resource or a threat so as to best accomplish the organization's objectives.

All technology strategies consist of two parts: An offense and a defense. The offense consists of maneuvers that acquire—i.e., co-production, joint development, license, R&D, the technology—and utilize the most effective worldwide technology. The defense consists of maneuvers to prevent the company's adversaries from acquiring the technologies the adversaries require and counter the adversaries['] effective utilization of the acquired technology.

The key to strategic level S&T planning is the integration of all of the maneuvers which acquire and utilize technology by the organization into a coherent plan that most effectively and efficiently utilizes the limited worldwide S&T resource. An effective technology strategy is philosophically the same as a winning military strategy. Both strategies are successful because they effectively utilize many small maneuvers in a highly orchestrated manner to exploit many small limited resources. This point was demonstrated by the U.S. military in Operation Desert Storm. Neither the military nor the business technology strategies is successful by deploying one single grand maneuver with one single resource.

Strategic level S&T planning has been developed and used by our foreign adversaries against the U.S. since the end of World War II. One result of their utilization of strategic level S&T planning has been their ability to locate their manufacturing and R&D facilities outside of their country that enable them to be competitive in the short and long term. They have been able to do this by balancing the acquisition, utilization, and protection of the technology and economic commodities they require to accomplish their objectives. The effective balancing of these two resources to gain a competitive advantage is not a simple task. It has taken Japan roughly 40 years to advance to the point in their technology strategies where they have a major competitive advantage over the U.S. The U.S companies and Government will not overcome this 40-plus year advantage in experience overnight. It will take a dedicated effort lasting many years.

Let me jump to the conclusion. In conclusion, to effectively understand and then address the globalization of manufacturing issue, the U.S decisionmakers, both industry and Government, must abandon their economic-based planning mentality and start examining the issue from a technology commodity perspective. Once this is accomplished, the U.S. decisionmakers will be in a position to start making and executing plans that enable the U.S companies to win at the global manufacturing game.

Thank you.

QUESTIONS TO CONSIDER

1. What was Sekora's view of globalization?
2. How did he propose to address globalization's impact? Does his argument make sense to you?

29.2 NATIONAL SECURITY COUNCIL, EXCERPT FROM "DEFENSE PLANNING GUIDANCE" (1992)

In addition to fears about globalization (see Reading 29.1), the U.S. government also began to formulate new military policies for the post–Cold War era. In March 1992, a few months after the dissolution of the Soviet Union, the Department of Defense formulated a set of guidelines for future U.S. foreign policy. The end of the Cold War clearly affected the document, as much of it revolved around future American unilateral action or preemptive military strikes. American leaders seemed to prepare for a world in which the United States was the only superpower. The *New York Times* obtained the initial document, which sparked an outcry in response to its support of imperialist ideas. Subsequently, U.S. Secretary of Defense Dick Cheney and Chairman of the Joint Chiefs of Staff Colin Powell rewrote the document and softened its language. The following document is excerpted from the revised version. This version, however, still provides insight into the mindset of American military leaders after the Cold War.

This Defense Planning Guidance addresses the fundamentally new situation which has been created by the collapse of the Soviet Union—the disintegration of the internal as well as the external empire, and the discrediting of Communism as an ideology with global pretensions and influence. The new international environment has also been shaped by the victory of the United States and its Coalition allies over Iraqi aggression—the first post–Cold War conflict and a defining event in U.S. global leadership. In addition to these two great successes, there has been a less visible one, the integration of the leading democracies into a U.S.-led system of collective security and the creation of a democratic "zone of peace."

Our fundamental strategic position and choices are therefore very different from those we have faced in the past. The policies that we adopt in this new situation will set the nation's direction for the next century. Guided by a fundamentally new defense strategy, we have today a compelling opportunity to meet our defense needs at lower cost. As we do so, we must not squander the position of security we achieved at great sacrifice through the Cold War, nor eliminate our ability to shape the future security environment in ways favorable to us and those who share our values.

I. DEFENSE POLICY GOALS

The national security interests of the United States are enduring, as outlined in the President's 1991 National Security Strategy Report: the survival of the United States as a free and independent nation, with its fundamental values intact and its institutions and people secure; a healthy and growing U.S economy to ensure opportunity for individual prosperity and resources for national endeavors at home and abroad; healthy, cooperative and politically vigorous relations with allies and friendly nations; and a stable and secure world, where political and economic freedom, human rights and democratic institutions flourish.

These national security interests can be translated into four mutually supportive strategic goals that guide our overall defense efforts:

- Our most fundamental goal is to deter or defeat attack from whatever source, against the United States, its citizens and forces, and to honor our historic and treaty commitments.

Source: "Defense Planning Guidance, FY 1994–1999," https://www.archives.gov/files/declassification/iscap/pdf/2008-003-docs1-12.pdf (Accessed June 15, 2018).

- The second goal is to strengthen and extend the system of defense arrangements that binds democratic and like-minded nations together in common defense against aggression, builds habits of cooperation, avoids the renationalization of security policies, and provides security at lower costs and with lower risks for all. Our preference for a collective response to preclude threats or, if necessary, to deal with them is a key feature of our regional defense strategy.

- The third goal is to preclude any hostile power from dominating a region critical to our interests, and also thereby to strengthen the barriers against the reemergence of a global threat to the interests of the U.S. and our allies. These regions include Europe, East Asia, the Middle East/Persian Gulf, and Latin America. Consolidated, nondemocratic control of the resources of such a critical region could generate a significant threat to our security.

- The fourth goal is to reduce sources of regional instability and limit violence should conflict occur, by encouraging the spread and consolidation of democratic government and open economic systems, and discouraging the spread of destructive technology, particularly of weapons of mass destruction and the means to deliver them. To this end, we must encourage other nations to respect the rule of law and each other's economic, social, ethnic, and political interests.

To reach these goals, the United States must show the leadership necessary to encourage sustained cooperation among major democratic powers. The alternative would be to leave our critical interests and the security of our friends dependent upon individual efforts that could be duplicative, competitive, or ineffective. We must also encourage and assist Russia, Ukraine, and the other new republics of the former Soviet Union in establishing democratic political systems and free markets so they too can join the democratic "zone of peace."

A collective response will not always be timely and, in the absence of U.S. leadership, may not gel. While the United States cannot become the world's policeman and assume responsibility for solving every international security problem, neither can we allow our critical interests to depend solely on international

mechanisms that can be blocked by countries whose interests may be very different from our own. Where our allies['] interests are directly affected, we must expect them to take an appropriate share of the responsibility, and in some cases play the leading role; but we must maintain the capabilities for addressing selectively those security problems that threaten our own interests. Such capabilities are essential to our ability to lead, and should international support prove sluggish or inadequate, to act independently, as necessary, to protect our critical interests. . . .

We cannot lead if we fail to maintain the high quality of our forces as we reduce and restructure them. As a nation we have never before succeeded in pacing reductions without endangering our interests. We must proceed expeditiously, but at a pace that avoids breaking the force or sending misleading signals about our intentions to friends or potential aggressors. An effective reconstitution capability is important as well, since it signals that no potential rival could quickly or easily gain a predominant military position.

At the end of World War I, and again to a lesser extent at the end of World War II, the United States as a nation made the mistake of believing that we had achieved a kind of permanent security, that a transformation of the security order achieved through extraordinary American sacrifice could be sustained without our leadership and significant American forces. Today, a great challenge has passed; but other threats endure, and new ones will arise. If we reduce our forces carefully, we will be left with a force capable of implementing the new defense strategy. We will have given ourselves the means to lead common efforts to meet future challenges and to shape the future environment in ways that will give us greater security at lower cost.

II. THE REGIONAL DEFENSE STRATEGY

A. REGIONAL FOCUS

The demise of the global threat posed by Soviet Communism leaves America and its allies with an unprecedented opportunity to preserve with greater ease a security environment within which our democratic ideals can prosper. We can shift our defense planning from a focus on the global threat posed by the Warsaw Pact to a focus on the less demanding regional threats and challenges we are more likely to face in the future.

In this way, we can work to shape the future environment and to preclude hostile nondemocratic powers from dominating regions critical to us. This same approach will also work to preclude the emergence of a hostile power that could present a global security threat comparable to the one the Soviet Union presented in the past. In so doing we can provide the underpinnings of a peaceful international order in which nations are able to pursue their legitimate interests without fear of military domination.

In this more secure international environment there will be enhanced opportunities for political, economic, environmental, social, and security issues to be resolved through new or revitalized international organizations, including the United Nations, or regional arrangements. But the world remains unpredictable and well-armed, causes for conflict persist, and we have not eliminated age-old temptations for nondemocratic powers to turn to force or intimidation to achieve their ends. We must not stand back and allow a new global threat to emerge or leave a vacuum in a region critical to our interests. Such a vacuum cold make countries there feel vulnerable, which in turn can lead to excessive military capabilities and an unsteady balance of one against another. If we do stand back it will be much harder to achieve the enhanced international cooperation for which we hope. . . .

Shaping the Future Security Environment. America cannot base its future security merely on a shaky record of prediction or even a prudent recognition of uncertainty. Sound defense planning seeks as well to help shape the future. Our strategy is designed to anticipate and to encourage trends that advance U.S. security objectives in the future. This is not simply within our means; it is critical to our future security.

The containment strategy we pursued for the past forty years successfully shaped the world we see today. By our refusal to be intimidated by Soviet military power, we and our allies molded a world in which Communism was forced to confront its contradictions. Even as we and our allies carried the defense burden required in the Cold War, democracy was able to develop and flourish.

One of the primary tasks we face today in shaping the future is carrying long standing alliances into the new era, and turning old enmities into new cooperative relationships. If we and other leading democracies continue to build a democratic security community, a much safer world is likely to emerge. If we act separately, many other problems could result. If we can assist former Warsaw Pact countries, including republics of the former Soviet Union, particularly Russia and Ukraine, in choosing a steady course of democratic progress and reduced military forces subject to responsible, civilian democratic control, we will have successfully secured the fruits of forty years of effort. Our goal should be to bring a democratic Russia and the other new democracies into the defense community of democratic nations, so that they can become a force for peace not only in Europe but also in other critical regions of the world.

Cooperative defense arrangements enhance security, while reducing the defense burden for everyone. In the absence of effective defense cooperation, regional rivalries cold lead to tensions or even hostilities that would threaten to bring critical regions under hostile domination. It is not in our interest or those of the other democracies to return to earlier periods in which multiple military powers balanced one another off in what passed for security structures, while regional, or even global peace hung in the balance. As in the past, such struggles might eventually force the U.S. at much higher cost to protect its interests and counter the potential development of a new global threat.

Maintaining highly capable forces is critical to sustaining the U.S. leadership with which we can shape the future. Such leadership supports collective defense arrangements and precludes hostile competitors from challenging our critical interests. Our fundamental belief in democracy and human rights gives other nations confidence that we will use our significant military power only as a force for peaceful democratic progress.

Strategic Depth. America's strategic position is stronger than it has been for decades. Today, there is no global challenger to a peaceful democratic order. There are no significant hostile alliances. To the contrary, the strongest and most capable countries in the world remain our friends. The threat of global, even nuclear war, once posed by massive Warsaw Pact forces poised at the inner German border, first receded hundreds of miles east and has since transformed into the promise of a new era of strategic cooperation.

Not only has our position improved markedly with respect to the passing of a global challenge, but our strategic position has improved in regional contexts as well. Today, no region of the world critical to our interests is under hostile, nondemocratic domination. Near-term threats in critical regions are small, relative to our capabilities and those of our friends and allies. Soviet Communism no longer exacerbates local conflicts, and we need no longer be concerned that an otherwise remote problem could affect the balance of power between us and a hostile global challenger. We have won great depth for our strategic position.

In this regard, it is important to note the effect on our strategy of the fact that the international system is no longer characterized by Cold War bi-polarity. The Cold War required the United States and its allies to be prepared to contain the spread of Soviet power on a global basis. Developments in even remote areas could affect the United States' relative position in the world, and therefore often required a U.S. response. The United States remains a nation with global interests, but we must reexamine in light of the new defense strategy whether and to what extent particular challenges engage our interests. These changes and the growing strength of our friends and allies will allow us to be more selective in determining the extent to which U.S. forces must be committed to safeguard shared interests.

The first major conflict of the post–Cold War era preserved our strategic position in one of the regions of the world critical to our interests. Our success in organizing an international coalition in the Persian Gulf against Saddam Hussein kept a critical region from the control of a ruthless dictator bent on developing nuclear, biological and chemical weapons and harming Western interests. Instead of a more radical Middle East/ Persian Gulf region under Saddam's influence, Saddam struggles to retain control in Iraq, Iraq's dangerous military has been greatly damaged, our ties with moderate states are stronger, oil flows in adequate amounts at reasonable prices, and Arabs and Israelis have for the first time in many years met to discuss peace.

Our strategy is designed to preserve this position by keeping our alliances strong and our threats small. Our tools include political and economic measures and others such as security assistance, military-to-military

contacts, humanitarian aid and intelligence assistance, as well as security measures to prevent the emergence of a nondemocratic aggressor in critical regions. We bring to this task our considerable moral influence as the world's leading democracy. We can provide more security at a reduced cost. If a hostile power sought to present a regional challenge again, or if a new, antagonistic global threat or alliance emerged in the future, we would have the ability to counter it. But the investments required to maintain the strategic depth that we won through forty years of the Cold War are much smaller than those it took to secure this strategic depth or those that would be required if we lost it.

Continued U.S. Leadership. U.S. leadership, essential for successful resolution of the Cold War, remains critical to achieving our long-term goals in this new era. The United States continues to prefer to address hostile, nondemocratic threats to our interests wherever possible through collective security efforts that take advantage of the strength of our allies and friends. However, sustained U.S. leadership will be essential for maintaining those alliances and for otherwise protecting our interests.

The sense that regional aggression could be opposed by the U.S. will be an important factor in inducing nations to work together to stabilize crises and resist or defeat aggression. For most countries, a general interest in international stability and security will not be enough to induce them to put themselves at risk simply in the hope that others will join them. Only a nation that is strong enough to act decisively can provide the leadership needed to encourage others to resist aggression. Collective security failed in the 1930s because no strong power was willing to provide the leadership behind which less powerful countries could rally against Fascism. It worked in the Gulf because the United States was willing and able to provide that leadership. Thus, even when a broad potential coalition exists, leadership will be necessary to actualize it.

The perceived capability of the U.S. to act independently, if necessary, is thus an important factor even in those cases where we do not actually do so. It will not always be incumbent upon us to assume a leadership role. In some cases, we will promote the assumption of leadership by others, such as the United Nations or regional organizations. But we will not ignore the need to be prepared to protect our critical interests and honor our commitments with only limited additional help, or even alone, if necessary. A future President will thus need to have options that will allow him to lead and, where the international reaction proves sluggish or inadequate, to act to protect our critical interests. In the end, there is no contradiction between U.S. leadership and multilateral action; history shows it is precisely U.S. leadership [that] is the necessary prerequisite for effective international action.

As a nation, we have paid dearly in the past for letter our capabilities fall and our will be questioned. There is a moment in time when a smaller, ready force can preclude an arms race, a hostile move or a conflict. Once lost, that moment cannot be recaptured by many thousands of soldiers poised on the edge of combat. Our efforts to rearm and to understand our danger before World War II come too late to spare us and others a global conflagration. Five years after our resounding global victory in World War II, we were nearly pushed off the Korean peninsula by a third rate power. We erred in the past when we failed to plan forces befitting our role in the world. And we paid dearly for our error. . .

In the decade ahead, we must adopt the right combination of deterrent forces, tactical and strategic, while creating the proper balance between offense and active defense to mitigate risk from weapons of mass destruction and their means of delivery, whatever the source. For now this requires retaining ready forces for a secure nuclear deterrent, including tactical forces. In addition, we must complete needed offensive modernization and upgrades. These offensive forces need to be complemented with early introduction of ballistic missile defenses.

Forward Presence. Our forward presence helps to shape the evolving security environment. We will continue to rely on forward presence of U.S. forces to show U.S. commitment and lend credibility to our alliances, to deter aggression, enhance regional stability, promote U.S. influence and access, and, when necessary, provide an initial crisis response capability. Forward presence is vital to the maintenance of the system of collective defense by which the United States has been able to work with our friends and allies to protect our security interests, while minimizing the burden of defense spending and of unnecessary arms competition. . . .

We should plan to continue a wide range of forward presence activities, including not only overseas basing of forces, but prepositioning and periodic deployments, exercises, exchanges or visits. Forward basing of forces and the prepositioning of equipment facilitate rapid reinforcement and enhance the capability to project forces into vital strategic areas.

QUESTIONS TO CONSIDER

1. What strategies does the document most highlight?
2. Do the strategies make sense to you for the post–Cold War world?

29.3 NEWT GINGRICH, SPEECH TO CONGRESS INTRODUCING THE "CONTRACT WITH AMERICA" (1995)

During his first two years in office, President Bill Clinton tried and failed to implement comprehensive health care reform, and the economy lagged. Republicans seized the opportunity and, in the 1994 midterm elections, experienced a wave election, which ushered the Republican Party into the House of Representatives majority for the first time in forty years. Newt Gingrich, a Republican Congressman from Georgia, led the charge and would become Speaker of the House of Representatives after Republicans won the majority. While campaigning, Gingrich disseminated a "Contract with America," which, he promised, Republicans would implement if they took the House majority. Much of the Contract involved diminishing the size of government—lowering taxes, reforming welfare, and deregulating parts of the economy, among other things. After Republicans took control, Gingrich reintroduced the Contract during his first speech as Speaker of the House. In the end, Gingrich did not manage to implement much of the Contract, and he eventually resigned from Congress in 1999 after his leadership shutdown the government and a House investigation disciplined him for ethics violations. The "Contract with America," however, provides crucial insight into the ideals that propelled the conservative revolution of the 1980s and 1990s.

Let me say first of all that I am deeply grateful to my good friend, DICK GEPHARDT. When my side maybe overreacted to your statement about ending 40 years of Democratic rule. I could not help but look over at Bob Michel, who has often been up here and who knows that everything DICK said was true. This is difficult and painful to lose, and on my side of the aisle, we have for 20 elections been on the losing side. Yet there is something so wonderful about the process by which a free people decides things.

In my own case, I lost two elections, and with the good help of my friend VIC FAZIO came close to losing two others. I am sorry, guys, it just did not quite work out. Yet I can tell you that every time when the polls closed and I waited for the votes to come in, I felt good. Because win or lose, we have been part of this process.

In a little while, I am going to ask the dean of the House, JOHN DINGELL, to swear me in, to insist on the bipartisan nature of the way in which we together work in this House. JOHN'S father was one of the great stalwarts of the New Deal, a man who, as an FDR Democrat, created modern America. I think that JOHN and his father represent a tradition that we all have to recognize and respect, and recognize that the America we are now going to try to lead grew from that tradition and is part of that great heritage. . . .

This is a historic moment. I was asked over and over, how did it feel, and the only word that comes close to adequate is overwhelming. I feel overwhelmed in every way, overwhelmed by all the Georgians who came up, overwhelmed by my extended family that is here, overwhelmed by the historic moment. I walked out and stood on the balcony just outside of the Speaker's office, looking down the Mall this morning, very early. I was just overwhelmed by the view, with two men I will introduce and know very, very well. Just

Source: New Gingrich Speech to the House of Representatives, 104th Congress, 1st Session, *Congressional Record* (January 4, 1995): 442–446.

the sense of being part of America, being part of this great tradition, is truly overwhelming.

I have two gavels. Actually, DICK happened to use one. Maybe this was appropriate. This was a Georgia gavel I just got this morning, done by Dorsey Newman of Tallapoosa. He decided that the gavels he saw on TV weren't big enough or strong enough, so he cut down a walnut tree in his backyard, made a gavel, put a commemorative item on it, and sent it up here.

So this is a genuine Georgia gavel, and I am the first Georgia Speaker in over 100 years. The last one, by the way, had a weird accent, too. Speaker Crisp was born in Britain. His parents were actors and they came to the United States—a good word, by the way, for the value we get from immigration. . . .

We are starting the 104th Congress. I do not know if you have ever thought about this, but for 208 years, we bring together the most diverse country in the history of the world. We send all sorts of people here. Each of us could find at least one member we thought was weird. I will tell you, if you went around the room the person chosen to be weird would be different for virtually every one of us. Because we do allow and insist upon the right of a free people to send and extraordinary diversity of people here.

Brian Lamb of C-SPAN read to me Friday a phrase from de Tocqueville that was so central to the House. I have been reading Remini's biography of Henry Clay and Clay, as the first strong Speaker, always preferred the House to the Senate although he served in both. He said the House is more vital. More active. More dynamic, and more common.

This is what de Tocqueville wrote: "Often there is not a distinguished man in the whole number. Its members are almost all obscure individuals whose names bring no associations to mind. They are mostly village lawyers, men in trade, or even persons belonging to the lower classes of society."

If we include women. I do not know that we would change much. But the word "vulgar" in de Tocqueville's time had a very particular meaning. It is a meaning the world would do well to study in this room. You see, de Tocqueville was an aristocrat. He lived in a world of kings and prices. The folks who come here do so by the one single act that their citizens freely chose them. I do not care what your ethnic background is, or your ideology. I do not care if you are born in America of if you

are a naturalized citizen. Every one of the 435 people have equal standing because their citizens freely sent them. Their voice should be heard and they should have a right to participate. It is the most marvelous act of a complex giant country trying to argue and talk. And, as DICK GEPHARDT said, to have a great debate, to reach great decisions, not through a civil war, not by bombing one of our regional capitals, not by killing a half million people, and not by having snipers. Let me say unequivocally, I condemn all acts of violence against the law by all people for all reasons. This is a society of law and a society of civil behavior.

Here we are as commoners together, to some extent Democrats and Republicans, to some extent liberals and conservatives, but Americans all. STEVE GUNDERSON today gave me a copy of the "Portable Abraham Lincoln." He suggested there is much for me to learn about our party, but I would also say that it does not hurt to have a copy of the portable F.D.R.

This is a great country of great people. If there is any one factor or acts of my life that strikes me as I stand up here as the first Republican in 40 years to do so. When I first became whip in 1989, Russia was beginning to change, the Soviet Union as it was then. Into my whip's office one day came eight Russians and a Lithuanian, members of the Communist Party, newspaper editors. They asked me, "What does a whip do?"

They said, "In Russia we have never had a free parliament since 1917 and that was only for a few months, so what do you do?"

I tried to explain, as DAVE BONIOR or TOM DELAY might now. It is a little strange if you are from a dictatorship to explain you are called the whip but you do not really have a whip, you are elected by the people you are supposed to pressure—other members. If you pressure them too much they will not reelect you. On the other hand, if you do not pressure them enough they will not reelect you. Democracy is hard. It if frustrating.

So our group came into the Chamber. The Lithuanian came into the Chamber. The Lithuanian was a man in his late sixties, and I allowed him to come up here and sit and be Speaker, something many of us have done with constituents. Remember, this is the very beginning of perestroika and glasnost. When he came out of the chair, he was physically trembling. He was almost in tears. He said, "Ever since World War II, I have remembered what the Americans did and I have never believed the propaganda. But I have to tell you, I did not think in my life that I would be able to sit at the center of freedom."

It was one of the most overwhelming, compelling moments of my life. It struck me that something I could not help but think of when we were here with President Mandela. I went over and saw RON DELLUMS and thought of the great work RON had done to extend freedom across the planet. You get that sense of emotion when you see something so totally different than you had expected. Here was a man who reminded me first of all that while presidents are important, they are in effect an elected kingship, that this and the other body across the way are where freedom has to be fought out. That is the tradition I hope that we will take with us as we go to work. . . .

I want to read just a part of the Contract With America. I don't mean this as a partisan act, but rather to remind all of us what we are about to go through and why. Those of us who ended up in the majority stood on these steps and signed a contract, and here is part of what it says:

On the first day of the 104th Congress the new Republican majority will immediately pass the following reforms aimed at restoring the faith and trust of the American people in their government: First, require all laws that apply to the rest of the country also to apply equally to the Congress. Second, select a major, independent auditing firm to conduct a comprehensive audit of the Congress for waste, fraud or abuse. Third, cut the number of House committees and cut committee staffs by a third. Fourth, limit the terms of all committee chairs. Fifth, ban the casting of proxy votes in committees. Sixth, require committee meetings to be open to the public. Seven, require a three-fifths majority vote to pass a tax increase. Eight, guarantee an honest accounting of our federal budget by implementing zero baseline budgeting.

Now, I told DICK GEPHARDT last night that if I had to do it over again we would have pledged within 3 days that we will do these things, but that is not what we said. So we have ourselves in a little bit of a box here.

Then we go a step further. I carry the T.V. Guide version of the contract with me at all times.

We then say that within the first 100 days of the 104th Congress we shall bring to the House floor the following bills, each to be given full and open debate, each to be given full and clear vote, and each to be immediately available that day. We listed 10 items. A balanced budget amendment and line-item veto, a bill to stop violent criminals, emphasizing among other things an effective and enforceable death penalty. Third was welfare reform. Fourth, legislation protecting our kids. Fifth was to provide tax cuts for families. Sixth was a bill to strengthen our national defense. Seventh was a bill to raise the senior citizens' earning limit. Eighth was legislation rolling back Government regulations. Ninth was a commonsense legal reform bill, and tenth was congressional term limits legislation.

Our commitment on our side, and this is an absolute obligation, is first of all to work today until we are done. I know that is going to inconvenience people who have families and supporters. But we were hired to do a job, and we have to start today to prove we will do it. Second, I would say to our friends in the Democratic Party that we are going to work with you, and we are really laying out a schedule working with the minority leader to make sure that we can set dates certain to go home. That does mean that if 2 or 3 weeks out we are running short we will, frankly, have longer sessions on Tuesday, Wednesday, and Thursday. We will try to work this out on a bipartisan basis to, in a workmanlike way, get it done. It is going to mean the busiest early months since 1933.

Beyond the Contract I think there are two giant challenges. I know I am a partisan figure. But I really hope today that I can speak for a minute to my friends in the Democratic Party as well as my own colleagues, and speak to the country about these two challenges so that I hope we can have a real dialog. One challenge is to achieve a balanced budget by 2002. I think both Democratic and Republican Governors will say we can do that but it is hard. I do not think we can do it in a year or two. I do not think we ought to lie to the American people. This is a huge, complicated job.

The second challenge is to find a way to truly replace the current welfare state with an opportunity society.

Let me talk very briefly about both challenges. First, on the balanced budget I think we can get it done. I think the baby boomers are now old enough that we can have an honest dialog about priorities, about resources, about what works, and what does not work. Let me say I have already told Vice President GORE that we are going to invite him to address a Republican conference. We would have invited him in December but he had to go to Moscow. I believe there are grounds for us to talk together and to work together, to have hearings together, and to have task forces together. If we set priorities, if we apply the principles of Edwards Deming and of Peter Drucker we can build on the Vice President's reinventing government effort and we can focus on transforming, not just cutting. The choice becomes not just do you want more or do you want less but are there ways to do it better? Can we learn from the private sector, can we learn from Ford, IBM, from Microsoft, from what General Motors has had to go through? I think on a bipartisan basis we owe it to our children and grandchildren to get this Government in order and to be able to actually pay our way. I think 2002 is a reasonable timeframe. I would hope that together we could open a dialog with the American people.

I have said that I think Social Security ought to be off limits, at least for the first 4 to 6 years of the process, because I think it will just destroy us if we try to bring it into the game. But let me say about everything else, whether it is Medicare, or it is agricultural subsidies, or it is defense or anything that I think the greatest Democratic President of the 20th century, and in my judgment the greatest President of the 20th century, said it right. On March 4, 1933, he stood in braces as a man who had polio at a time when nobody who had that kind of disability could be anything in public life. He was President of the United States. and he stood in front of this Capitol on a rainy March day and he said, "We have nothing to fear but fear itself." I want every one of us to reach out in that spirit and pledge to live up to that spirit, and I think frankly on a bipartisan basis. I would say to Members of the Black and Hispanic Caucuses that I would hope we could arrange by late spring to genuinely share districts. You could have a Republican who frankly may not know a thing about your district agree to come for a long weekend with you, and you will agree to go for a long weekend with them. We begin a dialog and an openness that is totally different than people are used to seeing in politics in America. I believe if we do that we can then create a dialog that can lead to a balanced budget.

But I think we have a greater challenge. I do want to pick up directly on what DICK GEPHARDT said, because he said it right. No Republican here should kid

themselves about it. The greatest leaders in fighting for an integrated America in the 20th century were in the Democratic Party. The fact is it was the liberal wing of the Democratic Party that ended segregation. The fact is that it was Franklin Delano Roosevelt who gave hope to a Nation that was in distress and could have slid into dictatorship. Every Republican has much to learn from studying what the Democrats did right.

But I would say to my friends in the Democratic Party that there is much to what Ronald Reagan was trying to get done. There is much to what is being done today by Republicans like Bill Weld, and John Engler, and Tommy Thompson, and George Allen, and Christy Whitman, and Pete Wilson. There is much we can share with each other.

We must replace the welfare state with an opportunity society. The balanced budget is the right thing to do. But it does not in my mind have the moral urgency of coming to grips with what is happening to the poorest Americans.

I commend to all Marvin Olasky's "The Tragedy of American Compassion." Olasky goes back for 300 years and looked at what has worked in America. how we have helped people rise beyond poverty, and how we have reached out to save people. He may not have the answers, but he has the right sense of where we have to go as Americans.

I do not believe that there is a single American who can see a news report of a 4-year-old thrown off of a public housing project in Chicago by other children and killed and not feel that a part of your heart went, too. I think of my nephew in the back, Kevin, and how all of us feel about our children. How can any American read about an 11-year-old buried with his teddy bear because he killed a 14-year-old, and then another 14-year-old killed him, and not have some sense of "My God, where has this country gone?" How can we not decide that this is a moral crisis equal to segregation, equal to slavery? How can we not insist that every day we take steps to do something?

I have seldom been more shaken than I was after the election when I had breakfast with two members of the Black Caucus. One of them said to me, "Can you imagine what it is like to visit a first-grade class and realize that every fourth or fifth young boy in that class may be dead or in jail within 15 years? And they are your constituents and you are helpless to change it?" For some reason. I do not know why, maybe because I visit a lot schools, that got through. I mean, that personalized it. That made it real, not just statistics, but real people.

Then I tried to explain part of my thoughts by talking about the need for alternatives to the bureaucracy, and we got into what I think frankly has been a pretty distorted and cheap debate over orphanages.

Let me say, first of all, my father, who is here today, was a foster child. He was adopted as a teenager. I am adopted. We have relatives who were adopted. We are not talking out of some vague impersonal Dickens "Bleak House" middle-class intellectual model. We have lived the alternatives.

I believe when we are told that children are so lost in the city bureaucracies that there are children who end up in dumpsters, when we are told that there are children doomed to go to schools where 70 or 80 percent of them will not graduate, when we are told of public housing projects that are so dangerous that if any private sector ran them they would be put in jail, and the only solution we are give is, "Well, we will study it. we will get around to it," my only point is that this is unacceptable. We can find ways immediately to do things better, to reach out, break through the bureaucracy and give every young American child a better chance.

Let me suggest to you Morris Schectman's new book. I do not agree with all of it, but it is fascinating. It is entitled "Working Without a Net." It is an effort to argue that in the 21st century we have to create our own safety nets. He draws a distinction between caring and caretaking. It is worth every American reading.

He said caretaking is when you bother me a little bit, and I do enough, I feel better because I think I took care of you. That is not any good to you at all. You may be in fact an alcoholic and I just gave you the money to buy the bottle that kills you, but I feel better and go home. He said caring is actually stopping and dealing with the human being, trying to understand enough about them to genuinely make sure you improve their life, even if you have to start with a conversation like, "If you will quit drinking, I will help you get a job." This is a lot harder conversation than, "I feel better. I gave him a buck or 5 bucks."

I want to commend every Member on both sides to look carefully. I say to those Republicans who believe in total privatization, you cannot believe in the Good Samaritan and explain that as long as business is making money we can walk by a fellow American who is hurt and not do something. I would say to my friends on the left who believe there has never been a government program that was not worth keeping, you cannot look at some of the results we now have and not want to reach out to the humans and forget the bureaucracies. . . .

But I want to close by reminding all of us of how much bigger this is than us. Because beyond talking with the American people, beyond working together, I think we can only be successful if we start with our limits. I was very struck this morning with something Bill Emerson used, a very famous quote of Benjamin Franklin, at the point where the Constitutional Convention was deadlocked. People were tired, and there was a real possibility that the Convention was going to break up. Franklin, who was quite old and had been relatively quiet for the entire Convention, suddenly stood up and was angry and he said:

> I have lived, sir, a long time, and the longer I live the more convincing proofs I see of this truth, that God governs in the affairs of men, and if a sparrow cannot fall to the ground without His notice, is it possible that an empire can rise without His aid?

At that point the Constitutional Convention stopped. They took a day off for fasting and prayer.

Then, having stopped and come together, they went back, and they solved the great question of large and small States. They wrote the Constitution, and the United States was created. All I can do is pledge to you that, if each of us will reach out prayerfully and try to genuinely understand each other, if we will recognize that in this building we symbolize America, and that we have an obligation to talk with each other, then I think a year from now we can look on the 104th Congress as a truly amazing institution without regard to party, without regard to ideology. We can say, "Here, America comes to work, and here we are preparing for those children a better future."

Thank you. Good luck and God bless you.

QUESTIONS TO CONSIDER

1. What kinds of things did Gingrich emphasize?
2. Why do you think the "Contract with America" was popular?

29.4 BILL CLINTON, SECOND INAUGURAL ADDRESS (1997)

After the Republican wave election in 1994, Bill Clinton did not seem to have great prospects for reelection. Clinton had won handily the 1992 election over George H. W. Bush by projecting an image of charismatic vitality and American optimism. As mentioned in the introduction to Reading 29.4, however, his first term did not produce his promised health care reform, and the Republicans took the House of Representatives for the first time in forty years. Two years later, though, the economy improved, and Clinton benefited from the lackluster campaign of Republican Bob Dole and the third-party candidacy of Ross Perot and the Reform Party. The Republican Party did maintain majorities in the Senate and the House of Representative, so as Clinton took to the stage for his second inaugural address, he did not necessarily claim a mandate. Instead, he struck an optimistic and bipartisan tone based on a faith in American progress. Clinton would serve out his second term—including surviving an impeachment trial after he lied about an affair with twenty-two-year-old intern Monica Lewinsky—and depart from office as one of the most popular presidents in American history.

My fellow citizens, at this last Presidential Inauguration of the 20th century, let us lift our eyes toward the challenges that await us in the next century. It is our great good fortune that time and chance have put us not only at the edge of a new century, in a new millennium, but on the edge of a bright new prospect in human affairs, a moment that will define our course and our character for decades to come. We must keep our old democracy forever young. Guided by the ancient vision of a promised land, let us set our sights upon a land of new promise.

The promise of America was born in the 18th century out of the bold conviction that we are all created equal. It was extended and preserved in the 19th century, when our Nation spread across the continent, saved the Union, and abolished the awful scourge of slavery.

Then, in turmoil and triumph, that promise exploded onto the world stage to make this the American Century. And what a century it has been. America became the world's mightiest industrial power, saved the world from tyranny in two World Wars and a long cold war, and time and again reached out across the globe to millions who, like us, longed for the blessings of liberty.

Along the way, Americans produced a great middle class and security in old age, built unrivaled centers of learning and opened public schools to all, split the atom and explored the heavens, invented the computer and the microchip, and deepened the wellspring of justice by making a revolution in civil rights for African-Americans and all minorities and extending the circle of citizenship, opportunity, and dignity to women.

Now, for the third time, a new century is upon us and another time to choose. We began the 19th century with a choice: to spread our Nation from coast to coast. We began the 20th century with a choice: to harness the industrial revolution to our values of free enterprise, conservation, and human decency. Those

Source: "William Clinton: Second Inaugural Address," http://www.presidency.ucsb.edu/ws/index.php?pid=54183 (Accessed May 21, 2018).

choices made all the difference. At the dawn of the 21st century, a free people must now choose to shape the forces of the information age and the global society, to unleash the limitless potential of all our people, and yes, to form a more perfect Union.

When last we gathered, our march to this new future seemed less certain than it does today. We vowed then to set a clear course to renew our Nation. In these 4 years, we have been touched by tragedy, exhilarated by challenge, strengthened by achievement. America stands alone as the world's indispensable nation. Once again, our economy is the strongest on Earth. Once again, we are building stronger families, thriving communities, better educational opportunities, a cleaner environment. Problems that once seemed destined to deepen, now bend to our efforts. Our streets are safer, and record numbers of our fellow citizens have moved from welfare to work. And once again, we have resolved for our time a great debate over the role of Government. Today we can declare: Government is not the problem, and Government is not the solution. We—the American people—we are the solution. Our Founders understood that well and gave us a democracy strong enough to endure for centuries, flexible enough to face our common challenges and advance our common dreams in each new day.

As times change, so Government must change. We need a new Government for a new century, humble enough not to try to solve all our problems for us but strong enough to give us the tools to solve our problems for ourselves, a Government that is smaller, lives within its means, and does more with less. Yet where it can stand up for our values and interests around the world, and where it can give Americans the power to make a real difference in their everyday lives, Government should do more, not less. The preeminent mission of our new Government is to give all Americans an opportunity, not a guarantee but a real opportunity, to build better lives.

Beyond that, my fellow citizens, the future is up to us. Our Founders taught us that the preservation of our liberty and our Union depends upon responsible citizenship. And we need a new sense of responsibility for a new century. There is work to do, work that Government alone cannot do: teaching children to read, hiring people off welfare rolls, coming out from behind locked doors and shuttered windows to help

reclaim our streets from drugs and gangs and crime, taking time out of our own lives to serve others.

Each and every one of us, in our own way, must assume personal responsibility not only for ourselves and our families but for our neighbors and our Nation. Our greatest responsibility is to embrace a new spirit of community for a new century. For any one of us to succeed, we must succeed as one America. The challenge of our past remains the challenge of our future: Will we be one Nation, one people, with one common destiny, or not? Will we all come together, or come apart?

The divide of race has been America's constant curse. And each new wave of immigrants gives new targets to old prejudices. Prejudice and contempt cloaked in the pretense of religious or political conviction are no different. These forces have nearly destroyed our Nation in the past. They plague us still. They fuel the fanaticism of terror. And they torment the lives of millions in fractured nations all around the world.

These obsessions cripple both those who hate and of course those who are hated, robbing both of what they might become. We cannot, we will not, succumb to the dark impulses that lurk in the far regions of the soul everywhere. We shall overcome them. And we shall replace them with the generous spirit of a people who feel at home with one another. Our rich texture of racial, religious, and political diversity will be a godsend in the 21st century. Great rewards will come to those who can live together, learn together, work together, forge new ties that bind together.

As this new era approaches, we can already see its broad outlines. Ten years ago, the Internet was the mystical province of physicists; today, it is a commonplace encyclopedia for millions of schoolchildren. Scientists now are decoding the blueprint of human life. Cures for our most feared illnesses seem close at hand. The world is no longer divided into two hostile camps. Instead, now we are building bonds with nations that once were our adversaries. Growing connections of commerce and culture give us a chance to lift the fortunes and spirits of people the world over. And for the very first time in all of history, more people on this planet live under democracy than dictatorship.

My fellow Americans, as we look back at this remarkable century, we may ask, can we hope not just to follow but even to surpass the achievements of the 20th century in America and to avoid the awful bloodshed that stained its legacy? To that question, every American here and every American in our land today must answer a resounding, "Yes!" This is the heart of our task. With a new vision of Government, a new sense of responsibility, a new spirit of community, we will sustain America's journey.

The promise we sought in a new land, we will find again in a land of new promise. In this new land, education will be every citizen's most prized possession. Our schools will have the highest standards in the world, igniting the spark of possibility in the eyes of every girl and every boy. And the doors of higher education will be open to all. The knowledge and power of the information age will be within reach not just of the few but of every classroom, every library, every child. Parents and children will have time not only to work but to read and play together. And the plans they make at their kitchen table will be those of a better home, a better job, the certain chance to go to college.

Our streets will echo again with the laughter of our children, because no one will try to shoot them or sell them drugs anymore. Everyone who can work, will work, with today's permanent under class part of tomorrow's growing middle class. New miracles of medicine at last will reach not only those who can claim care now but the children and hard-working families too long denied.

We will stand mighty for peace and freedom and maintain a strong defense against terror and destruction. Our children will sleep free from the threat of nuclear, chemical, or biological weapons. Ports and airports, farms and factories will thrive with trade and innovation and ideas. And the world's greatest democracy will lead a whole world of democracies.

Our land of new promise will be a nation that meets its obligations, a nation that balances its budget but never loses the balance of its values, a nation where our grandparents have secure retirement and health care and their grandchildren know we have made the reforms necessary to sustain those benefits for their time, a nation that fortifies the world's most productive economy even as it protects the great natural bounty of our water, air, and majestic land. And in this land of new promise, we will have reformed our politics so that the voice of the people will always speak louder than the din of narrow interests, regaining the participation and deserving the trust of all Americans.

Fellow citizens, let us build that America, a nation ever moving forward toward realizing the full potential of all its citizens. Prosperity and power, yes, they are important, and we must maintain them. But let us never forget, the greatest progress we have made and the greatest progress we have yet to make is in the human heart. In the end, all the world's wealth and a thousand armies are no match for the strength and decency of the human spirit.

Thirty-four years ago, the man whose life we celebrate today spoke to us down there, at the other end of this Mall, in words that moved the conscience of a nation. Like a prophet of old, he told of his dream that one day America would rise up and treat all its citizens as equals before the law and in the heart. Martin Luther King's dream was the American dream. His quest is our quest: the ceaseless striving to live out our true creed. Our history has been built on such dreams and labors. And by our dreams and labors, we will redeem the promise of America in the 21st century.

To that effort I pledge all my strength and every power of my office. I ask the Members of Congress here to join in that pledge. The American people returned to office a President of one party and a Congress of another. Surely they did not do this to advance the politics of petty bickering and extreme partisanship they plainly deplore. No, they call on us instead to be repairers of the breach and to move on with America's mission. America demands and deserves big things from us, and nothing big ever came from being small. Let us remember the timeless wisdom of Cardinal Bernardin, when facing the end of his own life. He said, "It is wrong to waste the precious gift of time on acrimony and division."

Fellow citizens, we must not waste the precious gift of this time. For all of us are on that same journey of our lives, and our journey, too, will come to an end. But the journey of our America must go on.

And so, my fellow Americans, we must be strong, for there is much to dare. The demands of our time are great, and they are different. Let us meet them with faith and courage, with patience and a grateful, happy heart. Let us shape the hope of this day into the noblest chapter in our history. Yes, let us build our bridge, a bridge wide enough and strong enough for every American to cross over to a blessed land of new promise.

May those generations whose faces we cannot yet see, whose names we may never know, say of us here that we led our beloved land into a new century with the American dream alive for all her children, with the American promise of a more perfect Union a reality for all her people, with America's bright flame of freedom spreading throughout all the world.

From the height of this place and the summit of this century, let us go forth. May God strengthen our hands for the good work ahead, and always, always bless our America.

QUESTIONS TO CONSIDER

1. What things did Clinton focus on most?
2. If you had listened to or watched the address, would you have felt optimistic about the next four years?

29.5 ABC NEWS INTERVIEW WITH OSAMA BIN LADEN (1998)

Osama Bin Laden (1957–2011) is most infamous for his planning of the September 11, 2001, attacks on the World Trade Center and the Pentagon, but he had been an internationally known terrorist figure long before those. Bin Laden created the terrorist organization al-Qaeda in 1988, and he began attacking American targets via bombings in 1992. In the following 1998 interview, Bin Laden outlined his views on the United States and defended his use of terrorism. American Special Forces eventually killed Bin Laden in a 2011 raid on his compound in Pakistan.

In the first part of this interview which occurred in May 1998, a little over two months before the U.S. embassy bombings in Kenya and Tanzania, Osama bin Laden answers questions posted to him by some of his followers as his mountaintop camp in southern Afghanistan. In the latter part of the interview, ABC reporter John Miller is asking the questions.

[QUESTIONS POSED BY FOLLOWERS]

. . . **What is the meaning of your call for Muslims to take arms against America in particular, and what is the message that you wish to send to the West in general?**

The call to wage war against America was made because America has spear-headed the crusade against the Islamic nation, sending tens of thousands of its troops to the land of the two Holy Mosques over and above its meddling in its affairs and its politics, and its support of the oppressive, corrupt and tyrannical regime that is in control. These are the reasons behind the singling out of America as a target. And not exempt of responsibility are those Western regimes whose presence in the region offers support to the American troops there. We know at least one reason behind the symbolic participation of the Western forces and that is to support the Jewish and Zionist plans for expansion of what is called the Great Israel. Surely, their presence is not out of concern over their interests in the region. . . . Their presence has no meaning save one and that is to offer support to the Jews in Palestine who are in need of their Christian brothers to achieve

Source: "Interview with Osama Bin Laden: May 1998," *PBS Frontline,* https://www.pbs.org/wgbh/pages/frontline/shows/binladen/who/interview.html (Accessed May 21, 2018). Reprinted with permission of ABC News. All rights reserved.

full control over the Arab Peninsula which they intend to make an important part of the so called Greater Israel. . . .

Many of the Arabic as well as the Western mass media accuse you of terrorism and of supporting terrorism. What do you have to say to that?

There is an Arabic proverb that says "she accused me of having her malady, then snuck away." Besides, terrorism can be commendable and it can be reprehensible. Terrifying an innocent person and terrorizing him is objectionable and unjust, also unjustly terrorizing people is not right.

Whereas, terrorizing oppressors and criminals and thieves and robbers is necessary for the safety of people and for the protection of their property. There is no doubt in this. Every state and every civilization and culture has to resort to terrorism under certain circumstances for the purpose of abolishing tyranny and corruption. Every country in the world has its own security system and its own security forces, its own police and its own army. They are all designed to terrorize whoever even contemplates to attack that country or its citizens. The terrorism we practice is of the commendable kind for it is directed at the tyrants and the aggressors and the enemies of Allah, the tyrants, the traitors who commit acts of treason against their own countries and their own faith and their own prophet and their own nation. Terrorizing those and punishing them are necessary measures to straighten things and to make them right. Tyrants and oppressors who subject the Arab nation to aggression ought to be punished. The wrongs and the crimes committed against the Muslim nation are far greater than can be covered by this interview. America heads the list of aggressors against Muslims. The recurrence of aggression against Muslims everywhere is proof enough. For over half a century, Muslims in Palestine have been slaughtered and assaulted and robbed of their honor and of their property. Their houses have been blasted, their crops destroyed. And the strange thing is that any act on their part to avenge themselves or to lift the injustice befalling them causes great agitation in the United Nations which hastens to call for an emergency meeting only to convict the victim and to censure the wronged and the tyrannized whose children have been killed and

whose crops have been destroyed and whose farms have been pulverized. . . .

In today's wars, there are no morals, and it is clear that mankind has descended to the lowest degrees of decadence and oppression. They rip us of our wealth and of our resources and of our oil. Our religion is under attack. They kill and murder our brothers. They compromise our honor and our dignity and dare we utter a single word of protest against the injustice, we are called terrorists. This is compounded injustice. And the United Nations insistence to convict the victims and support the aggressors constitutes a serious precedence which shows the extent of injustice that has been allowed to take root in this land. . . .

In your last statement, there was a strong message to the American government in particular. What message do you have for the European governments and the West in general?

Praise be Allah and prayers and peace upon Mohammed. With respect to the Western governments that participated in the attack on the land of the two Holy Mosques regarding it as ownerless, and in the siege against the Muslim people of Iraq, we have nothing new to add to the previous message. What prompted us to address the American government in particular is the fact that it is on the head of the Western and the crusading forces in their fight against Islam and against Muslims. The two explosions that took place in Riyadh and in Khobar recently were but a clear and powerful signal to the governments of the countries which willingly participated in the aggression against our countries and our lives and our sacrosanct symbols. It might be beneficial to mention that some of those countries have begun to move towards independence from the American government with respect to the enmity that it continues to show towards the Muslim people. We only hope that they will continue to move in that direction, away from the oppressive forces that are fighting against our countries. We[,] however, differentiate between the western government and the people of the West. If the people have elected those governments in the latest elections, it is because they have fallen prey to the Western media which portray things contrary to what they really are. And while the slogans raised by those regimes call for humanity, justice, and peace, the behavior of their governments is completely the opposite. It is not enough for their people to show pain when they see our children being killed in Israeli raids launched by American planes, nor does this serve the purpose. What they ought to do is change their governments which attack our countries. The hostility that America continues to express against the Muslim people has given rise to feelings of animosity on the part of Muslims against America and against the West in general. Those feelings of animosity have produced a change in the behavior of some crushed and subdued groups who, instead of fighting the Americans inside the Muslim countries, went on to fight them inside the United States of America itself.

The Western regimes and the government of the United States of America bear the blame for what might happen. If their people do not wish to be harmed inside their very own countries, they should seek to elect governments that are truly representative of them and that can protect their interests. . . .

The enmity between us and the Jews goes far back in time and is deep rooted. There is no question that war between the two of us is inevitable. For this reason it is not in the interest of Western governments to expose the interests of their people to all kinds of retaliation for almost nothing. It is hoped that people of those countries will initiate a positive move and force their governments not to act on behalf of other states and other sects. This is what we have to say and we pray to Allah to preserve the nation of Islam and to help them drive their enemies out of their land.

American politicians have painted a distorted picture of Islam, of Muslims and of Islamic fighters. We would like you to give us the true picture that clarifies your viewpoint. . . .

The leaders in America and in other countries as well have fallen victim to Jewish Zionist blackmail. They have mobilized their people against Islam and against Muslims. These are portrayed in such a manner as to drive people to rally against them. The truth is that the whole Muslim world is the victim of international terrorism, engineered by America at the United Nations. We are a nation whose sacred symbols have been looted and whose wealth and resources have

been plundered. It is normal for us to react against the forces that invade our land and occupy it. . . .

JOHN MILLER'S INTERVIEW BEGINS

You come from a background of wealth and comfort to end up fighting on the front lines. Many Americans find that unusual.

This is difficult to understand, especially for him who does not understand the religion of Islam. In our religion, we believe that Allah has created us for the purpose of worshipping him. He is the one who has created us and who has favored us with this religion. Allah has ordered us to make holy wars and to fight to see to it that His word is the highest and the uppermost and that of the unbelievers the lowermost. We believe that this is the call we have to answer regardless of our financial capabilities.

This too answers the claims of the West and of the secular people in the Arab world. They claim that this blessed awakening and the people reverting to Islam are due to economic factors. This is not so. It is rather a grace from Allah, a desire to embrace the religion of Allah. And this is not surprising. When the holy war called, thousands of young men from the Arab Peninsula and other countries answered the call and they came from wealthy backgrounds. Hundreds of them were killed in Afghanistan and in Bosnia and in Chechnya.

You have been described as the world's most wanted man, and there is word that the American government intends to put a price on your head—in the millions—when you are captured. Do you think they will do that? And does it bother you?

We do not care what the Americans believe. What we care for is to please Allah. Americans heap accusations on whoever stands for his religion or his rights or his wealth. . . . It does not scare us that they have put a price on my head. We as Muslims believe that our years on this earth are finite and predetermined. If the whole world gets together to kill us before it is our time to go, they will not succeed. We also believe that livelihoods are preordained. So no matter how much pressure American puts on the regime in Riyadh to freeze our assets and to forbid people from contributing to this great cause, we shall still have Allah to take care of us; livelihood is sent by Allah; we shall not want. . . .

Mr. bin Laden, you have issued a fatwah calling on Muslims to kill Americans where they can, when they can. Is that directed at all Americans, just the American military, just the Americans in Saudi Arabia?

Allah has ordered us to glorify the truth and to defend Muslim land, especially the Arab peninsula . . . against the unbelievers. After World War II, the Americans grew more unfair and more oppressive towards people in general and Muslims in particular. . . . The Americans started it and retaliation and punishment should be carried out following the principle of reciprocity, especially when women and children are involved. Through history, America has not been known to differentiate between the military and the civilians or between men and women or adults and children. Those who threw atomic bombs and used the weapons of mass destruction against Nagasaki and Hiroshima were the Americans. Can the bombs differentiate between military and women and infants and children? America has no religion that can deter her from exterminating whole peoples. Your position against Muslims in Palestine is despicable and disgraceful. America has no shame. . . . We believe that the worst thieves in the world today and the worst terrorists are the Americans. Nothing could stop you except perhaps retaliation in kind. We do not have to differentiate between military or civilian. As far as we are concerned, they are all targets, and this is what the fatwah says. . . . The fatwah is general (comprehensive) and it includes all those who participate in, or help the Jewish occupiers in killing Muslims. . . .

You've been painted in America as a terrorist leader. To your followers, you are a hero. How do you see yourself?

As I have said, we are not interested in what America says. We do not care. We view ourselves and our brothers like everyone else. Allah created us to worship Him and to follow in his footsteps and to be guided by His Book. I am one of the servants of Allah and I obey His orders. Among those is the order to fight for the word of Allah . . . and to fight until the Americans are driven out of all the Islamic countries. . . .

Many Americans believe that fighting army to army like what happened in Afghanistan is heroic for either army. But sending off bombs, killing civilians like in the World Trade Center is terrorism.

. . . After our victory over the Russians in Afghanistan, the international and the American mass media conducted fierce campaigns against us. . . . They called us terrorists even before the mujahedeen had committed any act of terrorism against the real terrorists who are the Americans. On the other hand, we say that American politics and their religion do not believe in differentiating between civilians and military, between infants and animals, or among any human groups. . . .

Our mothers and daughters and sons are slaughtered every day with the approval of America and its support. And, while America blocks the entry of weapons into Islamic countries, it provides the Israelis with a continuous supply of arms allowing them thus to kill and massacre more Muslims. Your religion does not forbid you from committing such acts, so you have no right to object to any response or retaliation that reciprocates your own actions. But, and in spite of this, our retaliation is directed primarily against the soldiers only and against those standing by them. Our religion forbids us from killing innocent people such as women and children. This, however, does not apply to women fighters. A woman who puts herself in the same trench with men, gets what they get. . . .

The American people, by and large, do not know the name bin Laden, but they soon likely will. Do you have a message for the American people?

I say to them that they have put themselves at the mercy of a disloyal government, and this is most evident in Clinton's administration. . . . We believe that this administration represents Israel inside America. Take the sensitive ministries such as the Ministry of Exterior and the Ministry of Defense and the CIA, you will find that the Jews have the upper hand in them. They make use of America to further their plans for the world, especially the Islamic world. American presence in the Gulf provides support to the Jews and protects their rear. And while millions of Americans are homeless and destitute and live in abject poverty, their government is busy occupying our land and building new settlements and helping Israel build new settlements in the point of departure for our Prophet's midnight journey to the seven heavens. America throws her own sons in the land of the two Holy Mosques for the sake of protecting Jewish interests. . . .

The American government is leading the country towards hell. . . . We say to the Americans as people and to American mothers, if they cherish their lives and if they cherish their sons, they must elect an American patriotic government that caters to their interests[,] not the interests of the Jews. If the present injustice continues with the wave of national consciousness, it will inevitably move the battle to American soil, just as Ramzi Yousef and others have done. This is my message to the American people. I urge them to find a serious administration that acts in their interest and does not attack people and violate their honor and pilfer their wealth. . . .

QUESTIONS TO CONSIDER

1. What does Bin Laden cite to defend his terrorism?
2. How does Islam factor into Bin Laden's expressed ideology?

CHAPTER 30

A NATION TRANSFORMED, THE TWENTY-FIRST CENTURY

30.1 HUGO CHAVEZ, SPEECH AT THE UNITED NATIONS (2006)

During the Presidency of George W. Bush, Hugo Chavez emerged as one of the foremost international opponents of American foreign policy. Chavez, a socialist who served as the President of Venezuela from 1999 to 2013, nationalized large portions of that country's economy. Internationally, he preached an ideology of anti-imperialism, opposed to the power of the United States in Central and South America. He asked other Latin American nations to join with Venezuela in rejecting American power. In the following speech at the United Nations in 2006, just one day after Bush spoke to the assembled nations, Chavez called Bush "the Devil" and attacked the United States. The speech provides a different outlook on American foreign policy in the early 2000s. Chavez died of cancer in 2013.

Madam President, Excellencies, Heads of State and Government, and high ranking representatives of governments from across the world. A very good day to you all. . . .

As the spokesperson for imperialism, he came to give us his recipes for maintaining the current scheme of domination, exploitation and pillage over the peoples of the world. His speech perfectly fit an Alfred Hitchcock movie, and I could even dare to suggest a title: "The Devil's Recipe." . . . We cannot allow this to

happen. We cannot allow a world dictatorship to be installed or consolidated.

The statement by the tyrannical president of the world was full of cynicism and hypocrisy. Basically, it is with imperial hypocrisy that he attempts to control everything. They want to impose upon us the democratic model they devised, the false democracy of elites. And, moreover, a very original democratic model, imposed with explosions, bombings, invasions and bullets. What a democracy! In light of this, Aristotle's

Source: "Statement By H. E. Hugo Chavez Frias, President of the Bolivarian Republic of Venezuela, at the 61st United Nations General Assembly," September 20, 2006, http://www.un.org/webcast/ga/61/pdfs/venezuela-e.pdf (Accessed June 16, 2018).

and those theories made by the first Greek thinkers who spoke about democracy shall be reviewed, so as to analyze what kind of democracy that is, one which imposes itself through marines, invasions, aggressions and bombs.

Yesterday, the United States' President said in this same Hall the following, I quote: *"Wherever you look at, you hear extremists telling you that violence, terror and torture can help you escape from misery and recover your dignity."* Wherever he looks he sees extremists. I am sure he sees you, my brother, with your skin color, and he thinks you are an extremist. With his color, the Honorable president of Bolivia, Evo Morales, who came here yesterday, is also an extremist. Imperialists see extremists everywhere. No, we are not extremists, what happens is that the world is waking up, and people are rising up everywhere. I have the feeling, Mister Imperialist Dictator, that you are going to live as if in a nightmare the rest of your days, because no matter where you look at, we will be rising up against the U.S. imperialism. They call us extremists, since we demand total freedom in the world, equality among the peoples, and respect for sovereignty of nations. We are rising up against the Empire, against its model of domination.

Then, the President continued to say, *"Today I want to talk directly to the populations in the Middle East My country desires peace."* It is true that people of the United States want peace; if you walk the streets of the Bronx, or through the streets of New York, Washington, San Diego, California, San Antonio, San Francisco, any city, and you ask people on the streets; definitely, all of them want peace. The difference lies on the fact that their government, the United States' Government, does not want peace; it seeks to impose its model of exploitation, plundering and its hegemony upon us under threat of war. That is the difference. People want peace, and then we wonder what is happening in Iraq? And what happened in Lebanon and Palestine? What has happened after 100 years in Latin America and the world; and most recently the threats against Venezuela, and new threats against Iran?

He addressed the people of Lebanon. *"Many of you—he said—have seen your homes and communities trapped in the middle of crossfire."* What cynicism! What capacity to blatantly lie before the world! Do you consider the bombs in Beirut, launched with such millimetric precision, as crossfire? I believe that the President is referring to those western movies in which cowboys dueled and someone ends up caught in the middle.

Imperialist fire! Fascist fire! Murderous Fire! Genocidal fire against the innocent people of Palestine and Lebanon by the Empire and Israel. That is the truth. Now, they say that "they are suffering" because they see their houses destroyed.

The President of the United States addressed the peoples of Afghanistan, the people of Lebanon and to the people of Iran. Well, one has to wonder, when listening to the U.S. President speak to those people: if those people could talk to him, what would they say?

I am going to answer on behalf of the peoples because I know their soul well, the soul of the peoples of the South, the downtrodden peoples would say: Yankee imperialist, go home! That would be the shout springing up everywhere, if the peoples of the world could speak in unison to the United States' Empire.

Therefore, Madam President, colleagues, and friends, last year we came to this same Hall, as every year over the last eight, and we said something that has been completely confirmed today. I believe that almost no one in this room would dare to stand up and defend the United Nations system, let us admit this with honesty: the United Nations system that emerged after World War II has collapsed, shattered, it does not work anymore.

Of course, the UN is good for coming here once a year to deliver speeches; that is what it is good for. And also to draft very long documents, make good reflections and listen to good speeches . . . But, this Assembly has been turned into a deliberative body, with no power to exert the slightest impact on the terrible reality the world is experiencing. That is why we propose once again, today the 20th of September to join our efforts to rebuild the United Nations. Madam President, last year we presented four modest proposals that we consider cannot be postponed; they must be taken into consideration and discussed by the Heads of State and Government, our Ambassadors and representatives.

First, the expansion of the Security Council—as it was also said by President Lula yesterday, in this same place—both in its permanent and nonpermanent membership categories, envisaging the entry of new developed and developing countries, which is the Third World, as new permanent members.

Secondly, achieve the implementation of effective methods of addressing and resolving world conflicts, transparent methods of debate and decision making.

Thirdly, we consider fundamental the immediate suppression of anti-democratic veto mechanism, the veto power on decisions of the Security Council. This is a common clamor. A recent example is the immoral veto of the U.S. Government, which openly allowed Israel forces to destroy Lebanon just before our eyes, by blocking a solution in the UN Security Council.

. . . .

They fear the truth. The Empire is afraid of the truth and of independent voices, accusing us of being extremists. They are the extremists! . . .

. . . [W]e went happily to Havana. We spent several days there and we could see the birth of a new era: The G-15 Summit, the NAM Summit, with a historical resolution, included in the final document. Don't worry. I am not going to read the whole document. However, this document lists several resolutions drafted in open discussions with transparency by more than 50 Heads of State. Havana was the capital of the South for a week. We have relaunched the Non Aligned Movement, and if there is anything I may ask to you all, my friends, brothers and sisters, is to please lend your support to strengthen the Non Aligned Movement, which has a paramount importance in the birth of a new era, to prevent hegemony and imperialism. Moreover, you all know that we have designated Fidel Castro, as President of the NAM, for a three-year term and we

are convinced that our friend, Fidel Castro, will lead it with much efficiency. For those who wanted Fidel Castro to die, they remained frustrated, because he is once again wearing his olive green uniform, and is now not only the President of Cuba but also the President of the Non Aligned Movement.

Madam President, distinguished colleagues, Presidents, a very strong movement of the South emerged there in Havana. We are men and women of the South. We are bearers of these documents, ideas, opinions, and reflections. I have already closed the folder. . . We attempt to bring new ideas for the salvation of the Planet, for saving it from the threat of imperialism, and god willing soon. Early in this century, we ourselves can see and experience with our children and grandchildren a peaceful world, under the fundamental principles of the United Nations Organization, which will be re-launched and relocated.

I believe the United Nations must be located in another country, in some city of the South. We have proposed this from Venezuela. You all know that my medical personnel had to remain inside the airplane as well as my Chief of Security. They both were denied to enter the United Nations. This is another abuse and an outrage, Madam President[,] that we request to be registered as a personal abuse by the Devil, it smells like sulfur, but God is with us.

A warn embrace and God bless us all.

Thank you.

QUESTIONS TO CONSIDER

1. Why do you think Chavez used such charged rhetoric?
2. How might his rhetoric have made Chavez popular in Venezuela?

30.2 BARACK OBAMA, "A MORE PERFECT UNION" (2008)

Going into the 2008 Presidential election, Barack Obama was a longshot candidate. A freshman U.S. Senator from Illinois, Obama had served in the Senate for just three years, after seven years spent in the Illinois State Senate. Moreover, Obama was also African American, and many commentators doubted if an African American candidate could win the Democratic nomination, much less the presidency. Obama had become more of a national figure after he gave a keynote speech at the 2004 Democratic National Convention, but New York Senator Hillary Clinton was the favorite to win the nomination. Despite this, during the early spring of 2008, Obama gained momentum—winning a slew of primaries in February, including Louisiana, Washington, Maryland, Virginia, and Wisconsin—and by early March, the two candidates were virtually tied in the delegate count. On March 14, 2008, however, the Obama campaign suffered a crisis when television stations aired video clips of his former pastor, Rev. Jeremiah Wright, saying, among other things, "God damn America." In response, Obama gave the following speech to answer the charges. The speech immediately became a sensation, and Obama pulled ahead of Clinton in the following months. Clinton eventually endorsed Obama on June 7th.

"We the people, in order to form a more perfect union . . ."—221 years ago, in a hall that still stands across the street, a group of men gathered and, with these simple words, launched America's improbable experiment in democracy. Farmers and scholars, statesmen and patriots who had traveled across an ocean to escape tyranny and persecution finally made real their declaration of independence at a Philadelphia convention that lasted through the spring of 1787.

The document they produced was eventually signed but ultimately unfinished. It was stained by this nation's original sin of slavery, a question that divided the colonies and brought the convention to a stalemate until the founders chose to allow the slave trade to continue for at least 20 more years, and to leave any final resolution to future generations.

Of course, the answer to the slavery question was already embedded within our Constitution—a Constitution that had at its very core the ideal of equal citizenship under the law; a Constitution that promised its people liberty and justice and a union that could be and should be perfected over time.

And yet words on a parchment would not be enough to deliver slaves from bondage, or provide men and women of every color and creed their full rights and obligations as citizens of the United States. What would be needed were Americans in successive generations who were willing to do their part—through protests and struggles, on the streets and in the courts, through a civil war and civil disobedience, and always at great risk—to narrow that gap between the promise of our ideals and the reality of their time.

This was one of the tasks we set forth at the beginning of this presidential campaign—to continue the long march of those who came before us, a march for a more just, more equal, more free, more caring and more prosperous America. I chose to run for president

Source: "Transcript: Barack Obama's Speech on Race," https://www.npr.org/templates/story/story.php?storyId=88478467 (Accessed May 21, 2018).

at this moment in history because I believe deeply that we cannot solve the challenges of our time unless we solve them together, unless we perfect our union by understanding that we may have different stories, but we hold common hopes; that we may not look the same and we may not have come from the same place, but we all want to move in the same direction—toward a better future for our children and our grandchildren.

This belief comes from my unyielding faith in the decency and generosity of the American people. But it also comes from my own story.

I am the son of a black man from Kenya and a white woman from Kansas. I was raised with the help of a white grandfather who survived a Depression to serve in Patton's Army during World War II and a white grandmother who worked on a bomber assembly line at Fort Leavenworth while he was overseas. I've gone to some of the best schools in America and lived in one of the world's poorest nations. I am married to a black American who carries within her the blood of slaves and slaveowners—an inheritance we pass on to our two precious daughters. I have brothers, sisters, nieces, nephews, uncles and cousins of every race and every hue, scattered across three continents, and for as long as I live, I will never forget that in no other country on Earth is my story even possible. . . .

The fact is that the comments that have been made and the issues that have surfaced over the last few weeks reflect the complexities of race in this country that we've never really worked through—a part of our union that we have not yet made perfect. And if we walk away now, if we simply retreat into our respective corners, we will never be able to come together and solve challenges like health care or education or the need to find good jobs for every American.

Understanding this reality requires a reminder of how we arrived at this point. As William Faulkner once wrote, "The past isn't dead and buried. In fact, it isn't even past." We do not need to recite here the history of racial injustice in this country. But we do need to remind ourselves that so many of the disparities that exist between the African-American community and the larger American community today can be traced directly to inequalities passed on from an earlier generation that suffered under the brutal legacy of slavery and Jim Crow.

Segregated schools were and are inferior schools; we still haven't fixed them, 50 years after *Brown v. Board of Education*. And the inferior education they provided, then and now, helps explain the pervasive achievement gap between today's black and white students.

Legalized discrimination—where blacks were prevented, often through violence, from owning property, or loans were not granted to African-American business owners, or black homeowners could not access FHA mortgages, or blacks were excluded from unions or the police force or the fire department—meant that black families could not amass any meaningful wealth to bequeath to future generations. That history helps explain the wealth and income gap between blacks and whites, and the concentrated pockets of poverty that persist in so many of today's urban and rural communities.

A lack of economic opportunity among black men, and the shame and frustration that came from not being able to provide for one's family contributed to the erosion of black families—a problem that welfare policies for many years may have worsened. And the lack of basic services in so many urban black neighborhoods—parks for kids to play in, police walking the beat, regular garbage pickup, building code enforcement—all helped create a cycle of violence, blight and neglect that continues to haunt us.

This is the reality in which Reverend Wright and other African-Americans of his generation grew up. They came of age in the late '50s and early '60s, a time when segregation was still the law of the land and opportunity was systematically constricted. What's remarkable is not how many failed in the face of discrimination, but how many men and women overcame the odds; how many were able to make a way out of no way, for those like me who would come after them.

For all those who scratched and clawed their way to get a piece of the American Dream, there were many who didn't make it—those who were ultimately defeated, in one way or another, by discrimination. That legacy of defeat was passed on to future generations—those young men and, increasingly, young women who we see standing on street corners or languishing in our prisons, without hope or prospects for the future. Even for those blacks who did make it, questions of race and racism continue to define their worldview in fundamental ways. For the men and women of Reverend Wright's generation, the memories of humiliation and doubt and fear have not gone away; nor has the anger and the bitterness of those years. That anger may not get expressed in public, in front of white co-workers or white friends. But it does find voice in the barbershop or the beauty shop or around the kitchen table. At times, that anger is exploited by politicians, to gin up votes along racial lines, or to make up for a politician's own failings.

And occasionally it finds voice in the church on Sunday morning, in the pulpit and in the pews. The fact that so many people are surprised to hear that anger in some of Reverend Wright's sermons simply reminds us of the old truism that the most segregated hour of American life occurs on Sunday morning. That anger is not always productive; indeed, all too often it distracts attention from solving real problems; it keeps us from squarely facing our own complicity within the African-American community in our condition, and prevents the African-American community from forging the alliances it needs to bring about real change. But the anger is real; it is powerful. And to simply wish it away, to condemn it without understanding its roots, only serves to widen the chasm of misunderstanding that exists between the races.

In fact, a similar anger exists within segments of the white community. Most working- and middle-class white Americans don't feel that they have been particularly privileged by their race. Their experience is the immigrant experience—as far as they're concerned, no one handed them anything. They built it from scratch. They've worked hard all their lives, many times only to see their jobs shipped overseas or their pensions dumped after a lifetime of labor. They are anxious about their futures, and they feel their dreams slipping away. And in an era of stagnant wages and global competition, opportunity comes to be seen as a zero sum game, in which your dreams come at my expense. So when they are told to bus their children to a school across town; when they hear an African-American is getting an advantage in landing a good job or a spot in a good college because of an injustice that they themselves never committed; when they're told that their fears about crime in urban neighborhoods are somehow prejudiced, resentment builds over time.

Like the anger within the black community, these resentments aren't always expressed in polite company. But they have helped shape the political landscape for at least a generation. Anger over welfare and affirmative action helped forge the Reagan Coalition. Politicians routinely exploited fears of crime for their own electoral ends. Talk show hosts and conservative commentators built entire careers unmasking bogus claims of racism while dismissing legitimate discussions of racial injustice and inequality as mere political correctness or reverse racism.

Just as black anger often proved counterproductive, so have these white resentments distracted attention from the real culprits of the middle class squeeze—a corporate culture rife with inside dealing, questionable accounting practices and short-term greed; a Washington dominated by lobbyists and special interests; economic policies that favor the few over the many. And yet, to wish away the resentments of white Americans, to label them as misguided or even racist, without recognizing they are grounded in legitimate concerns—this too widens the racial divide and blocks the path to understanding.

This is where we are right now. It's a racial stalemate we've been stuck in for years. Contrary to the claims of some of my critics, black and white, I have never been so naïve as to believe that we can get beyond our racial divisions in a single election cycle, or with a single candidacy—particularly a candidacy as imperfect as my own.

But I have asserted a firm conviction—a conviction rooted in my faith in God and my faith in the American people—that, working together, we can move beyond some of our old racial wounds, and that in fact we have no choice if we are to continue on the path of a more perfect union.

For the African-American community, that path means embracing the burdens of our past without becoming victims of our past. It means continuing to insist on a full measure of justice in every aspect of American life. But it also means binding our particular grievances—for better health care and better schools and better jobs—to the larger aspirations of all Americans: the white woman struggling to break the glass ceiling, the white man who has been laid off, the immigrant trying to feed his family. And it means taking full responsibility for our own lives—by demanding more from our fathers, and spending more time with our children, and reading to them, and teaching them that while they may face challenges and discrimination in their own lives, they must never succumb to despair or cynicism; they must always believe that they can write their own destiny. . . .

For we have a choice in this country. We can accept a politics that breeds division and conflict and cynicism. We can tackle race only as spectacle—as we did in the O.J. trial—or in the wake of tragedy—as we did in the aftermath of Katrina—or as fodder for the nightly news. We can play Reverend Wright's sermons on every channel, every day and talk about them from now until the election, and make the only question in this campaign whether or not the American people think that I somehow believe or sympathize with his most offensive words. We can pounce on some gaffe by a Hillary supporter as evidence that she's playing the race card, or we can speculate on whether white men will all flock to John McCain in the general election regardless of his policies.

We can do that.

But if we do, I can tell you that in the next election, we'll be talking about some other distraction. And then another one. And then another one. And nothing will change.

That is one option. Or, at this moment, in this election, we can come together and say, "Not this time." This time, we want to talk about the crumbling schools that are stealing the future of black children and white children and Asian children and Hispanic children and Native American children. This time, we want to reject the cynicism that tells us that these kids can't learn; that those kids who don't look like us are somebody else's problem. The children of America are not those kids, they are our kids, and we will not let them fall behind in a 21st century economy. Not this time.

This time we want to talk about how the lines in the emergency room are filled with whites and blacks and Hispanics who do not have health care, who don't have the power on their own to overcome the special interests in Washington, but who can take them on if we do it together.

This time, we want to talk about the shuttered mills that once provided a decent life for men and women of every race, and the homes for sale that once belonged to Americans from every religion, every region, every walk of life. This time, we want to talk about the fact that the real problem is not that someone who doesn't look like you might take your job; it's that the corporation you work for will ship it overseas for nothing more than a profit.

This time, we want to talk about the men and women of every color and creed who serve together and fight together and bleed together under the same proud flag. We want to talk about how to bring them home from a war that should have never been authorized and should have never been waged. And we want to talk about how we'll show our patriotism by caring for them and their families, and giving them the benefits that they have earned.

I would not be running for President if I didn't believe with all my heart that this is what the vast majority of Americans want for this country. This union may never be perfect, but generation after generation has shown that it can always be perfected. And today, whenever I find myself feeling doubtful or cynical about this possibility, what gives me the most hope is the next generation—the young people whose attitudes and beliefs and openness to change have already made history in this election.

There is one story in particularly that I'd like to leave you with today—a story I told when I had the great honor of speaking on Dr. King's birthday at his home church, Ebenezer Baptist, in Atlanta.

There is a young, 23-year-old white woman named Ashley Baia who organized for our campaign in Florence, South Carolina. She had been working to organize a mostly African-American community since the beginning of this campaign, and one day she was at a roundtable discussion where everyone went around telling their story and why they were there.

And Ashley said that when she was 9 years old, her mother got cancer. And because she had to miss days of work, she was let go and lost her health care. They had to file for bankruptcy, and that's when Ashley decided that she had to do something to help her mom.

She knew that food was one of their most expensive costs, and so Ashley convinced her mother that what she really liked and really wanted to eat more than anything else was mustard and relish sandwiches—because that was the cheapest way to eat. That's the mind of a 9-year-old.

She did this for a year until her mom got better. So she told everyone at the roundtable that the reason she joined our campaign was so that she could help the millions of other children in the country who want and need to help their parents, too.

Now, Ashley might have made a different choice. Perhaps somebody told her along the way that the source of her mother's problems were blacks who were on welfare and too lazy to work, or Hispanics who were coming into the country illegally. But she didn't. She sought out allies in her fight against injustice.

Anyway, Ashley finishes her story and then goes around the room and asks everyone else why they're supporting the campaign. They all have different stories and different reasons. Many bring up a specific issue. And finally they come to this elderly black man who's been sitting there quietly the entire time. And Ashley asks him why he's there. And he does not bring up a specific issue. He does not say health care or the economy. He does not say education or the war. He does not say that he was there because of Barack Obama. He simply says to everyone in the room, "I am here because of Ashley."

"I'm here because of Ashley." By itself, that single moment of recognition between that young white girl and that old black man is not enough. It is not enough to give health care to the sick, or jobs to the jobless, or education to our children.

But it is where we start. It is where our union grows stronger. And as so many generations have come to realize over the course of the 221 years since a band of patriots signed that document right here in Philadelphia, that is where the perfection begins.

QUESTIONS TO CONSIDER

1. How did Obama use American history in his argument?
2. Why do you think the speech was so popular?

30.3 JOHN MCCAIN, ACCEPTANCE SPEECH AT THE REPUBLICAN NATIONAL CONVENTION (2008)

The Democratic primary was competitive until the summer of 2008 (see Reading 30.2), but the Republican primary concluded much more quickly. McCain—a Senator from Arizona who spent five and a half years being tortured in a Vietnamese prisoner-of-war camp after his plane was shot down during a bombing mission in 1967—had become known as something of a "maverick," who would occasionally defy the Republican Party leadership. McCain handily defeated his major primary competitors, Mike Huckabee and Mitt Romney, in a series of contests on "Super Tuesday," January 31, 2008, which essentially gave him the nomination. McCain gave the following speech at the 2008 Republican National Convention in St. Paul, Minnesota. In it, he recounted his history and outlined a future vision of America based on limited government and a robust civil society. On Election Day, Obama easily defeated McCain, but McCain would remain a Senator and an important voice of the Republican Party nationally.

Thank you. Thank you all very much. Thank you.

Tonight, I have a privilege given few Americans: the privilege of accepting our party's nomination for president of the United States. [*applause*] . . .

These are tough times for many of you. You're worried about keeping your job or finding a new one, and you're struggling to put food on the table and stay in your home. [*applause*]

All you've ever asked of your government is to stand on your side and not in your way. And that's what I intend to do: stand on your side and fight for your future. [*applause*] . . .

And let me just offer an advance warning to the old, big-spending, do-nothing, me-first, country-second crowd: Change is coming. [*applause*]

I'm not—I'm not in the habit of breaking my promises to my country, and neither is Governor Palin. And when we tell you we're going to change Washington and stop leaving our country's problems for some unluckier generation to fix, you can count on it.

And we've . . . [*applause*]

We've got a record of doing just that, and the strength, experience, judgment, and backbone to keep our word to you. [*applause*]

You well know I've been called a maverick, someone who . . . [*applause*] . . . someone who marches to the beat of his own drum. Sometimes it's meant as a compliment; sometimes it's not. What it really means is I understand who I work for. I don't work for a party. I don't work for a special interest. I don't work for myself. I work for you. [*applause*]

I've fought corruption, and it didn't matter if the culprits were Democrats or Republicans. They violated their public trust, and they had to be held accountable.

I've fought the big spenders . . . [*applause*]

I've fought the big spenders in both parties, who waste your money on things you neither need nor want, and the first big-spending pork-barrel earmark bill that comes across my desk, I will veto it. I will make them famous, and you will know their names. You will know their names. [*applause*]

Source: "John McCain: Address Accepting the Presidential Nomination at the Republican National Convention in Saint Paul," http://www.presidency.ucsb.edu/ws/index.php?pid=78576 (Accessed May 21, 2018).

We're not going to allow that while you struggle to buy groceries, fill your gas tank, and make your mortgage payment. I've fought to get million-dollar checks out of our elections. I've fought lobbyists who stole from Indian tribes. I've fought crooked deals in the Pentagon.

I've fought tobacco companies and trial lawyers, drug companies and union bosses. [*applause*]

I've fought for the right strategy and more troops in Iraq when it wasn't the popular thing to do. [*applause*]

And when the pundits said—when the pundits said my campaign was finished, I said I'd rather lose an election than see my country lose a war. [*applause*]

And thanks—thanks to the leadership of a brilliant general, David Petraeus, and the brave men and women he has the honor to command . . . [*applause*] . . . that—that strategy succeeded, and it rescued us from a defeat that would have demoralized our military, risked a wider war, and threatened the security of all Americans. [*applause*]

I don't mind a good fight. For reasons known only to God, I've had quite a few tough ones in my life. But I learned an important lesson along the way: In the end, it matters less that you can fight. What you fight for is the real test. [*applause*]

I fight for Americans. I fight for you. I fight for Bill and Sue Nebe from Farmington Hills, Michigan, who lost . . . [*applause*] . . . lost their real estate investments in the bad housing market. Bill got a temporary job after he was out of work for seven months. Sue works three jobs to help pay the bills.

I fight for Jake and Toni Wimmer of Franklin County, Pennsylvania. Jake . . . [*applause*]

Jake works on a loading dock, coaches Little League, and raises money for the mentally and physically disabled. Toni is a schoolteacher, working toward her master's degree. They have two sons. The youngest, Luke, has been diagnosed with autism. Their lives should matter to the people they elect to office. And they matter to me. And they matter to you.

I fight for the family of Matthew Stanley of Wolfeboro, New Hampshire. [*applause*]

Matthew died serving our country in Iraq. I wear his bracelet and think of him every day. I intend to honor their sacrifice by making sure the country their son loved so well and never returned to remains safe from its enemies. [*applause*]

I fight to restore the pride and principles of our party. We were elected to change Washington, and we let Washington change us.

We lost—we lost the trust of the American people when some Republicans gave in to the temptations of corruption. We lost their trust when rather than reform government, both parties made it bigger.

We lost their trust when instead of freeing ourselves from a dangerous dependence on foreign oil, both parties—and Senator Obama—passed another corporate welfare bill for oil companies. We lost their trust when we valued our power over our principles.

We're going to change that. [*applause*]

We're going to recover the people's trust by standing up again to the values Americans admire. The party of Lincoln, Roosevelt and Reagan is going to get back to basics. [*applause*]

In this country, we believe everyone has something to contribute and deserves the opportunity to reach their God-given potential, from the boy whose descendants arrived on the Mayflower to the Latina daughter of migrant workers. We're all God's children, and we're all Americans. [*applause*]

We believe—we believe in low taxes, spending discipline, and open markets. We believe in rewarding hard work and risk-takers and letting people keep the fruits of their labor.

We believe . . . [*applause*]

We believe—we believe in a strong defense, work, faith, service, a culture of life . . . [*applause*] . . . personal responsibility, the rule of law, and judges who dispense justice impartially and don't legislate from the bench. [*applause*]

We believe in the values of families, neighborhoods, and communities. We believe in a government that unleashes the creativity and initiative of Americans, government that doesn't make your choices for you, but works to make sure you have more choices to make for yourself. [*applause*]

I will keep taxes low and cut them where I can. My opponent will raise them. I will open . . . [*audience boos*]

I will open new markets to our goods and services. My opponent will close them. [*audience boos*]

I will cut government spending. He will increase it. [*audience boos*]

My tax cuts will create jobs; his tax increases will eliminate them. [*audience boos*]

My health care plan will make it easier for more Americans to find and keep good health care insurance. His plan will force small businesses to cut jobs, reduce wages, and force families into a government-run health care system where a bureaucrat . . . [*audience boos*] . . . where a bureaucrat stands between you and your doctor. [*audience boos*]

We all know that keeping taxes low helps small businesses grow and create new jobs. Cutting the second-highest business tax rate in the world will help American companies compete and keep jobs from going overseas. [*applause*]

Doubling the child tax exemption from $3,500 to $7,000 will improve the lives of millions of American families. [*applause*]

Reducing government spending and getting rid of failed programs will let you keep more of your own money to save, spend, and invest as you see fit. [*applause*]

Opening new markets and preparing workers to compete in the world economy is essential to our future prosperity.

I know some of you have been left behind in the changing economy, and it often seems that your government hasn't even noticed. Government assistance for the unemployed workers was designed for the economy of the 1950s. That's going to change on my watch. [*applause*]

Now, my opponent promises to bring back old jobs by wishing away the global economy. We're going to help workers who've lost a job that won't come back find a new one that won't go away. [*applause*]

We will prepare them for the jobs of day—of today. We will use our community colleges to help train people for new opportunities in their communities. [*applause*]

For workers in industries—for workers in industries that have been hard-hit, we'll help make up part of the difference in wages between their old job and a temporary, lower paid one, while they receive re-training that will help them find secure new employment at a decent wage. [*applause*]

Education—education is the civil rights issue of this century. [*applause*]

Equal access to public education has been gained, but what is the value of access to a failing school? We need . . . [*applause*] . . . We need to shake up failed school bureaucracies with competition, empower parents with choice. [*applause*]

Let's remove barriers to qualified instructors, attract and reward good teachers, and help bad teachers find another line of work. [*applause*]

When a public school fails to meet its obligations to students, parent—when it fails to meet its obligations to students, parents deserve a choice in the education of their children. And I intend to give it to them. [*applause*]

Some may choose a better public school. Some may choose a private one.

Many will choose a charter school. But they will have the choice, and their children will have that opportunity. [*applause*]

Senator Obama wants our schools to answer to unions and entrenched bureaucrats. I want schools to answer to parents and students. [*applause*]

And when I'm president, they will. [*applause*]

My fellow Americans, when I'm president, we're going to embark on the most ambitious national project in decades.

We're going to stop sending $700 billion a year to countries that don't like us very much, and some of that money . . . [*applause*]

We'll attack—we'll attack the problem on every front. We'll produce more energy at home. We will drill new wells off-shore, and we'll drill them now. We'll drill them now. [*applause*]

We'll—we'll—my friends, we'll build more nuclear power plants.

We'll develop clean-coal technology. We'll increase the use of wind, tide, solar, and natural gas. We'll encourage the development and use of flex-fuel, hybrid and electric automobiles. [*applause*]

Senator Obama thinks we can achieve energy independence without more drilling and without more nuclear power. But Americans know better than that. [*applause*]

We must use all resources and develop all technologies necessary to rescue our economy from the damage caused by rising oil prices and restore the health of our planet.

My friends . . . [*applause*] . . . it's an ambitious plan, but Americans are ambitious by nature, and we've faced greater challenges. It's time for us to show the world again how Americans lead. [*applause*] . . .

My friends, when I was 5 years old, a car pulled up in front of our house. A Navy officer rolled down the window and shouted at my father that the Japanese had bombed Pearl Harbor. I rarely saw my father again for four years.

My grandfather came home from that same war exhausted from the burdens he had borne and died the next day.

In Vietnam, where I formed the closest friendships of my life, some of those friends never came home with me.

I hate war. It's terrible beyond imagination.

I'm running for president to keep the country I love safe and prevent other families from risking their loved ones in war as my family has.

I will draw on all my experience with the world and its leaders, and all the tools at our disposal—diplomatic, economic, military, and the power of our ideals—to build the foundations for a stable and enduring peace. [*applause*]

In America, we change things that need to be changed. Each generation makes its contribution to our greatness. The work that is ours to do is plainly before us; we don't need to search for it.

We need to change the way government does almost everything: from the way we protect our security to the way we compete in the world economy; from the way we respond to disasters to the way we fuel our transportation network; from the way we train our workers to the way we educate our children.

All these functions of government were designed before the rise of the global economy, the information technology revolution, and the end of the Cold War. We have to catch up to history, and we have to change the way we do business in Washington. [*applause*]

The—the constant partisan rancor that stops us from solving these problems isn't a cause. It's a symptom. It's what happens when people go to Washington to work for themselves and not for you. [*applause*]

Again and again—again and again, I've worked with members of both parties to fix problems that need to be fixed. That's how I will govern as president. I will reach out my hand to anyone to help me get this country moving again.

My friends . . . [*applause*] . . . I have that record and the scars to prove it. Senator Obama does not. [*applause*] . . .

On an October morning, in the Gulf of Tonkin, I prepared for my 23rd mission over North Vietnam. I hadn't any worry I wouldn't come back safe and sound. I thought I was tougher than anyone. I was pretty independent then, too. [*laughter*]

I liked to bend a few rules and pick a few fights for the fun of it.

But I did it for my own pleasure, my own pride. I didn't think there was a cause that was more important than me.

Then I found myself falling toward the middle of a small lake in the city of Hanoi, with two broken arms, a broken leg, and an angry crowd waiting to greet me. [*laughter*]

I was dumped in a dark cell and left to die. I didn't feel so tough anymore.

When they discovered my father was an admiral, they took me to a hospital. They couldn't set my bones properly, so they just slapped a cast on me. And when I didn't get better and was down to about a hundred pounds, they put me in a cell with two other Americans.

I couldn't do anything. I couldn't even feed myself. They did it for me. I was beginning to learn the limits of my selfish independence.

Those men saved my life. [*applause*]

I was in solitary confinement when my captors offered to release me. I knew why. If I went home, they would use it as propaganda to demoralize my fellow prisoners.

Our code said we could only go home in the order of our capture, and there were men who had been shot down long before me. I thought about it, though. I wasn't in great shape, and I missed everything about America, but I turned it down.

A lot of prisoners had it much worse . . . [*applause*]

A lot of—a lot of prisoners had it a lot worse than I did. I'd been mistreated before, but not as badly as many others. I always liked to strut a little after I'd been roughed up to show the other guys I was tough enough to take it.

But after I turned down their offer, they worked me over harder than they ever had before, for a long time, and they broke me.

When they brought me back to my cell, I was hurt and ashamed, and I didn't know how I could face my fellow prisoners. The good man in the cell next door to me, my friend, Bob Craner, saved me.

Through taps on a wall, he told me I had fought as hard as I could. No man can always stand alone. And then he told me to get back up and fight again for my country and for the men I had the honor to serve with, because every day they fought for me. [*applause*]

I fell in love with my country when I was a prisoner in someone else's. I loved it not just for the many comforts of life here. I loved it for its decency, for its faith in the wisdom, justice, and goodness of its people.

I loved it because it was not just a place, but an idea, a cause worth fighting for. I was never the same again; I wasn't my own man anymore; I was my country's. [*applause*]

I'm not running for president because I think I'm blessed with such personal greatness that history has anointed me to save our country in its hour of need. [*applause*]

My country saved me. My country saved me, and I cannot forget it. And I will fight for her for as long as I draw breath, so help me God. [*applause*]

My friends, if you find faults with our country, make it a better one.

If you're disappointed with the mistakes of government, join its ranks and work to correct them. Enlist . . . [*applause*]

Enlist in our Armed Forces. Become a teacher. Enter the ministry. Run for public office. Feed a hungry child. Teach an—an illiterate adult to read. Comfort the afflicted. Defend the rights of the oppressed.

Our country will be the better, and you will be the happier, because nothing brings greater happiness in life than to serve a cause greater than yourself. [*applause*]

I'm going to fight for my cause every day as your president. I'm going to fight to make sure every American has every reason to thank God, as I thank him, that I'm an American, a proud citizen of the greatest country on Earth. And with hard work—with hard work, strong faith, and a little courage, great things are always within our reach.

Fight with me. Fight with me. [*applause*]

Fight for what's right for our country. Fight for the ideals and character of a free people. [*applause*]

Fight for our children's future. Fight for justice and opportunity for all. [*applause*]

Stand up to defend our country from its enemies. Stand up for each other, for beautiful, blessed, bountiful America. [*applause*]

Stand up, stand up, stand up, and fight. [*applause*]

Nothing is inevitable here. We're Americans, and we never give up. [*applause*]

We never quit. [*applause*]

We never hide from history. We make history. [*applause*]

Thank you, and God bless you, and God bless America.

QUESTIONS TO CONSIDER

1. In which ways did McCain use his personal history, and American history, in his argument?
2. How would you describe McCain's vision for America?

30.4 OCCUPY WALL STREET MANIFESTO (2011) AND THE MOVEMENT FOR BLACK LIVES PLATFORM (2017)

The twenty-first century has seen a slew of grassroots movements gain power by fighting against established hierarchies. Two such movements are Occupy Wall Street and Black Lives Matter. Occupy Wall Street started in September 2011, when a group of about 1,000 protesters began camping in Zuccotti Park in Lower Manhattan. The protesters charged that the American financial system was rigged for the upper one percent of Americans. Wall Street, then, stood as a symbol for the injustices of the American economy writ large, as you will read in the following manifesto, which Occupy issued on September 30, 2011. Over the next two months, the protesters continued to camp in Zuccotti Park and raised national attention to their cause. Eventually, even President Obama issued a statement in support of Occupy. On November 15th, the New York Police Department forcibly cleared the protesters from Zuccotti Park, and the movement slowly fizzled. Their concerns, however, became integrated into mainstream political debates.

The Movement for Black Lives began in June 2015. It is a coalition group, which incorporated #BlackLivesMatter, an informal movement that protested the murder of seventeen-year-old Trayvon Martin by George Zimmerman in 2013, as well as criminal justice reform, education, and youth organizations. The Movement for Black Lives started in response to the police killings of eighteen-year old Michael Brown in Ferguson, Missouri; forty-three-year-old Eric Garner, in New York City; twenty-five-year-old Freddie Gray in Baltimore, Maryland; and twelve-year Tamir Rice in Cleveland, Ohio. The Movement for Black Lives Platform, as you will read, focuses on six demands. The movement further protested the police killings of Laquan McDonald, a seventeen-year-old in Chicago, Illinois, whose death the Chicago Police initially covered up; Sandra Bland, a twenty-eight-year-old woman who died in a jail cell after being pulled over for a traffic stop in Prairie View, Texas; and Aiyana Jones, a seven-year-old girl shot during a raid in Detroit, Michigan. The Movement for Black Lives continues to impact modern politics, especially since prominent National Football League players began kneeling during the pre-game national anthem in support of the movement in the 2016 season.

DECLARATION AND MANIFESTO OF OCCUPY WALL STREET MOVEMENT

As we gather together in solidarity to express a feeling of mass injustice, we must not lose sight of what brought us together. We write so that all people who feel wronged by the corporate forces of the world can know that we are your allies.

As one people, united, we acknowledge the reality: that the future of the human race requires the cooperation of its members; that our system must protect our

Sources: "Declaration and Manifesto of Occupy Wall Street Movement," http://www.declarationproject.org/?p=166 (Accessed May 21, 2018); "The Movement for Black Lives Platform," https://policy.m4bl.org/platform/ (Accessed May 21, 2018).

rights, and upon corruption of that system, it is up to the individuals to protect their own rights, and those of their neighbors; that a democratic government derives its just power from the people, but corporations do not seek consent to extract wealth from the people and the Earth; and that no true democracy is attainable when the process is determined by economic power.

We come to you at a time when corporations, which place profit over people, self-interest over justice, and oppression over equality, run our governments. We have peaceably assembled here, as is our right, to let these facts be known.

- They have taken our houses through an illegal foreclosure process, despite not having the original mortgage.
- They have taken bailouts from taxpayers with impunity, and continue to give Executives exorbitant bonuses.
- They have perpetuated inequality and discrimination in the workplace based on age, the color of one's skin, sex, gender identity and sexual orientation.
- They have poisoned the food supply through negligence, and undermined the farming system through monopolization.
- They have profited off of the torture, confinement, and cruel treatment of countless animals, and actively hide these practices.
- They have continuously sought to strip employees of the right to negotiate for better pay and safer working conditions.
- They have held students hostage with tens of thousands of dollars of debt on education, which is itself a human right.
- They have consistently outsourced labor and used that outsourcing as leverage to cut workers' healthcare and pay.
- They have influenced the courts to achieve the same rights as people, with none of the culpability or responsibility.
- They have spent millions of dollars on legal teams that look for ways to get them out of contracts in regards to health insurance.

- They have sold our privacy as a commodity.
- They have used the military and police force to prevent freedom of the press. They have deliberately declined to recall faulty products endangering lives in pursuit of profit.
- They determine economic policy, despite the catastrophic failures their policies have produced and continue to produce.
- They have donated large sums of money to politicians, who are responsible for regulating them.
- They continue to block alternate forms of energy to keep us dependent on oil.
- They continue to block generic forms of medicine that could save people's lives or provide relief in order to protect investments that have already turned a substantial profit.
- They have purposely covered up oil spills, accidents, faulty bookkeeping, and inactive ingredients in pursuit of profit.
- They purposefully keep people misinformed and fearful through their control of the media.
- They have accepted private contracts to murder prisoners even when presented with serious doubts about their guilt.
- They have perpetuated colonialism at home and abroad. They have participated in the torture and murder of innocent civilians overseas.
- They continue to create weapons of mass destruction in order to receive government contracts.*

"To the people of the world,

We, the New York City General Assembly occupying Wall Street in Liberty Square, urge you to assert your power.

Exercise your right to peaceably assemble; occupy public space; create a process to address the problems we face, and generate solutions accessible to everyone.

To all communities that take action and form groups in the spirit of direct democracy, we offer support, documentation, and all of the resources at our disposal.

Join us and make your voices heard!"

---

* NOTE—These grievances are not all-inclusive.

THE MOVEMENT FOR BLACK LIVES PLATFORM

Black humanity and dignity requires Black political will and power. Despite constant exploitation and perpetual oppression, Black people have bravely and brilliantly been the driving force pushing the U.S. towards the ideals it articulates but has never achieved. In recent years we have taken to the streets, launched massive campaigns, and impacted elections, but our elected leaders have failed to address the legitimate demands of our Movement. We can no longer wait.

In response to the sustained and increasingly visible violence against Black communities in the U.S. and globally, a collective of more than 50 organizations representing thousands of Black people from across the country have come together with renewed energy and purpose to articulate a common vision and agenda. We are a collective that centers and is rooted in Black communities, but we recognize we have a shared struggle with all oppressed people; collective liberation will be a product of all of our work.

We believe in elevating the experiences and leadership of the most marginalized Black people, including but not limited to those who are women, queer, trans, femmes, gender nonconforming, Muslim, formerly and currently incarcerated, cash poor and working class, disabled, undocumented, and immigrant. We are intentional about amplifying the particular experience of state and gendered violence that Black queer, trans, gender nonconforming, women and intersex people face. There can be no liberation for all Black people if we do not center and fight for those who have been marginalized. It is our hope that by working together to create and amplify a shared agenda, we can continue to move towards a world in which the full humanity and dignity of all people is recognized.

While this platform is focused on domestic policies, we know that patriarchy, exploitative capitalism, militarism, and white supremacy know no borders. We stand in solidarity with our international family against the ravages of global capitalism and anti-Black racism, human-made climate change, war, and exploitation. We also stand with descendants of African people all over the world in an ongoing call and struggle for reparations for the historic and continuing harms of colonialism and slavery. We also recognize and honor the rights and struggle of our Indigenous family for land and self-determination.

We have created this platform to articulate and support the ambitions and work of Black people. We also seek to intervene in the current political climate and assert a clear vision, particularly for those who claim to be our allies, of the world we want them to help us create. We reject false solutions and believe we can achieve a complete transformation of the current systems, which place profit over people and make it impossible for many of us to breathe.

Together, we demand an end to the wars against Black people. We demand that the government repair the harms that have been done to Black communities in the form of reparations and targeted long-term investments. We also demand a defunding of the systems and institutions that criminalize and cage us. This document articulates our vision of a fundamentally different world. However, we recognize the need to include policies that address the immediate suffering of Black people. These policies, while less transformational, are necessary to address the current material conditions of our people and will better equip us to win the world we demand and deserve.

We recognize that not all of our collective needs and visions can be translated into policy, but we understand that policy change is one of many tactics necessary to move us towards the world we envision. We have come together now because we believe it is time to forge a new covenant. We are dreamers and doers and this platform is meant to articulate some of our vision. The links throughout the document provide the stepping-stones and roadmaps of how to get there. The policy briefs also elevate the brave and transformative work our people are already engaged in, and build on some of the best thinking in our history of struggle. This agenda continues the legacy of our ancestors who pushed for reparations, Black self-determination and community control; and also propels new iterations of movements such as efforts for reproductive justice, holistic healing and reconciliation, and ending violence against Black cis, queer, and trans people.

DEMANDS

END THE WAR ON BLACK PEOPLE

We demand an **end to the war against Black people**. Since this country's inception there have been named and unnamed wars on our communities. We demand an end to the criminalization, incarceration, and killing of our people. This includes:

1. An immediate end to the criminalization and dehumanization of Black youth across all areas of society including, but not limited to; our nation's justice and education systems, social service agencies, and media and pop culture. This includes an end to zero-tolerance school policies and arrests of students, the removal of police from schools, and the reallocation of funds from police and punitive school discipline practices to restorative services.
2. An end to capital punishment.
3. An end to money bail, mandatory fines, fees, court surcharges and "defendant funded" court proceedings.
4. An end to the use of past criminal history to determine eligibility for housing, education, licenses, voting, loans, employment, and other services and needs.
5. An end to the war on Black immigrants including the repeal of the 1996 crime and immigration bills, an end to all deportations, immigrant detention, and Immigration and Custom Enforcement (ICE) raids, and mandated legal representation in immigration court.
6. An end to the war on Black trans, queer and gender nonconforming people including their addition to anti-discrimination civil rights protections to ensure they have full access to employment, health, housing and education.
7. An end to the mass surveillance of Black communities, and the end to the use of technologies that criminalize and target our communities (including IMSI catchers, drones, body cameras, and predictive policing software).
8. The demilitarization of law enforcement, including law enforcement in schools and on college campuses.
9. An immediate end to the privatization of police, prisons, jails, probation, parole, food, phone and all other criminal justice related services.
10. Until we achieve a world where cages are no longer used against our people we demand an immediate change in conditions and an end to all jails, detention centers, youth facilities and prisons as we know them. This includes the end of solitary confinement, the end of shackling of pregnant people, access to quality healthcare, and effective measures to address the needs of our youth, queer, gender nonconforming and trans families. . . .

REPARATIONS

We demand **reparations for past and continuing harms**. The government, responsible corporations and other institutions that have profited off of the harm they have inflicted on Black people—from colonialism to slavery through food and housing redlining, mass incarceration, and surveillance—must repair the harm done. This includes:

1. Reparations for the systemic denial of access to high quality educational opportunities in the form of full and free access for all Black people (including undocumented and currently and formerly incarcerated people) to lifetime education including: free access and open admissions to public community colleges and universities, technical education (technology, trade and agricultural), educational support programs, retroactive forgiveness of student loans, and support for lifetime learning programs.
2. Reparations for the continued divestment from, discrimination toward and exploitation of our communities in the form of a guaranteed minimum livable income for all Black people, with clearly articulated corporate regulations.
3. Reparations for the wealth extracted from our communities through environmental racism, slavery, food apartheid, housing discrimination and racialized capitalism in the form of corporate and government reparations focused on healing ongoing physical and mental trauma, and ensuring our access and control of food sources, housing and land.

4. Reparations for the cultural and educational exploitation, erasure, and extraction of our communities in the form of mandated public school curriculums that critically examine the political, economic, and social impacts of colonialism and slavery, and funding to support, build, preserve, and restore cultural assets and sacred sites to ensure the recognition and honoring of our collective struggles and triumphs.

5. Legislation at the federal and state level that requires the United States to acknowledge the lasting impacts of slavery, establish and execute a plan to address those impacts. This includes the immediate passage of H.R.40, the "Commission to Study Reparation Proposals for African-Americans Act" or subsequent versions which call for reparations remedies. . . .

INVEST-DIVEST

We demand **investments in the education, health and safety of Black people**, instead of investments in the criminalizing, caging, and harming of Black people. We want investments in Black communities, determined by Black communities, and **divestment from exploitative forces** including prisons, fossil fuels, police, surveillance and exploitative corporations. This includes:

1. A reallocation of funds at the federal, state and local level from policing and incarceration (JAG, COPS, VOCA) to long-term safety strategies such as education, local restorative justice services, and employment programs.

2. The retroactive decriminalization, immediate release and record expungement of all drug related offenses and prostitution, and reparations for the devastating impact of the "war on drugs" and criminalization of prostitution, including a reinvestment of the resulting savings and revenue into restorative services, mental health services, job programs and other programs supporting those impacted by the sex and drug trade.

3. Real, meaningful, and equitable universal health care that guarantees: proximity to nearby comprehensive health centers, culturally competent services for all people, specific services for queer, gender nonconforming, and trans people, full bodily autonomy, full reproductive services, mental health services, paid parental leave, and comprehensive quality child and elder care.

4. A constitutional right at the state and federal level to a fully-funded education which includes a clear articulation of the right to: a free education for all, special protections for queer and trans students, wrap around services, social workers, free health services (including reproductive body autonomy), a curriculum that acknowledges and addresses students' material and cultural needs, physical activity and recreation, high quality food, free daycare, and freedom from unwarranted search, seizure or arrest.

5. A divestment from industrial multinational use of fossil fuels and investment in community- based sustainable energy solutions.

6. A cut in military expenditures and a reallocation of those funds to invest in domestic infrastructure and community well-being. . . .

ECONOMIC JUSTICE

We demand **economic justice for all** and a reconstruction of the economy to ensure Black communities have collective ownership, not merely access. This includes:

1. A progressive restructuring of tax codes at the local, state, and federal levels to ensure a radical and sustainable redistribution of wealth.

2. Federal and state job programs that specifically target the most economically marginalized Black people, and compensation for those involved in the care economy. Job programs must provide a living wage and encourage support for local workers centers, unions, and Black-owned businesses which are accountable to the community.

3. A right to restored land, clean air, clean water and housing and an end to the exploitative privatization of natural resources—including land and water. We seek democratic control over how resources are preserved, used and distributed and do so while honoring and respecting the rights of our Indigenous family.

4. The right for workers to organize in public and private sectors especially in "On Demand Economy" jobs.

5. Restore the Glass-Steagall Act to break up the large banks, and call for the National Credit Union Administration and the U.S. Department of the Treasury to change policies and practices around regulation, reporting and consolidation to allow for the continuation and creation of black banks, small and community development credit unions, insurance companies and other financial institutions.

6. An end to the Trans-Pacific Partnership and a renegotiation of all trade agreements to prioritize the interests of workers and communities.

7. Through tax incentives, loans and other government directed resources, support the development of cooperative or social economy networks to help facilitate trade across and in Black communities globally. All aid in the form of grants, loans or contracts to help facilitate this must go to Black led or Black supported networks and organizations as defined by the communities.

8. Financial support of Black alternative institutions including policy that subsidizes and offers low-interest, interest-free or federally guaranteed low-interest loans to promote the development of cooperatives (food, residential, etc.), land trusts and culturally responsive health infrastructures that serve the collective needs of our communities.

9. Protections for workers in industries that are not appropriately regulated including domestic workers, farm workers, and tipped workers, and for workers—many of whom are Black women and incarcerated people—who have been exploited and remain unprotected. This includes the immediate passage at the Federal and state level of the Domestic Workers Bill of Rights and extension of worker protections to incarcerated people. . . .

COMMUNITY CONTROL

We demand a world where those most impacted in our **communities control the laws, institutions, and policies that are meant to serve us**—from our schools to our local budgets, economies, police departments, and our land—while recognizing that the rights and histories of our Indigenous family must also be respected. This includes:

1. Direct democratic community control of local, state, and federal law enforcement agencies, ensuring that communities most harmed by destructive policing have the power to hire and fire officers, determine disciplinary action, control budgets and policies, and subpoena relevant agency information.

2. An end to the privatization of education and real community control by parents, students and community members of schools including democratic school boards and community control of curriculum, hiring, firing and discipline policies.

3. Participatory budgeting at the local, state and federal level. . . .

POLITICAL POWER

We demand **independent Black political power and Black self-determination** in all areas of society. We envision a remaking of the current U.S. political system in order to create a real democracy where Black people and all marginalized people can effectively exercise full political power. This includes:

1. An end to the criminalization of Black political activity including the immediate release of all political prisoners and an end to the repression of political parties.

2. Public financing of elections and the end of money controlling politics through ending super PACs and unchecked corporate donations.

3. Election protection, electoral expansion and the right to vote for all people including: full access, guarantees, and protections of the right to vote for all people through universal voter registration, automatic voter registration, pre-registration for 16-year-olds, same day voter registration, voting day holidays, Online Voter Registration (OVR), enfranchisement of formerly and presently incarcerated people, local and state resident voting for undocumented people, and a ban on any disenfranchisement laws.

4. Full access to technology including net neutrality and universal access to the internet without discrimination and full representation for all.

5. Protection and increased funding for Black institutions including Historically Black Colleges and Universities (HBCU's), Black media and cultural, political and social formations. . . .

QUESTIONS TO CONSIDER

1. In the introduction to the Platform, how does Occupy Wall Street movement support its argument?
2. What stands out in the Movement for Black Lives' "Demands"?

30.5 EXCERPTS FROM THE THIRD TRUMP-CLINTON PRESIDENTIAL DEBATE (2016)

The 2016 election featured two historically unpopular candidates. The Republican nominee, real estate developer Donald Trump, fought claims that he had sexually assaulted multiple women and bragged about it, that he was benefitting from and colluding with the Russian hacking of Clinton aides' email accounts, and that he had expressed racist attitudes toward Mexican immigrants. The Democratic nominee, former Senator and Secretary of State Hillary Clinton, fought claims that she had illegally maintained her private email server as Secretary of State, that the Clinton Foundation (run by her and her husband, former President Bill Clinton) was corrupt, and that she would be soft on illegal immigration. On October 19th, just weeks before the election, the two candidates debated for the final time at the University of Nevada, Las Vegas. Unsurprisingly, the debate again turned into a series of attacks by both candidates, and moderator Chris Wallace struggled to control the event. The two candidates debated widely but especially focused on immigration and Russian intervention in the election. On November 6, 2016, two days before the election, FBI Director James Comey announced he was reopening an investigation into Clinton's emails, which did not subsequently uncover any wrongdoing. Comey's action, however, likely lent Trump the razor-thin margin he needed to win on Election Day. As of this writing (September 2018), Special Counsel investigation led by former FBI Director Robert Mueller continues to investigate the Trump Campaign's ties to the Russian government.

Chris Wallace: All right. Let's move on to the subject of immigration. And there is almost no issue that separates the two of you more than the issue of immigration. Actually there are many issues that separate the two of you. Mr. Trump. You want to build a wall. Secretary Clinton, you have offered no specific plan for how you want to secure our southern border. Mr. Trump, you are calling for major deportations. Secretary Clinton, you say that within your first 100 days as president, you're going to offer a package that includes a pathway to citizenship. The question really is why are you right and your opponent wrong? Mr. Trump, you go first in this segment, you have two minutes.

Trump: Well first of all, she wants to give amnesty, which is a disaster. And very unfair to all of the people waiting in line for many, many years. We need strong borders. In the audience we have four mothers of—I mean, these are unbelievable people that I've gotten to know over a period of years whose children have been killed, brutally killed, by people that came into the country illegally. You have thousands of mothers and fathers and relatives all over the country.

They're coming in illegally. Drugs are pouring in through the border. We have no country if we have no border. Hillary wants to give amnesty. She wants to have open borders. As you know, the border patrol agents, sixteen thousand five hundred plus ICE endorsed me. First time they've endorsed a candidate. It means their job is tougher. But they know what's going on. They know it than anybody. They want strong borders. They feel we have to have strong

Source: "Full Transcript: Third 2016 Presidential Debate," https://www.politico.com/story/2016/10/full-transcript-third-2016-presidential-debate-230063 (Accessed September 10, 2018).

borders. I was up in New Hampshire the other day. The biggest complaint they have, it's with all the problems going on in the world, many of the problems caused by Hillary Clinton and Barack Obama. All of the problems. The single biggest problem, is heroin that pours across our southern borders. Just pouring and destroying their youth. It is poisoning the blood of their youth and plenty of other people. We have to have strong borders. We have to keep the drugs out of our country. Right now, we're getting the drugs, they're getting the cash. We need strong borders. We need absolute, we cannot give amnesty. Now, I want to build a wall. We need the wall. The border patrol, ICE, they all want the wall. We stopped the drugs; we shore up the border. One of my first acts will be to get all of the drug lords, all of the bad ones, we have some bad, bad people in this country that have to go out. We're going to get them out. We're going to secure the border. And once the border is secure, at a later date, we'll make its determination as to the rest. But we have some bad hombres here that we're going to get them out.

Wallace: Mr. Trump, thank you. Same question to you, Secretary Clinton. Basically why are you right and Mr. Trump is wrong?

Clinton: As he was talking I was thinking about a young girl I met here in Las Vegas, Carla, who was very worried that her parents might he be deported because she was born in this country but they were not. They work hard. They do everything they can to get give her a good life. And you're right. I don't want to rip families apart. I don't want to be sending parents away from children. I don't want to see the deportation force that Donald has talked about in action in our country. We have eleven million undocumented people. They have four million American citizen children. Fifteen million people. He said as recently as a few weeks ago in Phoenix, that every undocumented person will be subject to deportation. Now here's what that means. It means you would have to have a massive law enforcement presence where law enforcement officers would be going school to school, home to home, business to business. Rounding up people who are undocumented. And we would then have to put them on trains, on buses to get them out of our country. I think that is an idea that is not in

keeping with who we are as a nation. I think it is an idea that would rip our country apart. I have been for border security for years. I voted for border security in the United States Senate. And my comprehensive immigration reform plan, of course[,] includes border security. But I want to put our resources where I think they're most needed. Getting rid of any violent person, anybody who should be deported, we should deport them. When it comes to the wall that Donald talks about building. He went to Mexico. He had a meeting with Mexican President. —He didn't even raise it. He choked. And then he got into a Twitter war because the Mexican president said we're not paying for that wall. So I think we are both a nation of immigrants and we are a nation of laws and that we can act accordingly and that's why I am introducing comprehensive immigration reform within the first hundred days with a path to citizenship. . . .

Wallace: Secretary Clinton, I want to clear up your position on this issue because in a speech you gave to a Brazilian bank, for which you were paid $225,000, we've learned from the Wikileaks that you said this, and I want to quote "My dream is a hemispheric common market with open trade and open borders."

Trump: Thank you.

Wallace: That is the question, please quiet everybody. Is that your dream? Open borders?

Clinton: Well, if you went on to read the rest of the sentence, I was talking about energy. You know, we trade more energy with our neighbors then we trade with rest of the world combined. And I do want us to have an electric grid, an energy system that crosses borders. I think I would be a great benefit to us. But you are very clearly quoting from WikiLeaks. What is really important about that is that the Russian government has engaged in espionage against Americans. They have hacked American websites, American accounts of private people, of institutions. Then they have given that information to WikiLeaks for the purpose of putting it on the Internet. This has come from the highest levels of the Russian government. Clearly from Putin himself in an effort, as seventeen of our intelligence agencies have confirmed, to influence our election. So I actually think the most important question of this evening, Chris, is finally, will Donald Trump admit and condemn that the Russians are doing this, and make it clear that he will not have the help of Putin in this election. That he rejects Russian espionage against Americans, which he actually encouraged in the past. Those are the questions we need answered. We had never had anything like this happen in any of our elections before.

Trump: That was a great pivot off of the fact that she wants open borders. Okay? When did we get off to Putin?

Wallace: Hold on, folks. Because this is going to end up getting out of control. Let's try to keep it quiet. For the candidates and for the American people.

Trump: Just to finish on the borders, she wants open borders. People are going to pour into our country. People are going to come in from Syria. She wants five hundred and fifty percent more people than Barack Obama. And he has thousands and thousands of people. They have no idea where they come from. And you see, we are going to stop radical Islamic terrorism in this country. She won't even mention the words and neither will President Obama. So I just want to tell you. She wants open borders. Now we can talk about Putin. I don't know Putin. He said nice things about me. If we got along well, that would be good. If Russia and the United States got along well and went after ISIS, that would be good. He has no respect for her. He has no respect for our president. And I'll tell you what, we're in very serious trouble. Because we have a country with tremendous numbers of nuclear warheads, eighteen hundred by the way where they expanded and we didn't. Eighteen hundred nuclear warheads and she is playing chicken. Look.

Clinton: Wait.

Trump: Putin from everything I see has no respect for this person.

Clinton: Well, that's because he'd rather have a puppet as a president of the United States.

Trump: No puppet. You're the puppet. . . .

Wallace: . . . [Mr. Trump,] I would like to ask you this direct question. The top national security officials of this country do believe that Russia has been behind these hacks. Even if you don't know for sure whether they are, do you condemn any interference with Russia in the American election?

Trump: By Russia or anybody else.

Wallace: Do you condemn their interference?

Trump: Of course I condemn, of course I condemn. I don't know Putin. . . . I never met Putin. This is not my best friend. But if the United States got along with Russia, it wouldn't so bad. Let me tell you, Putin has outsmarted her and Obama at every single step of the way. Whether it is Syria. You name it. Missiles. Take a look at the start-up that they signed. The Russians have said, according to many, many reports, I can't believe they allowed us to do this. They create warheads and we can't. The Russians can't believe it. She has been outsmarted by Putin and all you have to do is look at the Middle East. They've taken over. We have spent six trillion dollars, they've taken over the Middle East. She has been outsmarted and outplayed worse than anybody I've ever seen in any government whatsoever.

Wallace: We are a long way away from immigration . . .

. . .We are going to get to foreign hotspots in a few moments, but the next segment is fitness to be president of the United States. Mr. Trump, at the last debate, you said your talk about grabbing women was just that, talk, and that you'd never actually done it. And since then, as we all know, nine women have come forward and said that you either groped them or kissed them without their consent. Why would so many different women from so many different circumstances over so many different years, why would they all in this last couple of weeks make up—you deny this. Why would they all make up these stories? And since this is a question for both of you, Secretary Clinton, Mr. Trump says what your husband did and you defended was even worse. Mr. Trump, you go first.

Trump: Well, First of all, the stories have been largely debunked. Those people, I don't know those people. I have a feeling how they came. I believe it was her campaign that did it just like if you look at what came out today on the clips where I was wondering what happened with my rally in Chicago and other rallies where we had such violence? She's the one in Obama that caused the violence. They hired people. They payed them fifteen hundred dollars, and they're on tape saying be violent, cause fights, do bad things. I would say the only way—because those stories are all totally false. I have to say that, and I didn't even apologize to my wife who is sitting right here because I didn't do anything. I didn't know any of these women.

I didn't see these women. These women, the woman on the plane, the woman on the—I think they want either fame or her campaign did it. And I think it's her campaign because what I saw what they did, which is a criminal act, by the way, where there telling people to go out and start fistfights and start violence—and I'll tell you what. In particular, in Chicago, people were hurt and people could have [been] killed in that riot. And that was now all on tape started by her. I believe, Chris, that she got these people to step forward. If it wasn't, they get there ten minutes of fame, but they were all totally—it was all fiction. It was lies and it was fiction.

Clinton: Well—

Wallace: Secretary Clinton?

Clinton: At the last debate, we heard Donald talking about what he did to women, and after that a number of women have come forward saying that's exactly what he did to them. Now, what was his response? Well, he held a number of big rallies where he said that he could not possibly have done those things to those women because they were not attractive enough for—

Trump: I did not say that.

Clinton: —them to be assaulted.

Trump: I did not say that.

Clinton: In fact, he went on to say—

Wallace: Her two minutes. Sir, her two minutes.

Trump: I did not say that.

Wallace: Her two minutes.

Clinton: He went on to say, "Look at her. I don't think so." About another woman, he said, "that wouldn't be my first choice." He attacked the woman reporter writing the story, called her disgusting, as he has called a number of women during this campaign. Donald thinks belittling women makes him bigger. He goes after their dignity, their self-worth, and I don't think there is a woman anywhere doesn't know what that feels like. So we now know what Donald thinks and what he says and how he acts toward women. That's who Donald is. I think it's really up to all of us to demonstrate who we are and who our country is, and to stand up and be very clear about what we expect from our next president, how we want to bring our country together, where we don't want to have the kind of pitting of people one against the other, where instead we celebrate our diversity, we lift

people up, and we make our country even greater. America is great because America is good. And it really is up to all of us to make that true now and in the future and particularly for our children and our grandchildren.

Wallace: Mr. Trump—

Trump: Nobody has more respect for women than I do, nobody.

(Laughter)

Wallace: Please, everybody.

Trump: And frankly, those stories have been largely debunked. And I really want to just talk about something slightly different. She mentions this, which is all fiction, all fictionalized, probably or possibly started by her and her very sleazy campaign. But I will tell you what isn't fictionalized are her e-mails, where she destroyed thirty-three thousand e-mails criminally, criminally after getting a subpoena from the United States Congress. What happened to the FBI, I don't know. We have a great general, four-star general, today you read it in all the papers going to potentially serve five years in jail for lying to the FBI, one lie. She's lied hundreds of times to the people, to Congress, and to the FBI. He's going to probably go to jail. This is a four-star general and she gets away with it and she can run for the presidency of the United States? . . .

Wallace: This is the final time, probably to both of your delight, that you're going to be on the stage together in this campaign. I would like to end it on a positive note. You had not agreed to closing statements, but it seems to be in a funny way that might make it more interesting because you haven't prepared closing statements. So I would like you each to take—and we're going to put a clock up—a minute as a final question, in the final debate, to tell the American people why they should elect you to be the next president. This is another new mini-segment. Secretary Clinton, it's your turn to go first.

Clinton: Well, I would like to say to everyone watching tonight that I am reaching out to all Americans, Democrats, Republicans and Independents, because we need everybody to help make our country what it should be, to grow the economy, to make it fairer, to make it work for everyone. We need your talents, your skills, your commitment, your energy, your ambition. You know, I've been privileged to see the presidency up close. And I know the awesome responsibility of protecting our country and the incredible opportunity of working to try to make life better for all of you. I have made the cause of children and families really my life's work. That's what my mission will be in my presidency. I will stand up for families against powerful interests, against corporations. I will do everything that I can to make sure that you have good jobs with rising incomes, that your kids have good educations from preschool through college. I hope you will give me a chance to serve as your president.

Wallace: Secretary Clinton, thank you. Mr. Trump?

Trump: She's raising the money from the people she wants to control. Doesn't work that way. But when I started this campaign, I started it very strongly. It's called Make America Great Again. We're going to make America great. We have a depleted military. It has to be helped. It has to be fixed. We have the greatest people on earth in our military. We don't take care of our veterans. We take care of illegal immigrants, people that come into the country illegally better than we take care of our vets. That can't happen. Our policemen and women are disrespected. We need law and order, but we need justice too. Our inner cities are a disaster. You get shot walking to the store. They have no education. They have no jobs. I will do more for African-Americans and Latinos than she can ever do in ten lifetimes. All she's done is talk to the African-Americans and to the Latinos, but they get the vote and then they come back, they say, "We'll see you in four years." We are going to make America strong again, and we are going to make America great again and it has to start now. We cannot take four more years of Barack Obama, and that's what you get when you get her.

QUESTIONS TO CONSIDER

1. How would you characterize the debate between Clinton and Trump?
2. Whose attacks were more effective?

30.6 TIMES UP MOVEMENT, RESPONSE LETTER TO THE ALIANZA NACIONAL DE CAMPESINAS (2018)

In October 2017, the #MeToo movement spread on the social media website Twitter to show how widespread sexual assault was in America. First used by African American activist Tarana Burke in 2006, #MeToo grew rapidly in response to the sexual assault allegations against major Hollywood producer Harvey Weinstein. Subsequent investigations in the entertainment industry implicated, among many others, comedian Louis C. K., newscaster Charlie Rose, and *Today* host Matt Lauer. In November 2017, the Alianza Nacional de Campesinas (the National Farmworkers Women's Alliance) wrote an open letter to entertainment industry women involved in the #MeToo movement. The organization's letter referenced the harassment and assault faced by women in less public industries and pledged to stand united with every person who stood up against such abuse. In response, on January 1, 2018, a group of #MeToo activists in the entertainment industry founded the Times Up organization to advocate for victims and raise money to pay the legal fees of any woman mounting a case regarding sexual harassment in the workplace. Times Up's open letter to the Alianza Nacional de Campesinas illustrates the power of grassroots activism.

Dear Sisters,

We write on behalf of over 300 women who work in film, television and theater. A little more than two months ago, courageous individuals revealed the dark truth of ongoing sexual harassment and assault by powerful people in the entertainment industry. At one of our most difficult and vulnerable moments, Alianza Nacional de Campesinas (the National Farmworker Women's Alliance) sent us a powerful and compassionate message of solidarity for which we are deeply grateful.

To the members of Alianza and farmworker women across the country, we see you, we thank you, and we acknowledge the heavy weight of our common experience of being preyed upon, harassed, and exploited by those who abuse their power and threaten our physical and economic security. We have similarly suppressed the violence and demeaning harassment for fear that we will be attacked and ruined in the process of speaking out. We share your feelings of anger and shame. We harbor

fear that no one will believe us, that we will look weak or that we will be dismissed; and we are terrified that we will be fired or never hired again in retaliation.

We also recognize our privilege and the fact that we have access to enormous platforms to amplify our voices. Both of which have drawn and driven widespread attention to the existence of this problem in our industry that farmworker women and countless individuals employed in other industries have not been afforded.

To every woman employed in agriculture who has had to fend off unwanted sexual advances from her boss, every housekeeper who has tried to escape an assaultive guest, every janitor trapped nightly in a building with a predatory supervisor, every waitress grabbed by a customer and expected to take it with a smile, every garment and factory worker forced to trade sexual acts for more shifts, every domestic worker or home health aide forcibly touched by a client, every

Source: "Times Up Letter of Solidarity to Alianza Nacional de Campesinas," https://www.timesupnow.com/ (Accessed June 16, 2018). Reprinted here with permission of TIME'S UP.

immigrant woman silenced by the threat of her un-documented status being reported in retaliation for speaking up and to women in every industry who are subjected to indignities and offensive behavior that they are expected to tolerate in order to make a living: We stand with you. We support you.

Now, unlike ever before, our access to the media and to important decision makers has the potential of leading to real accountability and consequences. We want all survivors of sexual harassment, everywhere, to be heard, to be believed, and to know that account-ability is possible.

We also want all victims and survivors to be able to access justice and support for the wrongdoing they have endured. We particularly want to lift up the voices, power, and strength of women working in low-wage industries where the lack of financial stability makes them vulnerable to high rates of gender-based violence and exploitation.

Unfortunately, too many centers of power—from legislatures to boardrooms to executive suites and management to academia—lack gender parity and women do not have equal decision-making author-ity. This systemic gender-inequality and imbalance of power fosters an environment that is ripe for abuse and harassment against women. Therefore, we call for a significant increase of women in positions of leader-ship and power across industries. In addition, we seek equal representation, opportunities, benefits and pay for all women workers, not to mention greater repre-sentation of women of color, immigrant women, dis-abled women, and lesbian, bisexual, and transgender women, whose experiences in the workforce are often significantly worse than their white, cisgender, straight peers. The struggle for women to break in, to rise up

the ranks and to simply be heard and acknowledged in male-dominated workplaces must end; time's up on this impenetrable monopoly.

We are grateful to the many individuals—survivors and allies—who are speaking out and forcing the con-versation about sexual harassment, sexual assault, and gender bias out of the shadows and into the spotlight. We fervently urge the media covering the disclosures by people in Hollywood to spend equal time on the myriad experiences of individuals working in less glamorized and valorized trades.

Harassment too often persists because perpetra-tors and employers never face any consequences. This is often because survivors, particularly those working in low-wage industries, don't have the resources to fight back. As a first step towards helping women and men across the country seek justice, the signatories of this letter will be seeding a legal fund to help survivors of sexual assault and harassment across all industries challenge those responsible for the harm against them and give voice to their experiences.

We remain committed to holding our own work-places accountable, pushing for swift and effective change to make the entertainment industry a safe and equitable place for everyone, and telling women's sto-ries through our eyes and voices with the goal of shift-ing our society's perception and treatment of women.

QUESTIONS TO CONSIDER

1. How did Times Up choose to response to the Alianza Nacional de Campesinas?
2. What does the Times Up letter demonstrate about grassroots activism and contemporary power dynamics?